World Economic and Financial Surveys

W9-DEN-053

WORLD ECONOMIC OUTLOOK
September 2011

Slowing Growth, Rising Risks

International Monetary Fund

Cover and Design: Luisa Menjivar and Jorge Salazar
Composition: Maryland Composition

Cataloging-in-Publication Data

World economic outlook (International Monetary Fund)
   World economic outlook : a survey by the staff of the International Monetary Fund. —
Washington, DC : International Monetary Fund, 1980–
   v. ; 28 cm. — (1981–1984: Occasional paper / International Monetary Fund, 0251-6365).
— (1986– : World economic and financial surveys, 0256-6877)

Semiannual. Some issues also have thematic titles.
Has occasional updates, 1984–

   1. Economic development — Periodicals. 2. Economic forecasting — Periodicals.
3. Economic policy — Periodicals. 4. International economic relations — Periodicals.
I. International Monetary Fund. II. Series: Occasional paper (International Monetary Fund).
III. Series: World economic and financial surveys.

HC10.80

ISBN 978-1-61635-119-9

Please send orders to:
International Monetary Fund, Publication Services
P.O. Box 92780, Washington, D.C. 20090, U.S.A.
Tel.: (202) 623-7430 Fax: (202) 623-7201
E-mail: publications@imf.org
www.imfbookstore.org

CONTENTS

Tables

Online Tables

Figures

ASSUMPTIONS AND CONVENTIONS

A number of assumptions have been adopted for the projections presented in the *World Economic Outlook.* It has been assumed that real effective exchange rates remained constant at their average levels during July 18–August 15, 2011, except for the currencies participating in the European exchange rate mechanism II (ERM II), which are assumed to have remained constant in nominal terms relative to the euro; that established policies of national authorities will be maintained (for specific assumptions about fiscal and monetary policies for selected economies, see Box A1 in the Statistical Appendix); that the average price of oil will be $103.20 a barrel in 2011 and $100.00 a barrel in 2012 and will remain unchanged in real terms over the medium term; that the six-month London interbank offered rate (LIBOR) on U.S. dollar deposits will average 0.4 percent in 2011 and 0.5 percent in 2012; that the three-month euro deposit rate will average 1.3 percent in 2011 and 1.2 percent in 2012; and that the six-month Japanese yen deposit rate will yield on average 0.5 percent in 2011 and 0.3 percent in 2012. These are, of course, working hypotheses rather than forecasts, and the uncertainties surrounding them add to the margin of error that would in any event be involved in the projections. The estimates and projections are based on statistical information available through early September 2011.

The following conventions are used throughout the *World Economic Outlook:*

. . .   to indicate that data are not available or not applicable;

—   between years or months (for example, 2010–11 or January–June) to indicate the years or months covered, including the beginning and ending years or months;

/   between years or months (for example, 2010/11) to indicate a fiscal or financial year.

"Billion" means a thousand million; "trillion" means a thousand billion.

"Basis points" refer to hundredths of 1 percentage point (for example, 25 basis points are equivalent to ¼ of 1 percentage point).

Data for Estonia are now included in the aggregates for the euro area and advanced economies.

As in the April 2011 *World Economic Outlook,* WEO aggregated data exclude Libya for the projection years due to the uncertain political situation.

Starting with the September 2011 *World Economic Outlook,* Guyana and Suriname are classified as members of the South America region and Belize as a member of the Central America region. Previously, they were members of the Caribbean region.

For Sudan, the projections for 2011 and later exclude South Sudan.

In figures and tables, shaded areas indicate IMF staff projections.

If no source is listed on tables and figures, data are drawn from the WEO database.

When countries are not listed alphabetically, they are ordered on the basis of economic size.

Minor discrepancies between sums of constituent figures and totals shown reflect rounding.

As used in this report, the terms "country" and "economy" do not in all cases refer to a territorial entity that is a state as understood by international law and practice. As used here, the term also covers some territorial entities that are not states but for which statistical data are maintained on a separate and independent basis.

Composite data are provided for various groups of countries organized according to economic characteristics or region. Unless otherwise noted, country group composites represent calculations based on 90 percent or more of the weighted group data.

The boundaries, colors, denominations, and any other information shown on the maps do not imply, on the part of the International Monetary Fund, any judgment on the legal status of any territory or any endorsement or acceptance of such boundaries.

This version of the *World Economic Outlook* is available in full on the IMF's website, www.imf.org. Accompanying it on the website is a larger compilation of data from the WEO database than is included in the report itself, including files containing the series most frequently requested by readers. These files may be downloaded for use in a variety of software packages.

The data appearing in the *World Economic Outlook* are compiled by the IMF staff at the time of the WEO exercises. The historical data and projections are based on the information gathered by the IMF country desk officers in the context of their missions to IMF member countries and through their ongoing analysis of the evolving situation in each country. Historical data are updated on a continual basis, as more information becomes available, and structural breaks in data are often adjusted to produce smooth series with the use of splicing and other techniques. IMF staff estimates continue to serve as proxies for historical series when complete information is unavailable. As a result, WEO data can differ from other sources with official data, including the IMF's *International Financial Statistics*.

The WEO data and metadata provided are "as is" and "as available," and every effort is made to ensure, but not guarantee, their timeliness, accuracy, and completeness. When errors are discovered, there is a concerted effort to correct them as appropriate and feasible. For details on the terms and conditions for usage of the WEO database, please refer to the IMF Copyright and Usage website, http://www.imf.org/external/terms.htm.

Inquiries about the content of the *World Economic Outlook* and the WEO database should be sent by mail, forum, or fax (telephone inquiries cannot be accepted) to

World Economic Studies Division
Research Department
International Monetary Fund
700 19th Street, N.W.
Washington, D.C. 20431, U.S.A.
Forum address: www.imf.org/weoforum Fax: (202) 623-6343

PREFACE

The analysis and projections contained in the *World Economic Outlook* are integral elements of the IMF's surveillance of economic developments and policies in its member countries, of developments in international financial markets, and of the global economic system. The survey of prospects and policies is the product of a comprehensive interdepartmental review of world economic developments, which draws primarily on information the IMF staff gathers through its consultations with member countries. These consultations are carried out in particular by the IMF's area departments—namely, the African Department, Asia and Pacific Department, European Department, Middle East and Central Asia Department, and Western Hemisphere Department—together with the Strategy, Policy, and Review Department; the Monetary and Capital Markets Department; and the Fiscal Affairs Department.

The analysis in this report was coordinated in the Research Department under the general direction of Olivier Blanchard, Economic Counsellor and Director of Research. The project was directed by Jörg Decressin, Senior Advisor, Research Department and Rupa Duttagupta, Deputy Division Chief, Research Department. The primary contributors to this report are Abdul Abiad, John Bluedorn, Jaime Guajardo, Thomas Helbling, Daniel Leigh, Andrea Pescatori, Shaun Roache, Marco E. Terrones, Petia Topalova, and John Simon. Other contributors include Ali Alichi, Luis Catão, Ondra Kamenik, Heejin Kim, Michael Kumhof, Douglas Laxton, Prakash Loungani, Gian Maria Milesi-Ferretti, Rafael Portillo, and Felipe Zanna. Toh Kuan, Gavin Asdorian, Shan Chen, Angela Espiritu, Laura Feiveson, João Jalles, Murad Omoev, Katherine Pan, David Reichsfeld, Marina Rousset, Andy Salazar, Min Kyu Song, Ercument Tulun, and Su Wang provided research assistance. Kevin Clinton provided comments and suggestions. Tingyun Chen, Mahnaz Hemmati, Emory Oakes, Rajesh Nilawar, and Steve Zhang managed the database and the computer systems. Shanti Karunaratne, Skeeter Mathurin, and Cristina Tumale were responsible for word processing. Linda Griffin Kean of the External Relations Department edited the manuscript and coordinated the production of the publication. External consultants Anastasia Francis, Aleksandr Gerasimov, Wendy Mak, Shamiso Mapondera, Nhu Nguyen, and Pavel Pimenov provided additional technical support.

The analysis has benefited from comments and suggestions by staff from other IMF departments, as well as by Executive Directors following their discussion of the report on August 31, 2011. However, both projections and policy considerations are those of the IMF staff and should not be attributed to Executive Directors or to their national authorities.

FOREWORD

Relative to our previous *World Economic Outlook* last April, the economic recovery has become much more uncertain. The world economy suffers from the confluence of two adverse developments. The first is a much slower recovery in advanced economies since the beginning of the year, a development we largely failed to perceive as it was happening. The second is a large increase in fiscal and financial uncertainty, which has been particularly pronounced since August. Each of these developments is worrisome—their combination and their interactions more so. Strong policies are urgently needed to improve the outlook and reduce the risks.

Growth, which had been strong in 2010, decreased in 2011. This slowdown did not initially cause too much worry. We had forecast some slowdown, due to the end of the inventory cycle and fiscal consolidation. One-time events, from the earthquake and tsunami in Japan to shocks to the supply of oil, offered plausible explanations for a further slowdown. And the initial U.S. data understated the size of the slowdown itself. Now that the numbers are in, it is clear that more was going on.

What was going on was the stalling of the two rebalancing acts, which we have argued in many previous issues of the *World Economic Outlook* are needed to deliver "strong, balanced, and sustainable growth."

Take first internal rebalancing: What is needed is a shift from fiscal stimulus to private demand. Fiscal consolidation is indeed taking place in most advanced economies (although not in Japan). But private demand is not taking the relay. The reasons vary, depending on the country. But tight bank lending, the legacy of the housing boom, and high leverage for many households all turn out to be putting stronger brakes on the recovery than we anticipated.

Turn to external rebalancing: Advanced economies with current account deficits, most notably the United States, need to compensate for low domestic demand through an increase in foreign demand. This implies a symmetric shift away from foreign demand toward domestic demand in emerging market economies with current account surpluses, most notably China. This rebalancing act is not taking place. While imbalances decreased during the crisis, this was due more to a large decrease in output in advanced relative to emerging market economies than to structural adjustment in these economies. Looking forward, the forecast is for an increase rather than a decrease in imbalances.

Now turn to the second adverse development, increased fiscal and financial uncertainty: Markets have clearly become more skeptical about the ability of many countries to stabilize their public debt. For some time, their worries were mostly limited to a few small countries on the periphery of Europe. As time has passed, and as growth prospects have dimmed, their worries have extended to more European countries and to countries beyond Europe—from Japan to the United States. Worries about sovereigns have translated into worries about the banks holding these sovereign bonds, mainly in Europe. These worries have led to a partial freeze of financial flows, with banks keeping high levels of liquidity and tightening lending. Fear of the unknown is high. Stock prices have fallen. These will adversely affect spending in the months to come. Indeed, August numbers indicate that this is already happening.

Low underlying growth and fiscal and financial linkages may well feed back on each other, and this is where the risks are. Low growth makes it more difficult to achieve debt sustainability and leads markets to worry even more about fiscal stability. Low growth also leads to more nonperforming loans and weakens banks. Front-loaded fiscal consolidation in turn may lead to even lower growth. Weak banks and tight bank lending may have the same effect. Weak banks and the potential need for more capital lead to more worry about fiscal stability. Downside risks are very real.

I have been focusing so far on advanced economies. The reason is that, until now, emerging market economies have been largely immune to these adverse developments. They have had to deal with volatile capital flows, but in general have continued to sustain high growth. Indeed, some are close to overheating, although prospects are more uncertain again for many others. Under the risk scenarios, they may well suffer more adverse export conditions and even more volatile capital flows. Low exports and, perhaps, lower commodity prices will also create challenges for low-income countries.

In light of the weak baseline and high downside risks, strong policy action is of the essence. It must rely on three main legs.

The first leg is fiscal policy. Fiscal consolidation cannot be too fast or it will kill growth. It cannot be too slow or it will kill credibility. The speed must depend on individual country circumstances, but the key continues to be credible medium-term consolidation. Some countries need substantial outside help to succeed. Going beyond fiscal policy, measures to prop up domestic demand, ranging from continued low interest rates, to increased bank lending, to resolution programs for housing, are also of the essence.

The second leg is financial measures. Fiscal uncertainty will not go away overnight. And even under the most optimistic assumptions, growth in advanced economies will remain low for some time. During that time, banks have to be made stronger, not only to increase bank lending and baseline growth, but also—and more important—to reduce risks of vicious feedback loops. For a number of banks, especially in Europe, this is likely to require additional capital buffers, either from private or from public sources.

The third leg is external rebalancing. It is hard to see how, even with the policy measures listed above, domestic demand in the United States and other economies hit by the crisis can, by itself, ensure sufficient growth. Thus, exports from the United States and crisis-hit economies must increase, and, by implication, net exports from the rest of the world must decrease. A number of Asian economies, in particular China, have large current account surpluses and have indicated plans to rebalance from foreign to domestic demand. These plans cannot be implemented overnight. But they must be implemented as fast as possible. Only with this global rebalancing can we hope for stronger growth in advanced economies and, by implication, for the rest of the world.

Olivier Blanchard
Economic Counsellor

EXECUTIVE SUMMARY

The global economy is in a dangerous new phase. Global activity has weakened and become more uneven, confidence has fallen sharply recently, and downside risks are growing. Against a backdrop of unresolved structural fragilities, a barrage of shocks hit the international economy this year. Japan was struck by the devastating Great East Japan earthquake and tsunami, and unrest swelled in some oil-producing countries. At the same time, the handover from public to private demand in the U.S. economy stalled, the euro area encountered major financial turbulence, global markets suffered a major sell-off of risky assets, and there are growing signs of spillovers to the real economy. The structural problems facing the crisis-hit advanced economies have proven even more intractable than expected, and the process of devising and implementing reforms even more complicated. The outlook for these economies is thus for a continuing, but weak and bumpy, expansion. Prospects for emerging market economies have become more uncertain again, although growth is expected to remain fairly robust, especially in economies that can counter the effect on output of weaker foreign demand with less policy tightening.

World Economic Outlook (WEO) projections indicate that global growth will moderate to about 4 percent through 2012, from over 5 percent in 2010. Real GDP in the advanced economies is projected to expand at an anemic pace of about 1½ percent in 2011 and 2 percent in 2012, helped by a gradual unwinding of the temporary forces that have held back activity during much of the second quarter of 2011. However, this assumes that European policymakers contain the crisis in the euro area periphery, that U.S. policymakers strike a judicious balance between support for the economy and medium-term fiscal consolidation, and that volatility in global financial markets does not escalate. Moreover, the removal of monetary accommodation in advanced economies is now expected to pause. Under such a scenario, emerging capacity constraints and policy tightening, much of which has already happened, would lower growth rates in emerging and developing economies to a still very solid pace of about 6 percent in 2012.

The risks are clearly to the downside, and two warrant particular attention from policymakers:

- The first is that the crisis in the euro area runs beyond the control of policymakers, notwithstanding the strong policy response agreed at the July 21, 2011, EU summit. Policymakers must swiftly ratify the commitments made at the July summit, and in the meantime, the European Central Bank (ECB) must continue to intervene strongly to maintain orderly conditions in sovereign debt markets. Leaders must stand by their commitments to do whatever it takes to preserve trust in national policies and the euro. Furthermore, given declining inflation pressure and heightened financial and sovereign tensions, the ECB should lower its policy rate if downside risks to growth and inflation persist.

- The second is that activity in the United States, already softening, might suffer further blows— for example, from a political impasse over fiscal consolidation, a weak housing market, rapid increases in household saving rates, or deteriorating financial conditions. Deep political divisions leave the course of U.S. policy highly uncertain. There is a serious risk that hasty fiscal cutbacks will further weaken the outlook without providing the long-term reforms required to reduce debt to more sustainable levels. News from the housing market has been disappointing, with no end in sight to the overhang of excess supply and declining prices, and equity prices have corrected sharply. These or other developments could prompt households to accelerate their pace of deleveraging, by raising their saving rates further. Given growing downside risks to U.S. activity, the Federal Reserve should stand ready to deploy more unconventional support, and the pace of fiscal consolidation could become more back-loaded provided credible medium-term measures are adopted.

Either one of these eventualities would have severe repercussions for global growth. The renewed stress could undermine financial markets and institutions in advanced economies, which remain unusually vulnerable. Commodity prices and global trade and capital flows would likely decline abruptly, dragging down growth in emerging and developing economies. The extent to which this could lower global growth is illustrated in more detail in a downside scenario—the euro area and the United States could fall back into recession, with activity some 3 percentage points lower in 2012 than envisaged in WEO projections. Damage to other economies would also be significant.

Homegrown risks in emerging and developing economies seem less severe. Signs of overheating still warrant close attention, particularly from the monetary and prudential authorities. Risks related to commodity prices and social and political unrest in some parts of the world continue to loom large.

The uneven nature of the expansion and the many risks that threaten activity are symptomatic of a global economy that continues to struggle to accomplish the two rebalancing acts identified in earlier issues of the *World Economic Outlook*. First, private demand must take over from public demand. On this front, many economies have made considerable progress, but the major advanced economies lag behind. Second, economies with large external surpluses must rely increasingly on domestic demand, whereas those with large deficits must do the opposite. This rebalancing act has gone only halfway.[1] Key advanced and emerging market economies need to strengthen their policies to advance rebalancing and hedge against the many downside risks. Policies must be calibrated to reflect the transformed global environment, including lower potential output in many advanced and crisis-hit emerging market economies, unusually vulnerable financial sectors, high public deficits and debt and more sovereign credit risk differentiation among advanced economies, and the greater economic resilience of many emerging economies.

Rebalancing from public to private demand: Policymakers in crisis-hit economies must resist the temptation to rely mainly on accommodative monetary policy to mend balance sheets and accelerate repair and reform of the financial sector. Fiscal policy must navigate between the twin perils of losing credibility and undercutting recovery. Fiscal adjustment has already started, and progress has been significant in many economies. Strengthening medium-term fiscal plans and implementing entitlement reforms are critical to ensuring credibility and fiscal sustainability and to creating policy room to support balance sheet repair, growth, and job creation. Better short-term real sector prospects, in turn, would help make medium-term adjustment plans more credible. Should the macroeconomic environment deteriorate substantially, countries with more room for fiscal policy maneuvering should allow automatic stabilizers to operate fully and could choose a more back-loaded adjustment profile.

- In the euro area, the adverse feedback loop between weak sovereign and financial institutions needs to be broken. Fragile financial institutions must be asked to raise more capital, preferably through private solutions. If these are not available, they will have to accept injections of public capital or support from the EFSF, or be restructured or closed. Medium-term plans for fiscal consolidation are appropriately ambitious. In the economies of the periphery, a major task will be to find the right balance between fiscal consolidation and structural reform on the one hand and external support on the other, so as to ensure that adjustment in these economies can be sustained.

- The top priorities in the United States include devising a medium-term fiscal consolidation plan to put public debt on a sustainable path and to implement policies to sustain the recovery, including by easing the adjustment in the housing and labor markets. The American Job Act would provide needed short-term support to the

[1]See Blanchard, Oliver, and Gian Maria Milesi-Ferretti, 2011, "(Why) Should Current Account Balances Be Reduced?" IMF Staff Discussion Note No. 11/03 (Washington: International Monetary Fund); and Lane, Philip, and Gian Maria Milesi-Ferretti, 2011, "External Adjustment and the Global Crisis," IMF Working Paper No. 11/197 (Washington: International Monetary Fund), for further discussion of this challenge.

economy, but it must be flanked with a strong medium-term fiscal plan that raises revenues and contains the growth of entitlement spending.

- In Japan, the government should pursue more ambitious measures to deal with the very high level of public debt while attending to the immediate need for reconstruction and development in the areas hit by the earthquake and tsunami.

In all these economies, major progress with respect to entitlement and tax reform would create more room to adapt the pace of near-term fiscal consolidation to the strength of domestic demand and thereby limit further weakening of the recovery.

Rebalancing from external to domestic demand: Progress on this front has become even more important to sustain global growth. Some emerging market economies are contributing more domestic demand than is desirable (for example, several economies in Latin America); others are not contributing enough (for example, key economies in emerging Asia). The first set needs to restrain strong domestic demand by considerably reducing structural fiscal deficits and, in some cases, by further removing monetary accommodation. The second set of economies needs significant currency appreciation alongside structural reforms to reduce high surpluses of savings over investment. Such policies would help improve their resilience to shocks originating in the advanced economies as well as their medium-term growth potential.

The Great Recession amplified a number of real-sector problems, especially in advanced economies. The United States could be facing a very sluggish recovery of employment. Although unemployment is below post–World War II highs, job losses during the crisis were unprecedented and came on top of lackluster employment performance during the preceding decade. Households are more worried about future income prospects than at any time since the early 1980s. Priorities include easing adjustment in the housing market and strengthening active labor market policies. In many ways, however, the problem is so large that it warrants a drastic change in macroeconomic policy: major entitlement and tax reform with a view to creating more room for fiscal policy to sustain the recovery in the short term. In the euro area, abstracting from the large

problems posed by the financial turbulence, the situation is more mixed. Households generally seem less concerned than in the United States, and job destruction has been much less severe, except in the crisis-hit economies of the periphery. The key structural challenge is for the economies in the periphery to adopt reforms that improve their capacity to rebuild and maintain their competitiveness.

Structural challenges elsewhere in the world vary widely. Large capital inflows in some emerging market economies underscore the need to improve their absorptive capacity by further opening product and services markets to foreign capital and strengthening financial stability frameworks. In addition, high food prices underscore the need for many emerging and developing economies to develop well-targeted social safety nets.

In view of the slow pace of global demand rebalancing, high commodity prices, and the modest growth outlook for advanced economies, long-term interest rates for key sovereigns are likely to stay low. This may foster risk taking in other economies—previous episodes of money recycling on a massive scale have rarely been without financial accidents. Symptoms of excessive risk taking are in fact evident in a few advanced and a number of emerging market economies: very high credit growth, booming real estate markets, and large flows into financial markets. More generally, the financial crisis brought to the fore the extraordinary vulnerability of the global financial system to disruptions in wholesale funding markets. At the national level, central banks have responded by putting in place temporary mechanisms that inject liquidity if wholesale funding threatens to dry up. There are, however, no such mechanisms at the international level. In general, the latest financial crisis illustrates the urgent need to beef up the size and scope of international risk-sharing mechanisms, which have fallen far behind the size of international financial markets.

To ensure that trade remains supportive of the global recovery, policymakers must continue to resist protectionist pressures. Just as important, with negotiations on the long-running World Trade Organization (WTO) Doha Round of trade talks at a pivotal juncture, political leaders need to muster the will and high-level attention to devise a credible plan to move the negotiations forward, including by strongly communicating the benefits to the public. Failure of the round could lead to fragmentation of the global trading system and a weakening of the WTO and multilateralism.

Unless policies are strengthened, especially in advanced economies, nothing beyond a weak and bumpy recovery is in the cards. There are potential major benefits to a stronger, collaborative policy response. As explained in a separate IMF report for the G20 Mutual Assessment Program, adopting growth-friendly medium-term fiscal consolidation programs in advanced economies, policies to rebalance demand in emerging market surplus economies, and structural reforms to boost poten-

tial growth everywhere could provide a considerable fillip to global GDP.[2] Perhaps even more important, together with measures to facilitate balance sheet adjustment by households and banks, such policies would forestall a lost decade of growth in advanced economies, which would be very detrimental for all. However, achieving this will require that policymakers tackle difficult political economy challenges at home and resuscitate the strong collaborative spirit that prevailed at the height of the crisis.

---

[2]See Group of Twenty, 2010, "G20 Mutual Assessment Process—Alternative Policy Scenarios," report prepared by staff of the International Monetary Fund for the G-20 Mutual Assessment Process, G-20 Toronto Summit, Toronto, Canada, June 26–27 (Washington: International Monetary Fund). www.imf.org/external/np/g20/pdf/062710a.pdf.

Slowing Global Activity

Activity has weakened significantly (Figure 1.1), following a number of quarters of growth broadly in line with *World Economic Outlook* (WEO) projections. The slowdown reflects both anticipated and unanticipated developments. The strong cyclical rebound in global industrial production and trade in 2010 was never expected to persist. However, in crisis-hit advanced economies, especially the United States, the handover from public to private demand is taking more time than anticipated. In addition, sovereign debt and banking sector problems in the euro area have proven much more tenacious than expected. Furthermore, the disruptions resulting from the Great East Japan earthquake and tsunami, as well as the spreading unrest in the Middle East and North Africa (MENA) region and the related surge in oil prices, were major surprises.

The shocks to Japan and the oil supply have had a temporary effect on global growth, which is beginning to unwind. Various considerations suggest that they may have lowered output in advanced economies by ½ percentage point, mostly in the second quarter of 2011.

- According to some estimates, the number of cars manufactured worldwide may have dropped by up to 30 percent in the two months following the Japanese earthquake and tsunami because of supply-chain disruptions. For the United States, some estimates put losses on the order of 1 percentage point of GDP in the second quarter of 2011;[1] others report smaller effects of about ½ percentage point of GDP.[2]
- During the second quarter of 2011, oil prices briefly rose more than 25 percent above the levels that prevailed in January 2011. It is hard to determine the extent to which prices were driven up by

stronger demand or by lower supply (for example, from Libya). Assuming that a significant share of the price increase reflected lower supply, it may have reduced output in advanced economies by ¼ to ½ percentage point of GDP.

At the same time, emerging and developing economies performed broadly as forecast, with considerable variation across regions. Activity began to rebound fairly strongly in the crisis-hit economies of central and eastern Europe (CEE) and the Commonwealth of Independent States (CIS), helped in the latter by buoyant commodity prices. Surging commodity prices also propelled Latin America to high growth rates. Activity in developing Asia weakened modestly in response to global supply-chain disruptions and destocking in the face of more uncertain demand from advanced economies. Sub-Saharan Africa (SSA) continued to expand at a robust pace. By contrast, economic activity in the MENA region suffered from political and social conflict, although strong revenues boosted the economies of oil exporters. The net result of the various developments in advanced and emerging market economies was unexpectedly weak global activity during the second quarter (Figure 1.1, bottom panel).

Renewed Financial Instability

Recently, financial volatility has again increased drastically, driven by concerns about developments in the euro area and the strength of global activity, especially in the United States. Policy indecision has exacerbated uncertainty and added to financial strains, feeding back into the real economy. The September 2011 *Global Financial Stability Report* observes that renewed doubts about the prospects for addressing the problems in the euro area resurfaced in spring 2011 and have since deepened, notwithstanding the strong measures agreed at the July 21, 2011, EU summit. It is worrisome that investors have significantly pushed up sovereign risk premiums for Belgium, Italy, and Spain, and—to a much lesser extent—France (Figure

---

[1]See Macroeconomic Advisers (2011). Based on manufacturers' announced plans, they argue that rising car assembly could add 1¼ percentage points to GDP in the third quarter.

[2]See IMF (2011).

Table 1.1. Overview of the *World Economic Outlook* Projections

(Percent change unless noted otherwise)

| | | | Year over Year | | | | Q4 over Q4 | | |
| | | | Projections | | Difference from June 2011 WEO Projections | | Estimates | Projections | |
	2009	2010	2011	2012	2011	2012	2010	2011	2012
World Output[1]	**−0.7**	**5.1**	**4.0**	**4.0**	**−0.3**	**−0.5**	**4.8**	**3.6**	**4.1**
Advanced Economies	**−3.7**	**3.1**	**1.6**	**1.9**	**−0.6**	**−0.7**	**2.9**	**1.4**	**2.2**
United States	−3.5	3.0	1.5	1.8	−1.0	−0.9	3.1	1.1	2.0
Euro Area	−4.3	1.8	1.6	1.1	−0.4	−0.6	2.0	1.1	1.6
Germany	−5.1	3.6	2.7	1.3	−0.5	−0.7	3.8	1.6	2.0
France	−2.6	1.4	1.7	1.4	−0.4	−0.5	1.4	1.4	1.7
Italy	−5.2	1.3	0.6	0.3	−0.4	−1.0	1.5	0.4	0.4
Spain	−3.7	−0.1	0.8	1.1	0.0	−0.5	0.6	0.7	1.7
Japan	−6.3	4.0	−0.5	2.3	0.2	−0.6	2.5	0.5	2.0
United Kingdom	−4.9	1.4	1.1	1.6	−0.4	−0.7	1.5	1.5	1.7
Canada	−2.8	3.2	2.1	1.9	−0.8	−0.7	3.3	1.4	2.5
Other Advanced Economies[2]	−1.1	5.8	3.6	3.7	−0.4	−0.1	4.8	3.8	3.9
Newly Industrialized Asian Economies	−0.7	8.4	4.7	4.5	−0.4	0.0	6.0	5.2	4.7
Emerging and Developing Economies[3]	**2.8**	**7.3**	**6.4**	**6.1**	**−0.2**	**−0.3**	**7.4**	**6.4**	**6.4**
Central and Eastern Europe	−3.6	4.5	4.3	2.7	−1.0	−0.5	5.3	2.9	2.7
Commonwealth of Independent States	−6.4	4.6	4.6	4.4	−0.5	−0.3	4.6	3.8	3.9
Russia	−7.8	4.0	4.3	4.1	−0.5	−0.4	4.4	4.0	3.6
Excluding Russia	−3.0	6.0	5.3	5.1	−0.3	0.0	. . .	. . .	. . .
Developing Asia	7.2	9.5	8.2	8.0	−0.2	−0.4	9.0	8.1	8.1
China	9.2	10.3	9.5	9.0	−0.1	−0.5	9.8	9.3	9.1
India	6.8	10.1	7.8	7.5	−0.4	−0.3	9.2	7.0	7.5
ASEAN-5[4]	1.7	6.9	5.3	5.6	−0.1	−0.1	6.0	5.4	5.6
Latin America and the Caribbean	−1.7	6.1	4.5	4.0	−0.1	−0.1	5.4	4.1	3.9
Brazil	−0.6	7.5	3.8	3.6	−0.3	0.0	5.0	3.8	3.8
Mexico	−6.2	5.4	3.8	3.6	−0.9	−0.4	4.2	3.7	3.2
Middle East and North Africa	2.6	4.4	4.0	3.6	−0.2	−0.8	. . .	. . .	. . .
Sub-Saharan Africa	2.8	5.4	5.2	5.8	−0.3	−0.1	. . .	. . .	. . .
Memorandum									
European Union	−4.2	1.8	1.7	1.4	−0.3	−0.7	2.1	1.3	1.9
World Growth Based on Market Exchange Rates	−2.3	4.0	3.0	3.2	−0.4	−0.5	. . .	. . .	. . .
World Trade Volume (goods and services)	**−10.7**	**12.8**	**7.5**	**5.8**	**−0.7**	**−0.9**	. . .	. . .	. . .
Imports									
Advanced Economies	−12.4	11.7	5.9	4.0	−0.1	−1.1	. . .	. . .	. . .
Emerging and Developing Economies	−8.0	14.9	11.1	8.1	−1.0	−0.9	. . .	. . .	. . .
Exports									
Advanced Economies	−11.9	12.3	6.2	5.2	−0.6	−0.9	. . .	. . .	. . .
Emerging and Developing Economies	−7.7	13.6	9.4	7.8	−1.8	−0.5	. . .	. . .	. . .
Commodity Prices (U.S. dollars)									
Oil[5]	−36.3	27.9	30.6	−3.1	−3.9	−2.1	. . .	. . .	. . .
Nonfuel (average based on world commodity export weights)	−15.7	26.3	21.2	−4.7	−0.4	−1.4	. . .	. . .	. . .
Consumer Prices									
Advanced Economies	0.1	1.6	2.6	1.4	0.0	−0.3	1.6	2.5	1.3
Emerging and Developing Economies[3]	5.2	6.1	7.5	5.9	0.6	0.3	6.2	6.9	5.1
London Interbank Offered Rate (percent)[6]									
On U.S. Dollar Deposits	1.1	0.5	0.4	0.5	−0.2	−0.3	. . .	. . .	. . .
On Euro Deposits	1.2	0.8	1.3	1.2	−0.4	−1.4	. . .	. . .	. . .
On Japanese Yen Deposits	0.7	0.4	0.5	0.3	0.0	0.1	. . .	. . .	. . .

Note: Real effective exchange rates are assumed to remain constant at the levels prevailing during July 18–August 15, 2011. When economies are not listed alphabetically, they are ordered on the basis of economic size. The aggregated quarterly data are seasonally adjusted.

[1]The quarterly estimates and projections account for 90 percent of the world purchasing-power-parity weights.

[2]Excludes the G7 (Canada, France, Germany, Italy, Japan, United Kingdom, United States) and Euro Area countries.

[3]The quarterly estimates and projections account for approximately 80 percent of the emerging and developing economies.

[4]Indonesia, Malaysia, Philippines, Thailand, and Vietnam.

[5]Simple average of prices of U.K. Brent, Dubai, and West Texas Intermediate crude oil. The average price of oil in U.S. dollars a barrel was $79.03 in 2010; the assumed price based on futures markets is $103.20 in 2011 and $100.00 in 2012.

[6]Six-month rate for the United States and Japan. Three-month rate for the Euro Area.

1.2, top panels); and that Cyprus has come under major pressure. Interbank markets are again under strain, and some banks reportedly are finding it difficult to continue to obtain funding (Figure 1.2, center-right panel). With accumulating signs of weakness in key advanced economies, notably bad news about the U.S. economy over the past couple of months, equity markets have fallen sharply and equity price volatility has jumped up (Figure 1.3, top panels); also, prices for strong sovereign bonds and gold have risen—all signs that investors have become much more cautious about the prospects for the major advanced economies.

More Uneven Expansion

Worryingly, various consumer and business confidence indicators in advanced economies have retreated sharply, rather than strengthened as might have been expected in the presence of mostly temporary shocks that are unwinding. Accordingly, the IMF's Growth Tracker (Figure 1.4, top panel) points to low growth over the near term. WEO projections assume that policymakers keep their commitments and the financial turmoil does not run beyond their control, allowing confidence to return as conditions stabilize. The return to stronger activity in advanced economies will then be delayed rather than derailed by the turmoil. Projections thus point to a modest pickup of activity in advanced economies and robust growth in emerging and developing economies during 2011–12 (Figure 1.5; Table 1.1). Global growth is expected to be about 4 percent. Real GDP growth in the major advanced economies—the United States, euro area, and Japan—is forecast to rise modestly, from about ¾ percent in the first half of 2011 to about 1½ percent in 2012, as the effects of temporary disturbances abate and the fundamental drivers of expansion slowly reassert themselves. Activity will be more robust in a number of other advanced economies, especially in those with close ties to emerging Asia. In emerging and developing economies, capacity constraints, policy tightening, and slowing foreign demand are expected to dampen growth to varying extents across countries. As a result, growth in these economies will drop from about 7 percent in the first half of 2011 to about 6 percent in 2012. Risks are mainly to the downside over the near term.

Figure 1.1. Global Indicators[1]

(Annualized percent change of three-month moving average over previous three-month moving average unless noted otherwise)

Global trade and industrial production lost momentum during the second quarter of 2011, partly because an earthquake and tsunami in Japan disrupted global supply chains and high oil prices slowed consumption in advanced economies. As a result, global growth turned out weaker than expected, mainly in advanced economies.

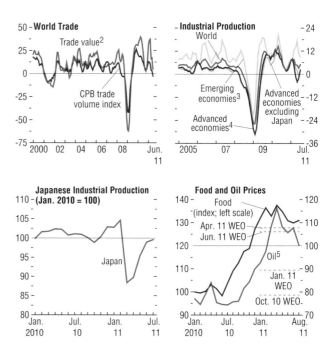

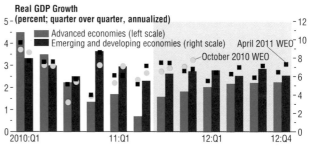

Sources: Bureau of Economic Analysis; U.S. Treasury; European Central Bank; Haver Analytics; Netherlands Bureau for Economic Policy Analysis for CPB trade volume index; and IMF staff estimates.
[1]Not all economies are included in the regional aggregations. For some economies, monthly data are interpolated from quarterly series.
[2]In SDR terms.
[3]Argentina, Brazil, Bulgaria, Chile, China, Colombia, Hungary, India, Indonesia, Latvia, Lithuania, Malaysia, Mexico, Pakistan, Peru, Philippines, Poland, Romania, Russia, South Africa, Thailand, Turkey, Ukraine, and Venezuela.
[4]Australia, Canada, Czech Republic, Denmark, euro area, Hong Kong SAR, Israel, Japan, Korea, New Zealand, Norway, Singapore, Sweden, Switzerland, Taiwan Province of China, United Kingdom, and United States.
[5]U.S. dollars a barrel; right scale; simple average of spot prices of U.K. Brent, Dubai Fateh, and West Texas Intermediate crude oil.

Figure 1.2. Financial Strains in Europe and the United States

The crisis in the euro area has deepened and broadened. Spreads on sovereign bonds of economies in the periphery have reached new highs. Concurrently, spreads of several other economies have also widened to varying degrees. Stock prices have suffered sharp corrections, dragged down by concerns about weak activity and financial sectors in advanced economies. Strains have resurfaced in interbank markets. At the same time, credit default swap (CDS) spreads on U.S. government bonds have moved up. This contrasts with the decline in U.S. bond rates. Both the euro and U.S. dollar depreciated against the Swiss franc until recently.

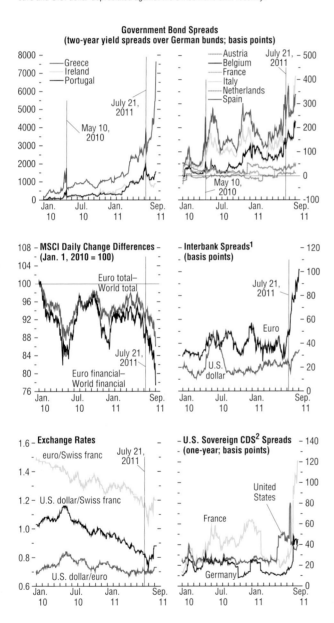

Sources: Bloomberg Financial Markets; and IMF staff calculations.
[1]Three-month London interbank offered rate minus three-month government bill rate.
[2]CDS = credit default swap.

Some expansionary forces are expected to return

Key drivers of stronger activity over the near term include the rebound of activity in Japan, the drop in oil and food prices (Appendix 1.1), and solid demand growth in key emerging market economies.

- Reports from Japan confirm a rapid recovery in both output and domestic spending. Industrial production is now growing rapidly, business sentiment is improving sharply, and household spending is recovering quickly. Although electricity shortages will likely weigh on production throughout the summer, and the government's rebuilding program could suffer further delays, a V-shaped short-term rebound seems to be under way.

- Oil prices are back where they were at the dawn of unrest in the MENA region (Appendix 1.1). They ended the second quarter at about $105 a barrel, after peaking at about $120 by the end of April, helped partly by more supply from other members of the Organization of Petroleum Exporting Countries (OPEC) and the release of crude oil and petroleum stocks from strategic emergency reserves by International Energy Agency (IEA) members. The IMF base metal price index declined by about 9 percent from its first-quarter peak in February. However, the decline in food prices has been much more limited, amounting to about 4 percent, mainly because food crops are now expected to be below earlier estimates.

Activity is likely to receive further support from several sources. The pace of inventory reduction should slow with the repair of global supply chains (Figure 1.6, middle-right panel). Investment in machinery and equipment has been expanding at a fairly solid pace in both advanced and emerging market economies (Figure 1.6, bottom-right panel) and is forecast to continue to do so, helped by strong corporate profitability and relatively healthy corporate balance sheets.

But consumption in major advanced economies is expected to lag behind

Consumption in emerging market economies has been going strong for some time, propelled by rapidly expanding employment and incomes. But consumption in advanced economies is likely to remain anemic for these key reasons:

- Unemployment is likely to stay high for some time. Employment may well exhibit more weakness during much of the summer, even if purchasing managers' index (PMI) survey indicators for employment have so far shown greater resilience than those for production (Figure 1.6, top panels). Neither a significant acceleration nor a large drop in employment seems in the offing.

- Sluggish wages and low funding costs have boosted corporate profits, but this is not directly benefiting households with a high propensity to consume. Concerns about income prospects are particularly elevated in the United States, where an extraordinarily large loss of jobs has added to an ongoing trend decline in the pace of employment creation (see below). Meanwhile, the share of corporate profits in income has returned to about 10 percent, which is close to the high precrisis levels. A similar conclusion about jobs and incomes emerges from an analysis of sectoral output and employment (Box 1.1).

- House prices show no signs of stabilizing in key crisis-hit economies such as the United States and Spain (Figure 1.7, bottom-left panel). A large overhang of unsold properties with underwater mortgages continues to present a major downside risk to consumption in the United States. House prices are rising again in other advanced economies, such as France and Germany, and remain high in Canada. However, households everywhere have recently suffered significant losses in stock market wealth.

Financial volatility could hold back activity

As discussed in the September 2011 *Global Financial Stability Report,* financial stability risks have once again increased dramatically. The IMF staff's financial conditions indices, which consider developments in equity and bond prices, spreads, and bank lending volume in the United States and the euro area, have tightened noticeably lately (see Figure 1.3, bottom panel), reflecting mainly lower stock prices and tighter spreads. How financial markets will evolve—and how they will affect real sectors in advanced economies—is still unclear.

Figure 1.3. Recent Financial Market Developments

Equity markets have retreated, and volatility has been on the rise. Investors have taken flight in government bonds of perceived "safe-haven" countries. There were signs that credit was bottoming until recently. Financial conditions indices have tightened lately, but projections assume gradual easing.

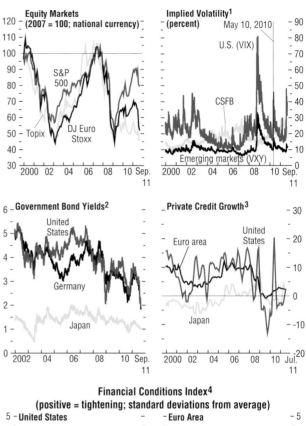

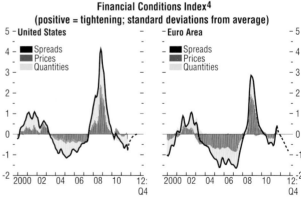

Sources: Bank of America/Merrill Lynch; Bank of Japan; Bloomberg Financial Markets; European Central Bank; Federal Reserve; Haver Analytics; Thomson Datastream; and IMF staff calculations.

[1]VIX = Chicago Board Options Exchange Market Volatility Index; VXY = JPMorgan Emerging Market Volatility Index; CSFB = Credit Suisse Fear Barometer.

[2]Ten-year government bonds.

[3]Annualized percent change of three-month moving average over previous three-month moving average. After January 2009, loans adjusted for sales and securitization are used for the euro area. Spike for the United States in late 2010 is due to securitized credit card assets that banks owned, which were brought onto their balance sheets in 2010.

[4]Historical data are monthly, and forecasts (dashed lines) are quarterly.

Figure 1.4. Prospects for Near-Term Activity

The IMF staff's Growth Tracker points to moderating growth in the very near term, while the Inflation Tracker suggests still elevated price pressure in several emerging market economies. This reflects both high commodity prices and rising core inflation.

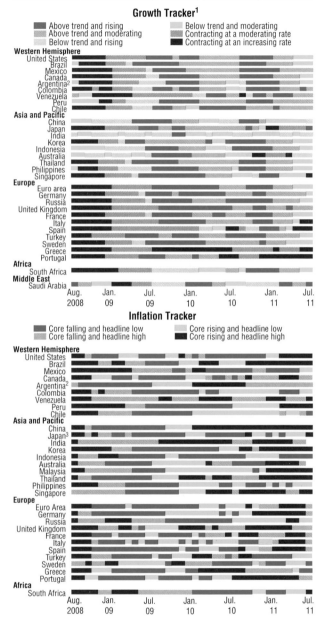

Sources: Haver Analytics; and IMF staff estimates.

[1] The Growth Tracker is described in Matheson (2011). Within regions, countries are listed by economic size.

[2] Figures are based on the official GDP and consumer price index (CPI) data. The authorities have committed to improve the quality of Argentina's official GDP and CPI, so as to bring them into compliance with their obligations under the IMF's Articles of Agreement. Until the quality of data reporting has improved, IMF staff will also use alternative measures of GDP growth and inflation for macroeconomic surveillance, including estimates by: private analysts which have been, on average, significantly lower than official GDP growth from 2008 onward, and provincial statistical offices and private analysts, which have shown inflation considerably higher than the official inflation rate from 2007 onward.

[3] The method gauges inflation pressure relative to historical trends. In Japan, inflation is higher than recent trends but still very low.

WEO forecasts assume that the latest bout of volatility will not lead to large increases in saving rates and that it will delay, rather than derail, the normalization of lending conditions. Spreads on corporate lending in capital markets and on emerging market sovereigns are still relatively low. IMF staff projections assume that banks can do without a sharp and sustained tightening of lending conditions, in some cases thanks to liquidity support from central banks. However, weaker growth prospects pose threats to public and private balance sheets and significantly increase the challenge of coping with heavy debt burdens.

Financial conditions remain supportive of growth in emerging and developing economies, notwithstanding higher volatility (Figure 1.8). In most of these economies, bank credit is still going strong (Figure 1.9, top panels). Search for yield is spurring capital inflows and magnifying already ample domestic liquidity. But flows are volatile (Figure 1.8, bottom panels). WEO forecasts see net private capital flows to most regions rising further, assuming policymakers in advanced economies forestall a cycle of deteriorating sovereign and financial sector prospects. The effect of strong growth and tighter monetary conditions in emerging market economies would then outweigh the effect of more elevated risk aversion among investors. However, as noted in the *Global Financial Stability Report,* with global downside risks rising, emerging markets could also face a sharp reduction in demand, a reversal in capital flows, and a rise in funding costs that could impact the financial soundness of domestic banks.

Monetary policy will continue to support activity

Monetary policy remains highly accommodative in many advanced economies (Figure 1.10, top panels), notwithstanding the end of the second round of quantitative easing (QE2) in the United States and rate hikes in a number of advanced economies, including the euro area. The financial turmoil has already affected monetary policymaking. The central banks of Japan and Switzerland have recently taken steps to further ease monetary conditions, amid rising deflation pressure on account of appreciating currencies. The Federal Reserve has indicated that it expects economic conditions to warrant exceptionally low policy rates at least through mid-2013. The European Central Bank (ECB) has expanded its liquidity operations and stepped up its Securities Market Program. More generally, markets have been pushing out their expectations for rate hikes much further into the future. Despite monetary tightening by many central banks in emerging market economies and other measures to slow credit growth, real interest rates are still low and credit is growing strongly in a number of these economies (Figure 1.10, bottom panels).

But fiscal consolidation will dampen short-term growth

Fiscal consolidation will weigh increasingly on activity (Figure 1.11, middle-left panel). In advanced economies, fiscal policy was neutral in 2010, with loosening in Canada, Germany, Japan, and the United States broadly offset by tightening elsewhere. In many economies, there was significant progress toward fiscal adjustment: policy tightened further in the first half of 2011, and the pace of consolidation is now estimated to be appreciably above earlier estimates. In particular, the structural fiscal balance of the United States is now expected to improve by about ½ percent of GDP in 2011, implying a 1 percentage point of GDP fiscal withdrawal relative to the April 2011 WEO projection. Fiscal policy will tighten further in 2012, mainly on account of tightening in the United States, but also because of sizable consolidation in various euro area economies. IMF staff analysis suggests that the switch from fiscal stimulus to consolidation will dampen short-term activity.[3]

Expansionary forces are expected to offset contractionary forces

On balance, the evidence points to continued, uneven growth. Relative to the June 2011 *WEO Update*, the most noteworthy revision is the reduction in the real GDP growth forecast for the

[3]See Chapter 3 of the October 2010 *World Economic Outlook.*

Figure 1.5. Global Outlook

(Real GDP; quarterly percent change from one year earlier unless noted otherwise)

Global growth is forecast to regain some momentum during the second half of 2011. Real GDP growth in the advanced economies is expected to gradually return to about 2 percent. Activity in emerging and developing economies is expected to decelerate in the face of capacity constraints and tightening policies, settling at a still high rate of about 6 percent in 2012. Growth is expected to remain very elevated in emerging Asia, notably in China and India, followed by sub-Saharan Africa.

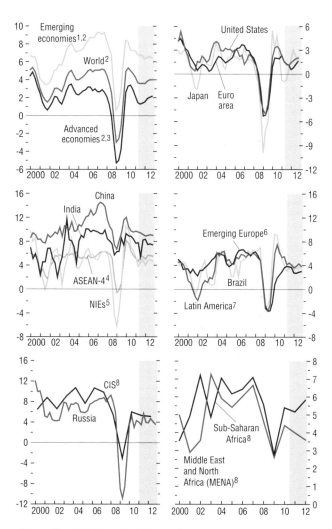

Sources: Haver Analytics; and World Economic Outlook database.
[1]Comprises China, India, Russia, South Africa, Turkey, and economies listed in footnotes 4, 6, and 7.
[2]Includes only economies that report quarterly data.
[3]Australia, Canada, Czech Republic, Denmark, euro area, Hong Kong SAR, Israel, Japan, Korea, New Zealand, Norway, Singapore, Sweden, Switzerland, Taiwan Province of China, United Kingdom, and United States.
[4]Indonesia, Malaysia, Philippines, and Thailand.
[5]Newly industrialized Asian economies (NIEs) comprise Hong Kong SAR, Korea, Singapore, and Taiwan Province of China.
[6]Bulgaria, Hungary, Latvia, Lithuania, and Poland.
[7]Argentina, Brazil, Chile, Colombia, Mexico, Peru, and Venezuela.
[8]CIS = Commonwealth of Independent States. Annual percent change from one year earlier. MENA data exclude Libya for the forecast years due to the uncertain political situation.

Figure 1.6. Current and Forward-Looking Growth Indicators[1]

(Annualized percent change of three-month moving average over previous three-month moving average unless noted otherwise)

Manufacturing and Services PMI indicators still stand above 50 and thus point to continued expansion in the near term but at a slower pace than in 2010. The indicators also suggest that cutbacks in payrolls are not expected. Data on retail sales and industrial production suggest that inventories have not been rebuilt to a major extent thus far. Further support from accelerated inventory building could be in the offing once uncertainty about prospects diminishes again. Private consumption has been strong in emerging economies and sluggish in advanced economies. Investment has grown fairly strongly, except in construction in advanced economies.

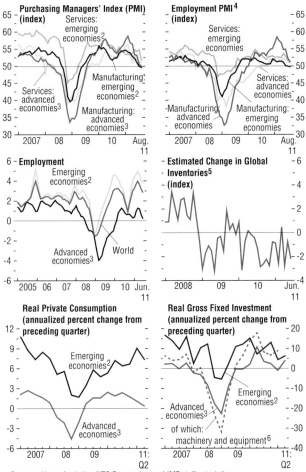

Sources: Haver Analytics; NTC Economics; and IMF staff calculations.

[1]Not all economies are included in the regional aggregations. For some economies, monthly data are interpolated from quarterly series.

[2]Argentina, Brazil, Bulgaria, Chile, China, Colombia, Hungary, India, Indonesia, Latvia, Lithuania, Malaysia, Mexico, Peru, Philippines, Poland, Romania, Russia, South Africa, Thailand, Turkey, Ukraine, and Venezuela.

[3]Australia, Canada, Czech Republic, Denmark, euro area, Hong Kong SAR, Israel, Japan, Korea, New Zealand, Norway, Singapore, Sweden, Switzerland, Taiwan Province of China, United Kingdom, and United States.

[4]Aggregated from available advanced and emerging economies' manufacturing employment PMI and services employment PMI data.

[5]Based on deviations from an estimated (cointegration) relationship between global industrial production and retail sales.

[6]Purchasing-power-parity-weighted averages of metal products and machinery for the euro area, plants and equipment for Japan, plants and machinery for the United Kingdom, and equipment and software for the United States.

United States, by 1 percentage point over 2011 and 2012. Other revisions for advanced economies generally range between ½ and 1 percentage point. The markdowns to most emerging and developing economies amount to about ½ percentage point. Growth will remain relatively robust in these economies because they can counter weaker foreign demand with less policy tightening. The forecast for CEE growth in 2011 has been lowered because of less buoyant (but still strong) growth in Turkey. In addition, prospects for the MENA region have been marked down further, by about ¾ percentage point for 2012.

- Among the advanced economies, real GDP growth in the United States is projected to pick up very gradually from about 1 percent in the second quarter of 2011 to about 2 percent later in 2012. Special factors that boosted activity in the euro area (notably in Germany) during the first quarter have already abated. Moreover, less foreign demand and tensions from the financial turmoil will weigh on investment and consumption, keeping real GDP growth at about ¼ percent during the remainder of 2011, before it rises gradually to about 1 percent during 2012. This assumes that national and euro area policies remain sufficiently strong to keep financial turmoil under control. The Japanese economy is set to expand vigorously during the second half of 2011 and, to a lesser extent, in the first half of 2012, as the economy recovers from the earthquake and tsunami.

- Real GDP growth in emerging and developing economies during the second half of 2011 is expected to be about 6¼ percent, down from about 7 percent during the first half of the year. Emerging Asia is forecast to continue to post strong growth of about 8 percent, propelled by China and India. In Latin America, growth is expected to moderate to 4 percent in 2012, from about 6 percent in 2010, as external demand slows and tighter macroeconomic policies begin to rein in strong domestic demand. With the rebound in the CEE and CIS regions losing some vigor in 2012, particularly in Turkey, real GDP growth in emerging and developing economies is expected to settle at about 6 percent.

Economic Slack alongside Signs of Overheating

The continued expansion of the global economy has come with increasing cyclical diversity. The picture is one of excess capacity in advanced economies and signs of overheating in emerging and developing economies. However, within each group there is significant diversity.

Despite permanent output losses, output gaps remain in advanced economies

By the end of the first half of 2011, many economies had returned to close to precrisis output levels (Figure 1.12, top-left panel). This includes a number of advanced and emerging economies that were hit severely by the crisis (for example, CEE and CIS economies). However, Italy and Spain continue to lag, and output in Japan was severely disrupted by the earthquake and tsunami. Other advanced economies in Asia, in contrast, are already far above precrisis output levels, as are many other emerging and developing economies.

Although the recession has ended, many economies continue to operate far below precrisis trends (Figure 1.12, top-right panel). Output losses relative to trends are largest for economies that were at the epicenter of the crisis, such as the United States and the United Kingdom, as well as for many CEE and CIS economies, notably Russia. In these economies output is some 10 percent below precrisis trends. Losses also persist in economies with very close economic linkages to crisis-hit economies, such as Canada and Mexico, which have close trade ties with the United States.

WEO estimates and forecasts suggest that crisis-related output losses will be long-lasting, even though output gaps remain (Figure 1.12, bottom-left panel).[4] For the United States, the gap is estimated at about 5½ percent of potential GDP in 2011; output is some 10 percent below precrisis trends. With the exception of Japan, output gaps in other major advanced economies are much lower, generally ranging between 2 and 3 percent. Incoming data confirm

[4]This is consistent with evidence on recoveries from financial crises in Chapter 4 of the October 2009 *World Economic Outlook.*

Figure 1.7. Balance Sheets and Saving Rates

(Percent unless noted otherwise)

The accumulation of household debt has been slowing, but there are now signs that this development is bottoming out. Although household debt is still contracting in Japan and the United States, the pace is stabilizing or diminishing. Household saving rates are forecast to move sideways, implying that disposable income growth will translate fully into consumption growth. Although household wealth has received a boost from the recovery of financial markets since 2009, house prices continue to decline in crisis-hit economies.

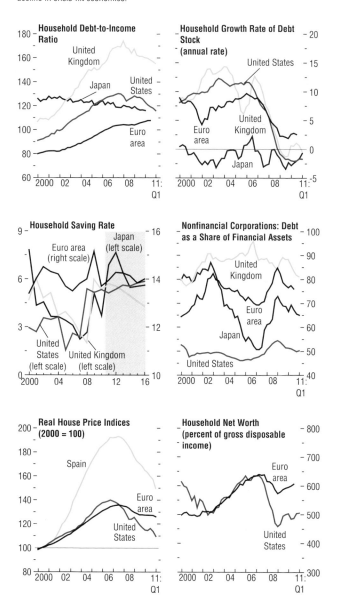

Sources: Haver Analytics; Organization for Economic Cooperation and Development; and IMF staff estimates.

Figure 1.8. Emerging Market Conditions

Equity prices in emerging markets have also retreated but are generally not far below precrisis levels. Interest rate spreads have moved up modestly lately. Flows into equities and bonds, however, have retreated noticeably of late.

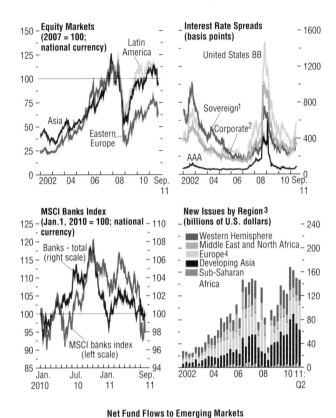

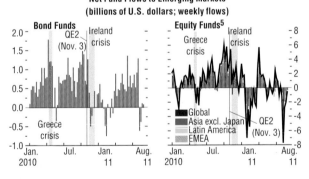

Sources: Bloomberg Financial Markets; Capital Data; EPFR Global; and IMF staff calculations.
[1]JPMorgan EMBI Global Index spread.
[2]JPMorgan CEMBI Broad Index spread.
[3]Total of equity, syndicated loans, and international bond issues.
[4]Central and eastern Europe and Commonwealth of Independent States.
[5]Black line = total. EMEA = Europe, Middle East, and Africa.

that most of the output lost in the euro area and the United States during the crisis will not be recovered (Figure 1.13). Emerging market economies that have been hit hard by the crisis appear to be suffering qualitatively similar output losses. Unemployment rates are higher than the typical rates during the 2002–08 expansion in only a few economies—these include the United Kingdom and the United States (Figure 1.12, bottom-right panel).

Underlying inflation pressure remains relatively elevated in emerging and developing economies

Headline and core inflation have been on the rise in many parts of the world until recently. The IMF's Inflation Tracker confirms that inflation pressure is still relatively elevated, especially in emerging and developing economies (Figure 1.4, bottom panel; and Figure 1.14). In the major advanced economies, however, headline and core inflation appear to be losing some momentum. Three factors will determine the path of inflation over the coming year:

- *Energy and food prices:* These were adding to inflation but have recently receded. Specifically, energy prices are currently far below their 2011 peaks. Food prices, which are particularly important for inflation in emerging and developing economies, have fallen to a much lesser extent. Forecasts assume a stabilization of energy and food prices at present levels. However, prospects are very uncertain, and previous forecasts based on futures markets have not proven accurate. Risks for prices are still tilted toward the upside. Emerging and developing economies are more likely to experience second-round effects on wages from past food and energy price hikes, because these account for a larger share of their consumption baskets (Chapter 3).
- *Output gaps:* In general, these are not exceptionally large. Two notable exceptions are Japan and the United States. However, even in the euro area, wage growth may well remain subdued for some time because employment is lagging the expansion of output. Evidence of labor market tightness is clearer for a number of smaller advanced economies and for many emerging and developing economies.

- *Policy and the credibility of policymakers:* Central bank credibility is well established in advanced economies but less so in many emerging and developing economies, and this is likely to amplify the second-round effects of external price increases (Chapter 3). In anticipation of such pressures, many central banks have begun to raise policy interest rates toward less accommodative levels.

Although headline inflation is projected to recede as food and energy prices moderate, underlying inflation pressure may well rise further, mainly in emerging and developing economies. In advanced economies, headline inflation is forecast to be about 2½ percent in 2011 but then to recede to close to 1½ percent in 2012, assuming that energy and food prices evolve as the markets expect. In emerging and developing economies, headline inflation is expected to settle at about 6 percent in 2012, down from over 7½ percent in 2011, as energy and food prices stabilize but demand pressures raise core inflation. Inflation is expected to stay high through 2011–12 in the CIS, MENA, and SSA regions, averaging 7 to 10 percent. Within the broad trends, some economies are seeing noticeably higher inflation than are their regional peers (for example, Argentina, India, Paraguay, Venezuela, and Vietnam).

Risks Are Clearly to the Downside

Downside risks to activity have increased noticeably since the June 2011 *WEO Update*. Four types of risk deserve particular attention and revolve around (1) weak sovereigns and banks in a number of advanced economies, (2) insufficiently strong policies to address the legacy of the crisis in the major advanced economies, (3) vulnerabilities in a number of emerging market economies, and (4) volatile commodity prices and geopolitical tensions. Various market indicators confirm the qualitative assessment that downside risks are now much higher than in June or April 2011. A downside scenario illustrates how the major advanced economies could fall back into recession and what damage this could inflict on emerging and developing economies.

Figure 1.9. Emerging Market Economies with Strong Credit Expansion[1]

Bank credit growth is high in a number of emerging market economies. In per capita terms, credit close to doubled in real terms during 2005–10. Credit has also grown much faster than nominal GDP in a number of economies. On the one hand, this indicates financial deepening, which is desirable. On the other hand, it raises concern, because the growth rates are so high that they are likely to come at the expense of deteriorating credit quality. Furthermore, high credit growth coincides with rapid increases in real estate prices in many emerging economies. These conditions are reminiscent of those experienced ahead of previous banking crises.

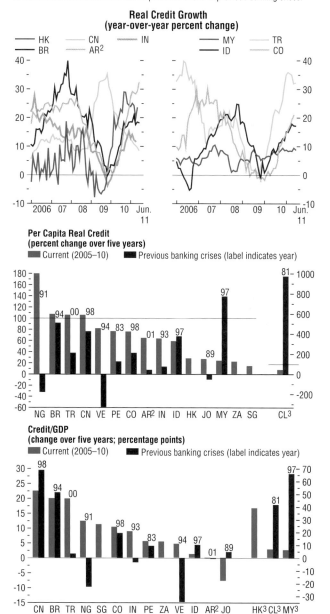

Sources: IMF, *International Financial Statistics;* and IMF staff calculations.
[1]AR: Argentina; BR: Brazil; CL: Chile; CN: China; CO: Colombia; HK: Hong Kong SAR; ID: Indonesia; IN: India; JO: Jordan; MY: Malaysia; NG: Nigeria; PE: Peru; SG: Singapore; TR: Turkey; VE: Venezuela; ZA: South Africa. Figure shows bank credit to the private sector.
[2]For Argentina, calculations are based on official GDP and CPI data.
[3]Right scale.

Figure 1.10. Measures of Monetary Policy and Liquidity in Selected Advanced and Emerging Market Economies
(Percent unless noted otherwise)

Policy rate hikes since the crisis have been limited thus far, except in Latin America, where in a number of countries capacity constraints appear tighter than elsewhere in the world. Nonetheless, short-term interest rates generally remain low in real terms, appreciably below precrisis levels, with the exception of Japan because of deflation. Expectations are for broadly stable policy rates in the advanced economies over the coming year.

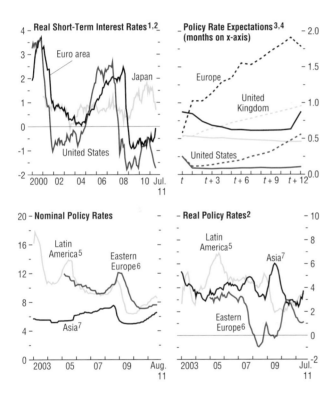

Sources: Bloomberg Financial Markets; Consensus Economics; Eurostat; Haver Analytics; and IMF staff calculations.

[1]Three-month treasury bill.

[2]Relative to core inflation (except for Argentina and Colombia, where headline inflation is used because of unavailable data on core inflation).

[3]Expectations are based on the federal funds rate for the United States, the sterling overnight interbank average rate for the United Kingdom, and the euro interbank offered forward rates for Europe; updated September 7, 2011.

[4]Dashed lines are from the April 2011 *World Economic Outlook*.

[5]Argentina, Brazil, Chile, Colombia, Mexico, and Peru.

[6]Bulgaria, Hungary, Poland, Romania, and Russia.

[7]China, India, Indonesia, Malaysia, Philippines, and Thailand.

Weak sovereign and banking sector balance sheets

The risks concerning weak sovereigns and their interaction with fragile banking systems and the real economy are discussed in depth in the September 2011 *Global Financial Stability Report*. Specifically, markets remain concerned about the euro area. With fragile balance sheets and debt sustainability influenced heavily by expectations, debt markets can become subject to multiple equilibriums. Vulnerable sovereigns are prone to a sudden loss of investor confidence in their debt sustainability if fundamentals deteriorate sharply. European banks are heavily exposed to economies that have recently seen sharply wider sovereign spreads. In this regard, a concern is that capitalization of euro area banks is relatively low, and they rely heavily on wholesale funding, which is prone to freezing during financial turmoil. Trouble in a few sovereigns could thus quickly spread across Europe. From there it could move to the United States—by way of U.S. institutional investors' holdings of European assets—and to the rest of the world.

Weak policy responses to the crisis

Additional risks surround weak policies in the euro area, Japan, and the United States. These give rise to two concerns, including the potential for (1) sudden investor flight from the public debt of systemically important economies and (2) brute force fiscal adjustment or loss of confidence because of a perceived lack of policy room. Under either scenario, major declines in consumer and business confidence are likely, leading to sharp increases in saving rates that undercut activity.

Investors could take flight from government debt of key sovereigns

There are few signs of flight from U.S. or Japanese sovereign debt thus far, and few substitute investments are available. Although sovereign credit default swap (CDS) spreads on U.S. debt have moved up lately and U.S. government debt experienced one rating downgrade, the impact on long-term interest rates of the end of the Federal Reserve's QE2 has been offset by inflows into Treasury securities. Interest rates on Japan's public debt remain very low, despite adverse shocks to the public finances resulting from the earthquake and tsunami. Nonetheless, without more ambitious fiscal consolidation, a sudden rise in government bond yields remains a distinct possibility as long as public debt ratios are projected to rise over the medium term. Long-term rates on the debt of France, Germany, and a few other economies are also very low. However, this could change if commitments at the national or euro area level are not met. The risks could play out in various ways:

- Investors could increasingly reallocate their portfolios to corporate or emerging market debt: This would be the least disruptive scenario, because it could spur demand, although not without potentially raising problems related to absorptive capacity.

- The term premium could rise as investors turn to short-term public debt: This would make the global economy more susceptible to funding shocks.

- Rates could move higher across the yield curve, with depreciation of the U.S. dollar or the Japanese yen (mild credit risk): This might materialize in the context of a broader sovereign rating downgrade that does not upset the status of the United States as the major provider of low-risk assets or an accelerated reduction in the home bias of Japanese investors.

- A strong increase in credit risk could quickly morph into a liquidity shock, as global investors take flight into precious metals and cash: This could occur if there were major political deadlock on how to move forward with consolidation in the United States or if the euro area crisis were to take a dramatic turn for the worse. The global repercussions of such shocks would likely be very severe.

Hasty fiscal adjustment and the absence of policy room could harm growth

In the systemically important advanced economies, activity and confidence are still fragile, and a sudden increase in household saving rates remains a distinct possibility. If fiscal consolidation were suddenly stepped up further at the expense of the disposable income of people with a high marginal propensity to consume, these economies could be thrown back into stagnation. For example, if (contrary to WEO assumptions) payroll tax relief and

Figure 1.11. General Government Fiscal Balances and Public Debt

(Percent of GDP unless noted otherwise)

Public deficits and debt rose sharply during the crisis, especially in advanced economies. Major adjustment is required, especially in Japan and the United States, to bring debt back down to prudent levels. Fiscal policy will turn increasingly contractionary in the advanced economies during 2012–13. Because of the low share of permanent consolidation measures in the United States relative to other countries, fiscal policy will do little to alleviate global current account imbalances. However, differences in fiscal policy stances will help reduce imbalances within the euro area.

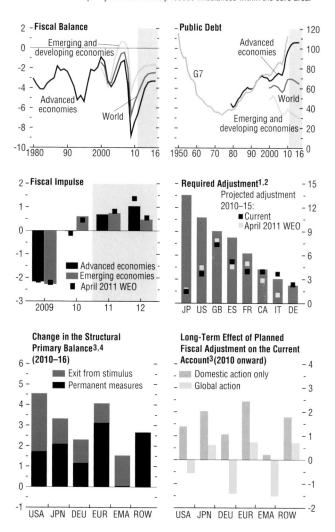

Sources: IMF, *Fiscal Monitor;* and IMF staff estimates.
[1] CA: Canada; DE: Germany; ES: Spain; FR: France; GB: United Kingdom; IT: Italy; JP: Japan; US: United States.
[2] Cyclically adjusted primary balance adjustment needed to bring the debt ratio to 60 percent of GDP by 2030. For Canada and Japan, the scenario assumes net debt targets (for Japan, a reduction in net debt to 80 percent of GDP, corresponding to a gross debt target of about 200 percent of GDP).
[3] Cumulative effect in percent of GDP during 2010–16; DEU: Germany; EMA: emerging Asia; EUR: euro area excluding Germany; JPN: Japan; ROW: rest of the world; USA: United States.
[4] The U.S. permanent measures shown in the figure are those planned in the president's February budget proposal.

Figure 1.12. Cyclical Conditions[1]

Output in major advanced economies has returned close to or above precrisis levels, with some notable exceptions. In emerging and developing economies, it is already well above precrisis levels, except in the CEE and CIS economies, which were hit hard by the financial crisis. Output in most advanced and CEE and CIS economies is still well below precrisis trends. However, much of the loss relative to trends is not expected to be recovered over the medium term. Accordingly, output gaps are generally much lower than losses relative to precrisis trends would suggest. Consistent with a view of generally limited output gaps, unemployment rates in most of the world are not much higher than precrisis averages—notable exceptions include the United States and the United Kingdom, which were at the epicenter of the crisis.

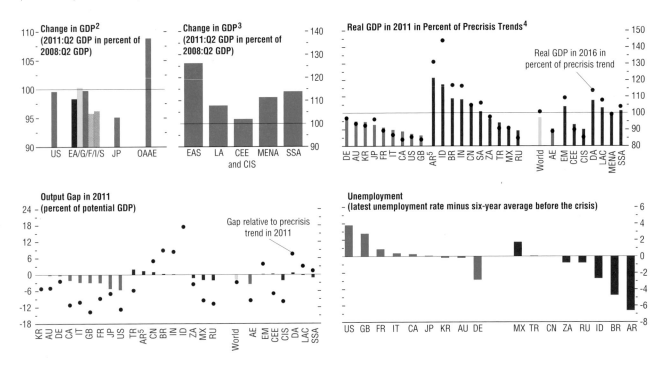

Source: IMF staff estimates.
[1]AR: Argentina; AE: advanced economies; AU: Australia; BR: Brazil; CA: Canada; CEE: central and eastern Europe; CIS: Commonwealth of Independent States; CN: China; DA: developing Asia; DE: Germany; EM: emerging economies; FR: France; GB: United Kingdom; ID: Indonesia; IN: India; IT: Italy; JP: Japan; KR: Korea; LAC: Latin America and the Caribbean; MENA: Middle East and North Africa; MX: Mexico; RU: Russia; SA: Saudi Arabia; SSA: sub-Saharan Africa; TR: Turkey; US: United States; ZA: South Africa.
[2]EA/G/F/I/S: euro area/Germany/France/Italy/Spain; OAAE: other advanced Asian economies.
[3]EAS: emerging Asia; LA: Latin America; CEE and CIS: central and eastern Europe and Commonwealth of Independent States; MENA: Middle East and North Africa; SSA: sub-Saharan Africa. Due to data limitations, annual data are used for MENA and SSA.
[4]Precrisis trend obtained by extrapolating 1996–2006 real GDP growth.
[5]Figures are based on official GDP data.

help for the unemployed in the United States are not prolonged, U.S. growth could be significantly lower. By the same token, if sound medium-term consolidation plans are not implemented, households and businesses may take an increasingly dim view of future prospects and drastically raise their saving rates. The result could be a lost decade for growth. Concerns among U.S. households about

future income prospects could be a symptom of such risks. Also, the September 2011 *Global Financial Stability Report* relates the latest bout of financial volatility to concerns in markets about policymakers' ability to rally support for strengthening public and banking sector balance sheets and growth-enhancing reforms. Moreover, as discussed in the September 2011 *Fiscal Monitor,* even with the plans currently in place, most major advanced economies will not achieve a large reduction in public debt over the medium term, which severely limits the ability of fiscal policy to stabilize output and employment in the future.

Vulnerabilities in emerging market economies

Overheating risks have become more differentiated since the April 2011 *World Economic Outlook*. These risks relate mainly to rapid credit growth and financial vulnerabilities. In a few cases, external vulnerabilities have begun to move into the foreground.

High credit and asset price growth could undermine financial stability

A number of major emerging and developing economies, and advanced economies with very close ties to them, continue to see buoyant credit and asset price growth (see Figure 1.9). Credit growth has been high in Brazil, Colombia, Hong Kong SAR, India, Indonesia, Peru, and Turkey. In China, however, real credit growth has continued to recede, to about 10 percent at an annual rate: housing market transactions and prices have fallen from exceptionally high levels, although construction is still going strong. Prices keep climbing rapidly in Hong Kong SAR and continue to rise in Brazil and Singapore. In India and Indonesia, by contrast, house price increases have been more contained, because credit is flowing mainly into infrastructure and industry. Financial stability risks in all these economies must be monitored for some time, given the sheer volume of credit growth over the past five years (see Figure 1.9, middle and bottom panels).

External vulnerabilities could cause an abrupt slowdown of capital inflows

So far, buoyant credit and asset price growth in emerging and developing economies has not led to a sharp acceleration in domestic demand or a precarious widening of current account imbalances. However, vulnerability is beginning to build, especially in economies where credit is spurred by capi-

Figure 1.13. Global Projection Model Estimates of the Output Gap

The recent financial crisis had a significant impact on the productive capacity of the economies at the epicenter: the United States and the euro area. Estimates of this unobservable variable are critical for policymakers, indicating the degree of economic slack and hence the appropriate policy stance. The top panels show the latest estimates of the output gap from the GPM[1] multivariate technique relative to those of the Congressional Budget Office, the European Commission, and the April 2011 *World Economic Outlook* (WEO), which also considers judgmental factors. New data and revisions to historical data have contributed to revisions in our estimate of the U.S. output gap. Revisions to historical GDP data have led to an increase in the estimate of excess supply at the trough of the recession. New data on inflation and capacity utilization have led to a reduction in the estimate of excess supply at the end of 2011:Q2 compared with our forecast of a year ago. For the euro area, faster than previously forecast growth is the primary source of the revision to our estimate of the amount of excess supply at the end of 2011:Q2.

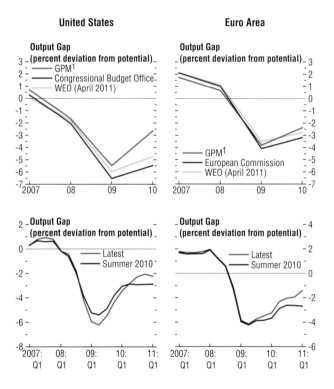

Source: IMF staff calculations.
[1]GPM = Global Projection Model.

Figure 1.14. Global Inflation

(Twelve-month change in the consumer price index unless noted otherwise)

Inflation has been moving up, reflecting the sharp recovery of commodity prices and emerging capacity constraints. However, core inflation remains low in the major advanced economies. In emerging market economies, by contrast, it has risen significantly but now shows signs of moderating. With commodity prices forecast to stabilize or retreat, headline inflation can be expected to decline. In emerging market economies, underlying inflation pressure is likely to continue to stay relatively elevated because of strong activity and relatively low unemployment.

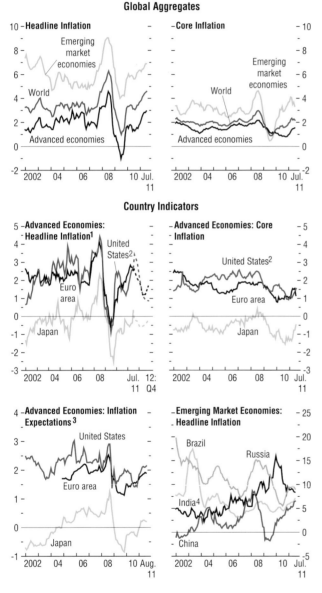

Sources: Consensus Economics; Haver Analytics; and IMF staff calculations.
[1]Historical data are monthly, and forecasts (dashed lines) are quarterly.
[2]Personal consumption expenditure deflator.
[3]One-year-ahead *Consensus Forecasts.* The December values are the average of the surrounding November and January values.
[4]Consumer price index for industrial workers.

tal inflows (Box 1.2). A key reason for the limited increase in current account deficits is the recovery in commodity prices. In fact, the current account surpluses of emerging and developing economies have been rising during the recovery, from 1½ percent of GDP in 2009 to 2½ percent in 2011. Energy-exporting MENA economies account for the bulk of this widening, followed by CIS economies, with SSA economies contributing to a small extent. By contrast, the Latin American economies have seen a widening of deficits, from ½ percent to 1½ percent of GDP. Against the backdrop of large terms-of-trade gains over this period, this development testifies to strong domestic demand pressures. The deficits are too low to present immediate stability concerns, but they could rapidly escalate if commodity prices fall significantly, potentially raising the threat of sudden stops. CEE economies also have seen some widening of their current account deficits as the sudden stop of capital inflows has gradually let up, which is a welcome development. However, in Turkey the deficit has reached disconcerting levels, and its funding is mostly short term.

Supply shocks in commodity markets could dent household real incomes

With tight demand-supply balances, commodity markets continue to present significant sources of downside risk to global activity. Disruptions to the global oil supply could seriously affect activity in advanced economies by cutting into the already sluggish real growth of household incomes. Rising food prices would do the same, with particularly deleterious consequences for developing economies. On both fronts, however, pressures have eased lately because prices have moderated.

Various quantitative indicators paint a deteriorating picture of risks (Figure 1.15). The Chicago Board Options Exchange Market Volatility Index (VIX) has recently reached very high levels again. Over the past year, the risk of a serious global slowdown—that is, global growth falling below 2 percent—was less than 5 percent, according to the IMF staff's fan chart. But now, according to the IMF staff's usual methodology, the probability of growth below 2 percent is substantially higher—more than

10 percent. Regarding the four risk factors underlying the fan chart computed with the usual methodology, three point to downside risks for growth and one points to upside risks for 2012 (Figure 1.15, middle panel):

- *Term spread:* There is now a significant risk that the yield curve flattens in 2012, indicating downside risks to growth. For 2011, the risks are roughly balanced, as they were in the April 2011 *World Economic Outlook.*[5]
- *Oil market:* Oil-related risks through 2012 remain to the upside for prices and thus to the downside for global growth, as in April.
- *Inflation:* Following significant upward revisions in inflation forecasts for 2011, inflation risks for the year are modestly to the downside, implying modest upside risks for growth. For 2012, there is now a downside risk to growth from higher inflation, unlike in April 2011,[6] possibly reflecting downward revisions to inflation forecasts.
- *S&P 500:* This risk factor still points to the upside for output for both 2011 and 2012.

New shocks could undercut the expansion

A downside scenario shows the repercussions of major financial turbulence in the euro area, combined with a downscaling of expectations for U.S. medium-term growth prospects and real-estate-related financial stress in emerging Asia (Figure 1.16). This scenario assumes that euro area banks need to suddenly absorb mark-to-market losses to such an extent that their bank capital falls by 10 percent, and that this triggers a new round of deleveraging. At the same time, markets revise medium-term growth prospects for the United States downward, while Asia experiences an increase in real-estate-lending-related losses.

[5]In this framework, a steepening yield curve is associated with higher growth prospects. Generally, the term spread captures the spread between long-term and short-term interest rates and is interpreted as reflecting growth prospects. It can also reflect sovereign default risks. The results are based on the simple average of Germany, Japan, the United Kingdom, and the United States. For further details on the construction of the fan chart, see Elekdag and Kannan (2009).

[6]An upside surprise in inflation would warrant higher interest rates and thus would entail lower growth. The results are based on market forecasts for inflation in the G7 economies as well as in Brazil, China, India, Mexico, and Russia.

Figure 1.15. Risks to the Global Outlook

Risks to the outlook remain large, and downside risks dominate upside risks. The probability of global growth below 2 percent is appreciably higher than in the April 2011 *World Economic Outlook* (WEO).

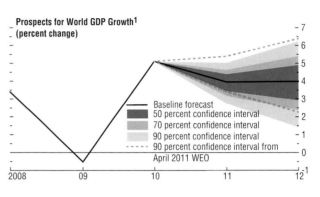

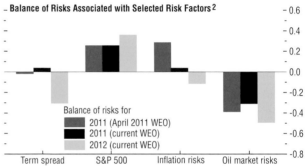

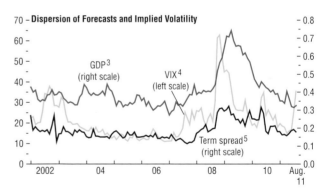

Sources: Bloomberg Financial Markets; Chicago Board Options Exchange; Consensus Economics; and IMF staff estimates.
[1]The fan chart shows the uncertainty around the WEO central forecast with 50, 70, and 90 percent confidence intervals. As shown, the 70 percent confidence interval includes the 50 percent interval, and the 90 percent confidence interval includes the 50 and 70 percent intervals. See Appendix 1.2 in the April 2009 *World Economic Outlook* for details.
[2]Bars depict the coefficient of skewness expressed in units of the underlying variables. The values for inflation risks and oil market risks are entered with the opposite sign, because they represent downside risks to growth.
[3]The series measures the dispersion of GDP forecasts for the G7 economies (Canada, France, Germany, Italy, Japan, United Kingdom, United States), Brazil, China, India, and Mexico.
[4]VIX: Chicago Board Options Exchange Market Volatility Index.
[5]The series measures the dispersion of term spreads implicit in interest rate forecasts for Germany, Japan, the United Kingdom, and the United States.

Figure 1.16. WEO Downside Scenario

(Deviation from control; years on x-axis)

This downside scenario uses a six-region version of the Global Economy Model (GEM) calibrated to represent the United States, Japan, the euro area, emerging Asia, Latin America, and the rest of the world. The scenario features shocks arising in three regions: the euro area, the United States, and emerging Asia. In the euro area, the shock is to bank capital, reflecting primarily recognition of losses on holdings of public debt but also of other losses on loans arising from the macroeconomic fallout. In the United States, the shock has two components. The first is slower potential output growth and the second is the resulting increase in loan losses (e.g., on the mortgage portfolio). The shock in emerging Asia is loan losses, reflecting poor lending decisions in the past. Furthermore, corporate risk premiums in emerging Asia, Japan, and Latin America are assumed to be correlated with the rise in risk premiums in the euro area and the United States, in a manner broadly consistent with what was observed during the collapse of Lehman Brothers. As a result of the large shock to global output, especially in the euro area and the United States, commodity prices plummet, dragging down activity in commodity exporters. The accompanying charts trace out the implications for GDP, firm net worth (in both the tradables and nontradables sectors), the effective interest rate faced by firms in the various regions, and commodity prices.

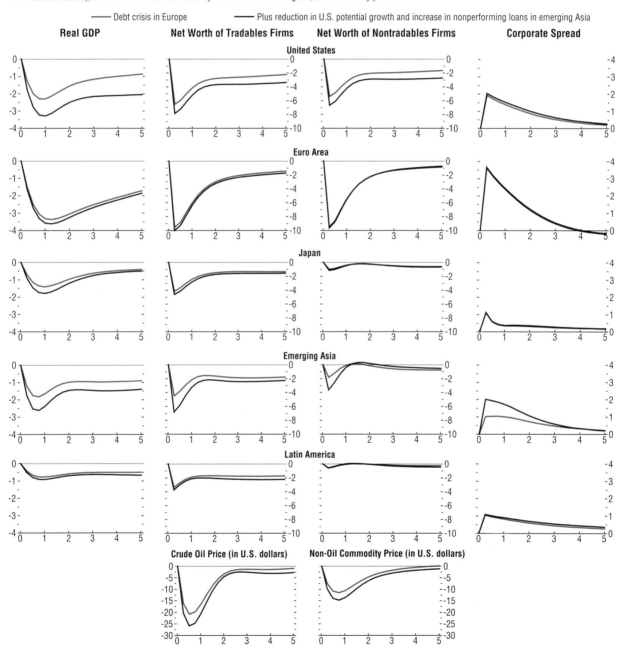

Source: GEM simulations.

Under such a scenario, global risk aversion would rise sharply, and funding rates for banks and nonfinancial corporations would shoot up to varying degrees. Emerging market economies would suffer from slumping commodity prices and a sudden reversal in capital flows. Given the limited room for monetary and fiscal policy in advanced economies to respond vigorously, a serious global slowdown would ensue, which would undo much of the progress since the end of the Great Recession. The United States and the euro area would fall back into recession, with output in 2012 more than 3 percent below WEO projections. Output in Japan would be some 1½ percent below the WEO projection; in emerging Asia it would be 2½ percent lower. Latin America would suffer higher risk premiums and lower commodity prices, which would drag output down almost 1 percent relative to the baseline.

Separately, in the advanced economies of the G7, recent falls in equity prices also point to a deterioration in growth prospects. As shown in Box 1.3, there is some evidence that drops in equity prices are associated with a greater chance of a new recession in a number of economies. Specifically, using the behavior of equity prices over the past quarter, a simple probabilistic model for these economies predicts an increased risk of a new recession from the third quarter of 2011 for the United States, and to a lesser extent for France and the United Kingdom.

Policy Challenges

With increasingly diverse cyclical and financial conditions, national policy requirements have increasingly diverged. In qualitative terms, requirements remain similar to those in recent issues of the *World Economic Outlook*. But on key fronts the difficulties are now greater, and even where there has been a policy response more needs to be done. This is perhaps most urgent in the euro area. In the meantime, global demand rebalancing, commodity markets, and financial system reform pose multilateral challenges.

Addressing the crisis in the euro area

The crisis in the euro area continues to deepen. The measures approved at the July 21, 2011, EU summit represent significant progress, but further

efforts are urgently needed. Once implemented, the measures imply that funding under the European Financial Stability Fund (EFSF) can also pay for debt buybacks or bank recapitalization, can be used on a precautionary basis, and will have much longer maturities and lower interest rates. There are three remaining challenges. The first is to quickly adopt the summit's decisions at the national level while sending a clear signal that euro area members will continue to do whatever it takes to preserve confidence in the euro. In the meantime, the ECB will need to continue to intervene forcefully (with suitable sovereign safeguards) to support orderly markets in sovereign debt. The second challenge involves advancing programs with economies in the periphery that strike the right balance between fiscal consolidation and structural reform on the one hand and external support on the other. The third challenge is to promptly finalize EU governance reforms. These probably will have to be strengthened over the medium term to ensure that the shared responsibility of all EU members for national macroeconomic policies is commensurate with increased risk sharing.

National Perspectives on Policy Challenges
Releasing the brakes on lagging economies

In many advanced economies, the priority remains fixing the financial system and, over the medium term, greatly reducing high public deficits. Repairing financial systems by strengthening incentives to build capital, including through public intervention, is essential to reestablishing trust and facilitating better pass-through of easy monetary conditions to economic activity—thereby unlocking a key brake on growth. In addition, a number of economies must deploy structural reforms that improve their macroeconomic performance. Such reforms may not boost growth in the short term, but they can help build confidence and improve medium-term prospects.

Continued monetary accommodation

Monetary policy can remain accommodative in many advanced economies. Given increasing risks to U.S. growth, the Federal Reserve should stand ready to deploy new unconventional support for the economy, provided inflation expectations stay subdued. Given declining inflation pressure and heightened financial and sovereign tensions, the ECB should lower its policy rate if downside risks to growth and inflation persist. Unconventional policies should continue until there is a durable reduction in financial stress, including resolution of the sovereign debt crisis. In Japan, rates can stay at their present levels, and unconventional policy support in the form of private asset purchases could be stepped up further to help accelerate the exit from deflation. Many other advanced economies have tightened to greater degrees already, because they are experiencing higher inflation pressure. They may have to do more but can stay on hold as long as downside risks are unusually high.

Strong fiscal consolidation and reform

Given still tepid activity in many advanced economies, immediate cutbacks to spending and tax increases should ideally be small while strong entitlement and tax reforms are being implemented that cut future deficits. Because major progress in cutting future spending has proved hard to achieve, however, postponing near-term consolidation is not an option in most advanced economies. But economies with relatively strong public balance sheets and strong medium-term plans could slow the pace of near-term adjustment if downside risks threaten to materialize. In crisis economies, gradual adjustment is not in the cards. Similarly, in economies that investors perceive to be vulnerable, it seems appropriate to err on the side of consolidation. In all economies, stronger fiscal rules and institutions can help rebuild credibility. The specific recommendations are discussed in the September 2011 *Fiscal Monitor*.

The key fiscal priority for major advanced economies—especially the United States and Japan—is to implement credible and well-paced medium-term consolidation programs focused on long-term debt sustainability. Addressing this is of paramount importance to regain room for more policy maneuvering.

- For the United States, the main priority is to soon launch a medium-term deficit reduction plan—including entitlement reform and tax reforms that gradually raise revenues—so as to stabilize the

debt ratio by mid-decade and gradually reduces it thereafter under realistic macroeconomic assumptions. This would allow for a short-term fiscal policy stance that is more attuned to the cycle—for example, through the adoption of measures targeted to labor and housing markets, state and local governments, and infrastructure spending. In this respect, the American Jobs Act would provide needed short-term support to the economy, but it must be flanked with a strong medium-term fiscal consolidation plan that raises revenues and contains the growth of entitlement spending. With a less ambitious medium-term fiscal strategy in place, fiscal consolidation should start in 2012, but its pace should reflect the need to sustain a weak recovery, and it should include the extension of unemployment insurance and payroll tax relief, with a fiscal withdrawal of 1 to 1½ percent of GDP.

- Similarly, for Japan a more ambitious fiscal strategy is needed—equivalent to a front-loaded 10 percent of GDP fiscal adjustment over 10 years—that brings the public debt ratio down decisively by the middle of the decade. Given the limited scope for cutting expenditures, fiscal adjustment will have to rely mainly on new revenue sources, limits on spending growth, and entitlement reform. Specifically, the strategy should be centered on a gradual increase in the consumption tax to 15 percent.

- The major euro area economies have made good progress in adopting and implementing strong medium-term consolidation plans. They are committed to reducing deficits to below 3 percent of GDP by 2013 and to stabilizing the level of public debt by 2015. Based on WEO macroeconomic projections, Spain still needs to identify new measures to achieve its objectives. France may have to do the same from 2013 onward, given the announcement in August of additional deficit-reduction measures for 2011–12. Italy has recently greatly strengthened its medium-term fiscal plan and is now expected to come fairly close to a structurally balanced budget in 2013. Adjustment in Germany during 2011–16 (at about ½ percent a year) is appropriately lower than elsewhere in the euro area—on present plans, the general government would be close to balance in 2014.

- Importantly, in all these economies adjustment will need to continue for some time, with a view to reaching surpluses that help bring down high public debt ahead of accelerated population aging. This will also be necessary to provide sufficient fiscal policy room to support balance sheet repair and growth and job creation.

More financial repair

As discussed in the September 2011 *Global Financial Stability Report*, financial repair is essential along two dimensions: injecting new capital and restructuring weak but viable banks while closing others, and repairing wholesale funding markets. Progress along both fronts has been slow, especially in Europe. In general, European banks tend to be less strongly capitalized and more reliant on wholesale funding than are their peers elsewhere. The stress in sovereign and interbank markets underscores the urgent need to address weakly capitalized banks. Symptoms of their difficulties include falling deposits or "deposit wars," in which banks aggressively bid up deposit rates; exclusion from wholesale markets; heavy reliance on ECB funding; and sluggish credit growth and tight lending conditions. Prudential authorities now need to foster private injections of capital in banks (as was done for some Spanish *cajas*) and promote consolidation and cross-border investment (as recently seen in Ireland). Absent these measures, they must make the case either for injecting public funds into weak banks or for closing them. They will need to ensure that these banks do not "gamble for resurrection" by offering very high deposit rates or engaging in very risky lending. Given prevailing balance sheet uncertainties, capital requirements should be set ambitiously high and be met well ahead of the Basel III timetable.

Facilitating gradual adjustment in housing markets

In the United States, the large number of underwater mortgages poses a risk for a downward spiral of falling house prices and distress sales that further undermines consumption and labor mobility. The challenge for policymakers is to facilitate gradual adjustment. Administrative complexity, capacity constraints, and conflicting incentives among banks, loan servicers, and bond investors have thus far hindered

potentially efficient loan modifications that would forestall at least some costly foreclosures. Taken together, these factors can provide justification for further policy action to mitigate distress sales, such as allowing mortgages to be modified in courts, expanding state programs that assist unemployed homeowners, and encouraging government-sponsored enterprises to participate in principal write-downs.

Putting the brakes on overheating economies

Since the April 2011 *World Economic Outlook*, many emerging and developing economies have implemented policy rate hikes or other measures to reduce credit growth. With a few exceptions, the overheating signals are mainly flashing yellow rather than red (Figure 1.17). Vulnerabilities related to strong credit expansion and, in some cases, buoyant domestic demand are still a concern.

- In economies with large capital inflows and appreciated exchange rates, such as in Latin America, fiscal tightening is urgently needed to roll back deficits that expanded during the crisis and to alleviate the burden of adjustment on monetary policy. Such tightening appears less warranted, however, in the emerging Asian economies with large external surpluses and relatively low fiscal deficits. In these economies, more exchange rate appreciation could help contain inflation pressure, while fiscal consolidation could be slowed with a view to supporting domestic consumption, should downside risks threaten to materialize.

- Regarding monetary policy, real interest rates remain low relative to precrisis levels in a number of economies, and more monetary tightening will be needed under WEO projections. However, requirements vary across countries, and some can afford to pause their rate hike cycle for as long as uncertainty remains exceptionally high.

More monetary tightening

The IMF staff's Global Projection Model (GPM) points to a need for rate increases of zero to 2 percentage points on average in Latin America and emerging Asia (Figure 1.18, top-left panel). However, requirements vary appreciably across countries. Simple Taylor rules, which are based on IMF

Figure 1.17. Overheating Indicators for the G20 Economies[1]

Among G20 economies, a number of emerging market economies are seeing buoyant activity, low unemployment, and relatively high inflation in comparison with precrisis norms. Output gap estimates of IMF country desks paint a more reassuring picture than the other indicators of internal balance. Indicators of external balance send mixed signals: terms of trade are very favorable for some emerging market economies, limiting the deterioration of current account balances in response to strong domestic demand. In others, domestic demand is not running far ahead of output. In a few, current account deficits have reached historically high levels. Indicators of financial developments raise concerns mainly due to high credit growth.

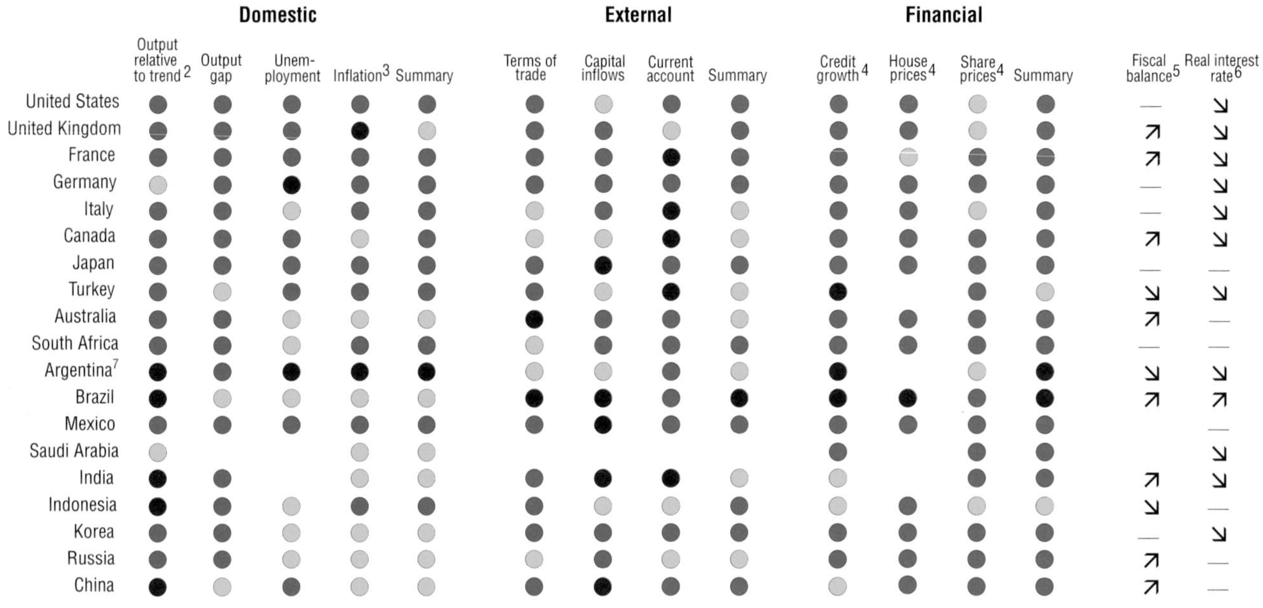

Sources: Australia Bureau of Statistics; Bank for International Settlements; CEIC China Database; Global Property Guide; Haver Analytics; IMF, *Balance of Payments Statistics;* IMF, *International Financial Statistics;* Organization for Economic Cooperation and Development; and IMF staff calculations.

[1]For each indicator, except as noted below, economies are assigned colors based on current predicted 2011 values relative to their precrisis (1997–2006) average. Blue indicates less than 0.5 standard deviation above the 1997–2006 average; yellow indicates greater than or equal to 0.5 but less than 1.5 standard deviations above the 1997–2006 average; red indicates greater than or equal to 1.5 standard deviations above the 1997–2006 average. Each indicator is scored as red = 2, yellow = 1, and blue = 0; summary scores are calculated as the sum of selected component scores divided by the maximum possible sum of those scores. Summary colors are assigned red if the summary score is greater than or equal to 0.66, yellow if greater than or equal to 0.33 but less than 0.66, and blue if less than 0.33.

[2]Output more than 2.5 percent above the precrisis trend is indicated by red. Output less than 2.5 percent below the trend is indicated by blue.

[3]For the following inflation-targeting countries, the target inflation rate was used instead of the 1997–2006 average in the calculation of the inflation indicator: Australia, Brazil, Canada, Indonesia, Korea, Mexico, South Africa, Turkey, United Kingdom. For the non-inflation-targeting countries, red is assigned if inflation is approximately 10 percent or higher, yellow if inflation is approximately 5 to 9 percent, and blue if inflation is less than 5 percent.

[4]The indicators for credit growth, house price growth, and share price growth are calculated relative to the 1997–2006 average of output growth.

[5]Arrows in the fiscal balance column represent the forecast change in the structural balance as a percent of GDP over the period 2010–11. An increase of more than 0.5 percent of GDP is indicated by an up arrow; a decrease of more than 0.5 percent of GDP is indicated by a down arrow.

[6]Real policy interest rates below zero are identified by a down arrow; real interest rates above 3 percent are identified by an up arrow.

[7]Figures are based on official GDP and CPI data.

staff forecasts for inflation in 2013 and output gap estimates for 2011, suggest that a few G20 economies would require larger rate hikes than suggested by GPM estimates (for example, Argentina, India, Russia); others need to tighten less or can afford to postpone further moves, given growing uncertainty.[7] However, even in economies in which interest rates are already relatively high, the monetary authorities will need to be vigilant.

- In emerging and developing economies where the credibility of monetary policy is less well established, high headline inflation could fuel greater than expected wage inflation. In fact, simple Taylor rules that use current headline inflation recommend more tightening than those that use IMF staff forecasts for inflation. Risks for commodity prices are tilted to the upside, and commodity price inflation may well be more persistent than expected. Thus, inflation forecasts for 2013 are subject to upside risk.

- Output gap estimates are notoriously unreliable, whether for advanced or for emerging and developing economies. They frequently overestimate the extent of slack following periods of strong growth, such as many emerging and developing economies have recently enjoyed. Replacing IMF staff output gap estimates with deviations of output from precrisis (1996–2006) trends reveals a need for much greater tightening, according to Taylor rules.[8]

- In a number of emerging and developing economies, credit growth and asset prices are still very buoyant. Related financial stability risks are best addressed with prudential measures. However, if such measures do not prove effective, monetary policy may need to be tighter than warranted from the perspective of inflation.

[7]Importantly, the quantitative indications of these simple rules should not be taken literally because they cannot do justice to country-specific factors, such as different objectives for inflation.

[8]Three notable exceptions are Mexico, Russia, and Turkey. However, Mexico and Russia are considered to have suffered some permanent output losses relative to trends: Mexico on account of close trade relations with the United States and Russia on account of financial turmoil. Precrisis output trends in Turkey were generally not sustainable.

Figure 1.18. Policy Requirements in Emerging Market Economies

Estimates obtained from the Global Projection Model (GPM) point to the need for further policy rate hikes in Latin America and emerging Asia. The GPM estimates assume that a number of emerging market economies in Asia also adopt other measures to tighten monetary conditions, such as controls on credit growth. Requirements differ across economies. Simple Taylor rules point to a need for major tightening in Argentina, India, Russia, and Turkey. In other economies, much less tightening may be needed or tightening can pause while uncertainty stays high. Also, in most economies structural fiscal balances should be brought back up to levels prevailing before the crisis.

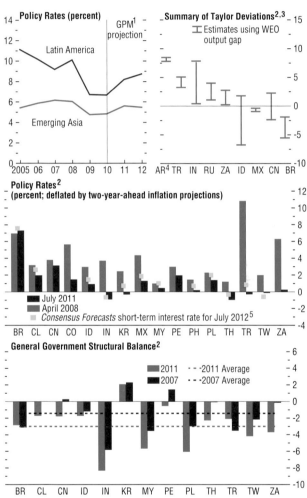

Sources: Bloomberg Financial Markets; Consensus Economics; Haver Analytics; and IMF staff calculations.
[1]GPM = Global Projection Model.
[2]AR: Argentina; BR: Brazil; CL: Chile; CN: China; CO: Colombia; ID: Indonesia; IN: India; KR: Korea; MX: Mexico; MY: Malaysia; PE: Peru; PH: Philippines; PL: Poland; RU: Russia; TH: Thailand; TR: Turkey; TW: Taiwan Province of China; ZA: South Africa.
[3]Taylor rule in the form of $i = infl + r^* + 0.5(infl - infl^*) + 0.5(ygap)$, where i is the policy rate (prescribed); $infl$ is actual inflation, core inflation, and two-year WEO projected inflation; r^* is the equilibrium real rate = 2; $infl^*$ is 2 percent for advanced economies and 4 percent for emerging economies; $ygap$ is the output gap (WEO) and output relative to the precrisis trend in percent.
[4]Figures are based on official GDP and CPI data. The policy rate is proxied by the short-term interbank lending rate.
[5]As of July 2011; overnight interbank rate for Turkey.

Figure 1.19. External Developments

(Index, 2000 = 100; three-month moving average unless noted otherwise)

Real effective exchange rates of major economies and regions have not moved much over the past six months; global current account imbalances appear to be widening again; and the buildup of international reserves continues unabated. However, some currencies are experiencing more pressure than others.

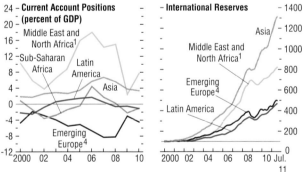

Sources: IMF, *International Financial Statistics;* and IMF staff calculations.
[1]Bahrain, Djibouti, Egypt, Islamic Republic of Iran, Jordan, Kuwait, Lebanon, Libya, Oman, Qatar, Saudi Arabia, Sudan, Syrian Arab Republic, United Arab Emirates, and Republic of Yemen.
[2]Botswana, Burkina Faso, Cameroon, Chad, Republic of Congo, Côte d'Ivoire, Equatorial Guinea, Ethiopia, Gabon, Ghana, Guinea, Kenya, Madagascar, Mali, Mauritius, Mozambique, Namibia, Niger, Nigeria, Rwanda, Senegal, South Africa, Tanzania, Uganda, and Zambia.
[3]Asia excluding China.
[4]Bulgaria, Croatia, Hungary, Latvia, Lithuania, Poland, Romania, and Turkey.
[5]Argentina, Brazil, Chile, Colombia, Mexico, Peru, and Venezuela.

More fiscal tightening

As discussed in more detail in the September 2011 *Fiscal Monitor*, public deficits must be rolled back to rebuild fiscal policy room and—in some cases—alleviate strong domestic demand pressure. Fiscal balances in emerging and developing economies are still some 2 percent of GDP below precrisis levels and are projected to stay there over the medium term (see Figure 1.11, top-left panel; Figure 1.18, bottom panel). Among G20 economies, the structural deficit is very large in India and appreciable in South Africa. Rolling back deficits in these economies and elsewhere (for example, Brazil, Poland, Turkey) is a major priority not only for alleviating upward pressure on inflation or the real exchange rate (and thus the burden on monetary policy) but also for rebuilding room for fiscal policy maneuvering. The experience of advanced economies shows how much policy room may be needed in the event the credit cycle suddenly turns. Elsewhere in emerging Asia, deficits and debt are less of a concern. In China, higher public spending has helped rebalance the economy toward more internal demand, and more can be done if downside risks materialize. Deficits and debt are high in many MENA economies. Although spending has been increased to address pressing social concerns, notably those raised by high food prices, ultimately the needs must be met by broadening the tax base or cutting back on low-priority expenditures.

Adjusting real effective exchange rates

Exchange rate misalignment relative to medium-term fundamentals persists, with little change over the past six months (Figure 1.19; Figure 1.20, middle-right panel). Also, reserves accumulation by emerging market economies has continued unabated (Figure 1.19, bottom-right panel).

- The euro and yen have appreciated somewhat in real effective terms since the April 2011 *World Economic Outlook,* but remain broadly in line with medium-term fundamentals. The Japanese authorities recently decided to intervene in the currency market to address excessive fluctuations and disorderly movements in the market. The Swiss authorities have adopted a minimum exchange rate target in response to strong appreciation pressures given its "safe haven" status. The U.S. dollar has weakened in recent months but still remains on the strong side of fundamentals; some further depreciation would contribute to global rebalancing and support the recovery.

- There has been no significant change for the various currencies of Asian economies with large external surpluses (for example, China), and they have continued to build up their foreign currency reserves. The renminbi still appears substantially undervalued. China's current account surplus is set to expand again. For Brazil and South Africa, the extent of overvaluation has remained broadly unchanged.

In various economies, domestic and external policy requirements point in the same direction. Further appreciation in the emerging surplus economies of Asia would help bring down both inflation and large current account surpluses. In other emerging market economies, however, monetary policy tightening could exacerbate overvaluation pressure. Economies with high fiscal and external deficits should alleviate domestic demand pressure by tightening fiscal policy. Whether this will significantly lower the pressure for their exchange rates to appreciate is unclear, but at least it will help create more room for fiscal policy to mitigate the repercussions of a sudden drop in capital inflows. Some have introduced measures designed specifically to manage capital inflows, such as taxes on certain inflows, minimum holding periods, and currency-specific reserve requirements. Recourse to such measures has been motivated by concerns about export competitiveness, financial stability, sterilization costs, and political constraints on fiscal policy. However, such measures should not be used as substitutes for macroeconomic tightening.

Implementing macrocritical structural reforms

Many economies are facing structural and social challenges. Crisis-hit economies need to reallocate labor away from construction and other struggling sectors. At the same time, they face declining

Figure 1.20. Global Imbalances

Emerging Asia is forecast to account for a rising proportion of global current account imbalances over the medium term, reflecting mainly a large increase in the surplus of China. Relative to precrisis levels, emerging market currencies have appreciated, and this seems appropriate, given their relatively better growth prospects. However, the appreciation has been distributed unevenly, worsening imbalances across emerging market economies. The real effective exchange rates of the yen and the euro remain broadly in line with fundamentals; the U.S. dollar is on the strong side of fundamentals; while Asian currencies (besides the yen) are undervalued (reflecting mainly the currencies of China and Korea).

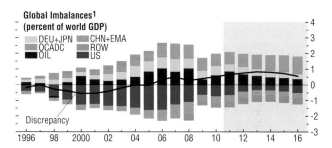

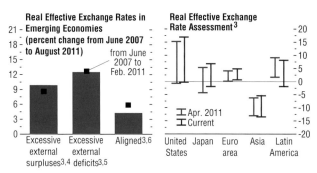

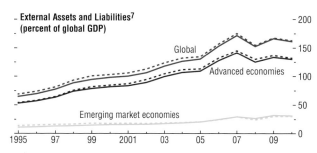

Sources: U.S. Federal Reserve; and IMF staff estimates.
[1]CHN+EMA: China, Hong Kong SAR, Indonesia, Korea, Malaysia, Philippines, Singapore, Taiwan Province of China, and Thailand; DEU+JPN: Germany and Japan; OCADC: Bulgaria, Croatia, Czech Republic, Estonia, Greece, Hungary, Ireland, Latvia, Lithuania, Poland, Portugal, Romania, Slovak Republic, Slovenia, Spain, Turkey, and United Kingdom; OIL: oil exporters; ROW: rest of the world; US: United States.
[2]Emerging Consultative Group on Exchange Rate Issues (CGER) economies only.
[3]Based on the IMF staff's CGER. CGER countries include Argentina, Australia, Brazil, Canada, Chile, China, Colombia, Czech Republic, euro area, Hungary, India, Indonesia, Israel, Japan, Korea, Malaysia, Mexico, Pakistan, Poland, Russia, South Africa, Sweden, Switzerland, Thailand, Turkey, United Kingdom, and United States. For a detailed discussion of the methodology for the calculation of exchange rates' over- or undervaluation, see Lee and others (2008).
[4]These economies account for 18.5 percent of global GDP.
[5]These economies account for 27.4 percent of global GDP.
[6]These economies account for 39.2 percent of global GDP.
[7]Solid lines are for assets and dashed lines are for liabilities.

Figure 1.21. Employment and Unemployment

The United States and the euro area face major employment challenges, but they differ appreciably. In the United States, the loss of jobs relative to long-term trends has been unprecedented and has also been much larger than in the euro area. Furthermore, it has added to a trend break in the employment-population ratio that seems to have occurred during the decade before the crisis. By contrast, that ratio was on the rise in the euro area during the same period. As a result, families' income expectations have hit an unprecedented low in the United States, unlike in the euro area. Labor market challenges loom large not only in the advanced economies but also in a number of emerging and developing economies, notably in the Middle East, North Africa, and the CEE and CIS.

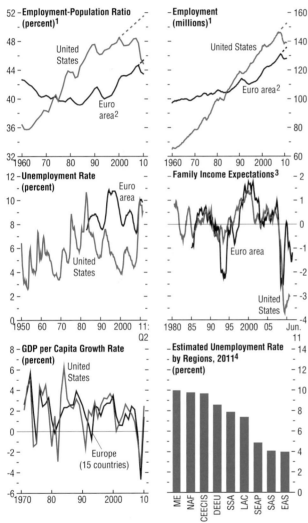

Sources: U.S. Bureau of Labor Statistics; European Commission; Haver Analytics; International Labor Organization; *OECD Economic Outlook;* Reuters; and IMF staff calculations.

[1]Dashed lines indicate trends.

[2]Euro area countries include Belgium, Finland, France, Germany, Italy, Netherlands, Portugal, and Spain.

[3]U.S. data are from Reuters/University of Michigan Surveys of Consumers and represent the difference between the percentage of people who think family income will go up and those who think it will go down. EU data are from the family financial situation index in the European Commission Business and Consumer Surveys. Both series are smoothed and harmonized.

[4]CEECIS: central and eastern Europe (non-EU) and Commonwealth of Independent States; DEEU: developed economies and European Union; EAS: east Asia; LAC: Latin America and the Caribbean; ME: Middle East; NAF: north Africa; SAS: south Asia; SEAP: southeast Asia and the Pacific; SSA: sub-Saharan Africa.

population growth or labor force participation rates, which exacerbates their fiscal problems.

- In the euro area periphery, reforms should reduce the growing gap between protected and unprotected workers, while improving employment prospects for the young, including through better education and vocational training. In addition, reforms should seek to eliminate wage-setting rigidity, which has caused sustained losses in competitiveness in the face of low productivity growth. More generally, the integration of euro area labor, goods, and services markets must continue, and obstacles to the free flow of equity capital must be eliminated. Progress on these fronts would facilitate financial restructuring and the transfer of skills and technology. This, in turn, would help raise productivity.

- In the United States, exceptionally high job losses during the crisis overlay lackluster employment generation during the previous decade. This left many households much more worried about future income prospects than during previous periods with similarly high unemployment rates (Figure 1.21). Persistently high unemployment (with more than 40 percent of the unemployed out of work for six months or more) may result in a permanent loss of work skills. Active labor market policies could help stem the rise in such structural unemployment, as could measures to expedite the adjustment in housing markets, given that weak housing market conditions can interact negatively with skill mismatches to raise unemployment. In many ways, however, the problem is so large that it warrants a sea change in macroeconomic policy: major entitlement and tax reform with a view to allowing less fiscal policy tightening.

- In many emerging and developing economies, rising food and commodity prices have exacerbated social problems posed by underemployment or high unemployment, especially among the young. Social safety nets need to be strengthened, and access to education and its quality need to be improved. In other economies, regulatory reforms would help ensure that capital inflows are used for productive, as opposed to speculative, investments. In China, a strengthened social safety net and a reorientation of the financial sector in favor of households would provide much-needed support to global demand rebalancing.

Multilateral Perspectives on Policy Challenges
Food and oil prices and policy spillovers

Food prices have risen for both temporary and more lasting reasons. Among the temporary reasons, which have begun to unwind with the new crop season, are poor harvests due to bad weather and low inventories. Among the more lasting reasons are high fossil fuel prices, which are driving up fertilizer costs. Over the medium term, high food prices can be expected to significantly increase agricultural output. Regarding oil, medium-term prospects appear more problematic. On the one hand, supply growth is expected to moderate to an annual pace of 1.3 percent during 2011–15, down from 1.8 percent during 1981–2005, according to IEA estimates. This is due to drag from maturing fields and a long period of reduced exploration.[9] On the other hand, at current prices and based on WEO growth forecasts, demand might expand at an annual pace anywhere between 1.3 and 3.0 percent, depending on whether estimates for short-term or long-term elasticity are used.[10] The extent to which futures prices reflect this is unclear. Tensions in oil markets are thus likely to remain elevated, notwithstanding the return of Libyan output. Over the medium term, more rapid than expected expansion of production in Iraq appears to be the only major downside factor for the price of oil, aside from lower global growth. Over the long term, other downside factors could come into play, such as technological innovation that reduces the production costs of alternative sources of energy or lowers energy consumption.

The current high and volatile level of commodity prices raises the risk of problems for global macroeconomic conditions, income inequality, and food security. Regarding the latter, direct interventions aimed at limiting price fluctuations, such as curbs on financial investment or trade restrictions, may be tempting, but such measures address symptoms rather than causes and are often ineffective if not harmful in the longer term. Instead, policymakers should focus on protecting the poor through targeted social safety nets. Over time, measures to strengthen the effectiveness of price signals and to enhance price discovery may result in more stable markets. In this regard, initiatives to improve the gathering of information on food and fuel markets need to be carried forward.

The influence of financial factors on commodity prices has come under close scrutiny. Low policy rates in advanced economies and a search for yield are seen in some quarters as having spurred large inflows into commodity derivative assets, raising concern about speculatively driven commodity price misalignments—that is, prices that are out of line with supply and demand fundamentals. The empirical evidence to date, however, points to limited, and mostly temporary, effects of "financialization" (Box 1.4). In particular, the main effects have not been on commodity price levels, or volatility, but rather on the pricing of risk in commodity markets. With the emergence of commodities as an asset class, markets increasingly price only systemic, rather than idiosyncratic, risks for individual commodities. Matters may change if this new asset class attracts a large proportion of uninformed traders, but any resulting problems would have to be addressed as part of the broader initiatives under way to improve investor education and protection.

Contrary to some claims, basing monetary policy on commodity prices would likely worsen, not improve, economic stability. As Chapter 3 explains, narrowly targeting headline inflation is likely to lead to policy errors, precisely because headline inflation is subject to some of the volatility in commodity prices. Instead, central banks should follow policy frameworks that seek to stabilize the rates of consumer price increases over the medium term, with due allowance for the lagged effect of monetary policy. This does not necessarily entail moving from targeting headline inflation to core (or, more precisely, value-added) inflation. Although clearly desirable on the basis of principle and simplicity, such a move could raise significant technical and communication challenges. Instead, central banks should explain clearly what economic agents should expect

---

[9]See Chapter 3 of the April 2011 *World Economic Outlook* for further details. Reduced exploration reflected relatively low demand during the 1990s—when the CEE and CIS economies collapsed and emerging Asia faced a major financial crisis—and restrictions on oil investment.

[10]See Chapter 3 of the April 2011 *World Economic Outlook* for further details.

(for example, stabilization of domestic inflation over a horizon of a couple of years) and what they should not expect (for example, monetary policy that responds directly to commodity price changes). Central banks should spell out the path of headline inflation to the desired rate over the forecasting horizon. If central banks are concerned that such a policy would raise inflation to unacceptable levels for their constituencies, they can offset the effect of long-term trends in the relative price of oil on the headline inflation rate by adjusting the operational targets for core inflation. If their constituents place a very high value on stabilizing fuel or food prices, central banks need to explain that this would come at the expense of more instability in output and employment.

Spillovers from low policy rates in advanced economies

The issue of distortions flowing from low interest rates in advanced economies is complex. Low interest rates can foster more risk taking, postpone needed balance sheet adjustment, and delay fiscal consolidation. In times of recession and financial turbulence, these distortions are welcome because they facilitate gradual adjustment. However, as economic expansion takes hold, policy efforts need to focus increasingly on raising capital buffers and fiscal consolidation. On both fronts, progress has been lacking to varying degrees across the major advanced economies. Although it is difficult to state with confidence, policy rates in these economies may therefore be lower than necessary because of the absence of strong bank capital or fiscal consolidation that strikes a good balance between near- and long-term consolidation (for example, by emphasizing major entitlement reforms). In addition, as discussed in the September 2011 *Global Financial Stability Report,* investors appear to be increasing their exposure to risk through such products as high-yield corporate bonds and emerging market assets. Low policy rates may be playing a role in this increased risk tolerance and thus may complicate the tasks of policymakers in some emerging market economies.

Are the adverse spillovers from low policy rates so large that they harm global output? All economies would probably be better off if advanced economies had implemented stronger financial and fiscal policies. Absent such policies, would many emerging and developing economies be better off if policy rates were higher and activity in advanced economies commensurately lower? Several emerging market economies have certainly had difficulty coping with large capital inflows, suggesting that the answer might be affirmative. But there are also reasons to reach the opposite conclusion. First, capital inflows are not exceptionally strong for the vast majority of emerging and developing economies (see Figure 1.8, lower panels). Only a few economies are experiencing strong enough pressure to keep their exchange rates in overvaluation territory (for example, Brazil, South Africa). Second, capital inflows are overwhelmingly a function of national rather than international factors, such as U.S. or euro area policy rates: evidence in Chapter 4 of the April 2011 *World Economic Outlook* suggests that the share of national factors in explaining the variability in net inflows into emerging market economies has been about 70 percent during the 2000s. Third, most of the theoretical and empirical evidence suggests that, as long as monetary policy successfully stabilizes macroeconomic conditions in advanced economies, overall spillovers to emerging and developing economies are not detrimental.[11] Fourth, with the exception of Japan, the world's major net exporters of capital have for many years been emerging market economies.

The best response to financial stability challenges posed by low interest rates lies in a sound framework of regulation and supervision. It is in each country's national interest to strengthen its domestic financial stability framework to control incentives for excessive risk taking by lenders and borrowers alike, including those that may arise on account of low policy rates. In addition, policymakers could look for ways to accelerate balance sheet restructuring, such as by improving insolvency frameworks, introducing new instruments for deleveraging (such as household debt-equity swaps), and direct intervention in undercapitalized institutions. Emerging and developing economies with appropriate macroeconomic

---

[11]This is summarized in Box 1.3 of the April 2011 *World Economic Outlook.*

policies that still struggle with speculative inflows can respond with supervisory, regulatory, or other measures. Others that are exporting large amounts of capital stand to benefit from policies that lower domestic saving and thereby help solve the underlying problem of global demand imbalances.[12]

Spillovers from global demand rebalancing

Emerging and developing economies are increasingly seen as the drivers of global growth. For the purpose of assessing their role in global demand rebalancing, domestic consumption provides a good gauge of global impact—consumption has an advantage over GDP for this purpose, in that the latter includes exports and therefore may overstate the extent to which an economy offers an outlet for other economies' exports.[13] To assess the contribution of each economy to the growth of the global market, it is appropriate to measure national aggregates in a common currency. The relative levels of consumption, measured for convenience in U.S. dollars, suggest that the effect of emerging and developing economies' growth on global demand rebalancing has been limited by their low share in global consumption (Figure 1.22, bottom-left panel). The contribution of consumption to growth in emerging market economies from 2011 through 2016 is smaller than before the crisis; for China it is about the same.[14] In short, these economies do not make up for the lower consumption contribution of advanced economies. Although the rebalancing journey may have started, based on announced policies it will likely take a long time to complete.

Current fiscal policy is unlikely to provide much help for global demand rebalancing. Chapter 4 finds that the lack of more permanent consolidation

---

[12]This advice does not necessarily apply to economies that are reinvesting proceeds from exports of exhaustible natural resources.

[13]Consumption in U.S. dollar terms offers the largest contrast to GDP in purchasing-power-parity terms. The conclusions are qualitatively quite similar for the sum of consumption and investment, as opposed to consumption alone. Notice that part of investment is geared toward exports.

[14]China's consumption in 2009 would have had to have been some 17 percent higher to fully make up for the lower contribution of U.S. consumption during 2008–09 relative to 2005–07. This would have required a drop in the savings-to-GDP ratio from about 54 percent to 45 percent.

Figure 1.22. Drivers of Global Growth and Rebalancing

Emerging and developing economies account for about half of global output and two-thirds of global growth in purchasing-power-parity (PPP) terms, much of which is accounted for by China and India. However, for purposes of demand rebalancing, the more relevant measure is not in PPP terms but, for example, in constant U.S. dollars. Furthermore, for demand rebalancing, consumption might be a better variable than GDP, considering that it is less related to exports. As shown, emerging and developing economies account for a much lower share of global consumption and consumption growth in U.S. dollar terms. Also, their contribution to global consumption growth fell during the crisis and is not expected to exceed precrisis levels because of large losses in the central and eastern European and Commonwealth of Independent States economies and few gains elsewhere, including in China.

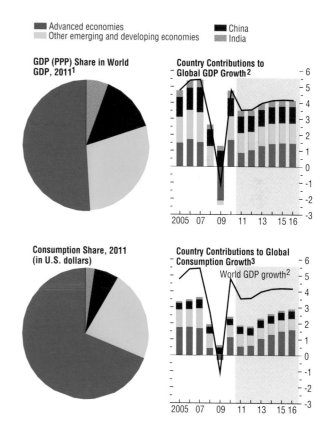

Source: IMF staff estimates.
[1]Shaded areas indicate IMF staff projections. Aggregates are computed on the basis of PPP weights.
[2]Based on 2007 PPP weights.
[3]Based on GDP at 2007 market exchange rates.

measures in the United States relative to elsewhere means that fiscal policy will contribute little to bringing down the U.S. external deficit (see Figure 1.11, bottom panels). This stands in contrast to what can be expected in the euro area, where large consolidation measures in other euro area economies relative to those adopted in Germany will help reduce imbalances within the region. However, unless demand picks up elsewhere, more consolidation in the United States would entail lower global activity. In sum, the challenges with respect to global demand rebalancing remain broadly unchanged: there is still a need for more ambitious medium-term fiscal consolidation in the United States and a boost in domestic demand in large emerging market surplus economies. Achieving the latter would be facilitated by nominal exchange rate appreciation, but it also requires further measures to boost social protection and to reform corporate governance and financial markets.

Vulnerabilities in the global financial system and the implications for spillovers

Some vulnerabilities in the global financial system are being addressed, but many others still are cause for concern. These issues are discussed in more depth in the September 2011 *Global Financial Stability Report*. First among these are institutions deemed too important to fail. Stronger prudential requirements for so-called systemically important financial institutions, including "living wills," would deter the pursuit of size solely for the sake of size and would foster more prudent behavior. The second vulnerability is the role of the shadow banking system. And third are the challenges presented by wholesale funding in the international money markets, which has grown rapidly over the past decade. The hope is that stronger capital and liquidity requirements, more transparency by moving over-the-counter activities to exchanges, and better incentives through "skin in the game" will help rebuild these markets and make them more stable. How successful such measures will be remains unclear. Recurring instability was a feature of financial systems until the advent of deposit insurance, and it is likely to be a feature of wholesale funding markets.

During the financial crisis, central banks had to resort to extraordinary mechanisms to provide liquidity to wholesale funding markets. There are no such mechanisms at the international level.

The challenges presented by wholesale funding have a major international dimension, implying that problems in some regions of the world can very quickly spill over to other regions. This international dimension also makes it very hard to address the underlying problems. In the decade ahead of the crisis, cross-border exposures grew very rapidly between advanced economies (see Figure 1.20, bottom panel). Large international short-term net financial liabilities play a major role in debt crises (Box 1.5), and they are a distinguishing feature of economies that have suffered severe financial stress in the euro area. Indeed, the euro area may well be a bellwether for problems that could arise if financial globalization continues apace. More generally, a number of fundamentally strong advanced economies have had to tap Federal Reserve swap lines as wholesale funding has dried up. Whether this is a sustainable solution is an open question. The stresses made apparent during the crisis illustrate that there is an urgent need to beef up the size and scope of international risk-sharing mechanisms, which have fallen far behind the growth of the international financial markets.

Reforming the global trade system

Trade has been an important driver of the global recovery. From its crisis-induced trough at the beginning of 2009, the volume of global trade has grown by 25 percent and recently surpassed precrisis peaks. To ensure that trade can continue to boost growth, it is vital that policymakers continue to keep protectionist pressures at bay. Just as important, one of the best ways to enhance and guarantee security in trade relationships, as well as safeguard the multilateral approach for trade negotiations, would be to conclude the long-running World Trade Organization (WTO) Doha Round of trade talks. Failure of the round would put at risk significant agreements reached during 10 years of negotiations, including on new market access in major markets, global farm trade reform, and recent unilateral trade liberalization. Moreover, failure could precipitate moves toward fragmentation of the global trading system, with further acceleration of bilateral preferential trade agreements, which would weaken both the WTO and multilateralism in general. In a worst-case scenario, a 19th-century-style Great Powers trade system could reemerge, and the poorest economies could lose their ability to negotiate on equal footing.

The negotiations for the Doha Round are at a pivotal juncture. In an attempt to break the persistent stalemate in talks, the focus shifted this year toward forging agreement soon on a partial package—at a minimum, aimed at helping the poorest or least developed countries (LDCs)—as a down payment for a more comprehensive package. However, momentum on the so-called LDC-plus package has stalled, largely because of disagreement over which "plus" (or non-LDC-specific) elements should be included. It is now vital that political leaders muster the will and high-level attention to move the negotiations forward, including by showing flexibility and making compromises. Leaders should also strongly communicate Doha's benefits to the public by arguing that trade liberalization is not a concession but instead spurs growth and is in a country's own best interest.

Appendix 1.1. Commodity Market Developments and Prospects

The authors of this appendix are Thomas Helbling, Shaun Roache, Joong Shik Kang, Marina Rousset, and David Reichsfeld.

Overview of Recent Developments and Prospects

After rising through April, prices of major commodities abruptly eased in two waves, first in May and June of 2011 and then again in August. The overall IMF commodity price index declined by 5 percent between April and July and another 5 percent in August. The index remains at high levels, from both a cyclical and a longer-term perspective. In August, it was about 9 percent above the level recorded in December 2010 and only about 14 percent below its most recent peak value in July 2008 (Figure 1.23, top-right panel).

The broad easing of commodity prices largely reflects common macroeconomic and financial factors that have led to a less favorable near-term outlook for the global economy and commodity demand. Incoming data suggest a stronger than expected slowing of global economic activity in the second quarter of 2011 and a gradual downgrade of near-term prospects, as discussed in detail in the main text of Chapter 1. Of particular relevance for global commodity markets was the policy response to rising inflation and surging housing prices in emerging market economies, in particular China, which accounts for about 40 percent of global metal consumption and 18 percent of energy consumption. The policy measures put in place since fall 2010 have reduced credit growth and succeeded in stabilizing economic growth at a more sustainable pace. Against this backdrop, China's import growth for many commodities—which is frequently considered a bellwether of global commodity demand conditions—has decelerated, which has reduced pressure on global demand-supply balances for some major commodities, notably base metals.

The increases in risk aversion in global financial markets, owing to renewed concerns about sovereign debt risks in the euro area periphery, and the related appreciation of the U.S. dollar likely also contributed to the broad decline in commodity prices. As usual, the effects of these financial factors on commodity

prices are difficult to distinguish from those related to global economic prospects, both because all these factors are partly driven by the same underlying forces and because the direction of their effects on prices is the same. Nevertheless, increases in risk aversion can have direct effects on commodity spot prices: inventory holdings become relatively less attractive unless there is an offset from higher expected future returns resulting from a decline in current spot prices.

The easing of commodity prices was associated with noticeable declines in net futures positions of noncommercial investors, including in the case of crude oil (Figure 1.23, middle-left panel). More generally, commodity assets under management declined by about 9 percent during May and June—reflecting lower prices and net outflows—ending the quarter at $410 billion (Figure 1.23, middle-right panel). Net outflows took place across all commodity groups, with agriculture and energy each accounting for about 34 percent of the overall decline and precious metals for about 27 percent. These net outflows of investor funds for the commodity asset class as a whole were larger than those during the Great Recession of 2008–09 (Figure 1.23, bottom-left panel).

Initially, the decline in commodity prices and the outflows from commodity assets, which preceded declines in prices of other assets, were widely perceived as a surprise, symptomatic of the recent financialization of commodity markets. With financialization, sudden shifts in large investor portfolios can cause abrupt changes in pricing that do not appear to have an immediate fundamental trigger. Nevertheless, subsequent incoming global economic and financial data provided the fundamental backdrop for the commodity price declines. And the experience of the past few years suggests that although sudden shifts in investor sentiment and prices are possible, such events do not appear to have long-lasting or destabilizing effects on commodity prices (Box 1.4).

Near-Term Outlook

Commodity prices already reflect a weaker near-term global growth outlook. Under the baseline projections in this issue of the *World Economic Outlook,* global growth is expected to rebound slightly in the second half of 2011, when the fundamental drivers of the expansion will reassert themselves. Nevertheless, this rebound is not expected to come with renewed strong upward pressure on commodity prices because it will be driven largely by a moderate, albeit still weaker than expected, earlier pickup in growth in advanced economies. In contrast, growth in emerging and developing economies, which have accounted for almost all commodity demand increases in recent years, is expected to slow modestly in the second half of 2011 and in 2012, because tightening policies should begin to affect domestic demand and prospects for external demand are less favorable. Much will also depend on commodity-specific demand and supply factors. For a growing number of commodities, upward pressure will likely also be contained by supply responses to higher prices that are estimated to be above long-term marginal cost in real terms—in the near term mainly in agriculture but increasingly also in metals.

The current commodity price forecasts are thus for broadly unchanged prices for 2011 as a whole. The IMF's average petroleum spot price (APSP) is expected to remain close to $100 a barrel for the remainder of 2011 and through 2012 (Figure 1.23, bottom-right panel). The IMF's nonfuel commodity price index is projected to moderate by about 5½ percent in the second half of 2011—largely owing to improved harvests for many food commodities and agricultural raw materials—as well as in 2012, when base metal prices are also expected to decline modestly because of improving supply conditions.

In the near term, broad commodity price risks seem more balanced than at the time of the October 2010 and April 2011 issues of the *World Economic Outlook*, because downside risks to global growth have risen. On the upside, price spikes due to supply factors remain the main concern. The balance of risks varies across commodities, however. Upside price risks remain most pertinent and most prominent for energy and food, the two commodity groups that matter most for global growth and inflation prospects. In oil markets, geopolitical factors are an important dimension of oil supply risks. More broadly, given generally price-inelastic supply in the short and medium term as well as recent declines in spare capacity, relatively small upward surprises to oil demand, such as the surge recorded last year,

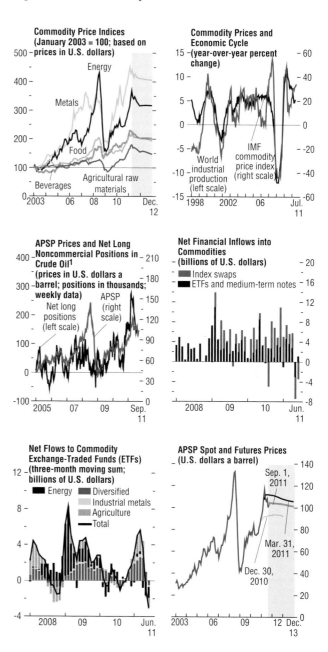

Figure 1.23. Commodity Prices

Sources: Barclays Capital; Bloomberg Financial Markets; and IMF staff estimates.
[1]APSP (average petroleum spot price) denotes an equally weighted average of three crude oil spot prices: West Texas Intermediate, Dated Brent, and Dubai Fateh.

Figure 1.24. World Energy Market Developments

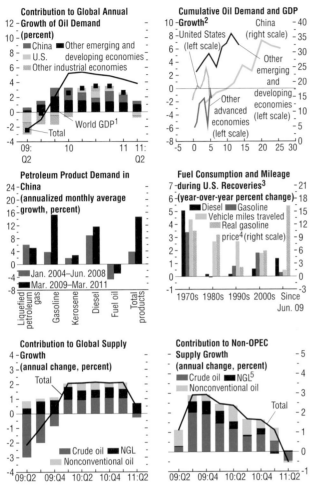

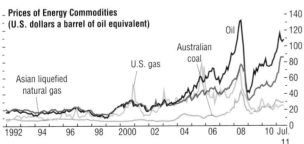

Sources: IMF Primary Commodity Price System; International Energy Agency, *Oil Market Report*, August 2011; Joint Oil Data Initiative; and IMF staff calculations.

[1]Annual change, in percent.

[2]Since 2009:Q1. Data are through 2011:Q2 for advanced economies and China; through 2011:Q1 for emerging economies. GDP growth is on x-axis, and oil demand growth is on y-axis, in percent.

[3]Average growth rates during the first 25 months of expansions according to National Bureau of Economic Research recession dates. Data are through May 2011 (23 months) for the expansion starting in June 2009.

[4]In 2011:Q1 U.S. dollars.

[5]NGL = natural gas liquids.

or adverse supply shocks can trigger large price increases. Oil market inflexibility thus continues to present risks to global growth and inflation. Given low global inventory levels for many crops, any significant adverse shocks—including this summer's heat wave in the United States—have the capacity to spike food prices higher.

Energy Market Developments and Prospects

After surging through April, and peaking at $120 a barrel at the end of that month, oil prices eased through the remainder of the second quarter and again in August, trading at about $100 a barrel since mid-August. During easing, the IMF's APSP—a simple average of the Brent, Dubai, and West Texas Intermediate (WTI) crude oil varieties—fell below the $100 threshold for some time and is expected to move sideways at about $100 throughout the projection period. Oil price volatility, as measured by the implied volatility embedded in the Chicago Board Options Exchange Crude Oil Volatility Index, spiked during the brisk price corrections in May and then again in August. On the latter occasion, the expected standard deviation of daily price changes temporarily rose above 50 percent (annualized), above the levels seen in March during the height of the Libya-related oil market disruption.

The easing in crude oil prices was driven primarily by the common macroeconomic and financial factors discussed in the overview of this appendix. These factors have underpinned concerns about oil demand prospects. Although slower global oil demand growth had been expected, given the overshooting in the second half of 2010, the slowing turned out to be stronger than projected in the second quarter of 2011, mirroring developments in global activity (Figure 1.24, top-left panel; Table 1.2). The main commodity-specific factor in the oil demand overshooting in the second half of 2010, the sharp acceleration in diesel demand growth in China due to power outages and cuts, was reversed as expected. Overall, oil demand growth in China has normalized to rates consistent with the past relationships between oil demand and economic activity (Figure 1.24, top-right panel). Nevertheless, gasoline consumption has grown at a higher rate over the past two years than

Table 1.2. Global Oil Demand and Production by Region
(Millions of barrels a day)

	2009	2010	2011 Proj.	2010 H2	2011 H1	Year-over-Year Percent Change							
						2004–06 Avg.	2007	2008	2009	2010	2011 Proj.	2010 H2	2011 H1
Demand													
Advanced Economies	45.0	45.7	45.4	46.2	45.0	0.6	−0.2	−3.5	−4.0	1.5	−0.6	2.7	−0.5
Of Which:													
United States	19.1	19.5	19.3	19.6	19.2	1.1	−0.1	−5.9	−3.7	2.2	−1.0	2.7	−0.4
Euro Area	10.6	10.6	10.4	10.7	10.2	0.1	−1.2	−0.4	−5.6	−0.1	−1.7	2.4	−1.6
Japan	4.4	4.5	4.5	4.5	4.4	−1.4	−3.1	−4.9	−8.2	1.3	1.1	1.7	−1.5
Newly Industrialized Asian Economies	4.6	4.8	4.8	4.8	4.7	2.3	4.4	−2.2	2.7	3.8	−0.1	4.1	−0.7
Emerging and Developing Economies	40.6	42.6	44.1	43.3	43.6	4.6	4.4	2.9	2.2	5.1	3.5	4.4	3.9
Of Which:													
Commonwealth of Independent States	4.2	4.5	4.7	4.6	4.6	1.5	2.1	2.3	−1.0	7.0	4.0	6.5	4.5
Developing Asia	23.4	24.8	26.0	24.9	26.1	4.9	5.1	1.5	4.6	6.0	4.6	3.8	5.3
China	8.1	9.1	9.6	9.3	9.5	9.4	4.6	2.2	4.1	12.5	6.1	10.2	7.5
India	3.3	3.3	3.5	3.3	3.5	3.8	6.7	4.0	4.7	2.4	3.6	2.1	3.5
Middle East and North Africa	9.0	9.2	9.4	9.4	9.3	5.8	4.2	5.1	3.9	3.2	2.1	2.9	2.3
Western Hemisphere	5.6	5.9	6.1	6.1	6.0	4.5	6.1	4.9	0.0	5.3	3.3	5.5	3.3
World	85.5	88.3	89.5	89.4	88.5	2.2	1.8	−0.7	−1.1	3.2	1.4	3.5	1.6
Production													
OPEC (current composition)[1,2]	34.1	34.8	36.5	35.2	35.4	4.6	−0.4	3.3	−5.8	2.2	4.8	2.8	2.7
Of Which:													
Saudi Arabia	9.5	9.8	. . .	9.9	10.4	2.4	−4.8	4.9	−9.5	3.1	. . .	4.6	8.7
Nigeria	2.2	2.5	. . .	2.6	2.6	2.6	−4.6	−7.6	−0.4	15.7	. . .	15.5	8.7
Venezuela	2.9	2.7	. . .	2.7	2.7	6.4	−1.3	0.8	−3.6	−4.8	. . .	−0.7	−1.8
Iraq	2.5	2.4	. . .	2.4	2.7	15.5	9.9	14.3	2.5	−2.2	. . .	−3.3	13.7
Non-OPEC[2]	51.6	52.6	53.0	52.9	52.5	0.6	0.7	−0.3	1.9	2.0	0.8	1.7	0.3
Of Which:													
North America	13.6	14.1	14.2	14.2	14.3	−1.2	−0.4	−3.6	2.1	3.5	0.8	3.5	2.1
North Sea	4.2	3.8	3.6	3.6	3.6	−6.8	−4.9	−5.0	−4.3	−8.7	−4.5	−10.1	−10.2
Russia	10.2	10.5	10.6	10.5	10.5	4.8	2.4	−0.7	2.0	2.4	1.0	1.7	1.2
Other Former Soviet Union[3]	3.1	3.1	3.1	3.1	3.1	8.9	11.6	3.1	8.7	1.3	−0.4	0.1	−0.4
Other Non-OPEC	20.5	21.1	21.5	21.4	21.0	1.3	0.7	3.0	2.1	3.2	1.7	2.9	0.8
World	85.6	87.4	89.5	88.0	87.9	2.2	0.2	1.2	−1.3	2.1	2.3	2.1	1.3
Net Demand[4]	**−0.1**	**0.9**	**0.0**	**1.4**	**0.6**	**−0.2**	**1.5**	**−0.3**	**−0.1**	**1.0**	**. . .**	**1.6**	**0.7**

Sources: International Energy Agency, *Oil Market Report*, August 2011; and IMF staff calculations.

[1]OPEC = Organization of Petroleum Exporting Countries. Includes Angola (subject to quotas since January 2007) and Ecuador, which rejoined OPEC in November 2007 after suspending its membership from December 1992 to October 2007.

[2]Totals refer to a total of crude oil, condensates, natural gas liquids, and oil from nonconventional sources.

[3]Other Former Soviet Union includes Azerbaijan, Belarus, Georgia, Kazakhstan, Kyrgyz Republic, Tajikistan, Turkmenistan, Ukraine, and Uzbekistan.

[4]Difference between demand and production. In the percent change columns, the figures are percent of world demand.

it did during the 2005–08 expansion (Figure 1.24, upper-middle-left panel), suggesting that the growing number of cars per household may have begun to change the slope of the gasoline demand path. In advanced economies, fuel demand turned out weaker than projected, declining in the second quarter. In the United States, fuel demand has been slightly weaker than expected, given the state of the cycle and retail fuel prices (Figure 1.24, upper-middle-right panel). This weakness reflects in part the higher fuel efficiency

of newer car models, which appears to be increasing the aggregate fuel efficiency of the U.S. car fleet, which had remained relatively unchanged for years.

Oil supply has expanded at a steady annual rate of about 2 percent since early 2010, although its relative contribution has changed (Figure 1.24, lower-middle-left panel). After expanding rapidly in 2010, supply growth from producers that are not members of the Organization of Petroleum Exporting Countries (OPEC) moderated in the first half of 2011. This slowdown reflects the end of the base effect of new capacity in the U.S. Gulf of Mexico in 2009 and temporary shutdowns of producing fields for maintenance and capacity expansion. This moderation was offset by increased OPEC production, although it took time for other OPEC producers to ramp up production after the disruption to Libyan production. Only in June did OPEC production reach the levels seen early in the first quarter, largely due to a production increase of about 12 percent in Saudi Arabia compared with the levels of the first quarter of this year (an increase equivalent to 1 percent of global oil supply). Production in all OPEC members except Libya has exceeded the December 2008 production quotas, which are still in effect, for some time, but at their most recent regular meeting in June, OPEC oil ministers failed to agree on quota increases.

Turning to the demand-supply balance, demand growth still exceeded supply growth through the first half of 2011. As in the second half of 2010, market clearing involved a strong draw on inventories. The release of emergency stocks by International Energy Agency members provided only very temporary price relief. By the end of June, Organization for Economic Cooperation and Development member inventories had declined to below-average levels over past cycles (in terms of stock-to-use ratios). With the decline in inventory buffers, futures curves for the Brent crude oil variety, the predominant price benchmark outside the North American market, have returned to the usual state of backwardation (spot prices exceed futures prices). In contrast, futures curves for U.S. WTI are still sloping upward at the front end, reflecting localized pockets of excess supply in landlocked areas of the North American oil supply system, as a result of increased production and still weak demand. Limited transportation capacity constrains the scope for arbitrage to reduce price differentials. These constraints are expected to persist for some time; current futures prices imply that markets expect WTI to be priced at a discount to Brent through 2016. Historically, WTI has traded at a premium, because it is a lighter and sweeter variety of crude oil. If this anomaly continues, use of the WTI price as a price benchmark will increasingly come under scrutiny.

Near-term oil market stability will depend heavily on two factors. First, oil demand growth is expected to moderate further after strong growth through 2010. On the supply side, the call on OPEC will increase further in the second half of 2011 and again in 2012 under the WEO baseline projections, given that non-OPEC supply growth is not expected to recover until late in 2011.[15] Higher OPEC production will thus be required for oil market stability, although some of the increases in the call on OPEC will be seasonal. There are risks on both sides. The extent of the moderation in oil demand growth will depend on whether global activity rebounds as expected. OPEC spare capacity has declined since the disruption to Libyan production, highlighting risks to supply, including for geopolitical reasons.

In the medium term, futures prices indicate that markets expect prices to remain high but also broadly constant in real terms. Such expectations are consistent with the view that at such prices supply can broadly keep up with relatively moderate growth in global oil demand on the order of 1 to 1½ percent a year. The global oil supply growth of about 2 percent observed over the past two years is unlikely to be sustained, because it was made possible by high postrecession spare capacity and other special factors. Nevertheless, the recent supply experience suggests that continued moderate net capacity expansion is possible. Thanks to oil prices of $100 a barrel in real terms, high-cost conventional and nonconventional oil reservoirs continue to be developed (Figure 1.24, lower-middle-right panel). Upstream oil investment in non-OPEC members has remained high, with continued exploration and development. As a result, production in these economies is already some 2½ million barrels a day above the previous peak in 2007, despite continued decline in the North Sea and Mexico. The increases in shale oil production in North Dakota in the United States highlight the scope for and the benefits of techno-

[15]The "call on OPEC" is the difference between global demand and supply from sources other than OPEC crude oil production, including OPEC natural gas liquids (NGL) production. In Table 1.2, the figure for OPEC production in 2011 reflects the call on OPEC and OPEC NGL production.

logical innovation.[16] Moreover, at such prices, efforts at decline management are likely to intensify.[17] Upstream investment in many OPEC members has remained relatively more subdued, although some major members are pursuing ambitious investment programs.

Price differences across fossil fuels continue to be large. Crude oil remains the most expensive fuel per unit of energy produced compared with coal and natural gas, reflecting differences in the extent of supply constraints (Figure 1.24, bottom panel). In the United States, shale gas development and exploration have continued at a broadly unchanged pace. Although costs and returns vary considerably across shale gas plays, many have turned out to be profitable at current gas prices of about $4 per 1,000 cubic feet. With such price differentials, recent energy demand patterns will continue. In particular, the decline in the share of crude oil in total use of fossil fuels and the generation of primary energy observed over the past three decades will continue. Whether the current higher price differentials will lead to faster decline in the share of crude oil is uncertain, however, in some sectors, notably transportation, where the extent of substitution in the short to medium term is limited (even though the technology to run vehicles on natural gas exists). On the other hand, in the U.S. power sector, natural gas has become a more attractive fuel input compared with coal, and its share in primary energy consumption is likely to increase. Natural gas could also play a more prominent role in the energy mix elsewhere, given that large shale gas deposits have also been identified in other regions. Although foreign oil and gas companies have acquired equity in U.S. shale gas producers, preparing the ground for technology transfer, exploration elsewhere has not really started yet.[18] Coal consumption also continued to increase at a rapid rate in the first half of 2011, reflecting lower costs compared with crude oil.

Metal Market Developments and Prospects

Base metal prices moved broadly sideways in the first half of 2011, with relatively minor ups and downs in sync with other commodity prices. In August, the IMF's base metal price index was down by 0.3 percent compared with December 2010 (Figure 1.25, middle-left panel).[19]

Metal prices started easing earlier than other major commodity group prices. This lead reflects two China-specific factors. First, with a market share of about 40 percent in global base metal markets, domestic demand developments in China are much more important for this commodity group than for others. The key development in this respect has been the Chinese authorities' policy tightening measures in response to rising inflation and surging house prices since the second half of 2010. As a result, activity in metal-intensive sectors has slowed. Fixed investment, which had surged along with policy stimulus and credit growth in 2009 and early 2010, has moderated since then. Although real estate investment has held up well, in part bolstered by ongoing expansion in the construction of housing for lower-income groups, industrial production growth has moderated to below the precrisis average (Figure 1.25, top-right panel). As a result, global base metal consumption growth moderated further in the first half of 2011, with China's contribution falling to unusually low levels compared with the past few years (Figure 1.25, middle-left panel).

The second China-related factor is the country-specific base metal inventory cycle, which had a hand in China's dominant contribution to global metal demand growth in 2009 and early 2010. This inventory cycle has gone from a bullish to a bearish force for metal prices over the past six to nine months. Following the 2009 policy stimulus, metal inventories in China surged in anticipation of higher demand, and local prices rose temporarily above world market prices. In addition, inventories in bonded warehouses started increasing because base metals, notably copper, were increasingly used as collateral for trade credit as policy tightening reduced

---

[16]Shale oil production is included in conventional oil in Figure 1.24 and Table 1.2.

[17]See Box 3.1 in the April 2011 *World Economic Outlook*.

[18]Box 3.2 in the April 2011 *World Economic Outlook* analyzes prospects for moving the U.S. shale gas "revolution" to the global stage.

[19]The price of gold rose strongly, by about 28 percent, during the first eight months of 2011.

Figure 1.25. Developments in Base Metal Markets

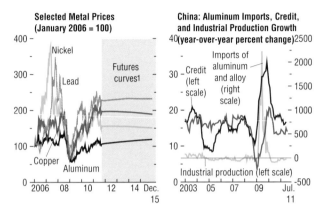

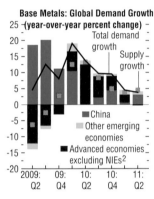

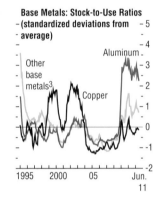

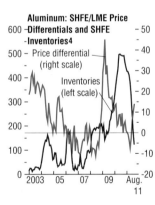

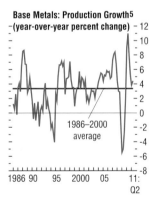

Sources: Bloomberg Financial Markets; London Metal Exchange; Thomson Datastream; World Bureau of Metal Statistics; and IMF staff estimates.

[1]Prices as of September 2, 2011.

[2]NIEs = newly industrialized Asian economies, which include Hong Kong SAR, Korea, Singapore, and Taiwan Province of China.

[3]Aggregate of aluminum, copper, lead, nickel, tin, and zinc.

[4]SHFE = Shanghai Futures Exchange; LME = London Metal Exchange. Price differentials are in percent; inventories are in thousands of tons.

[5]Index is composed of aluminum and copper until 1996; after 1996, nickel, tin, zinc, and lead were added. Weights are based on 2005 supply and price.

the supply of regular business credit.[20] Increased imports subsequently led to price equalization. With the slowing in demand and restrictive policies in place in some sectors, inventories have started to decline. This decline added to local supply, and metal import growth began to slow in the first half of 2011. In contrast, global metal inventory holdings (as measured by stock-to-use ratios) remain at high levels considering the stage of the global business cycle (Figure 1.25, middle-right panel).

Metal-specific supply developments have also shaped price behavior, with marked differences across metals, as evidenced in the recent increase in the dispersion of price changes across metals. Copper prices rebounded in June as supply disruptions in major mines due to strikes and adverse weather conditions worsened already tight demand-supply balances. Lead prices rose after one of the world's largest lead mine was closed indefinitely. Aluminum markets remained broadly balanced in the first half of this year, with record-high production levels matched by continued strong global demand. In contrast, nickel prices have stabilized despite tight supply conditions, because the production of nickel pig iron as a substitute for nickel has increased significantly, particularly in China.

Turning to the outlook, base metal consumption growth in China is expected to remain broadly stable at the rates seen in the first half of 2011, given prospects for economic activity overall. Economic growth in China is projected to remain robust, with a slowly increasing balance in contributions from investment and consumption, reaching 9.5 percent for 2011 as a whole and 9.0 percent in 2012 compared with 10.3 percent in 2010. On the other hand, although inventory destocking begun in late 2010 is expected to end, the overall impact on demand should be modest if inventories build up broadly in line with the rebound in consumption. Indeed, copper inventories at the Shanghai Futures Exchange (SHFE) have rebounded since June, and aluminum price differentials between the SHFE and the London Metal

[20]Markets have been concerned about reports of an increase share of copper imports being used as collateral in bank credit (through letters of credit to finance imports with deferred payment), although there are no official data to assess the scope of such deals.

Exchange have widened again, indicating tightening local supply-demand balances and some increases in base metal import growth (Figure 1.25, bottom-left panel).

Base metal prices are expected to remain broadly stable despite the moderate rebound in global economic growth in the second half of 2011. On the demand side, as noted above, base metal demand growth in China is expected to remain broadly stable, while base metal consumption in advanced economies, which was still 12½ percent below its precrisis peak in the second quarter, is expected to recover gradually in the context of subdued economic growth. On the supply side, production, which surged in the first half of 2010 following a sharp decline during the Great Recession, should remain close to its average rate of expansion of about 3½ percent (year over year)—with some variations across metals—making for broadly balanced market conditions at current high prices (Figure 1.25, bottom-right panel). Risks for base metals in general seem more balanced than for oil or food, mainly because overall supply does not seem as tightly constrained as for oil—with copper and lead being notable exceptions—and because of higher inventory levels (relative to consumption) than in food markets. Risks to energy prices also affect metal prices, however, given the high share of energy in the cost of metal refining.

Food Market Developments and Prospects

Food prices have retreated modestly from their peak in recent months, but they remain very high compared with the decade through 2010 (Figure 1.26, top panels). The IMF food price index during the third quarter to date of 2011 is about 20 percent higher than for the same quarter of 2010 and significantly above the average real price over the past 10 years. Grain and oilseed prices are particularly elevated, but prices of other food groups, including meat, are also well above their historical averages. A degree of respite from rising prices has been provided in recent months by improving near-term supply prospects for some important crops. Following the large weather-related supply setbacks during fall 2010, expectations for harvests in 2011 have

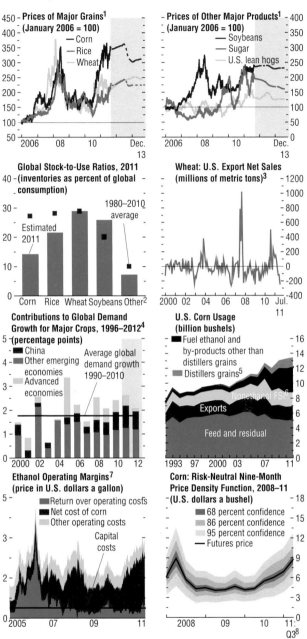

Figure 1.26. Recent Developments in Markets for Major Food Crops

Sources: Bloomberg Financial Markets; Chicago Mercantile Exchange; Iowa State University Center for Agriculture and Rural Development; U.S. Department of Agriculture; and IMF staff estimates.
[1]Futures prices for September 2011 through December 2012.
[2]Other grains and oilseeds.
[3]Sales adjusted for seasonal factors and long-term trends.
[4]Projections for 2011 and 2012 are by the U.S. Department of Agriculture.
[5]Distillers grains from dry mill fuel ethanol plants based on an estimated annual share of corn-based ethanol production from dry mills and on an assumption that distillers grains account for 17.5 pounds of each bushel of corn used in dry mill fuel ethanol production.
[6]FSI = food, seed, and industrial products.
[7]Ethanol operating margins are based on nearby futures and Iowa corn prices.
[8]As of September 6, 2011.

stabilized, and there are signs, based on projected acreage, that output growth will be relatively buoyant in 2012.

Food markets remain precariously balanced, however. Inventory buffers are very low for some important crops—notably corn—and this will keep prices very sensitive to changes in the supply and demand outlook (Figure 1.26, upper-middle-left panel). The most immediate risk is that key crops will suffer from another round of weather-related supply shocks. The recent pattern of extreme weather in major crop-growing regions seems to be continuing: following droughts in Europe and China, the United States has experienced a very wet spring followed by severe summer heat, leading to a reduction in projected corn yields. Even modest further downgrades to the supply outlook could trigger a large price response, cross-commodity spillovers, and higher volatility, similar to developments in early 2011. For example, rising supply uncertainty led to surging precautionary demand in physical markets by major food-importing economies during the first quarter of 2011, as reflected in U.S. export sales (Figure 1.26, upper-middle-right panel).

At the same time, demand growth momentum remains strong. Rapid increases in emerging market economy food consumption are showing no signs of moderating, reflecting income growth and a diet shifting toward higher-protein foods, including grain-fed meat (Figure 1.26, lower-middle-left panel). In advanced economies, notably the United States, overall demand growth is modest, but the use of food commodities as a biofuel feedstock continues to surpass expectations, most recently due to higher oil prices during the first half of 2011 and rising ethanol refining margins. Since 2000, ethanol has accounted for three-quarters of the 40 percent increase in the use of domestic corn output, with ethanol by-products accounting for the remainder

(Figure 1.26, lower-middle-right panel). Use of soybean oil in the production of biodiesel fuel is also increasing rapidly. High energy prices and policy support are bolstering biofuel production in Europe and other regions as well, but again, limited data availability continues to impede commodity market transparency (Figure 1.26, bottom-left panel). Overall, global demand for major crops during 2011–12 is anticipated to grow by about 2¼ percent, considerably above the 20-year average and almost entirely because of demand from China and other emerging market and low-income economies.

Food prices should decline modestly but remain high in real terms through 2012, assuming a return to more normal weather conditions and stable energy prices, which affect food prices through biofuel and production costs. This scenario is built into the futures prices of some key crops, notably corn, which currently reflect some easing as each new crop is harvested. Supply is responding to higher prices, albeit with a lag. In particular, rising global acreage should offset the medium-term moderation in yield growth due, in part, to emerging constraints in productive land and water. The balance of risks to food prices is still to the upside, however, and this is reflected in derivative market pricing, which shows market participants pricing in a higher-than-average probability of a price spike over the next nine months (Figure 1.26, bottom-right panel). A combination of low inventories, volatile weather, and demand uncertainties related to China and biofuels raises the prospect of further price spikes over the next 12 to 18 months. The renewed imposition of trade restrictions in the face of using prices and tighter demand-supply balances in physical markets—including through export bans by important producers—could exacerbate global supply conditions and heighten world price volatility.

Box 1.1. Slow Recovery to Nowhere? A Sectoral View of Labor Markets in Advanced Economies

Employment took a deep hit in many advanced economies during the Great Recession of 2008–09 and has been slow to recover, reflecting the still weak and uncertain recovery. But even after a cyclical recovery, structural trends that predate the Great Recession could dim labor market prospects. Skill-biased technological change and the increased prevalence of global supply chains have added to national income in advanced economies. But these trends also have been associated with a striking loss of middle-income and manufacturing jobs. This box describes these unequal impacts of technology and trade and their likely impact on potential output growth. The main policy message is that advanced economies need to address the human costs of these structural trends just as they took steps to lower the human costs of the Great Recession (Dao and Loungani, 2010).

Technology and Trade Effects on Employment

Technological change and trade are as old as civilization, but when it comes to their medium-term impacts on the labor market, each time can be different. In the two decades preceding the Great Recession, a salient feature of technological change was that it favored more highly skilled workers. This is not always the case: during some periods in history, technological change has replaced rather than complemented the highly skilled (Goldin and Katz, 2008).

The primary effect of trade on the labor market during these same two decades was an increasing reliance on global supply chains, a process helped by the availability of large pools of workers in emerging markets who previously had been outside the global production system. As Freeman (2007) notes, "almost all at once in the 1990s, China, India, and the ex-Soviet bloc joined the global economy," doubling the size of the global labor pool to nearly 3 billion. The concurrent advances in information and communication technology helped give many global businesses ready access to this expanded pool of labor.

As in the past, these trends in technology and trade have contributed to global welfare: millions have been lifted out of poverty in emerging markets; consumers everywhere have enjoyed the benefits of lower prices; and national income has expanded in advanced economies. But these trends have also increasingly been associated with diminished prospects for large groups of workers in advanced economies. As Spence (2011) notes, "until about a decade ago, the effects of globalization on the distribution of wealth and jobs were largely benign, [but now] it is changing the structures of individual economies in ways that affect different groups within countries differently. In advanced economies, it is redistributing employment opportunities and incomes."

Documenting these effects requires going beyond aggregates and looking at sectoral developments by skill level and industry.

Employment Shifts and Labor Productivity

Acemoglu and Autor (2010) document a shift in employment in the United States from medium-skill to low- and high-skill jobs during 1980–2007. Middle-income jobs declined significantly in other advanced economies between 1993 and 2006, including in the euro area, Japan, and the United Kingdom. Figure 1.1.1 suggests a shift away from middle-income jobs and from industries with high productivity levels and high productivity growth to industries with lower productivity levels and growth rates.

The top-left panel shows the striking hollowing out of medium-skill and middle-income jobs, many of which were lost from the manufacturing sector. In contrast, much of the services sector, which includes community, social, personal, and government services, remains dependent on low-skilled, low-income labor.[1]

The top-right panel of the figure shows the change in labor market share of various sectors during 2000–07 for selected advanced economies. All five economies experienced a decline in manufacturing and an increase in services. Even in Germany, which has had a trade surplus since 2001,

The main authors of this box are Prakash Loungani, Su Wang, Laura Feiveson, and João Jalles.

[1]For a fuller analysis of productivity developments in services, see Bosworth and Triplett (2007).

Box 1.1 *(continued)*

Figure 1.1.1. Trends in Employment and Labor Productivity

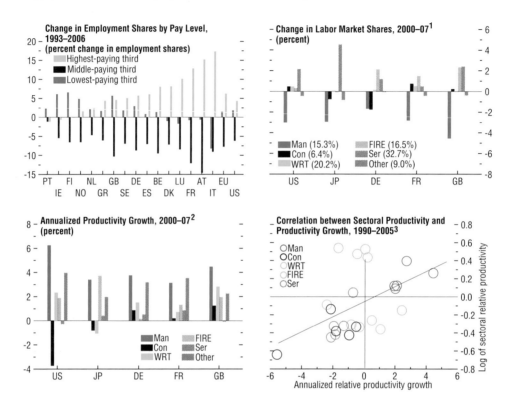

Sources: Autor (2010); Groningen Growth and Development Center (GGDC); Organization for Economic Cooperation and Development (OECD) STAN database; and IMF staff calculations.

Note: AT: Austria; BE: Belgium; DK: Denmark; EU: EU average; FI: Finland; FR: France; DE: Germany; GR: Greece; IE: Ireland; IT: Italy; JP: Japan; LU: Luxembourg; NL: Netherlands; NO: Norway; PT: Portugal; ES: Spain; SE: Sweden; GB: United Kingdom; US: United States. Con: construction; FIRE: finance, insurance, and real estate; Man: manufacturing; Ser: community, social, and personal services; WRT: wholesale and retail trade, hotels, and restaurants.

[1]Japanese data are taken from the GGDC database and are for 1996–2003.

[2]Japanese data are taken from the GGDC database and are for 1996–2003. Productivity is computed by dividing value added by hours worked. For the United Kingdom and Japan, it is computed by dividing value added by number of employees.

[3]The countries included in this panel are France, Germany, Japan, United Kingdom, and United States.

the manufacturing share of employment fell from 22 percent in 2000 to 20½ percent in 2007. The construction sector and the financial services sector (which includes finance, insurance, and real estate) also experienced large employment increases in most of these economies during the housing boom of the precrisis period.

Historically, reallocating labor from low-productivity to high-productivity sectors has been a primary channel through which advanced economies have increased national income (McMillan and Rodrik,

2011). But many observers fear that these economies are now at a stage in their structural transformation at which they could "slow down, stagnate, and decline" as labor is increasingly reallocated from high-productivity manufacturing to lower-productivity services (Duarte and Restuccia, 2010).

The bottom-left panel shows labor productivity growth by sector during 2000–07. Manufacturing was a high-productivity growth sector, whereas services sector productivity barely increased (or even declined) in every country during this period. There

Box 1.1 *(continued)*

was increased employment in construction, which experienced below-average productivity growth, and in financial services, which experienced average productivity growth.

The bottom-right panel shows that relative productivity levels and productivity growth are highly correlated. This occurs because sectoral productivity growth rates have been relatively consistent during the past decades.

Sectoral Productivity and Potential Output Growth

The likely impact of these employment shifts on aggregate productivity growth, and hence on potential output growth, can be illustrated through a simple accounting framework. The labor productivity of country i in year t can be expressed as follows:

$$A_{it} = \sum_j \theta_{ijt} \times P_{ijt}, \tag{1.1}$$

where θ_{ijt} is the share of labor input in industry j as a fraction of the economy-wide labor supply, P_{ijt} is per unit labor productivity, and the summation is over all industries j. The growth rate of productivity can be expressed as follows:

$$\frac{A_{it}^*}{A_{it}} = \frac{1}{A_{it}} \left(\sum_j \theta_{ijt}^* \times P_{ijt} + \sum_j \theta_{ijt} \times P_{ijt}^* \right). \tag{1.2}$$

An asterisk next to a variable indicates the change with respect to time.

Taking sectoral productivity growth as exogenous, this equation shows the impact on economy-wide productivity growth as employment starts to shift from an industry with high productivity and high productivity growth rates to a low-productivity (and low productivity growth) industry. During the shift, the first term on the right side of the equation is lower if there is a negative correlation between changes in labor share and productivity levels. This is referred to as a *compositional* or *structural* effect. Moreover, once the shift takes place, the second sum is also smaller, because there is now higher employment in sectors where productivity growth is lower and lower employment in sectors where productivity growth is higher. This is the *within-industry* effect.

Figure 1.1.2 illustrates these effects. The top-left panel shows the relationship between changes in

labor share and productivity levels for five advanced European economies from 2000 to 2007. There is a clear negative correlation between relative productivity and the change in the employment share, although the finance sector is an outlier. The top-right panel shows a similar and more striking negative correlation between changes in labor shares and productivity levels in the United States during 2000–07. The size of the bubbles represents the relative size of the sectors.

The bottom-left panel shows both the structural and within-industry effects on U.S. labor productivity growth for three typical years: 1991, 2000, and 2007. Each effect is the cumulative sum for six sectors, so that the sum of all 12 components is equal to the labor productivity growth rate for the year. Sectors differ greatly in the channels through which they contribute to aggregate labor productivity growth. The manufacturing sector has always had a negative structural component, due to its diminishing labor share. In contrast, the services sector has negative within-industry components for all three years, a sign of its sluggish productivity growth.[2]

Thus, shifts away from high-productivity industries have exerted a drag on per capita output growth due to both structural and within-industry effects.

Although the shifts in the labor market documented above predate the Great Recession, the evidence suggests that they persist. For instance, with respect to the polarization of jobs, Autor (2010) finds that "the Great Recession has quantitatively but not qualitatively changed the direction of the U.S. labor market." The bottom-right panel plots the level of productivity against the change in labor market share in the United States during 2007–09. The services sector continued to grow in terms of labor share and the manufacturing sector to decline—both at faster annual rates. Indeed, total employment fell 4½ percent and employment in manufacturing by 14 percent between 2007 and 2009, but employment in services increased by 2 percent.[3]

---

[2]See Peneder (2003) and Bosworth and Triplett (2007) for further discussion on the decomposition.

[3]The experiences of the United Kingdom and Spain were similar; Germany, however, had a slight increase in labor share in manufacturing and a slight decrease in services.

Box 1.1 *(continued)*

Figure 1.1.2. Sectoral Trends May Affect Potential Output Growth

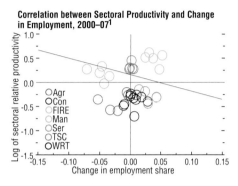

Correlation between Sectoral Productivity and Change in Employment, 2000–07[1]

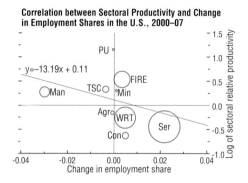

Correlation between Sectoral Productivity and Change in Employment Shares in the U.S., 2000–07

$y = -13.19x + 0.11$

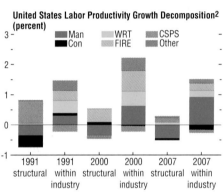

United States Labor Productivity Growth Decomposition[2] (percent)

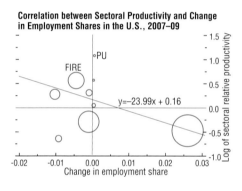

Correlation between Sectoral Productivity and Change in Employment Shares in the U.S., 2007–09

$y = -23.99x + 0.16$

Sources: Groningen Growth and Development Center; Organization for Economic Cooperation and Development; and IMF staff calculations.

Note: Agr: agriculture, forestry, and fishing; Con: construction; CSPS: community, social, and personal services; FIRE: finance, insurance, and real estate; Man: manufacturing; Min: mining and quarrying; PU: public utilities; Ser: community, social, and personal services; TSC: transport, storage, and communication; WRT: wholesale and retail trade, hotels, and restaurants.

[1]Trendline is drawn for sectors other than FIRE. The countries included in this panel are France, Germany, Japan, United Kingdom, and United States.

[2]Structural effect is the relationship between productivity level and labor share; within-industry effect is the relationship between productivity growth and labor share.

Where Are They Headed?

What impact will technology and trade trends have on labor markets in the coming years? Answering that question—and suggesting appropriate policy responses—requires some conjecture as to which of the two forces is likely to dominate, though it is not always easy to separate out their impacts. Early analyses of these developments, particularly explanations for the rising skill premium, tended to conclude that technological change was dominant (for example, Lawrence and Slaughter, 1993). And there

is no doubt that technology played an important role in the gradual decline of middle-income and manufacturing jobs since the 1970s. In particular, automation has decreased employment in industries with a higher share of routine tasks (Autor, Levy, and Murnane, 2003).

Other factors besides technological change also seem to be involved, however, not least because the sharp decline in jobs occurred well after the arrival of most new information and communication technology in the 1990s. Recent work therefore assigns greater importance to the role of trade, particu-

Box 1.1 *(continued)*

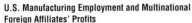

Figure 1.1.3. Employment, Profits, and Intermediate Goods Trade in the United States

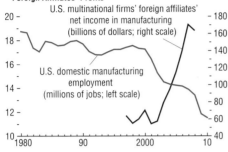

U.S. Manufacturing Employment and Multinational Foreign Affiliates' Profits

U.S. multinational firms' foreign affiliates' net income in manufacturing (billions of dollars; right scale)

U.S. domestic manufacturing employment (millions of jobs; left scale)

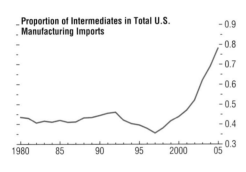

Proportion of Intermediates in Total U.S. Manufacturing Imports

Sources: Goel (2011); U.S. Bureau of Labor Statistics; Bureau of Economic Analysis; and IMF staff calculations.

larly to offshoring and soaring production within multinational firms.[4] These studies stress that it is no coincidence that the decline in manufacturing jobs accelerated during the 2000s and was accompanied by a huge increase in advanced economies' imports from low-income countries. Autor, Dorn, and Hanson (2011) estimate that at least one-third of the aggregate decline in U.S. manufacturing employment during 1990–2007 can be attributed to increased imports from emerging markets. The top panel of Figure 1.1.3 shows the sharp decline in U.S. manufacturing jobs and the increase in the profits of multinational firms during the 2000s.[5]

[4]See, for instance, Hanson, Mataloni, and Slaughter (2005).
[5]Over time, increasing labor costs in emerging market economies may partially reverse the offshoring trend. As multinationals and foreign firms begin to reopen some plants

The bottom panel shows the sharp acceleration in the share of intermediate goods imports in total imports over the same period (Goel, 2011), reflecting the establishment of global supply chains.

The consequences of job losses are amplified if there are interactions between international trade and technological innovations. If economies' comparative advantage is enhanced over time through learning-by-doing, as suggested by many authors, changes in patterns of specialization could persist over time.[6] Trade-induced technological changes would lead to similar effects.[7] As a result, the offshoring sectors with higher growth potential could dampen growth in the advanced economies in the long term.

Conclusions

This box documents the unequal impact on advanced economies of structural trends—namely, technological change and trade.[8] Over the past 20 years, these trends have lifted living standards in emerging markets and developing economies and conferred the benefits of lower prices on consumers everywhere. In advanced economies, technological innovation and the ability to take advantage of a global labor market have contributed to national income. But at the same time, there has been an adverse impact on a large class of workers in advanced economies, particularly in manufacturing, and prospects for this class remain dim. This adverse impact is reflected in increased income inequality; for example, the Gini coefficient of income inequality rose in six of the G7 economies

domestically, productivity growth may rebound. There are differing views on whether offshoring trends can continue. Blinder (2009) estimates that 25 percent of U.S. jobs are potentially offshorable. In contrast, Manyika and others (2011) and Deutsche Bank (2011) argue for a gradual shift from offshoring to "on-shoring" as labor costs continue to increase in coastal China and other emerging markets and as companies become aware of many hidden costs and risks intrinsic to doing business in emerging markets.
[6]See Krugman (1985), Lucas (1988), Boldrin and Scheinkman (1988), and Young (1991).
[7]See Acemoglu (2003) and Thoenig and Verdier (2003).
[8]The focus has been on medium-term trends rather than the question of how much current unemployment in advanced economies is structural (see Diamond, 2011).

Box 1.1 *(continued)*

between 1985 and 2008, according to the Organization for Economic Cooperation and Development. The calculations discussed in this box also suggest that, at least in the medium term, there could be a dampening effect on potential output growth from the ongoing shift in employment from industries with high productivity growth rates to those with low productivity growth rates.

The longer-term solutions to the hollowing out of middle-income jobs lie in retraining, better education, and increased productivity in nonmanu-facturing sectors. But more immediate action is also needed to cushion some of the human costs of structural change. As Spence (2011) argues, redistribution must be part of the policy response: the potential benefits include increased social cohesion and continued support for globalization. Spence cautions that if the employment challenges confronting the advanced economies are not tackled, countries may resort to "protectionist measures on a broad front [and] the global economy will be undermined."

Box 1.2. Credit Boom-Bust Cycles: Their Triggers and Policy Implications

Credit has been growing rapidly in a number of emerging market economies, raising concern in some quarters. Although there can be good reasons for credit to grow rapidly—cyclical upturns, financial deepening, and improved medium-term prospects—in some circumstances credit expansion can be excessive and can be followed by financial turbulence, as shown by the recent global financial crisis and the Asian crisis of the mid-1990s. Such credit expansion is often called a "credit boom."

What is a credit boom? It is an episode during which real credit to the private sector expands significantly more than during typical economic expansions.[1] During the upswing of a credit boom, economic activity expands strongly, housing and equity prices rise rapidly, leverage increases sharply, the real exchange rate appreciates, and current account deficits widen. The opposite is observed during the downswing of a boom: activity contracts sharply, housing and equity prices drop, leverage falls, the real exchange rate depreciates, and current account deficits narrow. Financial vulnerabilities heighten as a result of these large swings in macroeconomic and financial variables. In fact, there is a strong association between credit booms and currency crises, banking crises, and sudden stops (Figure 1.2.1, top panel).

Given the strong association between such credit boom-bust cycles and financial crises, it is important to understand what drives them. This box studies credit booms in 47 economies—19 advanced and 28 emerging market economies—during 1960–2010. We find that capital inflows are good predictors of credit booms and merit close monitoring not only because of their impact on competitiveness but also because of other implications for financial stability.

The main authors of this box are Jörg Decressin and Marco E. Terrones.

[1]Credit booms are defined as extreme episodes during which the cyclical component of credit is larger than 1.75 times its standard deviation—see Mendoza and Terrones (2008) for more details and an analysis of these episodes for advanced and emerging market economies. The focus on the cyclical component of credit assumes that the trend captures mostly healthy financial deepening.

Figure 1.2.1. Credit Booms

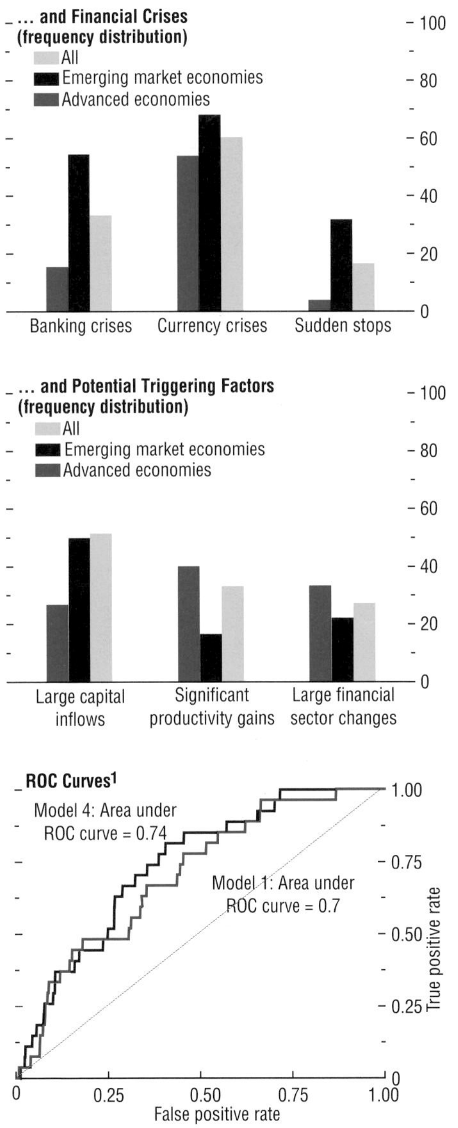

Sources: Mendoza and Terrones (2008); and IMF staff calculations.
[1]ROC = receiver operating characteristic. The ROC for a coin toss is indicated by the 45-degree line.

What Triggers a Credit Boom?

Credit booms can be driven by many factors. Three in particular garner considerable attention and are indeed strongly associated with credit booms:

Box 1.2 *(continued)*

surges in capital inflows, financial sector reforms, and productivity gains. In particular, credit booms in emerging market economies seem to be associated mostly with large capital inflows, whereas those in advanced economies often coincide with productivity gains (Figure 1.2.1, middle panel). Although this observation is useful, it does not indicate whether these factors can help predict credit boom-busts and which among these is most relevant. To address this issue, we use a simple probabilistic model of credit booms and the following factors:

- Past capital inflows: A surge in net private capital inflows typically leads to a rapid increase in loanable funds. Banks, in an attempt to allocate these funds, often lower their lending standards and extend credit to firms and households previously without access to financial markets. This can lead to an overly rapid expansion of credit.[2]

- Past financial sector reforms: In an attempt to improve their growth performance, countries around the world have implemented measures to eliminate financial repression and develop their financial sectors, which has frequently spurred credit growth. But the process of financial sector development—that is, the emergence of financial instruments, institutions, and markets—can involve risks, particularly when such development is not accompanied by adequate evolution of the regulatory and supervisory frameworks.

- Past productivity gains: Technological progress and innovation are often financed with external resources. Indeed, there is evidence that credit plays an important role in the process of technological innovation. Optimism about rapid technological progress and about future increases in the value of collateral assets often accompanies strong credit growth.[3]

Excessive credit expansion results in part from propagation mechanisms associated with financial market imperfections. One such mechanism is the financial accelerator (Bernanke, Gertler, and Gilchrist, 1999; and Kiyotaki and Moore, 1997): shocks to asset prices and relative prices are amplified through balance sheet effects. This propagation process can be exacerbated by inadequate regulatory and supervisory frameworks, including implicit government guarantees, and herd behavior by banks.

Main Findings

The econometric results confirm that net capital inflows, financial sector reform, and total factor productivity are good predictors of a credit boom.[4] Net capital inflows appear to have an important predictive edge over the other two factors.

The main econometric results are summarized in Table 1.2.1. This table shows the alternative specifications of a logit regression, with the dependent variable an episode dummy that takes the value of 1 if country i is experiencing a credit boom in year t, and zero otherwise. The estimated coefficients of the different triggering factors have the appropriate signs and are all statistically significant. We are interested in an assessment of the predictive power of various regression specifications, and for that purpose use the receiver operating characteristic (ROC) curve method.[5] The ROC curve is a plot of the true positive rate (TP) versus the false positive rate (FP). If the number of true positives equals the number of false positives, the three factors have the same predictive value as a coin toss—that is, none at all. Thus, the predictive value of the factors is given by the extent to which the ROC curve lies above the 45-degree line in the bottom panel of Figure 1.2.1. A summary measure of this curve—the so-called area under the curve (AUC) measure—is a useful statistic to rank the predictive performance

---

[2]Végh (2011) shows that the macroeconomic consequences of capital inflows are the same regardless of the nature of the shock driving the inflows—that is, push or pull.

[3]Zeira (1999), building on the idea of informational overshooting, shows how increased productivity for an unknown period of time could lead to financial booms and crashes.

[4]In the econometric model, the capital inflow variable is proxied by the five-year average of net capital inflows as a percent of GDP. Financial sector reforms correspond to the five-year average of the yearly changes in the financial reform index compiled by Abiad, Detragiache, and Tressel (2008). The data were extrapolated to 2008. The productivity measure was calculated using standard growth accounting methods (Kose, Prasad, and Terrones, 2009) using data from the Penn World Table 7.0.

[5]Berge and Jordà (2011) offer a detailed discussion of this method and an application to the U.S. business cycle. Jordà, Schularick, and Taylor (2010) use this method to examine the extent to which credit expansions help predict banking crises.

Box 1.2 *(continued)*

Table 1.2.1. What Triggers Credit Booms?
(Logit model; dependent variable—start of a credit boom: 1 if true, zero if false)

Explanatory Variables	(1)	(2)	(3)	(4)	(5)	(6)	(7)	(8)	(9)	(10)
Lagged Net Capital Inflows (percent of GDP, five-year average of yearly changes)	0.403*** [0.126]			0.379*** [0.121]		0.412*** [0.122]			0.388*** [0.127]	0.406* [0.246]
Lagged Financial Sector Reform (five-year average of yearly changes)		0.694*** [0.259]		0.592** [0.286]		0.686** [0.297]				
Lagged Total Factor Productivity Growth (five-year average)			0.177** [0.074]	0.132** [0.063]	0.118 [0.091]	0.081 [0.072]				
Lagged Total Factor Productivity Growth x Advanced Country Dummy					0.335** [0.148]	0.390** [0.155]				
Lagged Real U.S. Interest Rate (five-year average of yearly changes, 10-year Treasury bill)							−0.375 [0.294]		−0.285 [0.311]	
Lagged VIX (five-year average of yearly changes)								0.069 [0.139]		0.129 [0.153]
Advanced Economy Dummy					0.001 [0.328]	0.233 [0.360]				
Constant	−3.827*** [0.155]	−4.137*** [0.229]	−3.844*** [0.176]	−4.231*** [0.236]	−3.921*** [0.267]	−4.504*** [0.374]	−3.754*** [0.157]	−3.966*** [0.329]	−3.824*** [0.155]	−4.012*** [0.344]
Memorandum										
Number of Observations	1,180	1,180	1,180	1,180	1,180	1,180	1,180	472	1,180	472
Log Likelihood	−124.39	−125.97	−126.77	−121.20	−125.47	−118.92	−128.00	−44.49	−124.03	−43.35
Pseudo R^2	0.03	0.02	0.02	0.06	0.03	0.08	0.01	0.00	0.04	0.03
AUC	0.70	0.58	0.63	0.74	0.67	0.74	0.51	0.56	0.71	0.67

Sources: IMF, *International Financial Statistics;* Haver Analytics; Penn World Table 7.0; World Bank, *World Development Indicators;* and IMF staff calculations.

Note: *,**, and *** denote significance at the 10, 5, and 1 percent level, respectively. Significance is based on robust standard errors, which are in brackets. VIX = Chicago Board Options Exchange Market Volatility Index. AUC refers to the area under the curve. Broadly similar results are obtained when using the probit model.

of alternative specifications. If the ROC curve coincides with the 45-degree line, the AUC measure is 0.5 (half the square in Figure 1.2.1, bottom panel). Thus, an AUC of 0.5 indicates the predictive value of a coin toss. If the AUC is greater than 0.5, the respective factor (or combination of factors) has predictive value.

The results reveal that net capital inflows are the most helpful factor in predicting credit booms. Financial sector reforms and productivity gains also help predict these booms; however, their predictive value is lower. The predictive gains of combining

all these factors into a single model are marginal. The model with net capital inflows as a covariate (Table 1.2.1, column 1) shows that this variable is highly significant and possesses an AUC of 0.7. Past financial sector reforms and productivity gains are also important predictors of a credit boom (Table 1.2.1, columns 2 and 3); however, their significance level, fit, and AUC statistics are not as good as those of capital inflows. The model that includes all these factors simultaneously shows only marginal predictive gains vis-à-vis the model including only past net capital inflows (Table 1.2.1, column 4;

Box 1.2 *(continued)*

Figure 1.2.1, bottom panel). These results do not change materially if interaction terms are considered. The specification that includes an interaction term between productivity gains and the advanced economy dummy suggests that past productivity gains are strong predictors of credit booms in these economies, but not in emerging markets (Table 1.2.1, columns 5 and 6).

To explore the possibility that net capital inflows are capturing the effects of easy international financial conditions on domestic credit booms, we include in the regression analysis proxies for return (the real interest rate) and volatility (Chicago Board Options Exchange Market Volatility Index) in the United States. Although these variables have the expected signs, they are not statistically significant (Table 1.2.1, columns 7 and 8). Moreover, when included with net capital inflows, the predictive power of the volatility variable remains broadly unchanged (Table 1.2.1, columns 9 and 10).

What Are the Policy Implications?

Although net capital inflows have well-known benefits for long-term economic growth, they often raise concern among policymakers because they can undermine an economy's short-term competitiveness. The findings of this box suggest that they are also good predictors of credit booms and merit close monitoring for this reason alone. Given the high costs of credit boom-bust cycles, policymakers should closely monitor the joint behavior of capital inflows and domestic lending.[6] There is also evidence that financial sector reforms are predictors of credit boom-busts. Policymakers must ensure that financial liberalization programs are designed to strengthen financial stability frameworks. Last, there is evidence that large productivity gains increase the risk of a credit boom, particularly in advanced economies, driven perhaps by exuberant optimism in new sectors. Thus, even during particularly good periods for the economy, policymakers must be on the lookout for emerging threats to financial stability stemming from credit booms.

---

[6]Policymakers can use a combination of macroeconomic, exchange rate, prudential policy, and capital control measures to mitigate the adverse effects of large capital inflows. Ostry and others (2011) discuss in detail policymakers' diverse policy options for addressing different kinds of capital inflows, which is important in light of evidence that net debt flows are better predictors of credit booms than foreign direct investment flows.

Box 1.3. Are Equity Price Drops Harbingers of Recession?

The recent sharp drop in equity prices around the world has raised concerns about the possibility of a double-dip recession in a number of advanced economies. Several factors may have played a role in this fall in equity prices: the sovereign debt problems in the euro area; a downgrade of U.S. federal government debt; and the limited room for policy maneuver by advanced economies that are facing a weaker-than-expected economic recovery. To the extent that such factors simultaneously affect confidence and equity prices, an equity price drop can be indicative of a greater risk of recession, reflecting falling earnings expectations. In their own right, weak or falling equity prices can be a drag on consumption and investment through their effects on private sector wealth and borrowing constraints. Accordingly, many think that a double-dip recession in the United States and other advanced economies has become more likely. However, others have noted that equity price drops have not always been good predictors of recessions. As Paul Samuelson (1966) famously remarked, "The stock market has forecast nine of the last five recessions."

This box examines the performance of equity prices as coincident predictors of a new recession in France, Japan, the United Kingdom, and the United States.[1] Table 1.3.1 displays summary statistics on quarterly real equity price changes for these countries from the first quarter of 1970 through the first half of 2011. We find that real equity prices in these economies are useful predictors of recessions. However, in contrast with the existing literature, there is some evidence of important nonlinearities in the relationship between equity prices and recessions among those economies for which equity prices had predictive power. Equity price drops, defined as a quarterly decline in average

The main authors of this box are John C. Bluedorn, Jörg Decressin, and Marco E. Terrones.

[1]The beginnings of new recessions are defined according to the method of Harding and Pagan (2002), as implemented by Claessens, Kose, and Terrones (2011c). A cyclical peak or start of a new recession is defined to occur in a quarter if the level of real GDP is higher than during both the prior two quarters and the subsequent two quarters. For the United States, the Harding and Pagan–identified peaks exactly coincide with the NBER-identified peaks in four cases and precede the NBER peak by one quarter in the other two cases.

Table 1.3.1. Summary Statistics for Real Equity Price Growth
(Quarter-over-quarter, seasonally adjusted)

Statistic	France	Japan	United Kingdom	United States
Mean	1.1	0.8	1.2	1.4
Standard deviation	8.0	7.7	6.7	5.0
Median	1.5	1.5	1.8	1.9
10th Percentile	−10.0	−9.5	−7.1	−4.6
25th Percentile	−4.1	−3.1	−2.2	−1.4
75th Percentile	5.6	5.1	5.4	4.4
90th Percentile	10.6	9.2	8.7	8.4
Minimum	−22.2	−17.9	−23.1	−18.3
Maximum	25.4	27.1	18.8	14.0
Number of observations	138	141	135	132

Sources: Datastream; Haver Analytics; *IMF, International Financial Statistics*; and IMF staff calculations.

Note: The average nominal equity price index for each economy is converted to real terms using the respective consumer price index. The resulting average real equity price indices are then seasonally adjusted using the X12-ARIMA procedure.

real equity prices of 5 percent or more, significantly improve the accuracy of recession predictions for the United Kingdom and the United States but not for France and Japan.[2]

We also investigate whether the predictive power of equity prices in our simple probability model is materially changed by the addition of other financial variables, including a measure of spillovers from equity markets elsewhere, the term spread, real house price growth, real credit growth, or real oil price peaks. For Japan, the United Kingdom, and the United States, real equity prices remain an important and statistically significant coincident predictor of a new recession across all checks. This may be a reflection of the fact that these economies are home to the largest equity markets in the world. Apart from the case in which a measure of international equity prices is included, domestic equity prices are also an important predictor of a new recession in France.

Finally, we look at the predictive power of real equity price declines in the three other G7 economies. For Canada and Germany, there is no evidence

[2]The choice of 5 percent as the threshold is based on the evidence presented in Claessens, Kose, and Terrones (2011c) that equity price busts (the bottom quartile of periods characterized by equity price falls) have a median decline of about 5½ percent a quarter (Table 4, column 4).

Box 1.3 *(continued)*

that equity prices aid in predicting recessions, whereas for Italy, their predictive power is consistently superseded by the inclusion of additional financial market variables. Consequently, the remainder of the box focuses on the evidence for France, Japan, the United Kingdom, and the United States.[3]

Recession Forecasting

Real-time recession prediction remains an elusive endeavor (Hamilton, 2010). Forecasters are confronted with data limitations, changing economic relationships, and sometimes perverse incentive schemes (Loungani and Trehan, 2002). Although some leading indicator models find that equity prices help improve output growth forecasts for the United States, these models have failed to predict recent recessions (Stock and Watson, 2003).

More recent efforts to forecast the onset of a recession have used straightforward probabilistic models, such as logit or probit. These models take advantage of the fact that cyclical peaks can be modeled as binary indicators (with a value of 1 when the economy has reached its peak and zero otherwise). The most important finding of this literature is that the term spread (the difference between the long-term interest rate and the short-term interest rate) is an important predictor of recessions in the euro area (Moneta, 2003) and the United States (Estrella and Mishkin, 1998; Estrella, 2005; Wright, 2006; and Nyberg, 2010). A number of these studies also find that domestic equity prices can be useful in predicting recessions (Estrella and Mishkin, 1998; and Nyberg, 2010). This literature, however, does not examine in detail the role that other financial variables, such as international equity prices, house prices, and credit, play in forecasting recessions. Recent research indicates that developments in these markets are associated with the characteristics of recessions and recoveries (Claessens, Kose, and Terrones, 2011c).

Predicting the Probability of a New Recession

To explore how a particular variable helps predict new recessions in France, Japan, the United

Kingdom, and the United States, we use a simple probabilistic model for each economy. The explanatory variables included in our baseline logit model are the contemporaneous quarterly growth rate of the economy's average real equity price index, an indicator variable for whether the real equity price index dropped quarter-over-quarter by 5 percent or more, and the interaction (product) of these two variables. This model allows us to explore the relevance of nonlinearities in the information conveyed by equity price changes about the likelihood of a recession. In particular, sharp drops in equity prices are more likely to be followed by a new recession, reflecting both the destruction of private sector wealth and possible underlying weaknesses in the macroeconomy.

The following findings stand out (Table 1.3.2):

- In the United Kingdom and the United States, there is evidence of important nonlinearities in the information that equity prices convey about the probability of a new recession. This is shown in the statistical significance of equity price growth, the equity price drop indicator, and their interaction as predictors of a new recession. The in-sample performance of the baseline model for these economies is very strong, as reflected by AUC statistics of 0.85 and 0.90, respectively.[4] As seen in Table 1.3.2, column 3, the average probability of a new recession occurring in any quarter, conditional upon observing a drop in equity prices of 5 percent or more, is around 20 percent. By contrast, if no equity price drop is observed, the estimated average probability is insignificantly different from zero. To get a sense for how equity price growth, which is continuous, affects the probability of a new recession, we calculate the marginal effect on the average recession probability of a 1 percent fall in equity prices. As shown in Table 1.3.2, column 1, if only equity price growth is included, the marginal effect of

---

[3]The results for Canada, Germany, and Italy are available at www.imf.org/weoforum.

[4]The AUC statistic is the area under the receiver operating characteristic, which is described in Box 1.2. It is indicative of how well the model classifies the start of a recession versus the absence of recession observations in-sample, relative to a fair coin toss (which would have a 50 percent chance of correctly classifying the situation). A perfect classifier would have an AUC statistic of 1.

Box 1.3 *(continued)*

Table 1.3.2. Predicting New Recessions with Financial Market Variables
(Logit model, dependant variable—New recession starts with quarter t [1 if true and zero if false])

Explanatory Variable	France (1)	France (2)	France (3)	Japan (1)	Japan (2)	Japan (3)	United Kingdom (1)	United Kingdom (2)	United Kingdom (3)	United States (1)	United States (2)	United States (3)
Equity Price Change in Quarter *t* (Change in quarterly average equity price index)	-0.174** (0.0746)		-0.0984*** (0.024)	-0.258** (0.108)		-0.304*** (0.0444)	-0.153 (0.0598)		0.173*** (0.0367)	-1.181*** (0.0689)		-0.280* (0.169)
Equity Price Drop > 5% (Indicator is 1 if true and zero if false)		1.970** (0.945)	-3.014 (2.703)		2.648** (1.181)	-3.128 (2.722)		3.350*** (1.154)	3.767** (1.803)		2.691*** (0.898)	4.566*** (1.78)
Interaction of Equity Drop and Equity Price Change			-0.265 (0.211)			-0.145 (0.197)			-0.220* (0.13)			0.546** (0.268)
Constant	-3.970*** (0.801)	-4.007*** (0.716)	-3.766*** (0.723)	-4.967*** (1.269)	-4.727*** (1.008)	-4.525*** (1.011)	-3.624*** (0.616)	-4.736*** (1.008)	-5.644*** (1.004)	-3.186*** (0.431)	-3.672*** (0.587)	-3.529*** (0.616)
Number of Observations	138	138	138	141	1414	141	135	135	135	132	132	132
Pseudo R^2	0.209	0.101	0.251	0.303	0.167	0.33	0.163	0.264	0.287	0.124	0.16	0.233
Log Likelihood	-17	-19.33	-16.1	-12.69	-15.15	-12.18	-17.89	-15.75	-15.25	-21.39	-20.5	-18.71
AUC	0.8	0.71	0.824	0.902	0.788	0.911	0.773	0.835	0.892	0.829	0.715	0.84
Average Predicted Probabilities and Marginal Effects												
Average Predicted Probability if *No* Equity Price Drop > 5%		0.0179 (0.0126)	0.0156 (0.011)		0.00877 (0.00876)	0.00368 (0.00367)		0.0087 (0.00869)	0.00608 (0.00606)		0.0248* (0.0142)	0.0152 (0.0121)
Average Predicted Probability if Equity Price Drop > 5%		0.115* (0.0629)	0.0544 (0.0342)		0.111* (0.067)	0.0539 (0.0405)		0.200** (0.0898)	0.197* (0.0911)		0.273** (0.135)	0.228* (0.133)
Marginal Effect if Equity Price Rise of 1%	-0.00538** (0.00262)		-0.00614** (0.00309)	-0.00606** (0.00304)		-0.00869*** (0.00405)	-0.00491** (0.00226)		0.000157 (0.00315)	-0.00722* (0.00378)		-0.002 (0.00587)

Sources: Datastream; Haver Analytics; IMF, *International Financial Statistics*; Claessens, Kose, and Terrones (2011c); and IMF staff calculations.

Note: Robust standard errors are in parentheses underneath the estimates. *, **, and *** denote significance at the 10, 5, and 1 percent level, respectively.

Box 1.3 *(continued)*

a 1 percent fall is a rise in the estimated probability of a new recession by around 0.7 percent for the United States and around 0.5 percent for the United Kingdom. If the equity price drop indicator and its interaction with equity price growth are included, the marginal effect of equity price growth alone is tiny and no longer statistically significant in helping to predict a recession, revealing the importance of nonlinearities in the form of large equity price drops.

- Interestingly, this nonlinearity in the predictive power of equity prices is not evident for France and Japan. Instead, there appears to be a robust, linear relationship between equity price growth and the likelihood of a new recession—large equity price drops do not appear to convey any more information than small drops. The in-sample performance of this model is also strong, as reflected in an AUC of 0.82 for France and 0.91 for Japan. The marginal effect of a 1 percent fall in equity prices is associated with a rise in the probability of a new recession of between 0.5 and 0.6 percent for France and 0.6 and 0.9 percent for Japan.

As noted earlier, we also investigate whether the predictive power of equity prices is materially changed by the addition of other financial variables (such as the term spread, real house prices, and real credit) and real oil prices. Apart from one instance in the case of France, equity prices remain important, coincident predictors of new recessions. The additional financial variables that improve recession prediction differed across these economies. For the United States, a measure of spillovers from equity price movements in the G7, the term spread, and the change in real house prices are all significant predictors of new recessions.[5] For the United Kingdom,

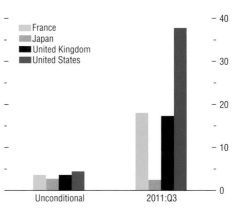

Figure 1.3.1. Predicted Probability of a New Recession in a Quarter

- France
- Japan
- United Kingdom
- United States

Unconditional   2011:Q3

Sources: Claessens, Kose, and Terrones (2011c); Haver Analytics; and IMF Staff Calculations.

Note: The equity price indices used in the estimation are: S&P 500 for the United States, FTSE All Shares for the United Kingdom, CAC All-Tradable for France, and the Nikkei 225 for Japan. The Claessens, Kose, and Terrones (2011c) recession indicator is used for the starts of recessions. Probability estimates are derived from a simple logit model for the recession indicator over the period 1970:Q1 to 2011:Q2, excluding periods during which the economy is already in recession and the quarter just after a recession concludes. The logit model takes as arguments the real equity price change, a dummy for large drops (> 5%) and their interaction. To calculate the average for 2011:Q3, we assume that the last, daily equity price index extends to the end of the quarter. We then calculate the quarterly average level for 2011:Q3 over these daily observations. Latest data are for August 24, 2011.

commodity prices appear to be important, with the peak real oil price growth serving as a significant predictor, while the measure of equity spillovers, the term spread, and real house prices do not.[6] For France, the measure of equity spillovers and the term spread are important predictors. In the model that includes the equity spillover measure, the domestic equity price variables are not statistically significant. For Japan, none of the additional financial variables are important—equity prices alone appear to convey information on the likelihood of a recession.

---

[5]The measure of spillovers from equity price movements is defined as the weighted average of quarter-over-quarter, real equity price growth in the G7 economies, with the weight being nominal GDP in U.S. dollars. The term spread is defined to be the difference between the interest rate on a 10-year government bond and that on a three-month Treasury bill. Real house price changes are calculated from real house price data supplied by the Organization for Economic Cooperation and Development. Real credit growth is calculated from the CPI-deflated credit (line 22d) in the IMF's *International Financial Statistics*. Peak real oil price growth is

calculated from the seasonally adjusted (X-12 ARIMA), U.S. CPI-deflated oil price index in the *World Economic Outlook*.

[6]The peak real oil price growth is defined according to Hamilton (2003). It is the maximum of either zero or the log difference between the current real oil price and the peak real oil price over the previous three years.

Box 1.3 *(continued)*

Despite the statistical significance of some of the additional financial variables, the in-sample performance (as measured by the AUC statistic) is not statistically significantly different from the baseline model (column 3 of Table 1.3.2) for any of the four economies.

What Does This Say about the Future?

This box examines the performance of sharp drops in equity prices in predicting new recessions in France, Japan, the United Kingdom, and the United States. The findings suggest that allowing for nonlinearities in the effects of equity prices can be useful in predicting recessions in the United Kingdom and the United States. Although there is no evidence of such nonlinearities in France and Japan, equity price changes still show up as useful coincident predictors of new recessions. These findings suggest that policymakers should be mindful of sharp drops in equity prices because

they are associated with an increased risk of a new recession.

An application of the baseline model paints a sobering picture about the likelihood of a double-dip recession in France, the United Kingdom, and the United States in light of the recent sharp drop in equity prices. As seen in Figure 1.3.1, the historical or unconditional probabilities of a new recession starting in the third quarter of 2011 are about 3½ percent for France and the United Kingdom and about 4½ percent for the United States. Assuming that the recent behavior of the equity markets in these economies during the third quarter of 2011 continues, the predicted likelihood of a new recession rises about fivefold for France and the United Kingdom (to about 18 percent and 17 percent, respectively) and eightfold for the United States (to about 38 percent). By contrast, the model for Japan indicates that there has been essentially no change in the likelihood of a new recession there.

Box 1.4. Financial Investment, Speculation, and Commodity Prices

Was financial speculation a major force behind the commodity price boom of 2003–08 and behind stubbornly high prices since the end of the Great Recession? This question continues to be widely debated against the backdrop of the financialization of commodity markets—that is, the greater role of noncommercial participants (including speculators and long-term investors) in commodity derivative markets and large increases both in trading volume and in outstanding stocks of derivatives (Figure 1.4.1).

There is an element of déjà vu to this debate, given the long tradition of attributing commodity price increases and booms to speculation.[1] In earlier episodes, however, the focus was on traditional speculation through inventory hoarding. This box reviews the financialization of commodity markets and its impact on commodity prices, building on recent research.[2] It argues that although financialization has influenced commodity price behavior, recent research does not provide strong evidence to suggest that it either destabilizes or distorts spot markets. In this light, policy efforts should focus on making markets work better at a time of structural change in global commodity markets.

The Case for Attributing High Commodity Prices to Financialization

Many arguments have been advanced to support the view that financialization has driven commodity spot prices over the past decade.[3] At the risk of oversimplifying, their essence is that commodity markets have had trouble adjusting to financialization because of one imbalance and two distortions.

- The imbalance is the continued large inflow into derivative markets by long-only investors seeking exposure to commodity prices. These inflows have led to an upward shift in the demand for commodity futures and upward pressure on

futures prices. Because commodity spot and futures prices are connected through price discovery linkages and arbitrage, spot prices could also be affected by this upward pressure.

- This imbalance contributes to the first distortion. After years of rapid growth, open positions and trading volumes in commodity derivative markets now exceed transactions in physical markets, suggesting that investors now dominate commodity price formation.[4]
- The second distortion arises from an investment strategy widely used by institutional investors—indexing—which is seen as having led to "noise trading" (trading by investors on the basis of erroneous beliefs or other reasons unrelated to market fundamentals or meaningful new information).The strategy builds exposure through a synthetic derivative, issued by a financial intermediary, which tracks returns on a fixed-weight portfolio of commodity futures. The noise trading arises through the intermediation process, which implies that demand simultaneously increases for the whole set of underlying futures, irrespective of specific market conditions and prospects for the individual commodities. It could thus affect both futures and spot prices, as above.

Together, the distortions imply that fundamentals may not fully explain recent commodity price increases, reflecting the destabilizing effects of noise traders.[5]

Recent Empirical Evidence Concerning Such Imbalances and Distortions

In the absence of a recognized fair value for commodities, recent research has tried to find evidence that apparent imbalances and distortions have destabilizing effects on prices. There is no general evidence of increased commodity price volatility since the onset of financialization in the early 2000s (Figure 1.4.2).

The main authors of this box are Thomas Helbling, Shaun Roache, and Joong Shik Kang.

[1]Jacks (2007) provides a historical perspective.

[2]This box draws on Helbling, Kang, and Roache (2011), which includes an extensive list of references in addition to those provided here.

[3]Irwin, Sanders, and Merrin (2009) survey the arguments.

[4]The well-known testimony of Masters (2008) at a U.S. congressional hearing exemplifies this view.

[5]The effects of noise trading in finance are examined by Shleifer and Summers (1990) and De Long and others (1990).

Box 1.4 *(continued)*

Figure 1.4.1. Commodity Market Financialization

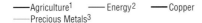

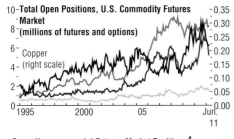

Sources: Bloomberg Financial; U.S. Commodity Futures Trading Commission; and IMF staff calculations.
[1] Includes corn, wheat, soybeans, and rice.
[2] Includes crude oil, gasoline, heating oil, and natural gas.
[3] Includes gold and silver.
[4] Gross noncommercial positions include long and short positions. Total gross positions include long and short commercial, noncommercial, and nonreportable positions. For agriculture, energy, and precious metal groups, average gross noncommercial positions are shown. Options are included in terms of futures equivalents: number of options multiplied by the previous day's risk factor for the option series.

Figure 1.4.2. Commodity Price Volatility, 1990–2011[1]

(Annual averages of estimates of conditional daily returns; annualized, in percent)

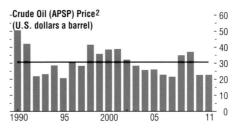

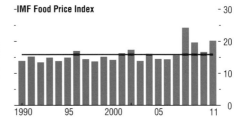

Sources: Bloomberg Financial; and IMF staff calculations.
[1] Conditional standard deviation from a GARCH (1,1) model estimated from daily data. Data are through July for 2011.
[2] APSP (average petroleum spot price) denotes an equally weighted average of three crude spot prices: West Texas Intermediate, Dated Brent, and Dubai Fateh.

If noise trading (and destabilizing speculation more generally) had become more important, commodity price volatility should have increased. On the other hand, if investors provide liquidity and facilitate price discovery, price volatility would be expected to decrease. Although there is no general evidence of increased price volatility across the 51 commodities included in the IMF's commodity price index, there are two points worth noting. First, there are occasional increases in volatility, before and after financialization. But in most cases, times of higher volatility can be attributed to specific factors, such as the Great Recession of 2008–09 or times of low inventories

Box 1.4 *(continued)*

(metal prices during 2005–07). Second, the price volatility of a number of major food commodities has increased over the past few years (see also Roache, 2010). Although fundamentals likely contributed to this increase (for example, low inventories and bad weather), it is difficult to establish statistically significant relationships in this respect.

Evidence based on other approaches to assessing the impact of financialization suggests the following.

- A large number of studies covering different time periods and commodities have not found evidence that changes in futures positions of financial ("noncommercial") investors in U.S. markets had statistically significant effects on subsequent futures price changes.[6] If order flows from commodity financial investment affected price dynamics beyond the usual horizon of a few hours to a few days, such predictive power should be apparent.[7]
- The forecast performance of futures prices—the success in predicting future spot prices—does not depend on whether markets are in a bull or a bear market phase (Roache and Reichsfeld, 2011).[8] If bull markets involved an element of price overshooting driven by the herd behavior of uninformed long-only investors, the forecast performance of futures prices would be expected to deteriorate during such market phases.
- Global macroeconomic factors explain a large and broadly stable share of commodity price fluctuations.[9] In addition, Kilian (2009) found that shocks to global activity explain a large part of the run-up in oil prices during 2003–08. If noise trading had become more important, the

unexplained share in econometric models of commodity price fluctuations would have increased. Because global macroeconomic factors influence all commodities to some extent, comovement in commodity prices over the past few years does not seem unusual.

- Inventories of major commodities did not rise steadily during the boom of 2003–08. If the price boom had reflected simply the unrealistically bullish expectations of uninformed investors, such a situation could be sustained only with increasing inventory hoarding. Otherwise, physical markets would not clear as consumption declined with ever-rising prices.[10] This stylized fact rules out simple bubble explanations of the 2003–08 commodity price boom, but it does not preclude short-lived price overshooting because of noise trading (given price-inelastic demand in the short term). It also does not preclude interaction between financialization and the cyclical behavior of the demand for commodity inventories, including because of changes in the cost of hedging.

Why Is the Empirical Evidence of These Imbalances and Distortions So Inconclusive?

Although recent research does not rule out spot price effects of commodity market financialization, it has not uncovered a smoking gun for obvious price misalignments or destabilizing effects due to financial speculation. This broad conclusion still seems counterintuitive to many. A number of factors can help reconcile evidence and intuition.

In practice, there is greater diversity among investors and investment strategies than the caricature of new market participants as index investors suggests. Hedge funds, which now account for a substantial share of the holdings of commodity derivatives in U.S. markets, often go long or short, depending on

---

[6]See, for example, Büyükşahin and others (2009). Singleton (2011) is a notable exception.

[7]This analysis, based on so-called Granger causality tests, long suffered from data shortcomings. But more recent studies based on disaggregated data that allow identification of trading behavior of specific investor categories (such as swap dealers) have corroborated earlier findings. Studies based on daily data have yielded similar results.

[8]Similarly, Alquist and Gervais (2011) do not find evidence that changes in investor positions have statistically significant effects on the spread between futures and spot prices. They would have such an effect if expectations of future spot prices embedded in futures prices were driven primarily by noise traders.

[9]See, for example, Vansteenkiste (2009); Helbling (2011); and Roache (2011).

[10]This argument was put forward in the oil market context by Krugman (2008), drawing on Jovanovic (2007). Alternatively, as noted by Hamilton (2009), if producers shared investors' expectations, they would lower current production to produce more later when prices are higher. But, again, if unrealistic expectations by investors were the initial driving force, they would ultimately be validated by fundamentals in the physical market.

Box 1.4 *(continued)*

circumstances.[11] They also pursue arbitrage strategies, which may offset distortions from indexing strategies.[12] Many of the large new investors are also well informed and follow supply and demand closely.

Supply constraints play very different roles in commodity futures markets compared with physical commodity markets. In the latter, they are the main reason for very small short-term supply price elasticities (see below), whereas in futures markets, limits to arbitrage by large informed investors and financial intermediaries are the main obstacle to highly elastic supply. Although arbitrage is sometimes limited—for example, because of capital or risk constraints—it usually is a strong force even though it may have occasional spillovers into physical markets.[13] As a result, price pressure from increased futures demand by index investors typically seems small in practice.

Commodity market fundamentals can also explain the large, abrupt price changes that are sometimes attributed to speculation. Because physical demand and supply are highly price-inelastic in the short and sometimes also in the medium term, unexpected small changes in demand or supply fundamentals, including, for example, in global activity, can trigger large rapid price changes. In other words, large initial price increases are often needed to induce the demand reduction and supply increases needed for market clearing (and vice versa). Temporary price spikes can be amplified if inventory or spare capacity buffers are low and consumers fear physical shortages. Such amplification, while not always present, can introduce regime-switching behavior in commodity prices.

Another consideration is that, even if commodity market financialization does influence pricing, it is not clear that the effects on spot prices are large, especially at cyclical horizons. The price changes

---

Figure 1.4.3. Commodity Futures Risk Premiums

(Based on 91-day futures; log difference between future and realized spot price)

— Two-year moving average

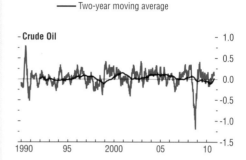

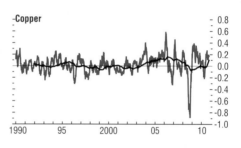

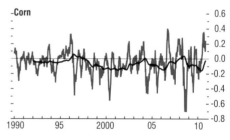

Sources: Bloomberg Financial; and IMF staff calculations.

---

[11]See Büyükşahin and Robe (2010), among others.

[12]Irwin and Sanders (2010) noted that the behavior of index investors is very predictable, thereby facilitating arbitrage.

[13]Spillovers are also possible because liquidity suppliers in futures markets may seek to arbitrage index investors without assuming additional risk by taking offsetting long spot and short futures positions.

---

would be the result of closer integration of commodity derivative markets into global financial markets.[14] A first obvious channel for change is that an expanding, broader set of market participants (which includes participants who also invest in other markets) means that unexpected changes in global factors may now be priced more rapidly and more in sync with other financial markets. Second,

[14]See, for example, Tang and Xiong (2011).

Box 1.4 *(continued)*

commodity prices might respond more to global risk premiums, as investors compare their risks and expected returns on commodities to those of other financial assets in their portfolios.

These changes in pricing can be expected to affect high-frequency price dynamics, but they may not affect commodity price behavior at monthly or quarterly frequencies. The reason is that these same underlying factors influenced commodity prices long before financialization. Factors such as prospects for global activity, for example, have always influenced prices through their effects on commodity supply and demand. Similarly, the risk premiums that compensate commodity futures investors—part of the well-known risk transfer function of futures markets—were present before financialization. Although they have not yet been closely scrutinized, there is no evidence of fundamental changes in commodity futures risk premiums (Figure 1.4.3).

Finally, research remains constrained by a lack of data. In particular, data that differentiate positions by type of trader have only recently become available and cover only U.S. markets for a five-year period. Such differentiation is needed to examine the impact of new investors on indicators of market performance such as futures returns and risk premiums, given the great diversity in trading strategies among traders and investors. Promising research along these lines has only begun.[14]

Does Commodity Market Financialization Call for Policy Action?

In sum, recent research does not provide strong evidence that commodity market financialization has had obvious destabilizing effects. On the other hand, there is evidence that it has added to market liquidity, which generally enhances rather than distorts price discovery. And a number of recent developments that are often perceived to be anomalies can be explained based on fundamentals. For example, after a recession, when evolving expectations about the path of global economic recovery are key factors in asset price fluctuations, high correlation between equity and commodity prices should not be a surprise. The conclusion is that commodity market financialization does not call for urgent policy intervention. Nevertheless, at a time of rapid structural change in global commodity markets—significant and largely permanent shifts in the sources and strength of demand for major commodities amid new supply challenges and changing market structures—it is important to ensure a framework for the proper functioning of globalized markets.

[14]Etula (2009) and Büyükşahin and Robe (2010) are recent examples.

Box 1.5. External Liabilities and Crisis Tipping Points

The extent to which the level of a country's net external liabilities affects the risk of a debt crisis is an important policy question. This is particularly true in economies in which rising fiscal and current account deficits have translated into an unprecedented accumulation of net foreign liabilities (NFLs), as in many advanced economies and some emerging markets in recent years. The aim of this box is to characterize whether there are in fact "thresholds" beyond which the risk of being tipped into an external crisis becomes nontrivial and accelerates with further exposure.

Such thresholds can be gauged by examining NFL levels around crisis episodes. Recent developments, particularly in Europe, suggest that such tipping points in external liabilities are not exclusive to emerging markets (EMs), so the analysis here includes both EMs and advanced economies. Debt crises are defined either as an outright external default or the disbursement of a large multilateral financial support package, including IMF support. The latter is considered large when net disbursements from a program's inception to its end are at least twice as large as the respective economy's IMF quota. The sample contains 62 crisis events in a panel of 74 economies over the period 1970–2010. Catão and Milesi-Ferretti (2011) provide additional information on the data and sample selection.

The top panel of Figure 1.5.1 plots the evolution of cross-country means of the ratio of net foreign assets (NFA) to GDP, within an eight-year window centered on the crisis outbreak, delimited by the upper and lower quartiles around the mean. Crisis events are split into two groups: one comprising crises occurring during 2007–10 and the other comprising crises over 1970–2007. One reason for this split is that the recent crises are ongoing, and so the full set of pre- and postcrisis observations is not yet available; the other reason is to allow comparison between recent and past crises.

The top panel of Figure 1.5.1 shows that the run-up period to external crises is typically characterized by a gradual NFA deterioration, which tends to be steeper during the two-year window before the event

The main authors of this box are Luis Catão and Gian Maria Milesi-Ferretti.

Figure 1.5.1. Net Foreign Asset Indicators in the Run-up to External Crises
(Percent; years on x-axis; t = 0 is the year of the crisis outbreak)

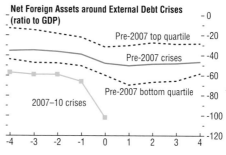

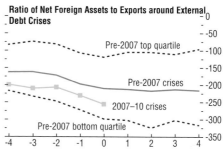

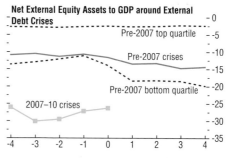

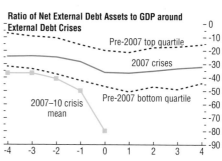

Source: IMF staff calculations.

Box 1.5 *(continued)*

for both pre-2007 and post-2007 crises. Recent crises were triggered at higher NFL levels: although the cross-country mean points to a tipping point threshold between 40 percent and 50 percent, recent crises point to a threshold around 60 percent.

Some models of debt and external crises emphasize that openness tends to raise the cost of default and that the ratio of exports to GDP is a rough gauge of an economy's capacity to generate revenues sufficient to repay its external liabilities. This suggests that exports of goods and services can serve as an alternative scaling variable for NFL. Such a metric is plotted in the second panel of Figure 1.4.1, which shows narrower differences in NFL positions between the pre- and post-2007 crises: both recent and past crises are now suggestive of a tipping point at about 200 percent of exports of goods and services. This is equivalent to an average NFL-to-GDP threshold of 60 percent once the exports-to-GDP ratio averages 30 percent. So the somewhat lower crisis threshold (about 50 percent) that typically characterized pre-2007 episodes appears attributable in part to lower trade openness.

Because debt liabilities—as opposed to equity liabilities—tend to be particularly burdensome in times of economic distress, including because for emerging markets they are often denominated in foreign currency, it seems important to disaggregate NFL into its debt and equity components.[1] Specifically, the net equity position is defined as the sum of a country's net foreign direct investment and portfolio equity positions, whereas the net debt position reflects the sum of the net position in other investment instruments (such as loans and deposits), portfolio debt instruments, and net foreign exchange reserves. The third panel of Figure 1.5.1 shows that crises have not typically been accompanied by a rise in net equity liabilities, but these have been on average much larger in recent crises than in pre-2007 crises. Still, debt liabilities appear to have a much stronger link to crises, and the bottom panel shows in particular how the 2007–10 crises were preceded by a dramatic increase in net external debt.

Although the above discussion has focused on individual NFL variables, to establish causality between

[1]Data that would allow calculation of countries' net foreign currency positions are unfortunately unavailable.

NFLs and debt crises allowance must be made for the role of other factors. In addition, it is important to examine econometrically whether the effect is in fact nonlinear—that is, whether it grows stronger closer to the crisis tipping points. To this end, the first column of Table 1.5.1 reports the results of a probit regression in which the dependent variable equals 1 when there is a crisis and zero otherwise. The estimated coefficient shows that as NFA decreases there is a statistically significant increase in crisis risk. As with probit models, the respective elasticity (marginal effect) varies nonlinearly with the level of NFL and approaches 1 percent on average around crises—that is, a 1 percentage point increase in NFL tends to increase the probability of crisis by roughly the same amount.

The second column in the table disaggregates NFA into the net position in debt instruments and equity instruments. As discussed earlier, the net debt position is far more important than the net equity position in accounting for crisis risk. (The estimated coefficient of 1.4 percent is statistically significant and some four times as large as that for equity.) The third column of Table 1.5.1 controls for a variety of variables that are widely held to affect crisis risk. Of these, the negative coefficient on foreign exchange reserves is notable. It implies that higher reserves reduce the probability of a crisis over and above their effects through an economy's NFA and net debt position. One rationale for this effect is that foreign exchange reserves are a tool under the direct control of a policymaker, unlike, say, private sector deposits overseas. As a result, foreign exchange reserves can provide a more effective offset to external liabilities than can private sector assets.

The effect of other variables is broadly consistent with what economic theory suggests. A higher current account balance relative to GDP lowers the probability of crisis, whereas appreciation (a rise in the index) of the real exchange rate relative to its five-year moving average increases the probability of a crisis. Economies that are historically more volatile (with volatility measured as the standard deviation of the output gap over a 10-year window) tend to be more prone to crisis, whereas richer countries (measured by their constant GDP per capita in thousands of U.S. dollars) are less so. Another important variable included in these regressions—not featured in previous studies in this

Box 1.5 *(continued)*

Table 1.5.1. Probit Estimates of Crisis Probability

	(1)	(2)	(3)	(4)
Net Foreign Assets to GDP	−0.89*** [0.190]			
Net Debt to GDP		−1.41*** [0.28]	−1.29*** [0.38]	−1.16*** [0.40]
Net Equity to GDP		−0.32 [0.278]	0.80** [0.394]	1.10** [0.477]
Foreign Exchange Reserves to GDP			−2.03* [1.12]	−2.45* [1.36]
Current Account to GDP			−5.99*** [1.66]	−5.29*** [1.65]
Real Exchange Rate Gap			2.03*** [0.50]	1.96*** [0.49]
Output Volatility			3.69 [3.00]	4.41 [2.95]
GDP per Capita			−0.08*** [0.01]	−0.09*** [0.01]
U.S. Corporate Spread			0.44*** [0.15]	0.40*** [0.15]
Net Debt to GDP, 2007–09				−0.74* [0.40]
Net Equity to GDP, 2007–09				−0.75 [0.67]
Observations	1,983	1,983	1,979	1,979
Pseudo R^2	0.06	0.08	0.27	0.28

Source: IMF staff calculations.

Note: Robust standards are in brackets under each estimate. *, **, and *** denote significance at the 10 percent, 5 percent, and 1 percent level, respectively.

literature—is the spread between U.S. AAA and AAB corporate bonds, which is a proxy for global financial conditions and attitudes toward risk. The estimates show that the higher such spreads, the higher the crisis probability. Interestingly, an independent role for fiscal variables such as public debt to GDP and general government deficits for GDP was considered but not found to be statistically significant. This suggests that the effect of these fiscal variables on crisis risk occurs via their effects on net foreign debt and/or the remaining explanatory variables.

The final column in Table 1.5.1 distinguishes between pre- and post-2007 crises by interacting the net debt and net equity variables, respectively, with a dummy variable, defined as 1 for 2007–10 and zero otherwise. The purpose is to gauge whether the effect of net foreign debt and net foreign equity positions on crisis risk has changed since 2007. The point estimate of −0.74 for the debt variable indi-

cates that higher debt positions have had a stronger effect during recent crises. A similar result is found for net equity positions, but the effect is not statistically significant at 5 percent.[2]

How well does this empirical model predict "out of sample" the most recent wave of crises? To address that question, the specification of column (3) was run for the period up to 2007, and fitted values were constructed for the probability of a crisis in the subsequent period. Results in Table 1.5.2 show that the model correctly predicts a "high" probability of crisis (10 percent or above) for 6 out of 11 economies that actually suffered a major debt crisis during 2008–10.[3]

[2]A fuller set of regressions and discussion, including a robustness analysis for an alternative crisis definition, is available from Catão and Milesi-Ferretti (2011).

[3]Because the unconditional probability of a crisis in the sample is about 3 percent (62 crisis events in close to 2,000 observations), a 10 percent probability of a crisis is quite elevated.

Box 1.5 *(continued)*

Table 1.5.2. Model's Predictive Power

Country	First Year of Crisis	Predictive Crisis Probability (percent)	Default or Multilateral Support	Growth in First Crisis Year (percent)	Growth in Second Crisis Year (percent)
Bulgaria	2009	13	No	−5.48	0.15
Dominican Republic	2009	10	Yes	3.45	7.75
Ecuador	2008	1	Yes	7.24	0.36
Estonia	2009	12	No	−13.90	3.11
Greece	2009	18	No	−2.34	−4.35
Greece	2010	23	Yes	−4.35	. . .
Hungary	2008	2	Yes	0.80	−6.69
Latvia	2008	16	Yes	−4.24	−17.95
Lithuania	2009	15	No	−14.74	1.32
Pakistan	2008	5	Yes	3.68	1.72
Portugal	2009	15	No	−2.51	1.33
Portugal	2010	20	Yes	1.33	. . .
Romania	2009	17	Yes	−3.72	−0.15
Serbia	2009	22	Yes	−3.50	0.95
Spain	2010	10	No	−3.72	−0.15
Turkey	2008	5	Yes	0.66	−4.83
Ukraine	2008	2	Yes	1.94	−14.46

Source: IMF staff estimates.

Moreover, several countries in the table designated as having "no crisis" according to our strict default/multilateral bailout definition (for example, Bulgaria, Estonia, Lithuania, Spain) did undergo severe output contractions (contemporaneously and/or a year later) and faced macroeconomic distress related to the need for broader external adjustment.

To sum up, once economies' NFL rises above 40 percent of GDP and is composed mostly of debt liabilities, the risk of crisis accelerates with further net liability exposure. There is also evidence that this threshold may have shifted upward—to the 50 to 60 percent range—in recent years, reflecting, at least in part, greater trade openness. The effect of net external debt on the probability of a crisis is strong even after controlling for other fundamentals such as real exchange rate appreciation, the current account balance, and the level of development. We also find evidence that higher reserves mitigate crisis risk, over and above their effects on the net debt position.

Among the G20 countries, the model generally finds crisis probabilities below or close to the unconditional sample crisis probability of 3 percent (62 crises/1,999 observations), with the

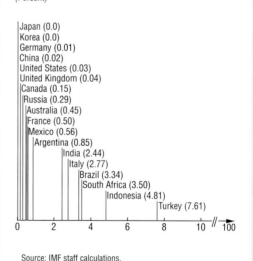

Figure 1.5.2. Model Estimate of Crisis Probabilities

(Percent)

Japan (0.0)
Korea (0.0)
Germany (0.01)
China (0.02)
United States (0.03)
United Kingdom (0.04)
Canada (0.15)
Russia (0.29)
Australia (0.45)
France (0.50)
Mexico (0.56)
Argentina (0.85)
India (2.44)
Italy (2.77)
Brazil (3.34)
South Africa (3.50)
Indonesia (4.81)
Turkey (7.61)

Source: IMF staff calculations.

one exception of Turkey (Figure 1.5.2). Of course, while the overall performance of the model is good, not all point estimates and orderings of country crisis probabilities are to be taken as pre-

Box 1.5 *(continued)*

cise assessments of external risks. Estimates rely on past information and historical crisis patterns and hence do not fully take into account the current and expected future trend behavior of some important variables (including, for example, public debt dynamics in the euro area, Japan, and the United States; the strong public sector balance sheet and external liabilities predominantly in domestic currency in Australia; as well as NFL in some current account deficit countries) and likely place too much weight on the mitigating effect of high per capita income on crisis risk (given the small number of external crises in advanced economies during the sample period).

References

Abiad, Abdul, Enrica Detragiache, and Thierry Tressel, 2008, "A New Database of Financial Reforms," IMF Working Paper 08/266 (Washington: International Monetary Fund).

Acemoglu, Daron, 2003, "Patterns of Skill Premia," *The Review of Economic Studies,* Vol. 70, No. 2, pp. 199–230.

———, and David Autor, 2010, "Skills, Tasks and Technologies: Implications for Employment and Earnings," in *Handbook of Labor Economics,* Vol. 4, ed. by Orley Ashenfelter and David E. Card (Amsterdam: Elsevier).

Alquist, Ron, and Olivier Gervais, 2011, "The Role of Financial Speculation in Driving the Price of Crude Oil," Discussion Paper No. 2011-6 (Ottawa: Bank of Canada).

Amiti, Mary, and Shang-Jin Wei, 2009, "Does Service Offshoring Lead to Job Losses? Evidence from the United States," in *International Trade in Services and Intangibles in the Era of Globalization,* ed. by Marshall Reinsdorf and Matthew J. Slaughter (Chicago: University of Chicago Press), pp. 227–43.

Autor, David, 2010, "*The Polarization of Job Opportunities in the U.S. Labor Market*" (Washington: Center for American Progress and Hamilton Project).

———, David Dorn, and Gordon Hanson, 2011, "The China Syndrome: Local Labor Market Effects of Import Competition in the United States," MIT Working Paper. (Cambridge, Massachusetts: Massachusetts Institute of Technology).

Autor, David, Frank Levy, and Richard Murnane, 2003, "The Skill Content of Recent Technological Change: An Empirical Exploration," *The Quarterly Journal of Economics,* Vol. 118, No. 4, pp. 1279–334.

Berge, Travis, and Òscar Jordà, 2011, "Evaluating the Classification of Economic Activity into Recessions and Expansions," *American Economic Journal: Macroeconomics,* Vol. 3, No. 2, pp. 246–77.

Bernanke, Ben S., Mark Gertler, and Simon Gilchrist, 1999, "The Financial Accelerator in a Quantitative Business Cycle Framework," in *Handbook of Macroeconomics,* Vol. 1, ed. by John. B. Taylor and Michael Woodford (Amsterdam: Elsevier), pp. 1341–93.

Blanchard, Olivier, and Gian Maria Milesi-Ferretti, 2009, "Global Imbalances: In Midstream?" IMF Staff Position Note No. 09/29 (Washington: International Monetary Fund).

———, 2011, "(Why) Should Current Account Balances Be Reduced?" IMF Staff Discussion Note No. 11/03 (Washington: International Monetary Fund).

Blinder, Alan S., 2009, "How Many U.S. Jobs Might Be Offshorable?" *World Economics,* Vol. 10, No. 2, pp. 41–78.

Boldrin, Michele, and Jose A. Scheinkman, 1988, "Learning-by-Doing, International Trade and Growth: A Note," UCLA Working Paper No. 462 (Los Angeles: University of California at Los Angeles Department of Economics).

Bosworth, Barry P., and Jack E. Triplett, 2007, "The Early 21st Century U.S. Productivity Expansion Is *Still* in Services," *International Productivity Monitor,* No. 14 (Spring), pp. 3–19.

Burda, Michael C., and Jennifer Hunt, 2011, "What Explains the German Labor Market Miracle in the Great Recession?" NBER Working Paper No. 17187 (Cambridge, Massachusetts: National Bureau of Economic Research).

Büyükşahin, Bahattin, Michael S. Haigh, Jeffrey H. Harris, James A. Overdahl, and Michel Robe, 2009, "Fundamentals, Trading Activity, and Derivative Pricing," paper presented at the 2009 Meeting of the European Finance Association.

Büyükşahin, Bahattin, and Michel Robe, 2010, "Does It Matter Who Trades? Hedge Fund Activity and Commodity-Equity Linkages" (unpublished; Washington: American University).

Catão, Luis, and Gian Maria Milesi-Ferretti, 2011, "External Liabilities and Crises" (unpublished; Washington: International Monetary Fund).

Claessens, Stijn, M. Ayhan Kose, and Marco E. Terrones, 2011a, "Financial Cycles: What? How? When?" IMF Working Paper 11/76 (Washington: International Monetary Fund).

———, 2011b, "Gyrations in Financial Markets," *Finance & Development,* Vol. 48, No. 1. www.imf.org/external/pubs/ft/fandd/2011/03/Claessens.htm.

———, 2011c, "How Do Business and Financial Cycles Interact?" IMF Working Paper 11/88 (Washington: International Monetary Fund).

Dao, Mai, and Prakash Loungani, 2010, "The Human Cost of Recessions: Assessing It, Reducing It," IMF Staff Position Note No. 10/17 (Washington: International Monetary Fund).

De Long, J. Bradford, Andrei Shleifer, Lawrence Summers, and Robert Waldmann, 1990, "Noise Trader Risk in Financial Markets," *Journal of Political Economy*, Vol. 98, pp. 703–38.

Deutsche Bank, 2011, *Is Outsourcing History?* (Frankfurt).

Diamond, Peter A., 2011, "Unemployment, Vacancies, Wages," *American Economic Review,* Vol. 101, No. 4, pp. 1045–72.

Duarte, Margarida, and Diego Restuccia, 2010, "The Role of the Structural Transformation in Aggregate Productivity," *The Quarterly Journal of Economics,* Vol. 125, No. 1, pp. 129–73.

Ebenstein, Avraham, Ann Harrison, Shannon Phillips, and Margaret McMillan, 2009, "Estimating the Impact of

Trade and Offshoring on American Workers Using the Current Population Surveys," NBER Working Paper No. 15107 (Cambridge, Massachusetts: National Bureau of Economic Research).

Elekdag, Selim, and Prakash Kannan, 2009, "Incorporating Market Information into the Construction of the Fan Chart," IMF Working Paper No. 09/178 (Washington: International Monetary Fund).

Estrada, Angel, and J. David López-Salido, 2004, "Sectoral and Aggregate Technology Growth in Spain," *Spanish Economic Review*, Vol. 6, No. 3, pp. 3–27.

Estrella, Arturo, 2005, "The Yield Curve and Recessions," *The International Economy* (Summer), pp. 8–9, 38.

———, and Frederic S. Mishkin, 1998, "Predicting U.S. Recessions: Financial Variables as Leading Indicators," *Review of Economics and Statistics*, Vol. 80, No.1, pp. 45–61.

Etula, Erkko, 2009, "Broker-Dealer Risk Appetite and Commodity Returns," Staff Report No. 406 (New York: Federal Reserve Bank).

Freeman, Richard B., 2007, "The Great Doubling: The Challenge of the New Global Labor Market," in *Ending Poverty in America: How to Restore the American Dream*, ed. by John Edwards, Marion G. Crain, and Arne L. Kalleberg (New York: New Press), Chapter 4.

Goel, Manisha, 2011, "Offshoring, Technology and Skill Premium," FREIT Working Paper (San Rafael, California: Forum for Research in Empirical International Trade). www.freit.org/WorkingPapers/Papers/Other/FREIT341.pdf.

Goldin, Claudia, and Lawrence F. Katz, 2008, "Transitions: Career and Family Life Cycles of the Educational Elite," *American Economic Review: Papers & Proceedings 2008*, Vol. 98, No. 2, pp. 363–36.

Goos, Maarten, Barbara Fraumeni, Alan Manning, and Anna Salomons, 2009, "Job Polarization in Europe," *American Economic Review*, Vol. 99, No. 2, pp. 58–63.

Hamilton, James, 2003, "What Is an Oil Shock?" *Journal of Econometrics*, Vol. 113, pp. 363–98.

———, 2009, "Causes and Consequences of the Oil Shock of 2007–08," *Brookings Papers on Economic Activity*, Vol. 1, pp. 215–61.

———, 2010, "Calling Recessions in Real Time" (unpublished; San Diego: University of California, San Diego). http://dss.ucsd.edu/~jhamilto/real_time.pdf.

Hanson, Gordon H., Raymond J. Mataloni, and Matthew J. Slaughter, 2005, "Vertical Production Networks in Multinational Firms," *The Review of Economics and Statistics*, Vol. 87, No. 4, pp. 664–78.

Harding, Don, and Adrian Pagan, 2002, "Dissecting the Cycle: A Methodological Investigation," *Journal of Monetary Economics*, Vol. 49, pp. 365–81.

Helbling, Thomas, 2011, "Commodity Prices and the Global Economy—A Retrospective," IMF Working Paper (Washington: International Monetary Fund).

———, Joong Shik Kang, and Shaun K. Roache, 2011, "Financial Investment, Speculation, and Commodity Prices," IMF Staff Discussion Note (Washington: International Monetary Fund).

Hummels, David, 2007, "Transportation Costs and International Trade in the Second Era of Globalization," *Journal of Economic Perspectives*, No. 21, Vol. 3, pp. 131–54.

International Monetary Fund (IMF), 2011, *Japan: Spillover Report for the 2011 Article IV Consultation and Selected Issues*, IMF Country Report No. 11/183 (Washington). www.imf.org/external/pubs/ft/scr/2011/cr11183.pdf.

Irwin, Scott, and Dwight Sanders, 2010, "The Impact of Index and Swap Funds on Commodity Futures Markets," OECD Food, Agriculture and Fisheries Working Paper No. 27 (Paris: Organization for Economic Cooperation and Development).

———, and Robert Merrin, 2009, "Devil or Angel? The Role of Speculation in the Recent Commodity Price Boom (and Bust)," *Journal of Agricultural and Applied Economics*, Vol. 41, No. 2 pp. 377–91.

Jacks, David S., 2007, "Populists versus Theorists: Futures Markets and the Volatility of Prices," *Explorations in Economic History*, Vol. 44, No. 2, pp. 342–62.

Jordà, Òscar, Mortiz Schularick, and Alan M. Taylor, 2010, "Financial Crises, Credit Booms, and External Imbalances: 140 Years of Lessons," NBER Working Paper No. 16567 (Cambridge, Massachusetts: National Bureau of Economic Research).

Jorgenson, Dale W., 1990, "Productivity and Economic Growth," in *Fifty Years of Economic Measurement: The Jubilee of the Conference on Research in Income and Wealth (National Bureau of Economic Research Studies in Income and Wealth)*, ed. by Ernst Berndt and Jack Triplett (Chicago: University of Chicago Press), pp. 19–118.

Jovanovic, Boyan, 2007, "Bubbles in Prices of Exhaustible Resources," NBER Working Paper No. 13320 (Cambridge, Massachusetts: National Bureau of Economic Research).

Kilian, Lutz, 2009, "Not All Oil Price Shocks Are Alike: Disentangling Demand and Supply Shocks in the Crude Oil Market," *American Economic Review*, Vol. 99, No. 3, pp. 1053–69.

Kiyotaki, Nobuhiro, and John Moore, 1997, "Credit Cycles," *Journal of Political Economy*, Vol. 105, No. 2, pp. 211–48.

Kolev, Alexandre, and Catherine Saget, 2010, "Are Middle-Paid Jobs in OECD Countries Disappearing? An Overview," ILO Working Paper No. 96 (Geneva: International Labor Office).

Kose, M. Ayhan, Eswar Prasad, and Marco E. Terrones, 2009, "Does Openness to International Flows Contribute to Productivity Growth?" *Journal of International Money and Finance*, Vol. 28, No. 4, pp. 549–738.

Krugman, Paul R., 1985, "Increasing Returns and the Theory of International Trade," NBER Working Paper No. 1752 (Cambridge, Massachusetts: National Bureau of Economic Research).

———, 1987, "The Narrow Moving Band, the Dutch Disease and the Competitive Consequences of Mrs. Thatcher: Notes on Trade in the Presence of Dynamic Scale Economies," *Journal of Development Economics,* No. 27 (October), pp. 41–55.

———, 2008, "The Oil Nonbubble," *The New York Times* (June 23).

Lane, Philip R., and Gian Maria Milesi-Ferretti, 2011, "External Adjustment and the Global Crisis," IMF Working Paper 11/197 (Washington: International Monetary Fund).

Lawrence, Robert Z., and Matthew J. Slaughter, 1993, "Trade and US Wages: Great Sucking Sound or Small Hiccup?" *Brookings Papers on Economic Activity: Microeconomics Vol. 2*, pp. 161–226.

Lee, Jaewoo, Gian Maria Milesi-Ferretti, Jonathan Ostry, Alessandro Prati, and Luca Antonio Ricci, 2008, *Exchange Rate Assessments: CGER Methodologies,* IMF Occasional Paper No. 261 (Washington: International Monetary Fund).

Loungani, Prakash, and Bharat Trehan, 2002, "Predicting When the Economy Will Turn," FRBSF Economic Letter, No. 2002–07. www.frbsf.org/publications/economics/letter/2002/el2002-07.htm.

Lucas, Robert E., 1988, "On the Mechanics of Economic Development," *Journal of Monetary Economics,* Vol. 22, No. 1, pp. 3–42.

Macroeconomic Advisers, 2011, *Macro Musings,* Vol. 4, No. 10 (July 8).

Manyika, James, Susan Lund, Byron Auguste, Lenny Mendonca, Tim Welsh, and Sreenivas Ramaswamy, 2011, *An Economy that Works: Job Creation and America's Future* (Seoul, San Francisco, London, and Washington: McKinsey Global Institute).

Masters, Michael W., 2008, "Testimony before the Committee on Homeland Security and Government Affairs, U.S. Senate" (May 20). http://hsgac.senate.gov/public/_files/052008Masters.pdf.

Matheson, Troy D., 2011, "New Indicators for Tracking Growth in Real Time, " IMF Working Paper 11/43 (Washington: International Monetary Fund).

McMillan, Margaret S., and Dani Rodrik, 2011, "Globalization, Structural Change, and Productivity Growth," NBER Working Paper No. 17143 (Cambridge, Massachusetts: National Bureau of Economic Research).

Mendoza, Enrique G., and Marco E. Terrones, 2008, "An Anatomy of Credit Booms: Evidence from Macro Aggregates and Micro Data," NBER Working Paper No. 14049 (Cambridge, Massachusetts: National Bureau of Economic Research).

Moneta, Fabio, 2003, "Does the Yield Spread Predict Recessions in the Euro Area?" European Central Bank Working Paper No. 294 (Frankfurt: European Central Bank).

Nyberg, Henri, 2010, "Dynamic Probit Models and Financial Variables in Recession Forecasting," *Journal of Forecasting,* Vol. 29, pp. 215–30.

Ostry, Jonathan D., Atish Ghosh, Karl Habermeier, Luc Laeven, Marcos Chamon, Mahvash S. Qureshi, and Annamaria Kokenyne, 2011, "Managing Capital Inflows: What Tools to Use?" IMF Staff Discussion Note No. 11/06 (Washington: International Monetary Fund).

Peneder, Michael R., 2003, "Industrial Structure and Aggregate Growth," *Structural Change and Economic Dynamics,* Vol. 14, No. 4, pp. 427–48.

Roache, Shaun K., 2010, "What Explains the Rise in Food Price Volatility?" IMF Working Paper 10/129 (Washington: International Monetary Fund).

———, 2011, "China's Impact on World Commodity Markets," IMF Working Paper (Washington: International Monetary Fund).

———, and David Reichsfeld, 2011, "Do Commodity Futures Help Predict Spot Prices?" IMF Working Paper (Washington: International Monetary Fund).

Samuelson, Paul, 1966, "Science and Stocks," *Newsweek* (September 9), pp. 92.

Shleifer, Andrei, and Lawrence H. Summers, 1990, "The Noise Trader Approach to Finance," *Journal of Economic Perspectives,* Vol. 4, pp. 19–33.

Singleton, Kenneth J., 2011, "Investor Flows and the 2008 Boom/Bust in Oil Prices," Working Paper Series, Social Science Research Network. http://ssrn.com/abstract=1793449.

Spence, Michael, 2011, "Globalization and Unemployment: The Downside of Integrating Markets," *Foreign Affairs* (July/August).

Stock, James H., and Mark W. Watson, 2003, "Forecasting Output and Inflation: The Role of Asset Prices," *Journal of Economic Literature,* Vol. 41 (September), pp. 788–829.

Tang, Ke, and Wei Xiong, 2011, "Index Investment and Finalization of Commodities" (unpublished; Princeton, New Jersey: Princeton University).

Thoenig, Mathias, and Thierry Verdier, 2003, "A Theory of Defensive Skill-Biased Innovation and Globalization," *The American Economic Review,* Vol. 93, No. 3, pp. 709–28.

Vansteenkiste, Isabel, 2009, "How Important Are Common Factors in Driving Non-Fuel Commodity Prices? A Dynamic Factor Analysis," ECB Working Paper No. 1072 (Frankfurt: European Central Bank).

Végh, Carlos A., 2011, "Open Macro in Developing Countries" (unpublished; College Park: University of Maryland). http://econweb.umd.edu/~vegh/book/book.htm.

Wind, Serge L., 2011, "Unemployment: Structural versus Cyclical and the Impact of Globalization," Working Paper Series, Social Science Research Network. http://ssrn.com/abstract=1838365.

Wright, Jonathan H., 2006, "The Yield Curve and Predicting Recessions," Finance and Economics Discussion Series No. 2006–07 (Washington: Board of Governors of the Federal Reserve System).

Young, Alwyn, 1991, "Invention and Bounded Learning by Doing," NBER Working Paper No. 3712 (Cambridge, Massachusetts: National Bureau of Economic Research).

Zeira, Joseph, 1999, "Informational Overshooting, Booms, and Crashes," *Journal of Monetary Economics,* Vol. 43, pp. 237–57.

The global economy has slowed, financial volatility and investor risk aversion have sharply increased, and performance has continued to diverge across regions (Figure 2.1). In the United States, weak growth and the lack of a credible medium-term fiscal plan to reduce debt are draining confidence. Europe is gripped with financial strains from the sovereign debt crisis in the euro area periphery. How these advanced economies confront their fiscal challenges will profoundly affect their economic prospects. Emerging and developing economies as a group continue to expand, a few at rates well above their precrisis averages. However, growth will likely moderate as the slowdown in major advanced economies weighs on external demand. Finally, inflation remains elevated (Figure 2.2). Although this is explained mainly by resurgent commodity prices in the first half of the year, in some economies, demand pressures—stoked by accommodative policies, strong credit growth, and capital

inflows—have contributed as well. Policy tightening, to eliminate inflation pressure and strengthen fiscal accounts, is essential to sustain balanced growth in these economies. Where overheating and fiscal risks are not imminent, further tightening can wait until risks to global stability subside.

Almost three years after the crisis, the global economy continues to be challenged with intermittent volatility. Economic performance has become even more bipolar in nature, with anemic growth in economies with large precrisis imbalances and robust activity in many others. As discussed earlier, the unbalanced expansion reflects an inadequate transition from public to private demand in advanced economies and from external-demand-driven growth to domestic-demand-driven growth in key emerging and developing economies. Without progress on

Figure 2.1. Current Global Growth versus Precrisis Average
(Percentage point difference in compound annual rates of change between 2011–12 and 2000–07)

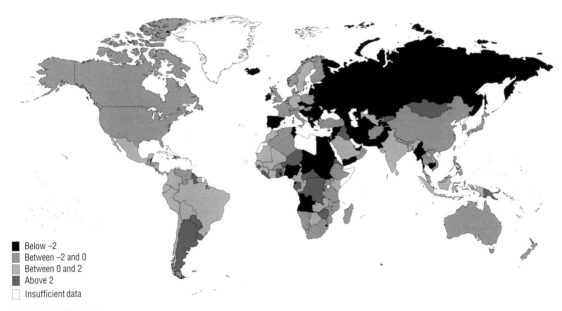

- ■ Below –2
- ▨ Between –2 and 0
- ▧ Between 0 and 2
- ▨ Above 2
- □ Insufficient data

Source: IMF staff estimates.
Note: There are no data for Libya in the projection years due to the uncertain political situation. Projections for 2011 and later exclude South Sudan. Due to data limitations, data for Iraq are the growth differential between the average in 2011–12 and 2005–07; for Afghanistan between the average in 2011–12 and 2003–07; and for Kosovo, Liberia, Malta, Montenegro, Tuvalu, and Zimbabwe between the average in 2011–12 and 2001–07.

Figure 2.2. Output Gaps and Inflation[1]

Economies that experienced the worst financial crises are still struggling with modest growth and persistent economic slack. Others are growing relatively strongly, with many emerging and developing economies hitting up against capacity constraints. Notwithstanding economic cycles, inflation remains elevated, reflecting resurgent commodity prices earlier in the year as well as demand pressures in some economies.

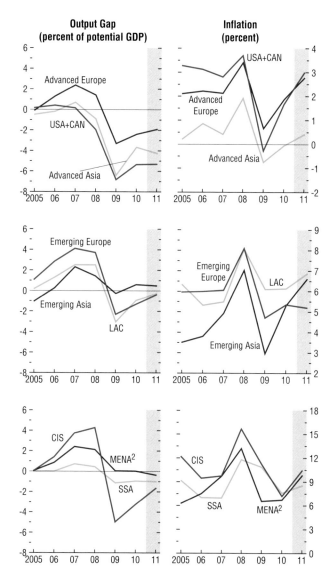

Source: IMF staff estimates.
[1]Advanced Asia: Australia, Japan, and New Zealand; CIS: Commonwealth of Independent States; LAC: Latin America and the Caribbean; MENA: Middle East and North Africa; SSA: sub-Saharan Africa; USA+CAN: United States and Canada. Regional aggregates are computed on the basis of purchasing-power-parity weights.
[2]Excludes Libya for the projection years due to the uncertain political situation. Projections for 2011 and later exclude South Sudan.

these fronts, global economic and financial stability will remain at risk.

This chapter outlines the variable global outlook by region. Growth in the United States has weakened with a sluggish transition from public to private demand. In Europe, spillover risks from the financial and economic woes in the euro area periphery have intensified. Elsewhere, growth is more solid, but the loss in U.S. and euro area momentum will weigh on prospects. The recovery of the Commonwealth of Independent States (CIS) is being helped in part by strong commodity prices thus far. Japan is successfully pulling out of its recession inflicted by the March Great East Japan earthquake and tsunami. In emerging Asia, activity is still robust, despite the supply-chain disruptions caused by the Japanese earthquake. South America also shows strong growth but the Caribbean and Central America less so. In sub-Saharan Africa (SSA), many economies are gaining momentum. In the Middle East and North Africa (MENA), social unrest has hurt growth in some economies, but solid oil prices have boosted output in the region's oil exporters.

The United States: Weakening Again amid Daunting Debt Challenges

The U.S. economy is struggling to gain a strong foothold, with sluggish growth (Figure 2.3) and a protracted job recovery. Downside risks weigh on the outlook given fiscal uncertainty, weakness in the housing market and household finances, renewed financial stress, and subdued consumer and business sentiment. Bold political commitment to put in place a medium-term debt reduction plan is imperative to avoid a sudden collapse of market confidence that could seriously disrupt global stability. At the same time, renewal of some of the temporary stimulus measures—within the medium-term fiscal envelope— and accommodative monetary policy can partly cushion private activity. The prompt implementation of the Dodd-Frank Act will minimize risks to financial stability from a prolonged period of low interest rates. In Canada, downdrafts from its southern neighbor will be offset in part by relatively healthy economic fundamentals and still supportive commodity prices.

U.S. economic activity has lost steam in 2011 (Figure 2.4). Growth slowed from an annual rate of

Figure 2.3. United States and Canada: Current Growth versus Precrisis Average
(Percentage point difference in compound annual rates of change between 2011–12 and 2000–07)

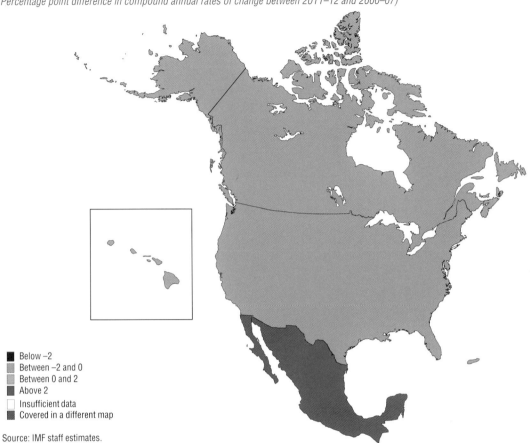

■ Below −2
■ Between −2 and 0
■ Between 0 and 2
■ Above 2
□ Insufficient data
■ Covered in a different map

Source: IMF staff estimates.

2¾ percent in the second half of 2010 to 1 percent in the first half of 2011. Although a slowdown was expected—given the automotive supply disruptions resulting from the Japanese earthquake and tsunami and the drag on domestic demand from steep oil price gains until April—the deceleration in activity was deeper than projected in the June 2011 *WEO Update.* In the meantime, household and business confidence have markedly deteriorated and market volatility significantly increased on concerns about the tepid recovery, the recent downgrade in the U.S. sovereign credit rating, and rising tensions from Europe. Inflation appears to have peaked with the recent retreat in commodity prices. Weak job growth and persistent economic slack are holding back wages.

Economic growth is projected to average 1½ to 1¾ percent in 2011–12 (Table 2.1). The forecast assumes that the negative effects of the Japanese earthquake and energy prices will taper off in the second half of the year and that the temporary payroll tax cuts and increase in unemployment insurance will be renewed in 2012. However, the damage to consumer and business confidence from the ongoing equity market losses, weak house prices (which are assumed to pick up slowly from the second half of 2012), and, last but not least, the pressure to deleverage imply that growth will be modest relative to historical averages for years to come. Unemployment, currently at 9.1 percent, is expected to remain high through 2012. The sustained output gap will keep inflation in check, with headline inflation receding from 3 percent in 2011 to 1¼ percent in 2012, in line with the pullback in commodity prices.

In Canada, growth is forecast to moderate from 3¼ percent in 2010 to 2 percent during 2011–12, reflecting ongoing fiscal withdrawal and downdrafts from the U.S. slowdown. Although jobs

Figure 2.4. United States: Struggling to Gain a Foothold

Growth has weakened, and growing concerns about the recovery and uncertain fiscal stance have undermined confidence and financial stability. Fiscal policy needs to achieve medium-term debt sustainability while supporting the recovery through the renewal of temporary stimulus measures beyond 2011. Current fiscal plans will not help reduce external imbalances over the medium term, given more durable fiscal tightening projected for the largest U.S. trading partners.

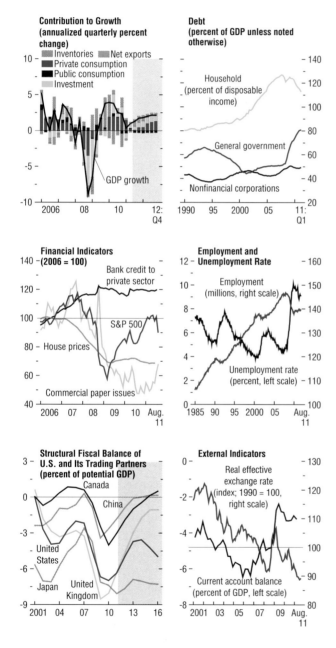

Sources: Haver Analytics; and IMF staff estimates.

have rebounded at a faster pace than in the United States, a slower pace of recovery over the near term is expected to keep unemployment at 7½ to 7¾ percent during 2011–12.

Downside risks to the U.S. outlook have significantly increased. Growth will suffer if the temporary payroll tax cuts and increased unemployment insurance are not continued into 2012. Also, failure to reach political consensus on the design of debt reduction by this fall will result in more front-loaded deficit cuts than currently assumed, with attendant negative effects on growth. More fundamentally, delays in accomplishing an adequate medium-term debt-reduction plan could suddenly induce an increase in the U.S. risk premium, with major global ramifications. As recently observed, shocks to the U.S. bond and stock markets tend to reverberate through major economies, and U.S. interest rate shocks have a strong bearing on emerging market spreads.[1] Other risks include a more protracted house price recovery than assumed under the baseline, sustained losses in equity markets, and upside risks on commodity prices, which would further depress consumer spending. On the upside, growth in the second half of the year could be stronger if financial stability and consumer and business confidence are restored sooner than anticipated. However, risks point down overall. These risks also shape Canada's outlook, through real and financial spillovers.

The first priority for the U.S. authorities is to commit to a credible fiscal policy agenda that places public debt on a sustainable track over the medium term, while supporting the near-term recovery. For this, the fiscal consolidation plan should be based on realistic macroeconomic assumptions and should comprise entitlement reform and revenue-raising measures (for example, gradual removal of loopholes and deductions in the tax system and enhanced indirect taxes).[2] This would allow the near-term fiscal policy stance to be more attuned to the cycle, for example, through temporary stimulus to support labor and housing markets, state and local governments, and infrastructure spending. With a less

[1]See IMF (2011f).

[2]In the past decade, Japan, followed by the United States, had the lowest share of government tax revenue in GDP among G7 economies.

Table 2.1. Selected Advanced Economies: Real GDP, Consumer Prices, Current Account Balance, and Unemployment
(Annual percent change unless noted otherwise)

	Real GDP			Consumer Prices[1]			Current Account Balance[2]			Unemployment[3]		
		Projections			Projections			Projections			Projections	
	2010	2011	2012	2010	2011	2012	2010	2011	2012	2010	2011	2012
Advanced Economies	**3.1**	**1.6**	**1.9**	**1.6**	**2.6**	**1.4**	**−0.2**	**−0.3**	**0.1**	**8.3**	**7.9**	**7.9**
United States	3.0	1.5	1.8	1.6	3.0	1.2	−3.2	−3.1	−2.1	9.6	9.1	9.0
Euro Area[4,5]	1.8	1.6	1.1	1.6	2.5	1.5	−0.4	0.1	0.4	10.1	9.9	9.9
Japan	4.0	−0.5	2.3	−0.7	−0.4	−0.5	3.6	2.5	2.8	5.1	4.9	4.8
United Kingdom[4]	1.4	1.1	1.6	3.3	4.5	2.4	−3.2	−2.7	−2.3	7.9	7.8	7.8
Canada	3.2	2.1	1.9	1.8	2.9	2.1	−3.1	−3.3	−3.8	8.0	7.6	7.7
Other Advanced Economies[6]	5.8	3.6	3.7	2.3	3.3	2.8	5.0	4.7	3.7	4.9	4.4	4.3
Memorandum												
Newly Industrialized Asian Economies	8.4	4.7	4.5	2.3	3.7	3.1	7.0	6.4	6.1	4.1	3.5	3.5

[1]Movements in consumer prices are shown as annual averages. December–December changes can be found in Table A6 in the Statistical Appendix.

[2]Percent of GDP.

[3]Percent. National definitions of unemployment may differ.

[4]Based on Eurostat's harmonized index of consumer prices.

[5]Current account position corrected for reporting discrepancies in intra-area transactions.

[6]Excludes the G7 economies (Canada, France, Germany, Italy, Japan, United Kingdom, United States) and Euro Area countries.

ambitious medium-term fiscal strategy in place, fiscal consolidation would need to be more front-loaded, comprising a withdrawal of 1 to 1½ percent of GDP in 2012, but including at least temporary payroll tax cuts and increased unemployment insurance through 2012 to contain the drag on near-term growth.[3]

For Canada, which is in a sounder fiscal and financial position than the United States, ongoing fiscal tightening can continue, but there is policy room to pause if downside risks to growth keep rising.

The much weaker than previously projected U.S. outlook calls for a more sustained period of accommodative interest rates, as recently announced by the Federal Reserve. The Federal Reserve should also stand ready to implement further unconventional support, as needed, as long as inflation expectations remain subdued.

[3]See Chapter 1 and IMF (2011g) for details. In September, President Obama proposed a package of additional stimulus measures that would extend unemployment benefits, extend and deepen payroll tax deductions for workers, introduce new payroll tax reductions for employers and special tax credits for hiring the long-term employed, and increase spending on infrastructure and on transfers to state and local governments. The equivalent of about 40 percent of this package was already incorporated in IMF staff forecasts. The proposed package would be financed through revenue measures, including a cap on tax deductions and exemptions for high-income earners. If the package were approved and implemented in full, the fiscal deficit reduction projected for 2012 would largely disappear, and it would also imply a sizable fiscal withdrawal in 2013 if policies assumed for that year were to remain unchanged.

Given the U.S. dollar's dominant role as a global monetary anchor, U.S. monetary policy changes have significant global spillovers, which underscore the importance of maintaining financial sector stability both at home and abroad. Indeed, low U.S. interest rates may be driving capital flows elsewhere, which can be challenging to absorb for economies that are operating at or above potential.[4] Moreover, recent volatility in global risk aversion may increase capital flow variability. At the same time, an insufficiently accommodative monetary policy could stall the U.S. recovery and, as a consequence, hurt the global economy. In this regard, the bigger concern from an accommodative U.S. monetary policy stems from whether it could induce excessive risk taking. Thus, a prompt implementation of the U.S. financial sector reforms—combined with similar action to enhance financial stability elsewhere—would contain the buildup of excessive financial leverage in a low interest rate environment. The Dodd-Frank Act should be implemented as planned, with timely allocation of resources to fund the needed enhancements in regulation and supervision. Progress also needs to be made in identifying systemically important institutions—including nonbank institutions—that would be subject to higher regulatory standards and in

[4]See Chapter 4 of the April 2011 *World Economic Outlook.*

addressing cross-border resolution issues involving them. Heightened focus on systemic risks is also critical in an environment in which the financial sector is at the front line of renewed market volatility.

Policies to achieve internal balance, centered on judicious fiscal consolidation, will also help reduce the U.S. current account deficit—which is key to broader global rebalancing—but there are constraints. Unless fiscal consolidation proves durable, the current account deficit will widen again over the medium term, even if not above precrisis levels. Moreover, the effects of fiscal tightening on the U.S. current account balance will be diminished by the fact that key U.S. trading partners, including Canada and the United Kingdom, have already embarked on more ambitious and permanent fiscal adjustments (see Chapter 4).

Europe: Enduring Economic and Financial Turbulence

High public deficits and debt, lower potential output, and mounting market tensions are weighing on growth in much of advanced Europe (Figure 2.5). In addition, there is a transition under way toward greater differentiation between the sovereign debt risks of the euro area members, a shift that is proceeding in fits and starts. Outside the euro area, many central and eastern European (CEE) economies are enjoying a fairly strong rebound from their deep recessions. Even so, the forecast is for a slowdown in activity for much of Europe, with risks to the downside (Figure 2.6; Table 2.2). The responses of policymakers to the euro area's debt crisis will shape the continent's near-term prospects. In particular, a speedy implementation of the July EU summit measures will be key to gaining market credibility. Increased sharing of risk will need to be matched, however, with increased sharing of responsibility for macroeconomic and financial policies.

Europe is grappling with renewed market volatility and sharply elevated risks to financial stability.[5] Spreads have risen to new highs in sovereigns and banks in the euro area periphery (especially Greece).

[5]See also the September 2011 *Global Financial Stability Report.*

Strains have proved contagious, with elevated spreads even in economies that had not been affected thus far (Belgium, Cyprus, Italy, Spain, and to a lesser extent France), and markets further differentiating sovereign risk within the euro area on the basis of individual countries' economic and fiscal challenges and their banks' exposure to sovereigns and banks in the periphery. Global risk aversion, as measured by the Chicago Board Options Exchange Market Volatility Index (VIX), recently surpassed levels reached at the onset of the Greek debt crisis in spring 2010. The European Banking Authority's July 2011 stress tests did little to stabilize bank stocks in the short term. Investors remain concerned, notwithstanding recent modifications to the European Financial Stability Facility (EFSF), the July 2011 package of measures to help Greece address its debt crisis, and extension of the European Central Bank's (ECB's) unconventional measures.

After a strong first quarter, growth in the euro area fell sharply in the second quarter of 2011, in part due to the pressure of high commodity prices on real disposable incomes and to ongoing fiscal tightening, but also because of the effect of the crisis on consumer and business confidence across the region, including in the core economies. Domestic demand growth generally lagged behind GDP growth in most advanced European economies, reflecting mainly sluggish household consumption. In contrast, domestic demand growth in many CEE economies remained strong in the first half of the year, either reflecting demand pressures amid accommodative policy conditions thus far (Turkey) or a strong rebound from the recent crisis (Lithuania). External demand slowed for much of Europe, and will likely continue to moderate in line with the midcycle global slowdown.

Real GDP growth in the euro area is expected to slow from an annual rate of about 2 percent in the first half of 2011 to ¼ percent in the second half, before rising to a bit above 1 percent in 2012. The ongoing financial turbulence will be a drag on activity through lower confidence and financing, even as the negative effects of temporary factors such as high commodity prices and supply disruptions from the Japanese earthquake diminish. However, the projections assume that European policymakers will

Figure 2.5. Europe: Current Growth versus Precrisis Average
*(Percentage point difference in compound annual rates of change
between 2011–12 and 2000–07)*

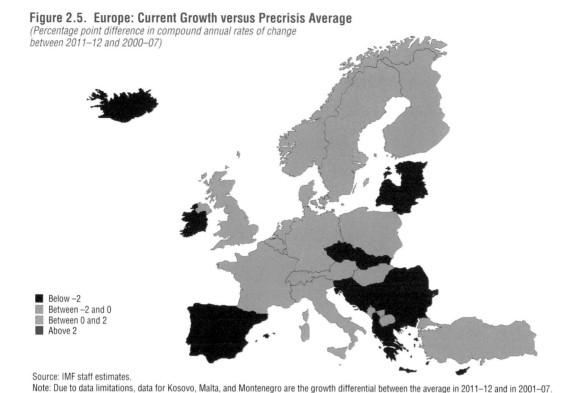

■ Below –2
■ Between –2 and 0
■ Between 0 and 2
■ Above 2

Source: IMF staff estimates.
Note: Due to data limitations, data for Kosovo, Malta, and Montenegro are the growth differential between the average in 2011–12 and in 2001–07.

contain the crisis in the euro area periphery, consistent with their commitments at the July EU summit. In the CEE economies, growth will slow from 4¼ percent in 2011 to about 2¾ percent in 2012, as both domestic and external demand moderate.

Economic performance will vary widely across Europe:

- A few economies are operating close to average precrisis rates, with little or no excess capacity (for example, Denmark, Germany, Netherlands, Poland, Sweden, Switzerland, Turkey), and in some cases unemployment rates are at or below typical precrisis levels. These economies avoided major precrisis imbalances and have benefited from the strong rebound in global manufacturing. Turkey, however, is experiencing a boom, driven to a large extent by overly accommodative policies.

- Some economies are noticeably below precrisis growth rates because of sharp economic adjustments in the context of financial crises. These include the euro area periphery countries that remain engulfed in deep sovereign debt crises (Greece, Ireland,

Portugal) with concurrent recessions or fragile growth. Others are recuperating from recent crises while addressing a number of challenges, including weak banking systems and/or high unemployment (Iceland, Latvia). These economies must steadfastly continue their balance sheet adjustment, which will likely keep output below capacity for some time.

- The rest of the region includes a wide spectrum of economies, most of which are likely to grow at less than precrisis averages. A few are shaken by contagion from the euro area periphery and are experiencing increasing market volatility and rising bond spreads (Italy, Spain), while others are less affected. Among the latter, some are projected to enjoy relatively solid growth (Bulgaria, Serbia); others continue to struggle (Croatia, United Kingdom).

Inflation pressure is expected to stay well contained, assuming receding commodity prices. Inflation in the euro area is expected to fall from 2½ percent in 2011 to about 1½ percent in 2012. In the CEE economies, the decline is expected to be from 5¼ percent in 2011 to 4½ percent in 2012.

Table 2.2. Selected European Economies: Real GDP, Consumer Prices, Current Account Balance, and Unemployment
(Annual percent change unless noted otherwise)

	Real GDP			Consumer Prices[1]			Current Account Balance[2]			Unemployment[3]		
		Projections			Projections			Projections			Projections	
	2010	2011	2012	2010	2011	2012	2010	2011	2012	2010	2011	2012
Europe	**2.2**	**2.0**	**1.5**	**2.4**	**3.1**	**2.1**	**0.3**	**0.1**	**0.4**	...	...	...
Advanced Europe	**1.8**	**1.6**	**1.3**	**1.9**	**2.8**	**1.7**	**0.8**	**0.8**	**1.0**	**9.4**	**9.2**	**9.1**
Euro Area[4,5]	1.8	1.6	1.1	1.6	2.5	1.5	−0.4	0.1	0.4	10.1	9.9	9.9
Germany	3.6	2.7	1.3	1.2	2.2	1.3	5.7	5.0	4.9	7.1	6.0	6.2
France	1.4	1.7	1.4	1.7	2.1	1.4	−1.7	−2.7	−2.5	9.8	9.5	9.2
Italy	1.3	0.6	0.3	1.6	2.6	1.6	−3.3	−3.5	−3.0	8.4	8.2	8.5
Spain	−0.1	0.8	1.1	2.0	2.9	1.5	−4.6	−3.8	−3.1	20.1	20.7	19.7
Netherlands	1.6	1.6	1.3	0.9	2.5	2.0	7.1	7.5	7.7	4.5	4.2	4.2
Belgium	2.1	2.4	1.5	2.3	3.2	2.0	1.0	0.6	0.9	8.4	7.9	8.1
Austria	2.1	3.3	1.6	1.7	3.2	2.2	2.7	2.8	2.7	4.4	4.1	4.1
Greece	−4.4	−5.0	−2.0	4.7	2.9	1.0	−10.5	−8.4	−6.7	12.5	16.5	18.5
Portugal	1.3	−2.2	−1.8	1.4	3.4	2.1	−9.9	−8.6	−6.4	12.0	12.2	13.4
Finland	3.6	3.5	2.2	1.7	3.1	2.0	3.1	2.5	2.5	8.4	7.8	7.6
Ireland	−0.4	0.4	1.5	−1.6	1.1	0.6	0.5	1.8	1.9	13.6	14.3	13.9
Slovak Republic	4.0	3.3	3.3	0.7	3.6	1.8	−3.5	−1.3	−1.1	14.4	13.4	12.3
Slovenia	1.2	1.9	2.0	1.8	1.8	2.1	−0.8	−1.7	−2.1	7.3	8.2	8.0
Luxembourg	3.5	3.6	2.7	2.3	3.6	1.4	7.8	9.8	10.3	6.2	5.8	6.0
Estonia	3.1	6.5	4.0	2.9	5.1	3.5	3.6	2.4	2.3	16.9	13.5	11.5
Cyprus	1.0	0.0	1.0	2.6	4.0	2.4	−7.7	−7.2	−7.6	6.4	7.4	7.2
Malta	3.1	2.4	2.2	2.0	2.6	2.3	−4.8	−3.8	−4.8	6.9	6.3	6.2
United Kingdom[5]	1.4	1.1	1.6	3.3	4.5	2.4	−3.2	−2.7	−2.3	7.9	7.8	7.8
Sweden	5.7	4.4	3.8	1.9	3.0	2.5	6.3	5.8	5.3	8.4	7.4	6.6
Switzerland	2.7	2.1	1.4	0.7	0.7	0.9	15.8	12.5	10.9	3.6	3.4	3.4
Czech Republic	2.3	2.0	1.8	1.5	1.8	2.0	−3.7	−3.3	−3.4	7.3	6.7	6.6
Norway	0.3	1.7	2.5	2.4	1.7	2.2	12.4	14.0	12.8	3.6	3.6	3.5
Denmark	1.7	1.5	1.5	2.3	3.2	2.4	5.1	6.4	6.4	4.2	4.5	4.4
Iceland	−3.5	2.5	2.5	5.4	4.2	4.5	−10.2	1.9	3.2	8.1	7.1	6.0
Emerging Europe[6]	**4.5**	**4.3**	**2.7**	**5.3**	**5.2**	**4.5**	**−4.6**	**−6.2**	**−5.4**	...	...	...
Turkey	8.9	6.6	2.2	8.6	6.0	6.9	−6.6	−10.3	−7.4	11.9	10.5	10.7
Poland	3.8	3.8	3.0	2.6	4.0	2.8	−4.5	−4.8	−5.1	9.6	9.4	9.2
Romania	−1.3	1.5	3.5	6.1	6.4	4.3	−4.3	−4.5	−4.6	7.6	5.0	4.8
Hungary	1.2	1.8	1.7	4.9	3.7	3.0	2.1	2.0	1.5	11.2	11.3	11.0
Bulgaria	0.2	2.5	3.0	3.0	3.8	2.9	−1.0	1.6	0.6	10.3	10.2	9.5
Serbia	1.0	2.0	3.0	6.2	11.3	4.3	−7.2	−7.7	−8.9	19.6	20.5	20.6
Croatia	−1.2	0.8	1.8	1.0	3.2	2.4	−1.1	−1.8	−2.7	12.2	12.7	12.2
Lithuania	1.3	6.0	3.4	1.2	4.2	2.6	1.8	−1.9	−2.7	17.8	15.5	14.0
Latvia	−0.3	4.0	3.0	−1.2	4.2	2.3	3.6	1.0	−0.5	19.0	16.1	14.5

[1]Movements in consumer prices are shown as annual averages. December–December changes can be found in Tables A6 and A7 in the Statistical Appendix.

[2]Percent of GDP.

[3]Percent. National definitions of unemployment may differ.

[4]Current account position corrected for reporting discrepancies in intra-area transactions.

[5]Based on Eurostat's harmonized index of consumer prices.

[6]Also includes Albania, Bosnia and Herzegovina, Kosovo, former Yugoslav Republic of Macedonia, and Montenegro.

In a highly uncertain environment dominated by tension from the euro area sovereign debt crisis, risks to growth are mainly to the downside. An overarching concern is whether investment will pull the recovery along, especially as higher sovereign and banking spreads in various euro area members are eventually transmitted to corporate funding costs. Moreover, should the periphery's debt crisis continue to propagate to core euro area economies, there could be significant disruption to global financial stability.[6] Although CEE economies' direct trade and financial exposure to the euro area periphery is limited, an escalation of sovereign debt and financial sector troubles to the core euro area would undermine

[6]See IMF (2011a and 2011e).

growth in emerging Europe, given tight financial and economic linkages. External risks also point down, with negative spillovers from a slower U.S. growth path or collapse in market confidence in U.S. fiscal policy resulting in a sharp retrenchment of capital inflows, or from rebounding commodity prices.

Fiscal policies are generally appropriate as currently planned in the euro area economies, although additional entitlement reform would help create more policy room. Recent announcements by several countries of measures to further tighten the fiscal stance and/or bring forward some measures are welcome and should be implemented as announced. However, some countries need to identify the measures that will be used to attain their medium-term fiscal targets (France, Spain). In some European countries (for example, Germany, Netherlands, Sweden), stronger fiscal prospects provide room to allow automatic stabilizers to work fully to deal with growth surprises. If activity were to undershoot current expectations, countries that face historically low yields should also consider delaying some of their planned adjustment (Germany, United Kingdom). Where the recovery has already been established (for example, Poland, Turkey), stepped-up fiscal consolidation is needed to strengthen fiscal accounts and build fiscal room in the event of a sustained reversal in capital inflows and also to stave off inflation pressure. Everywhere, fiscal consolidation should be supported by structural measures to bolster growth prospects.

In the euro area, given a weak recovery, declining inflation pressure, and an overall highly uncertain economic and financial environment, the ECB should lower its policy rate if downside risks to growth and inflation persist. Also, the ECB should maintain its unconventional support to contain market volatility at least until the implementation of the July EU summit commitments. Elsewhere, including in most CEE economies, monetary tightening could be more gradual in light of the significant weakening in the economic environment.

Strengthening the financial system remains a major priority. Efforts to raise capital from private sources to fill the gaps identified during the recent stress tests should move ahead immediately and should be more ambitious than supervisors deemed necessary. The objective should be to lift bank equity beyond

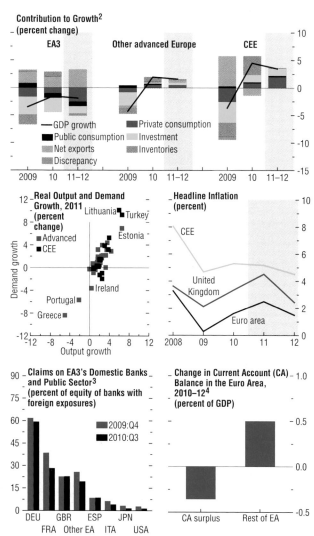

Figure 2.6. Europe: An Uneven Performance and Elevated Risks[1]

European economic performance has been unbalanced, with growth in many economies in the core euro area and emerging Europe stronger than in the euro area periphery. However, contagion pressures from the deteriorating situation in the latter are a rising concern, the containment of which is critical for regional and global stability. Current fiscal consolidation plans should help reduce intra-euro-area external imbalances.

Sources: Bankscope; BIS Consolidated Banking Statistics; and IMF staff estimates.
[1]Euro area (EA): Austria, Belgium, Cyprus, Estonia, Finland, France (FRA), Germany (DEU), Greece, Ireland, Italy (ITA), Luxembourg, Malta, Netherlands, Portugal, Slovak Republic, Slovenia, and Spain (ESP). Central and eastern Europe (CEE): Albania, Bosnia and Herzegovina, Bulgaria, Croatia, Hungary, Kosovo, Latvia, Lithuania, former Yugoslav Republic of Macedonia, Montenegro, Poland, Romania, Serbia, and Turkey. Aggregates for the external economy are sums of individual country data. Aggregates for all others are computed on the basis of purchasing-power-parity weights.
[2]EA3: Greece, Ireland, and Portugal. Other advanced Europe comprises non-EA3 euro area countries and Czech Republic, Denmark, Iceland, Portugal, Sweden, Switzerland, and United Kingdom (GBR). Due to data limitations, Kosovo is excluded from CEE.
[3]Other EA: Austria, Belgium, Ireland, Portugal, and Netherlands. Japan (JPN), United States (USA).
[4]CA surplus: Austria, Belgium, Finland, Germany, Ireland, Luxembourg, and Netherlands.

the Basel III minimums and well ahead of the Basel III timetable, while allowing flexibility in the use of macroprudential tools to address country-specific financial and systemic risks. Given the greater vulnerability of euro area banks to potentially impaired wholesale funding markets, the July EU summit commitments must be promptly adopted by fully implementing the EFSF's expanded mandate through purchasing securities from secondary markets and supporting bank capitalization. Among the crisis economies in the CEE, banking systems are gradually stabilizing, but financial sector vulnerability persists where asset quality and profitability remain low. In these cases, a slower withdrawal of crisis-related support measures is justified as the banking sector heals. Among others, including those that until recently experienced strong credit growth driven by capital flows, financial supervision should remain watchful for a possible worsening in banking system stability affected by a potential drying up of wholesale financing or deterioration in asset quality.

The overriding policy challenge, beyond containing the crisis, is to push forward with European integration. Stronger European governance frameworks are essential to aligning fiscal policies and limiting external imbalances. More integrated and flexible labor, product, and services markets would facilitate adjustment in response to shocks. This is particularly important for the financial sector, which urgently needs a truly integrated financial stability framework, featuring a single rules book, integrated supervision, and burden sharing. This offers the greatest hope for greater resilience against future shocks. Good progress has been made in putting in place a framework for sharing sovereign risk in the euro area.[7] The challenge is to ensure that any support disbursed through it is conditional on arrangements that foster sustained adjustment to better fiscal and external positions. Crucially, increased sharing of risk will need to be accompanied by increased sharing of responsibility for macroeconomic and financial policies. Countries must stand ready to sacrifice some policy autonomy for the common European good.

External rebalancing has progressed in the euro area, owing primarily to low domestic demand growth. However, current account deficits have narrowed much less in the crisis-hit euro area periphery, compared with some CEE economies during their 2008–09 crises (Latvia, Lithuania). In the former, private capital inflows have been replaced largely with ECB and official financing. In the latter, the reversal of capital flows forced a sharp adjustment in the current account deficits, which are now gradually unwinding. Therefore, in the euro area periphery, rebalancing will need to continue for some time with domestic adjustment programs and resulting weak growth fostering wage moderation and restructuring. In this regard, the current nature of euro area fiscal plans—with less adjustment in surplus economies and more in deficit economies, including use of permanent measures rather than simply the end of stimulus—supports further narrowing of intra-euro-area current account imbalances. In many other economies in emerging Europe (for example, Turkey) continued fiscal tightening remains key to reducing the risks of an unexpected sharp adjustment in the current account in the future.

Commonwealth of Independent States: Moderate Growth Performance

The recovery in the CIS region is taking hold even as ongoing household and financial sector deleveraging continues to bridle activity. Growth has thus far been supported by strong commodity prices, but downside risks have risen with the global slowdown. As in other emerging and developing economies, efforts should be focused on rebuilding fiscal room and keeping inflation in check. Major reforms are also needed to enhance the business environment, develop financial systems, and build strong institutions to raise the region's growth potential.

With strong commodity prices thus far, growth in the CIS region has continued to recover, although modestly compared with precrisis rates of expansion (Figure 2.7). Private demand is still subdued in economies with weak financial systems and ongoing deleveraging. Also, remittances and capital flows are well below their levels

[7]See the September 2011 *Fiscal Monitor* for important institutional reforms in other European economies.

during the run-up to the crisis, when many economies in the region were facing growing overheating pressures. The global economic slowdown and increase in investor risk aversion will challenge the region through a more subdued external financing environment.

Growth is expected to average 4½ percent during 2011–12 (Figure 2.8; Table 2.3). However, prospects vary considerably across the region:

- Growth in Russia is projected to reach about 4¼ percent during 2011–12. Prospects for oil prices, although still strong, are weaker than in the June 2011 *WEO Update.* Moreover, capital flows—which fueled credit, private demand, and growth before the crisis—have yet to return because investors remain wary of the political uncertainty in the run-up to presidential elections and the uninviting business climate.

- In most of the other energy-exporting economies, growth is also projected to moderate as energy prices recede somewhat in 2012. However, in Azerbaijan, maintenance-related disruptions in oil production will result in a sharp slowdown

in growth in 2011—despite an acceleration in non-oil GDP growth, reflecting a sizable supplementary budget approved in May—followed by a rebound next year. In general, growth of oil output is expected to decline over the medium term as existing fields approach their capacity. In Kazakhstan, the increase in oil production is expected to be lower than in previous years. Non-oil GDP growth is also expected to ease slightly from the strong rebound in 2010 in Kazakhstan as well as in Turkmenistan.

- Energy-importing economies, on average, are expected to expand at roughly the same pace as in 2010. However, various idiosyncratic factors will lift growth in some of these economies: a recovery from last year's poor harvest in Armenia and a rebound in the Kyrgyz Republic from the contraction caused by previous civil unrest and political turmoil. At the other end of the spectrum, Belarus is expected to experience a sharp slowdown as domestic demand contracts with the currency crisis and a reversal in capital flows.

Figure 2.7. Commonwealth of Independent States: Current Growth versus Precrisis Average
(Percentage point difference in compound annual rates of change between 2011–12 and 2000–07)

- Below −2
- Between −2 and 0
- Between 0 and 2
- Above 2
- Insufficient data
- Covered in a different map

Source: IMF staff estimates.
Note: Includes Georgia and Mongolia.

Figure 2.8. Commonwealth of Independent States: A Gradual Recovery[1]

The recovery in the CIS region is taking hold on the back of strong exports and a pickup in activity in Russia. Strong commodity prices have helped strengthen external and fiscal balances. However, the priority is to discontinue procyclical policies, build policy buffers, and increase the region's resilience to future shocks.

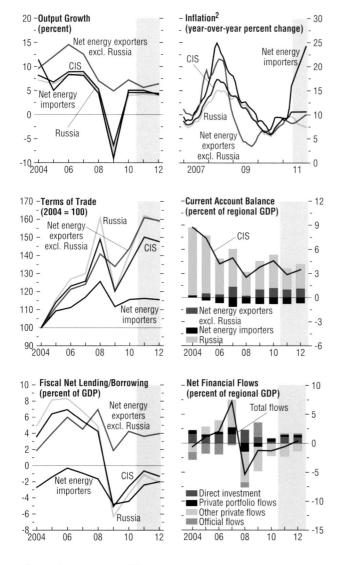

Sources: Haver Analytics; and IMF staff estimates.

[1]Net energy exporters: Azerbaijan, Kazakhstan, Russia, Turkmenistan, and Uzbekistan. Net energy importers: Armenia, Belarus, Georgia, Kyrgyz Republic, Moldova, Mongolia, Tajikistan, and Ukraine. Aggregates for the external economy are sums of individual country data. Aggregates for all others are computed on the basis of purchasing-power-parity weights.

[2]Due to data limitations, Turkmenistan and Uzbekistan are excluded from the group of net energy exporters excluding Russia.

Headline inflation has begun to pick up and is forecast to reach double digits in several of the region's economies. This reflects mostly the sharp uptick in commodity prices in the first half of the year and the high share of food in the consumption baskets, but in some cases, it is also due to current or recent demand pressure (Azerbaijan, Belarus, Kyrgyz Republic, Uzbekistan).

The CIS region is particularly vulnerable to spillovers from the rest of world, as evidenced by the economic collapse during the global financial crisis. Commodity prices largely determine the economic fortunes of most of the large economies in the region, whereas foreign funding has been crucial for growth in investment and consumption. In turn, economic performance in these economies, particularly in Russia, has major repercussions for many others in the region, notably through workers' remittances.[8]

Against this backdrop, net downside risks to the outlook have increased. On the upside, energy exporters stand to benefit from a further rise in oil prices, and higher import costs for energy importers will be somewhat cushioned by higher remittances from Russia. Conversely, a sharper global slowdown would further reduce commodity prices, dampening the prospects for the region. In addition, with elevated global risk aversion, capital flows may stay away from these economies for longer than expected, dragging down regional growth. Finally, the region's sociopolitical environment, with long-standing tensions and unresolved conflicts, remains a source of risk, further exacerbated by the possibility of spillovers from events in the MENA region.

It is time for the CIS region to discontinue procyclical policies and build on structural reforms to increase its resilience to future shocks. A number of countries have started raising interest rates to contain price pressure (for example, Azerbaijan, Kyrgyz Republic, Russia) and strengthening reserve and liquidity requirements. However, with increased uncertainty in the global outlook, the pace of monetary tightening could be slower in economies where overheating pressures are still well contained. In this light, increasing the transparency of monetary

[8]See the April 2011 *Regional Economic Outlook: Middle East and Central Asia.*

Table 2.3. Commonwealth of Independent States: Real GDP, Consumer Prices, Current Account Balance, and Unemployment

(Annual percent change unless noted otherwise)

	Real GDP			Consumer Prices[1]			Current Account Balance[2]			Unemployment[3]		
		Projections			Projections			Projections			Projections	
	2010	2011	2012	2010	2011	2012	2010	2011	2012	2010	2011	2012
Commonwealth of Independent States (CIS)[4]	**4.6**	**4.6**	**4.4**	**7.2**	**10.3**	**8.7**	**3.8**	**4.6**	**2.9**	. . .	. . .	. . .
Russia	4.0	4.3	4.1	6.9	8.9	7.3	4.8	5.5	3.5	7.5	7.3	7.1
Ukraine	4.2	4.7	4.8	9.4	9.3	9.1	−2.1	−3.9	−5.3	8.1	7.8	7.4
Kazakhstan	7.3	6.5	5.6	7.4	8.9	7.9	2.9	5.9	4.6	5.8	5.7	5.6
Belarus	7.6	5.0	1.2	7.7	41.0	35.5	−15.5	−13.4	−9.9	0.7	0.7	0.7
Azerbaijan	5.0	0.2	7.1	5.7	9.3	10.3	27.7	22.7	19.3	6.0	6.0	6.0
Turkmenistan	9.2	9.9	7.2	4.4	6.1	7.2	−11.7	−2.9	−2.6	. . .	. . .	. . .
Mongolia	6.4	11.5	11.8	10.2	10.2	14.3	−14.9	−15.0	−10.5	3.3	3.0	3.0
Low-Income CIS	**6.5**	**6.5**	**6.2**	**8.3**	**12.3**	**9.4**	**−0.7**	**−0.7**	**−0.7**	. . .	. . .	. . .
Uzbekistan	8.5	7.1	7.0	9.4	13.1	11.8	6.7	8.0	7.4	0.2	0.2	0.2
Georgia	6.4	5.5	5.2	7.1	9.6	5.0	−9.6	−10.8	−9.2	16.3	16.2	16.0
Armenia	2.1	4.6	4.3	7.3	8.8	3.3	−13.9	−11.7	−10.7	7.0	7.0	7.0
Tajikistan	6.5	6.0	6.0	6.5	13.6	10.0	2.1	−3.6	−6.7	. . .	. . .	. . .
Kyrgyz Republic	−1.4	7.0	6.0	7.8	19.1	9.4	−7.2	−7.7	−7.6	9.3	8.4	8.3
Moldova	6.9	7.0	4.5	7.4	7.9	7.8	−8.3	−9.9	−10.3	7.4	7.3	7.0
Memorandum												
Net Energy Exporters[5]	4.5	4.5	4.4	6.9	9.0	7.6	5.2	6.0	4.1	. . .	. . .	. . .
Excluding Russia	7.2	5.6	6.4	7.2	9.6	9.2	7.5	9.2	7.8	. . .	. . .	. . .
Net Energy Importers[6]	5.1	5.1	4.2	8.7	16.8	14.7	−6.5	−7.1	−7.0	. . .	. . .	. . .

[1]Movements in consumer prices are shown as annual averages. December–December changes can be found in Table A7 in the Statistical Appendix.

[2]Percent of GDP.

[3]Percent. National definitions of unemployment may differ.

[4]Georgia and Mongolia, which are not members of the Commonwealth of Independent States, are included in this group for reasons of geography and similarities in economic structure.

[5]Net Energy Exporters comprise Azerbaijan, Kazakhstan, Russia, Turkmenistan, and Uzbekistan.

[6]Net Energy Importers comprise Armenia, Belarus, Georgia, Kyrgyz Republic, Moldova, Mongolia, Tajikistan, and Ukraine.

policy—by more clearly communicating inflation developments and objectives—will also help anchor expectations.

Establishing a prudent fiscal stance is crucial for macroeconomic stability and sustained, balanced growth in the region. To ensure its durability, consolidation must be supported by strong fiscal frameworks and fundamental structural reforms, including in pensions, health care, and social protection. For energy exporters, the challenge will be to resist pressure to increase spending while there is still ample fiscal room and to improve the efficiency of public spending. Energy importers should start rebuilding the fiscal buffers depleted during the crisis to prepare for potential future needs and to ensure medium-term fiscal sustainability (for example, Kyrgyz Republic, Tajikistan).

Further action is also needed to restore financial system strength. In Russia, the financial system remains fragile due to the high share of nonperforming assets and inadequate provisioning. Regulatory gaps need to be addressed, including enhancing the central bank's authority to conduct effective supervision. In other economies (for example, Kazakhstan, Kyrgyz Republic, Tajikistan, Ukraine), impaired balance sheets still weigh on credit growth and efficient resource intermediation. Strengthened risk management practices, reforms in the legal and regulatory system to improve collateral recovery and increase bank competition, and an end to directed lending would prevent the recurrence of such impairments.

These immediate economic challenges should not distract from the region's longer-term objectives of reducing external vulnerability and raising potential growth through a more diversified pattern of economic development. Improving the business environment, increasing the role of the private sector, further developing the financial sector, and enhancing institutions are key to such efforts. These measures will also help increase the region's export potential and improve external balances—independent of commodity prices—and help attract more durable sources of external financing and capital flows.

Asia: Securing a More Balanced Expansion

Asia's track record during the crisis and the recovery has been enviable. Growth remains strong, although it is moderating with emerging capacity constraints and weaker external demand. Downdrafts from weaker activity in major advanced economies suggest that a pause in the policy tightening cycle may be warranted for some economies, and underscore the importance of rebalancing growth toward domestic sources. Greater exchange rate flexibility needs to be a key policy tool for much of the region to alleviate price pressures in goods and asset markets and—along with structural reforms— to foster more balanced growth in economies with persistent current account surpluses.

Activity in Asia remained solid but moderated somewhat in the first half of 2011 owing to the temporary disruption in supply chains from the Japanese earthquake and tsunami, especially in the automotive and electronics sectors. Some economies

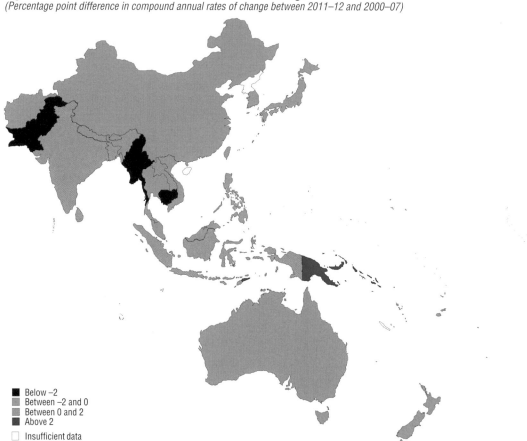

Figure 2.9. Asia: Current Growth versus Precrisis Average
(Percentage point difference in compound annual rates of change between 2011–12 and 2000–07)

- Below –2
- Between –2 and 0
- Between 0 and 2
- Above 2
- Insufficient data

Source: IMF staff estimates.
Note: Due to data limitations, data for the Islamic Republic of Afghanistan are the growth differential between the average in 2011–12 and 2003–07, and for Tuvalu between the average in 2011–12 and 2001–07.

Table 2.4. Selected Asian Economies: Real GDP, Consumer Prices, Current Account Balance, and Unemployment
(Annual percent change unless noted otherwise)

	Real GDP			Consumer Prices[1]			Current Account Balance[2]			Unemployment[3]		
		Projections			Projections			Projections			Projections	
	2010	2011	2012	2010	2011	2012	2010	2011	2012	2010	2011	2012
Asia	**8.2**	**6.2**	**6.6**	**4.1**	**5.3**	**4.0**	**3.3**	**2.9**	**2.9**	. . .	. . .	. . .
Advanced Asia	**5.4**	**1.7**	**3.3**	**0.8**	**1.6**	**1.3**	**3.3**	**2.5**	**2.3**	**4.8**	**4.4**	**4.4**
Japan	4.0	−0.5	2.3	−0.7	−0.4	−0.5	3.6	2.5	2.8	5.1	4.9	4.8
Australia	2.7	1.8	3.3	2.8	3.5	3.3	−2.7	−2.2	−4.7	5.2	5.0	4.8
New Zealand	1.7	2.0	3.8	2.3	4.4	2.7	−4.1	−3.9	−5.6	6.5	6.4	5.6
Newly Industrialized Asian Economies	**8.4**	**4.7**	**4.5**	**2.3**	**3.7**	**3.1**	**7.0**	**6.4**	**6.1**	**4.1**	**3.5**	**3.5**
Korea[4]	6.2	3.9	4.4	3.0	4.5	3.5	2.8	1.5	1.4	3.7	3.3	3.3
Taiwan Province of China	10.9	5.2	5.0	1.0	1.8	1.8	9.3	11.0	11.0	5.2	4.3	4.2
Hong Kong SAR	7.0	6.0	4.3	2.3	5.5	4.5	6.2	5.4	5.5	4.3	3.6	3.7
Singapore	14.5	5.3	4.3	2.8	3.7	2.9	22.2	19.8	18.5	2.2	2.3	2.3
Developing Asia	**9.5**	**8.2**	**8.0**	**5.7**	**7.0**	**5.1**	**3.3**	**3.3**	**3.4**	. . .	. . .	. . .
China	10.3	9.5	9.0	3.3	5.5	3.3	5.2	5.2	5.6	4.1	4.0	4.0
India	10.1	7.8	7.5	12.0	10.6	8.6	−2.6	−2.2	−2.2	. . .	. . .	. . .
ASEAN-5	**6.9**	**5.3**	**5.6**	**4.4**	**6.1**	**5.6**	**3.3**	**2.5**	**1.6**	. . .	. . .	. . .
Indonesia	6.1	6.4	6.3	5.1	5.7	6.5	0.8	0.2	−0.4	7.1	6.8	6.6
Thailand	7.8	3.5	4.8	3.3	4.0	4.1	4.6	4.8	2.5	1.0	1.2	1.2
Malaysia	7.2	5.2	5.1	1.7	3.2	2.5	11.5	11.3	10.8	3.3	3.2	3.1
Philippines	7.6	4.7	4.9	3.8	4.5	4.1	4.2	1.7	1.3	7.2	7.2	7.2
Vietnam	6.8	5.8	6.3	9.2	18.8	12.1	−3.8	−4.7	−3.8	5.0	5.0	5.0
Other Developing Asia[5]	**5.2**	**4.6**	**5.0**	**9.1**	**10.9**	**9.5**	**−0.4**	**−0.1**	**−1.3**	. . .	. . .	. . .
Memorandum												
Emerging Asia[6]	9.3	7.7	7.5	5.2	6.6	4.9	3.9	3.8	3.8	. . .	. . .	. . .

[1]Movements in consumer prices are shown as annual averages. December–December changes can be found in Tables A6 and A7 in the Statistical Appendix.

[2]Percent of GDP.

[3]Percent. National definitions of unemployment may differ.

[4]The 2011 annual GDP growth forecast is as of September 5, 2011. The recent revision of the second quarter GDP data would imply a revision of the 2011 annual GDP growth forecast to 4 percent.

[5]Other Developing Asia comprises Islamic Republic of Afghanistan, Bangladesh, Bhutan, Brunei Darussalam, Cambodia, Republic of Fiji, Kiribati, Lao People's Democratic Republic, Maldives, Myanmar, Nepal, Pakistan, Papua New Guinea, Samoa, Solomon Islands, Sri Lanka, Timor-Leste, Tonga, Tuvalu, and Vanuatu.

[6]Emerging Asia comprises all economies in Developing Asia and the Newly Industrialized Asian Economies.

in emerging Asia also experienced a slowdown in export growth, although domestic demand continued to be supported by relatively accommodative policies, solid growth in credit and asset prices in the first half of the year, firm consumer and business sentiment, and strong labor markets. Also, capital flows were sizable until recently, although more volatile in 2011. Activity in advanced Asia also bounced back fairly strongly after the initial setback caused by the natural disasters. However, the recent volatility in U.S. and euro area financial markets rippled through many Asian equity markets, which if sustained could affect the region's future economic prospects.

Growth is projected to decelerate but remain strong and self-sustained, assuming that the global financial tensions do not escalate (Figures 2.9–2.10; Table 2.4). For emerging Asia, although the slowdown in the United States and euro area will dampen external demand, domestic demand is expected to continue supporting growth. In advanced Asia, activity will be boosted by reconstruction investment.

The nature of expansion and the drivers of growth will differ significantly across the region:

• In China, growth will average 9 to 9½ percent during 2011–12, less than the average of 10½ percent during 2000–07, as ongoing policy tightening and a smaller contribution from net external demand moderate activity. Investment growth has decelerated with the unwinding of the fiscal stimulus, but it remains the principal contributor to growth. Although inflation pressure remains,

Figure 2.10. Asia: A Bright Spot in the World Economy[1]

Growth is expected to remain strong, with weaker external demand offset by still solid domestic demand. That said, there has been limited progress in external rebalancing that would durably enhance the role of domestic demand in growth—currencies have appreciated at a slower pace in economies with current account surpluses than in others, and these surpluses are projected to remain large or to widen further over the medium term.

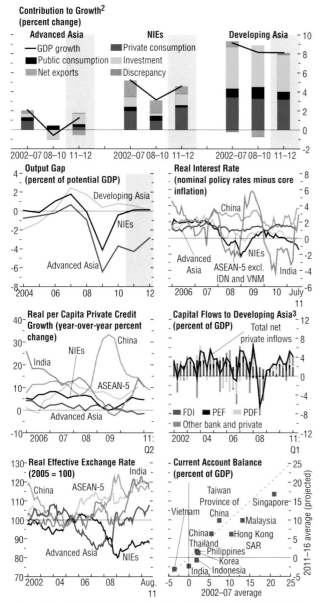

Sources: Haver Analytics; IMF, *International Financial Statistics;* and IMF staff estimates.
[1]Advanced Asia: Australia, Japan, and New Zealand; newly industrialized Asian economies (NIEs): Hong Kong SAR, Korea, Singapore, and Taiwan Province of China; developing Asia: rest of Asia; ASEAN-5: Indonesia (IDN), Malaysia, Philippines, Thailand, and Vietnam (VNM). Aggregates for the external economy are sums of individual country data. Aggregates for all others are computed on the basis of purchasing-power-parity weights.
[2]Excludes Bhutan, Brunei Darussalam, Republic of Fiji, Kiribati, Lao People's Democratic Republic, Maldives, Samoa, Timor-Leste, Tonga, Tuvalu, and Vanuatu due to data limitations.
[3]FDI: foreign direct investment; PEF: portfolio equity flows; PDF: portfolio debt flows.

efforts to withdraw credit stimulus—through administrative limits on credit growth, higher interest rates, and tighter reserve requirements—and to rein in property price inflation through loan-to-value limits in mortgage credit and restrictions on multiple home purchases have been gaining traction: property price inflation and credit growth have softened from recent record levels.

- In India, growth is forecast to average 7½ to 7¾ percent during 2011–12. Activity is expected to be led by private consumption. Investment is expected to remain sluggish, reflecting, in part, recent corporate sector governance issues and a drag from the renewed global uncertainty and less favorable external financing environment. A key challenge for policymakers is to bring down inflation, which is running close to double digits and has become generalized. Despite policy tightening, real interest rates are much lower than precrisis averages, and credit growth is still strong.

- In the newly industrialized Asian economies (NIEs), growth is expected to slow from almost 8½ percent in 2010 to a bit above 4½ percent during 2011–12, as activity moderates to close positive output gaps. The contribution from net exports is forecast to remain positive, in part due to limited appreciation of real effective exchange rates despite sustained current account surpluses.

- Near-term growth in the ASEAN-5[9] is projected to average 5½ percent, pulled by domestic demand—in particular, robust investment—which will offset the slowdown in export momentum. While commodity prices will remain supportive, they will provide less of a boost to growth for the commodity exporters (Indonesia, Malaysia).

- In Japan, the supply constraints from the March earthquake and tsunami have been easing, confidence has picked up, and activity is starting to rebound. The economy is expected to contract by ½ percent this year, but growth is forecast to reach 2¼ percent in 2012, with activity sharply rebounding on reconstruction investment.

- Recent natural disasters slowed growth only temporarily in Australia, and despite recent

[9]The Association of Southeast Asian Nations (ASEAN) includes Indonesia, Malaysia, Philippines, Thailand, and Vietnam.

earthquakes, New Zealand's recovery has gained traction, supported by strong terms of trade and positive trade spillovers from the region. Growth is forecast to pick up from 1¾ percent in 2011 to 3¼ percent in 2012 for Australia and from 2 percent to 3¾ percent for New Zealand.

Headline inflation in Asia is projected to average 5¼ percent in 2011, before receding to 4 percent in 2012, assuming commodity prices remain stable. However, inflation pressures are disparate across the region—higher in economies with sustained strong credit growth, positive output gaps, and/or relatively accommodative policies (for instance, India, Korea, Vietnam). For these economies, the risks around inflation continue to point up. For the rest of the region, risks are more balanced. In Japan, prices are expected to remain broadly flat, with little or no inflation. Property prices have also continued to rise (China, NIEs), although thanks to the use of a wide range of macroprudential measures, the pace has started to ease in many economies.

As elsewhere, the risks around the outlook point down, mainly due to the deterioration in the external environment. Upside risks from continued support from accommodative policies are more than offset by a potentially larger drag from external demand, potential pressure on commodity prices, and persistent financial shocks from the euro area and the United States that threaten to eventually impinge on domestic demand and regional financial stability. Conversely, if upside risks to inflation materialize, the authorities could be forced to sharply tighten policies and provoke a hard landing. Given Asia's rising systemic importance, a sharp deceleration in activity in some key Asian economies could stall regional and global activity through standard trade channels, a fall in demand for commodities and in their prices, or confidence effects.[10] In Japan, in addition to external negative risks from downbeat external demand and potentially sustained appreciation pressure from safe haven flows, longer than anticipated delays in correcting its supply-side disruptions and rebuilding electricity-generating capacity could undermine confidence and further restrain domestic demand. Despite its small share in global trade, the aftereffects of the earthquake were a

reminder of Japan's ability to originate and transmit shocks because of its role as a key supplier of sophisticated inputs in the global supply chain. Moreover, although Japanese government bond yields remain low, a loss of market confidence related to Japan's high public debt could lead to a rise in bond yields in other economies with similar problems.[11]

Against this backdrop, further exchange rate flexibility remains a key policy priority for emerging Asia. However, real effective exchange rates in many current account surplus economies (for example, China, Korea) have moved less than those in deficit economies (for example, India) and are lower than their precrisis levels, and foreign reserves have continued to build up. For these economies, a stronger exchange rate, combined with structural reforms (see below), would raise domestic purchasing power and allow external rebalancing, while also containing inflation pressure. More generally, exchange rate flexibility complemented with macroprudential tools would reduce the perception of a one-way exchange rate bet and slow the pace of debt-creating capital inflows and the buildup of short-term external liabilities (for example, in Korea).

Beyond further exchange rate appreciation in surplus economies, monetary policy requirements vary across Asia. Given the unusual uncertainty in the external environment, a wait-and-see approach may be warranted for some economies. However, inflation pressure needs to be carefully monitored. In some economies, despite nominal policy rate hikes, the real cost of capital is at historical lows because of elevated inflation (India, Korea, Vietnam), and inflation expectations are inching up. In these economies, the monetary tightening phase needs to be sustained for as long as the baseline scenario prevails. Elsewhere, tightening could be paused unless upside risks to inflation grow further. In China, the transparency and effectiveness of monetary policy should be enhanced by relying more on interest rates than quantitative measures of monetary control. In Japan, monetary policy should remain accommodative to eliminate the risk of deflation given a chronic output gap. In particular, the Bank of Japan could purchase more longer-dated public securities and expand its asset purchase program for private assets.

---

[10]See IMF (2011d).

[11]See IMF (2011b).

Although the region has made good progress in enhancing the strength of its financial system, significant growth in credit and property prices over the past few years raises financial stability risks. In many economies, banking systems are strong, thanks to comfortable capital positions and loan loss provisioning levels, high liquidity, and enhancement of domestic stress-testing frameworks (China, Indonesia, Korea). However, the rapid rise in nonbank intermediation means that the perimeter of financial supervision needs be widened to ensure that vulnerabilities are detected early and contained. In addition, financial sector development and liberalization still remain a top priority in some economies. For instance, in China further progress in financial liberalization, including the use of market-determined interest rates, will create incentives for financial institutions to better manage their market risks; remove the artificially low cost of capital, which favors investment over consumption; and, at the same time, strengthen the transmission of monetary policy.[12]

Fiscal policy priorities are also diverse across the region. Under baseline assumptions, increasing the pace of fiscal withdrawal is more urgent in economies with limited fiscal room and high public debt (for example, India, Vietnam). Fiscal savings will also create the room needed for funding infrastructure needs (for example, India, Indonesia, Malaysia). For Japan, although the immediate focus should be on infrastructure reconstruction, a comprehensive plan to put public debt on a sustainable footing over the medium term is essential. In this light, the proposed increase in the consumption tax to 10 percent by the middle of this decade is an important first step. However, a more ambitious deficit reduction plan—based on entitlement reform and a gradual increase of the consumption tax to 15 percent—is needed to put the debt ratio on a downward track. Adoption of a fiscal rule could help safeguard fiscal adjustment gains. In Australia, the planned return to surplus by 2012/13 is welcome, as it will increase fiscal room and take pressure off monetary policy and the exchange rate. The mining boom also provides an opportunity to build fiscal buffers further over the medium term and contribute to national saving. In New Zealand, while

the recent earthquake will adversely affect near-term fiscal balances, planned medium-term consolidation will help build policy room, contain the current account deficit, and put the budget in a stronger position to deal with rising costs related to aging and health care. If downside risks to growth materialize, however, most countries in the region have the fiscal room to slow or reverse the pace of fiscal consolidation.

Asia needs a durable and multifaceted approach to demand rebalancing. The narrowing of surpluses relative to precrisis highs is explained largely by the moderation in the global cycle and slower domestic demand growth in advanced economies. In key surplus economies (China), current account surpluses are set to remain high or widen again as the global expansion continues. In others, surpluses narrow very slowly over the medium term. Moreover, the ongoing fiscal stimulus withdrawal will likely boost external surpluses, with the exception of Thailand, where recently announced public policies target boosting domestic demand and in particular consumption. As a result, strong emphasis needs to be put on other elements of the policy agenda, including further exchange rate appreciation for some economies and structural reforms to enhance the role of domestic demand in growth. This would imply raising the contribution of household consumption for some (for example, China) and investment for others (for example, Indonesia, Korea, Malaysia).[13] Given Asia's large and rising systemic importance, steady and well-paced rebalancing in Asian economies would help foster more balanced growth in its trading partners as well.

Latin America and the Caribbean: Moving toward More Sustainable Growth

Much of the region has thus far benefited from strong terms of trade and easy external financing conditions. In many economies, activity is above potential, credit growth is high, inflation is trending near or above the upper target range, and current account deficits are widening despite supportive commodity prices. The outlook is still strong, although downside risks have come to the

[12]See IMF (2011c).

[13]See the October 2010 *World Economic Outlook*.

fore and commodity prices will provide less momentum in the future. Further macroeconomic tightening is still essential to rebuild room for policy maneuvering and to contain demand pressures. But in most economies, monetary tightening can pause until uncertainty abates.

The Latin American and Caribbean (LAC) region expanded rapidly in the first half of 2011, led by vibrant activity in many of the region's commodity exporters. Buoyant domestic demand underpinned by accommodative macroeconomic policies, strong capital inflows (although more volatile lately), and favorable terms of trade supported the momentum. The pace of expansion, however, has begun to mod-erate, as many economies have fully recovered from the global crisis, and macroeconomic policies are being tightened (Figure 2.11). Nonetheless, growth remains above potential, and a number of economic indicators—including positive output gaps, above-target inflation levels, deteriorating current account balances, rapid credit growth, strong asset prices, and sustained appreciation of real exchange rates—suggest that some economies may be overheating (Figure 2.12). Elsewhere, including in Central America and the Caribbean, economic activity is still subdued, reflecting stronger real linkages with the United States and other advanced economies, and in some cases, high levels of public debt.

Figure 2.11. Latin America and the Caribbean: Current Growth versus Precrisis Average
(Percentage point difference in compound annual rates of change between 2011–12 and 2000–07)

■ Below –2
■ Between –2 and 0
■ Between 0 and 2
■ Above 2
□ Insufficient data

Source: IMF staff estimates.

Figure 2.12. Latin America: Maintaining the Growth Momentum[1]

Growth in the region remains strong, supported by buoyant domestic demand, easy external financial conditions, and still favorable terms of trade. The key now is to maintain healthier growth momentum as macroeconomic policies move to a more neutral position. Boom-bust risks must be contained, including through tighter fiscal and macroprudential policies.

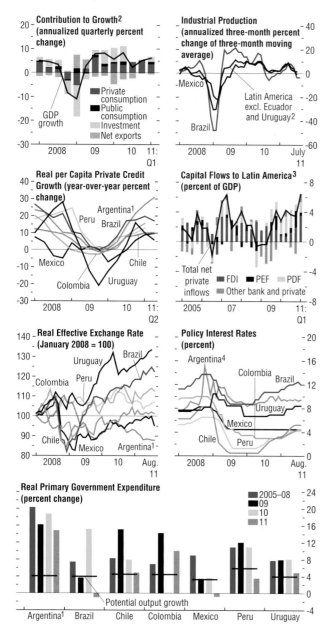

Sources: Bloomberg Financial Markets; Haver Analytics; IMF, *Balance of Payments Statistics;* IMF, *International Financial Statistics;* and IMF staff estimates.

[1]Calculations are based on the official consumer price index and GDP for Argentina.
[2]Argentina, Brazil, Chile, Colombia, Mexico, Peru, and Venezuela. Aggregates are computed on the basis of purchasing-power-parity weights.
[3]FDI: foreign direct investment; PEF: portfolio equity flows; PDF: portfolio debt flows.
[4]The policy rate is proxied by the short-term interbank lending rate.

Financial conditions have become somewhat more unsettled with the synchronized increase in volatility in global equity markets and the rise in global risk aversion, but the impact on the region has been limited thus far.

The LAC region is projected to expand by 4½ percent in 2011, moderating to about 4 percent in 2012, with output remaining above potential (Table 2.5). Economic growth is projected to slow, as domestic demand growth moderates in response to less accommodative macroeconomic policies and external demand weakens as projected. Overall, external conditions are projected to remain supportive, although with somewhat greater risk aversion and a weaker push from commodity prices. Near-term baseline growth prospects vary substantially across the region:

- Growth will be led by many of South America's commodity exporters—particularly Argentina, Chile, Paraguay, Peru, and Uruguay—all of which are expected to grow at levels near or above 6 percent in 2011. Growth in South America is projected to moderate toward potential in 2012, in the range of 3½ to 5½ percent. In the case of Brazil, growth has already begun to moderate, with activity expanding by 4 percent in the first half of 2011, compared with 7½ percent in 2010. Near-term growth is expected to slow below potential and bring inflation toward the target, in part reflecting the less favorable external outlook.

- In Mexico, growth was fairly robust during the first half of the year, despite weak U.S. growth and the effects on the automotive sector of the Japanese earthquake and tsunami. However, negative spillovers from the anemic U.S. recovery will keep growth around 3¾ percent for 2011–12.

- In Central America and the Caribbean, growth will continue to be constrained by a slow recovery in remittances and tourism, and in much of the Caribbean by the challenges posed by high public debt.

Inflation is forecast to recede from 6¾ percent in 2011 to 6 percent in 2012 as activity moderates and commodity prices stabilize, although with considerable intra-regional differences. In the inflation-targeting countries (Brazil, Chile, Colombia, Mexico, Peru, Uruguay), it is projected to stay within the target

Table 2.5. Selected Western Hemisphere Economies: Real GDP, Consumer Prices, Current Account Balance, and Unemployment
(Annual percent change unless noted otherwise)

	Real GDP			Consumer Prices[1]			Current Account Balance[2]			Unemployment[3]		
		Projections			Projections			Projections			Projections	
	2010	2011	2012	2010	2011	2012	2010	2011	2012	2010	2011	2012
North America	**3.3**	**1.8**	**2.0**	**1.9**	**3.0**	**1.5**	**–3.1**	**–3.0**	**–2.2**	. . .	. . .	. . .
United States	3.0	1.5	1.8	1.6	3.0	1.2	–3.2	–3.1	–2.1	9.6	9.1	9.0
Canada	3.2	2.1	1.9	1.8	2.9	2.1	–3.1	–3.3	–3.8	8.0	7.6	7.7
Mexico	5.4	3.8	3.6	4.2	3.4	3.1	–0.5	–1.0	–0.9	5.4	4.5	3.9
South America[4]	**6.6**	**4.9**	**4.1**	**6.7**	**7.9**	**7.0**	**–1.1**	**–1.3**	**–1.7**	. . .	. . .	. . .
Brazil	7.5	3.8	3.6	5.0	6.6	5.2	–2.3	–2.3	–2.5	6.7	6.7	7.5
Argentina[5]	9.2	8.0	4.6	10.5	11.5	11.8	0.8	–0.3	–0.9	7.8	7.3	6.9
Colombia	4.3	4.9	4.5	2.3	3.3	2.9	–3.1	–2.6	–2.5	11.8	11.5	11.0
Venezuela	–1.5	2.8	3.6	28.2	25.8	24.2	4.9	7.3	5.8	8.6	8.1	8.0
Peru	8.8	6.2	5.6	1.5	3.1	2.4	–1.5	–2.7	–2.8	7.9	7.5	7.5
Chile	5.2	6.5	4.7	1.5	3.1	3.1	1.9	0.1	–1.5	8.3	7.2	7.2
Ecuador	3.6	5.8	3.8	3.6	4.4	4.9	–3.3	–3.0	–3.1	7.6	7.3	7.5
Uruguay	8.5	6.0	4.2	6.7	7.7	6.5	–0.4	–1.6	–3.0	6.7	6.6	6.6
Bolivia	4.1	5.0	4.5	2.5	9.8	4.8	4.6	4.2	3.9	. . .	. . .	. . .
Paraguay	15.0	6.4	5.0	4.7	8.7	7.8	–2.8	–3.9	–3.7	6.1	5.8	5.6
Central America[6]	**3.7**	**3.9**	**4.0**	**3.9**	**6.0**	**5.7**	**–5.2**	**–6.3**	**–6.4**	. . .	. . .	. . .
Caribbean[7]	**3.3**	**3.3**	**4.3**	**7.1**	**7.8**	**5.9**	**–3.7**	**–3.6**	**–2.7**	. . .	. . .	. . .
Memorandum												
Latin America and the Caribbean[8]	6.1	4.5	4.0	6.0	6.7	6.0	–1.2	–1.4	–1.7	. . .	. . .	. . .
Eastern Caribbean Currency Union[9]	–1.1	1.1	2.0	2.5	3.5	3.0	–21.4	–23.3	–21.0	. . .	. . .	. . .

[1]Movements in consumer prices are shown as annual averages. December–December changes can be found in Tables A6 and A7 in the Statistical Appendix.

[2]Percent of GDP.

[3]Percent. National definitions of unemployment may differ.

[4]Also includes also Guyana and Suriname.

[5]Figures are based on the official GDP and consumer price index (CPI) data. The authorities have committed to improve the quality of Argentina's official GDP and CPI, so as to bring them into compliance with their obligations under the IMF's Articles of Agreement. Until the quality of data reporting has improved, IMF staff will also use alternative measures of GDP growth and inflation for macroeconomic surveillance, including estimates by: private analysts, which have shown growth that is, on average, significantly lower than official GDP growth from 2008 onward; and provincial statistical offices and private analysts, which have shown inflation considerably higher than the official inflation rate from 2007 onward.

[6]Central America comprises Belize, Costa Rica, El Salvador, Guatemala, Honduras, Nicaragua, and Panama.

[7]The Caribbean comprises Antigua and Barbuda, The Bahamas, Barbados, Dominica, Dominican Republic, Grenada, Haiti, Jamaica, St. Kitts and Nevis, St. Lucia, St. Vincent and the Grenadines, and Trinidad and Tobago.

[8]Latin America and the Caribbean comprises Mexico and economies from the Caribbean, Central America, and South America.

[9]Eastern Caribbean Currency Union comprises Antigua and Barbuda, Dominica, Grenada, St. Kitts and Nevis, St. Lucia, and St. Vincent and the Grenadines as well as Anguilla and Montserrat, which are not IMF members.

range during 2011, but near or above the upper bound (Brazil, Peru, Uruguay). In other economies, such as Argentina and Venezuela, inflation is projected to remain in double digits, reflecting expansionary policies.[14]

The risks to the near-term regional outlook point down. A sharper slowdown in advanced economies, notably the United States, would dampen growth, particularly in economies dependent on trade, tourism

[14]Private sector analysts estimate that consumer price inflation in Argentina since 2007 has been considerably higher than official estimates.

spending, and remittances (the Caribbean, Central America, Mexico). If global risk aversion continues to stay elevated, it could increase external financing risks for the region through a potential reversal in capital inflows and a sharp adjustment of current account imbalances and exchange rates. The strong presence of Spanish banks in the region could raise some risks in a tail scenario, but these risks should be offset by the existing subsidiary model. Last, potential spillovers from China could show up through trade—that is, manufacturing and commodity prices—in that a sharper policy-based slowdown in China could dampen the outlook for the region's commodity exporters. However, some upside risks still remain—domestic demand growth could exceed expectations if global risks unwind relatively quickly, resuming the strong wave of capital flows to the region and if macroeconomic policy tightening does not progress sufficiently.

Against this backdrop, policies need to be designed to address two offsetting forces: containing domestic overheating pressure and the buildup of financial vulnerabilities, while responding appropriately to the souring external environment. In this context, efforts thus far to normalize monetary policies to a neutral stance are welcome, although in countries where inflation pressure has lessened, a temporary pause in monetary tightening could be considered until uncertainty abates. Further monetary tightening is likely warranted in a few economies where overheating risks appear more imminent (Argentina, Paraguay, Venezuela). In Mexico, given firmly anchored inflation expectations along with potentially larger downdrafts from the United States, monetary policy can remain accommodative as long as inflation pressure and expectations remain at bay.

Fiscal consolidation should continue, however (especially where it is needed to maintain debt sustainability), while protecting social and infrastructure spending.[15] Fiscal policy in commodity-exporting countries needs to avoid procyclical spending, and consideration should be given to adopting structural fiscal targets (that control for the cycle and commodity prices) and binding medium-term plans. In Central America, policies should shift toward rebuilding the policy buffers used during the crisis and adopting structural reforms aimed at boosting medium-term growth. Greater resolve is required for reducing debt overhang in the Caribbean while addressing weak competitiveness.

The postcrisis rapid increase in credit and equity prices in many LAC economies, boosted in part by strong capital flows, calls for continued vigilance to limit the attendant risks to financial stability. The region has responded to capital flows and vibrant credit growth with a combination of policies. Countries mostly have allowed their currencies to

be flexible and have intervened in foreign exchange markets to different degrees (Brazil, Peru, and Uruguay more than Colombia and Mexico). Others have also introduced macroprudential measures, including tightening reserve requirements and raising capital requirements for certain consumer credit operations (Brazil, Peru). In some cases, these measures have been complemented with capital controls (Brazil). Overall, the banking system is strong, and prudential indicators have generally improved, including capital adequacy, the ratio of nonperforming loans, and provisioning levels.[16] That said, the sheer growth of credit points to a potential deterioration in credit quality, and banks' exposure to wholesale funding has increased, although from a small base. In this regard, it is important to continue to monitor potential financial sector vulnerabilities and strengthen financial sector supervision, including for nonbank financial intermediaries, to contain the buildup of excessive leverage and avoid boom-bust credit cycles.

The region's external current account deficits are set to widen slightly during 2011–12, despite the strength in commodity prices. Indeed, the reliance on capital flows to finance these deficits has increased the region's susceptibility to a sudden turnaround in investor sentiment. Enhanced macroprudential measures and supervision (discussed above) remain imperative for maintaining financial stability, and capital controls could provide some temporary relief in the face of strong capital inflows, but these measures should not substitute for needed macroeconomic adjustment. The greater use in the region of exchange rate flexibility as a shock absorber is indeed welcome, but more fiscal policy tightening is needed, not just to reduce fiscal vulnerability but also to abate the pressures on the real exchange rate and support external balances.

Sub-Saharan Africa: Sustaining the Expansion

The SSA region is showing solid macroeconomic performance, with many economies already growing at rates close to their precrisis averages (Figure 2.13). The global slowdown has not significantly affected the region thus far, but downside risks have risen. Inflation has

---

[15] See the September 2011 *Fiscal Monitor.*

[16] See the April 2011 *Western Hemisphere Regional Economic Outlook.*

Figure 2.13. Sub-Saharan Africa: Current Growth versus Precrisis Average
(Percentage point difference in compound annual rates of change between 2011–12 and 2000–07)

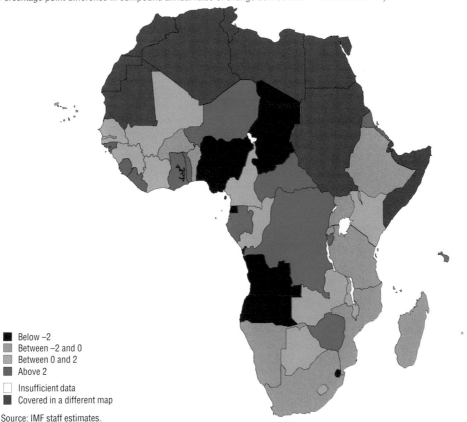

Below –2
Between –2 and 0
Between 0 and 2
Above 2

Insufficient data
Covered in a different map

Source: IMF staff estimates.
Note: Due to data limitations, data for Liberia and Zimbabwe are the growth differentials between the average in 2011–12 and 2001–07.

increased perceptibly in a number of countries in the region. *Under the baseline scenario, with a strong recovery under way, this is an opportune time to return to the region's long-standing priorities of improving policy and institutional frameworks, building resilience to commodity price swings, and developing financial markets, all of which would help lift the region's potential growth and alleviate poverty. In the event of a pronounced global downturn, countries that have policy buffers should aim to support growth.*

Real activity in the region expanded strongly in 2010 and so far in 2011. Robust private and public consumption underpinned this strength, as many countries used available macroeconomic policy room to help speed the recovery from the crisis-induced slowdown. The earlier surge in commodity prices fueled a rise in inflation. Reflecting the relatively accommodative monetary conditions, there are signs of nontrivial inflation pressure in some economies (including Ethiopia, Kenya, and Uganda). However, private capital flows, which had been gaining importance as a source of external financing before the crisis, have resumed only to a handful of emerging and frontier economies (Ghana, Mauritius, South Africa).

The region is poised for continued economic expansion in the near term, provided the recent rise in financial and economic instability in major advanced economies remains contained (Figure 2.14; Table 2.6). Real GDP growth in the SSA region is projected to average 5¼ to 5¾ percent during 2011–12, with considerable differences across the region:

- Largely shielded from the global financial crisis owing to their limited integration into global manufacturing and financial networks, most of the

Figure 2.14. Sub-Saharan Africa: Continued Strength[1]

Recovery is well under way, with growth in many economies back to the highs of the early 2000s. Strong domestic demand, closing output gaps, and rising inflation call for normalization of the fiscal stance. Building policy room is key to containing risks emanating from a further deterioration in the global outlook.

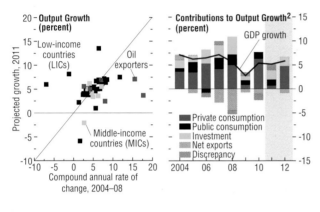

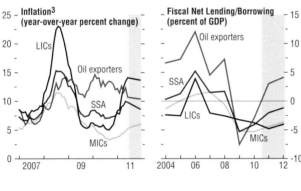

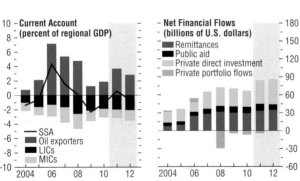

Sources: Haver Analytics; and IMF staff estimates.

[1]Aggregates for the external economy are sums of individual country data. Aggregates for all others are computed on the basis of purchasing-power-parity weights.

[2]Excludes Liberia and Zimbabwe due to data limitations.

[3]Due to data limitations, the following countries are excluded: Chad, Republic of Congo, and Equatorial Guinea from oil exporters; Burundi, Cameroon, Central African Republic, Comoros, Democratic Republic of Congo, Eritrea, Guinea, Guinea-Bissau, Liberia, Malawi, São Tomé and Príncipe, Togo, Zambia, and Zimbabwe from LICs.

region's low-income countries (LICs) have returned to their precrisis growth rates. The severe drought in the horn of Africa has precipitated a major humanitarian crisis in a few economies in the region and caused inflation to increase to sharply higher levels. Average growth for the LIC group is projected at 6 percent in 2011, on the back of strong domestic demand and accelerating exports. In 2012, growth is expected to gather speed to 6½ percent as investment strengthens in Kenya, economic activity normalizes in Côte d'Ivoire after severe disruption following the 2010 elections, and large oil and mining projects come online in Niger and Sierra Leone.

- Oil-exporting economies have a similarly positive outlook, with growth of about 6 percent in 2011, increasing to 7¼ percent in 2012. The acceleration in growth in 2012, despite lower oil prices than projected in the June 2011 *WEO Update*, reflects continued strength in domestic public investment spending, as well as some idiosyncratic factors, such as a strong rebound in oil production in Angola following a disruption in 2011.

- Middle-income countries (MICs), whose greater integration with global markets made them more vulnerable to the crisis, have yet to fully recover from its impact. A surge in unemployment, high household debt, low capacity utilization, the slowdown in advanced economies, and substantial real exchange rate appreciation are making for a hesitant recovery in South Africa, the largest economy in the region. Yet, over the next 12 months, its output gap is projected to close as growth picks up to about 3½ percent during 2011–12. Economic growth will be driven by private consumption and reinvigorated investment, supported by a low interest rate environment and a return to the issuance and renewal of mining licenses.

Across the SSA region, there has been a marked increase in inflation. The earlier surge in commodity prices risks fueling inflation further amid the limited economic slack of the LICs (for example, Uganda), especially in net staple importers (such as Ethiopia) or where there is significant pass-through from international to domestic food prices (for example, Kenya). Among oil exporters, inflation is projected to remain

Table 2.6. Selected Sub-Saharan African Economies: Real GDP, Consumer Prices, Current Account Balance, and Unemployment

(Annual percent change unless noted otherwise)

	Real GDP			Consumer Prices[1]			Current Account Balance[2]			Unemployment[3]		
		Projections			Projections			Projections			Projections	
	2010	2011	2012	2010	2011	2012	2010	2011	2012	2010	2011	2012
Sub-Saharan Africa	**5.4**	**5.2**	**5.8**	**7.5**	**8.4**	**8.3**	**−1.2**	**0.6**	**−0.6**	...	...	...
Oil Exporters	**7.3**	**6.0**	**7.2**	**12.3**	**10.5**	**9.4**	**6.0**	**11.1**	**8.6**	...	...	...
Nigeria	8.7	6.9	6.6	13.7	10.6	9.0	8.4	13.5	11.1	4.5	4.5	4.5
Angola	3.4	3.7	10.8	14.5	15.0	13.9	8.9	12.0	7.3	...	...	...
Equatorial Guinea	−0.8	7.1	4.0	7.5	7.3	7.0	−24.2	−9.6	−10.5	...	...	...
Gabon	5.7	5.6	3.3	1.4	2.3	3.4	10.5	14.8	12.3	...	...	...
Republic of Congo	8.8	5.0	7.0	5.0	5.9	5.2	5.1	7.4	9.7	...	...	...
Chad	13.0	2.5	6.9	−2.1	2.0	5.0	−31.3	−18.9	−13.0	...	...	...
Middle-Income	**3.1**	**3.5**	**3.7**	**4.4**	**6.0**	**5.1**	**−3.1**	**−3.0**	**−3.8**	...	...	...
South Africa	2.8	3.4	3.6	4.3	5.9	5.0	−2.8	−2.8	−3.7	24.9	24.5	23.8
Botswana	7.2	6.2	5.3	6.9	7.8	6.2	−4.9	−4.3	−1.7	...	...	...
Mauritius	4.2	4.2	4.1	2.9	6.7	5.3	−8.2	−9.9	−8.0	7.8	8.2	8.4
Namibia	4.8	3.6	4.2	4.5	5.0	5.6	−1.3	−0.7	−3.3	...	...	...
Swaziland	2.0	−2.1	0.6	4.5	8.3	7.8	−18.5	−11.8	−9.0	...	...	...
Cape Verde	5.4	5.6	6.4	2.1	5.0	4.9	−11.2	−12.9	−11.9	10.3	...	...
Low-Income[4]	**5.8**	**5.9**	**6.5**	**6.2**	**8.8**	**10.3**	**−6.3**	**−7.0**	**−7.0**	...	...	...
Ethiopia	8.0	7.5	5.5	2.8	18.1	31.2	−4.4	−6.3	−8.6	...	...	...
Kenya	5.6	5.3	6.1	4.1	12.1	7.4	−7.0	−8.9	−8.5	...	...	...
Ghana	7.7	13.5	7.3	10.7	8.7	8.7	−7.0	−6.5	−4.9	...	...	...
Tanzania	6.4	6.1	6.1	10.5	7.0	9.4	−8.8	−8.8	−10.2	...	...	...
Cameroon	3.2	3.8	4.5	1.3	2.6	2.5	−2.8	−3.8	−3.3	...	...	...
Uganda	5.2	6.4	5.5	9.4	6.5	16.9	−8.8	−4.0	−8.9	...	...	...
Côte d'Ivoire	2.4	−5.8	8.5	1.4	3.0	2.5	5.0	1.0	−0.4	...	...	...

[1]Movements in consumer prices are shown as annual averages. December–December changes can be found in Table A7 in the Statistical Appendix.

[2]Percent of GDP.

[3]Percent. National definitions of unemployment may differ.

[4]Also includes also Benin, Burkina Faso, Burundi, Central African Republic, Comoros, Democratic Republic of Congo, Eritrea, The Gambia, Ghana, Guinea, Guinea-Bissau, Lesotho, Liberia, Madagascar, Malawi, Mali, Mozambique, Niger, Rwanda, São Tomé and Príncipe, Senegal, Seychelles, Sierra Leone, Togo, Zambia, and Zimbabwe.

high, dominated by price developments in Nigeria and Angola, where rapid monetary expansion before the crisis (Nigeria) and a sharp increase in domestic fuel prices (Angola) fed into price increases. The incomplete recovery from the crisis in the region's MICs will limit the rise in inflation in these economies.

A further deterioration of the global economic environment could have substantial spillovers to the SSA region. A faltering U.S. or European recovery could undermine prospects for exports, remittances, official aid, and private capital flows. Asset market spillovers from continued market turbulence or spikes in risk aversion would likely be limited to the few frontier markets, as they were during the 2008–09 crisis, and the situation thus far is well contained. Finally, a sharp increase in oil prices, while boost-

ing growth in oil exporters, would pose significant challenges for oil importers.[17] Similarly, a continued surge in non-oil commodity prices would entail large social and fiscal costs for the region's net commodity importers. Other risks to the outlook are primarily domestic—for example, political uncertainty and weather shocks also have the potential to dampen growth prospects.

Under the baseline scenario, with growth recovering, especially among the LICs, rebuilding fiscal room and reorienting fiscal policy toward longer-term investment and poverty-reduction objectives should

[17]Simulations suggest that growth in oil-importing SSA economies would decline by 0.5 to 0.7 percent should oil prices increase to an average of $150 in 2011 (see the April 2011 *Sub-Saharan Africa Regional Economic Outlook*).

be a priority. For oil exporters, the challenge will be to manage the current revenue bonanza, especially given the somewhat weakened outlook for prices. Spending targets guided by absorption capacity and anchored within a medium-term fiscal framework will help. Targeted and time-bound policy interventions to mitigate the impact of high commodity prices on vulnerable groups should be considered. With inflation picking up, monetary policy should also revert to a more neutral stance, as is already happening in a number of economies (Kenya, Tanzania, Uganda).

Should global growth slow down significantly, economies with adequate policy buffers should aim to support growth. The likes of South Africa, for example, should allow automatic stabilizers to operate on the fiscal side and ease monetary conditions. LICs should also aim to support activity by using the available room for maneuvering—by protecting spending while allowing revenues to fluctuate with activity to the extent financing allows.

The region's aggregate external balance is expected to improve slightly in 2011, but to deteriorate in 2012. External current account surpluses in commodity exporters will narrow somewhat with the slight retreat in commodity prices. Current account deficits are projected to be sustained among the remaining economies, in line with the continued strength in their domestic demand, although they will remain contained over the medium term.

Middle East and North Africa: Growth Stalling amid Uncertainty

Commodity price movements and social unrest continue to shape the region's experience and prospects. The short-term outlook is still subject to unusually large uncertainties, stemming mainly from the fluid political and security situation in some MENA economies as well as growing uncertainty about external demand. Preserving macroeconomic stability while building social cohesion is a key immediate priority; restoring fiscal health and designing a growth model to achieve inclusive medium-term growth and employment also remain critical.

Elevated oil prices thus far have boosted the fortunes of the region's oil exporters, while creating challenges for oil importers. Among oil exporters, activity has also been spurred by broadly stimulatory macroeconomic policies. At the same time, activity in several MENA economies is being adversely affected by social unrest and ongoing conflict, which are weighing heavily on tourism receipts, capital flows, and investment.

Growth in oil-exporting economies is forecast to reach 5 percent in 2011 and about 4 percent in 2012 (Figures 2.15 and 2.16; Table 2.7)—with growth led by Qatar (driven by expanding natural gas exports), Iraq, and Saudi Arabia. The outlook for oil importers is much more subdued (especially for Egypt, Syrian Arab Republic, and Tunisia), with growth projected at 1½ percent in 2011. Activity in a few economies will be constrained by domestic social unrest and an associated slow recovery in tourism receipts and remittances. Oil importers' growth is projected to reach 2½ percent in 2012, underpinned by a slow recovery in investment.

MENA inflation will remain elevated in 2011 but will fall somewhat in 2012, reflecting receding commodity prices. Inflation is forecast to fall from 10¾ percent in 2011 to 7½ percent in 2012 for oil exporters, while staying under 8 percent during 2011–12 for oil importers.

The outlook is subject to large downside risks. External risks relate to the unfolding weaker outlook in the United States and Europe, which could sharply depress activity and hence commodity prices or further slow external financing flows to the region. However, most risks pertain to continued domestic instability, compounded by intraregional contagion. The political turmoil has seen risk premiums rise and private financing and tourism receipts fall—not only in those economies directly affected by the turmoil but throughout the region. Any intensification of the political crises would exacerbate the economic plight of the region, with the tail risk that MENA oil production could be further affected with ramifications for global energy markets. Global spillovers from the disruption of oil production in Libya until recently were mitigated by increased production from other MENA economies, notably Saudi Arabia.

The region faces serious policy challenges. Beyond securing economic and social stability, shorter-

Figure 2.15. Middle East and North Africa: Current Growth versus Precrisis Average
(Percentage point difference in compound annual rates of change between 2011–12 and 2000–07)

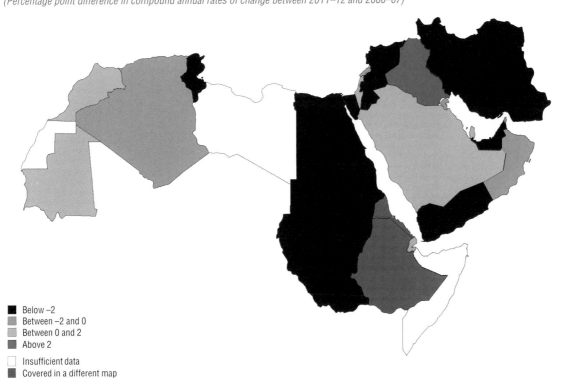

- Below −2
- Between −2 and 0
- Between 0 and 2
- Above 2
- Insufficient data
- Covered in a different map

Source: IMF staff estimates.
Note: There are no data for Libya in the projection years due to the uncertain political situation. Projections for 2011 and later exclude South Sudan.

term challenges focus on the need to place public finances on a sustainable footing. For oil exporters, governments need to seize the opportunity presented by high oil prices to move toward sustainable and more diversified economies. In addition, the social disruption seen in MENA countries highlights the need for an inclusive medium-term growth agenda that establishes strong institutions to stimulate private sector activity, opens up greater access to economic opportunities, and addresses chronically high unemployment, particularly among the young.

Fiscal policy priorities in MENA economies are quite diverse, with the need for fiscal consolidation greatest among oil-importing economies, which face growing concerns over fiscal sustainability. In all MENA countries, a key medium-term objective is the reorientation of fiscal policies to attain

poverty reduction and productive investment goals. However, governments recently have been under pressure to increase current spending—to support both increased social spending and commodity subsidies—and to address pressing social problems. Increased spending on fuel and food subsidies (with the Islamic Republic of Iran an important exception), along with pressures to raise civil service wages and pensions, is placing a strain on public finances (particularly for oil-importing economies), which will not be sustainable over the medium term. Moreover, procyclical fiscal expansion could further crowd out needed private investment, perpetuating the problems with job creation in the private sector.

The region's external balance is expected to remain high during 2011–12, although it will narrow somewhat in 2012 with the slight pullback in commodity

Figure 2.16. Middle East and North Africa: Weakening Activity in an Uncertain Environment[1]

The level of economic activity is slowing, with output moving further away from its potential. High unemployment, growing social unrest, and rising food prices are dampening growth prospects, especially in oil-importing economies. Oil-driven fiscal and current account surpluses (deficits) have widened for oil exporters (importers).

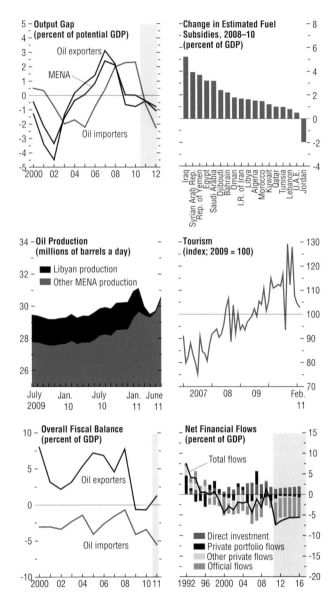

Sources: Haver Analytics; International Energy Agency; International Labor Organization; IMF, Primary Commodity Price System; national sources; and IMF staff estimates.
[1] Oil exporters: Algeria, Bahrain, Islamic Republic of Iran, Iraq, Kuwait, Libya, Oman, Qatar, Saudi Arabia, Sudan, United Arab Emirates (U.A.E.), and Republic of Yemen. Oil importers: Djibouti, Egypt, Jordan, Lebanon, Mauritania, Morocco, Syrian Arab Republic, and Tunisia. Aggregates for the external economy are sums of individual country data. Aggregates for all others are computed on the basis of purchasing-power-parity weights. Excludes Libya for the projection years due to the uncertain political situation. Projections for 2011 and later exclude South Sudan.

prices. Among oil exporters, high commodity prices will maintain strong external positions and enhance reserves. Current account deficits in oil importers will remain wide at about 4¾ percent amid pressing commodity import bills, declining remittances, and shrinking tourism receipts. Current account balances are projected to deteriorate most in the Mashreq (Jordan, Lebanon, Syrian Arab Republic). In terms of external financing in 2011, private capital inflows (chiefly foreign direct investment) will likely be insufficient to offset oil importers' growing current account deficits, resulting in a drawdown of international reserve cushions.

References

International Monetary Fund (IMF), 2011a, *Euro Area Policies: Spillover Report for the 2011 Article IV Consultation and Selected Issues,* IMF Country Report No. 11/185 (Washington: International Monetary Fund). www.imf.org/external/pubs/ft/scr/2011/cr11185.pdf.

———, 2011b, *Japan: Spillover Report for the 2011 Article IV Consultation and Selected Issues,* IMF Country Report No. 11/183 (Washington: International Monetary Fund). www.imf.org/external/pubs/ft/scr/2011/cr11183.pdf.

———, 2011c, *People's Republic of China: 2011 Article IV Consultation,* IMF Country Report No. 11/192 (Washington: International Monetary Fund). www.imf.org/external/pubs/ft/scr/2011/cr11192.pdf.

———, 2011d, *People's Republic of China: Spillover Report for the 2011 Article IV Consultation and Selected Issues,* IMF Country Report No. 11/193 (Washington: International Monetary Fund). www.imf.org/external/pubs/ft/scr/2011/cr11193.pdf.

———, 2011e, *United Kingdom: Spillover Report for the 2011 Article IV Consultation and Selected Issues,* IMF Country Report No. 11/225 (Washington: International Monetary Fund). www.imf.org/external/pubs/ft/scr/2011/cr11225.pdf.

———, 2011f, *The United States Spillover Report—2011 Article IV Consultation,* IMF Country Report No. 11/203 (Washington: International Monetary Fund). www.imf.org/external/pubs/ft/scr/2011/cr11203.pdf.

———, 2011g, *United States: Staff Report for the 2011 Article IV Consultation,* IMF Country Report No. 11/201 (Washington: International Monetary Fund). www.imf.org/external/pubs/ft/scr/2011/cr11201.pdf.

Table 2.7 in the printed version of the September 2011 *World Economic Outlook* contains inaccurate unemployment data for Sudan. The corrected table is below.

Table 2.7. Selected Middle East and North African Economies: Real GDP, Consumer Prices, Current Account Balance, and Unemployment

(Annual percent change unless noted otherwise)

	Real GDP			Consumer Prices[1]			Current Account Balance[2]			Unemployment[3]		
		Projections			Projections			Projections			Projections	
	2010	2011	2012	2010	2011	2012	2010	2011	2012	2010	2011	2012
Middle East and North Africa	**4.4**	**4.0**	**3.6**	**6.8**	**9.9**	**7.6**	**7.7**	**11.2**	**9.0**	...	...	...
Oil Exporters[4]	**4.4**	**4.9**	**3.9**	**6.6**	**10.8**	**7.6**	**10.6**	**15.0**	**12.4**	...	...	...
Islamic Republic of Iran	3.2	2.5	3.4	12.4	22.5	12.5	6.0	7.8	7.1	14.6	15.3	15.6
Saudi Arabia	4.1	6.5	3.6	5.4	5.4	5.3	14.9	20.6	14.2	10.0	...	...
Algeria	3.3	2.9	3.3	3.9	3.9	4.3	7.9	13.7	10.9	10.0	9.8	9.5
United Arab Emirates	3.2	3.3	3.8	0.9	2.5	2.5	7.0	10.3	9.2	...	...	...
Qatar	16.6	18.7	6.0	−2.4	2.3	4.1	25.3	32.6	30.1	...	...	...
Kuwait	3.4	5.7	4.5	4.1	6.2	3.4	27.8	33.5	30.4	2.1	2.1	2.1
Iraq	0.8	9.6	12.6	2.4	5.0	5.0	−3.2	−0.9	−1.2	...	...	...
Sudan[5]	6.5	−0.2	−0.4	13.0	20.0	17.5	−6.7	−7.3	−7.6	13.7	13.4	12.2
Oil Importers[6]	**4.5**	**1.4**	**2.6**	**7.6**	**7.5**	**7.7**	**−3.9**	**−4.8**	**−4.7**	...	...	...
Egypt	5.1	1.2	1.8	11.7	11.1	11.3	−2.0	−1.9	−2.2	9.0	10.4	11.5
Morocco	3.7	4.6	4.6	1.0	1.5	2.7	−4.3	−5.2	−4.0	9.1	9.0	8.9
Syrian Arab Republic	3.2	−2.0	1.5	4.4	6.0	5.0	−3.9	−6.1	−6.1	8.4	...	...
Tunisia	3.1	0.0	3.9	4.4	3.5	4.0	−4.8	−5.7	−5.5	13.0	14.7	14.4
Lebanon	7.5	1.5	3.5	4.5	5.9	5.0	−10.9	−14.7	−13.8	...	...	...
Jordan	2.3	2.5	2.9	5.0	5.4	5.6	−4.9	−6.7	−8.4	12.5	12.5	12.5
Memorandum												
Israel	4.8	4.8	3.6	2.7	3.4	1.6	2.9	0.3	0.7	6.7	5.9	5.8
Maghreb[7]	3.5	2.9	3.9	3.1	3.1	3.8	4.4	4.9	3.7	...	...	...
Mashreq[8]	4.9	0.8	1.9	9.6	9.6	9.5	−3.6	−4.5	−4.7	...	...	...

[1]Movements in consumer prices are shown as annual averages. December–December changes can be found in Tables A6 and A7 in the Statistical Appendix.
[2]Percent of GDP.
[3]Percent. National definitions of unemployment may differ.
[4]Also includes Bahrain, Libya, Oman, and Republic of Yemen. Excludes Libya for the projection years due to the uncertain political situation.
[5]Projections for 2011 and later exclude South Sudan.
[6]Includes also Djibouti and Mauritania.
[7]The Maghreb comprises Algeria, Libya, Mauritania, Morocco, and Tunisia. It excludes Libya for the projection years due to the uncertain political situation.
[8]The Mashreq comprises Egypt, Jordan, Lebanon, and Syrian Arab Republic.

TARGET WHAT YOU CAN HIT: COMMODITY PRICE SWINGS AND MONETARY POLICY

This chapter examines the inflationary effects of commodity price movements and the appropriate monetary policy response. Commodity prices tend to have stronger and longer-lasting effects on inflation in economies with high food shares in the consumption basket and in economies with less firmly anchored inflation expectations. The chapter's analysis suggests that central banks in these economies should set and communicate monetary policy based on developments in underlying inflation rather than headline inflation, where underlying inflation means a measure that reflects the changes in inflation that are likely to be sustained over the medium term. Because shocks to commodity price inflation are typically beyond the control of policymakers, hard to predict, and often not sustained, central banks seeking to establish credibility are generally better off setting and communicating their monetary policy in terms of underlying inflation rather than headline inflation. A headline framework may be preferred, however, if economic agents place a much higher value on the stability of headline inflation than on the stability of output. Finally, in emerging and developing economies with excess demand pressures and inflation already above target, a food price shock is likely to have larger second-round effects and require a more aggressive policy response than in the absence of such preexisting demand pressures.

International food prices have risen to levels last seen during the 2003–08 commodity price surge. After falling during the Great Recession, world food prices surged again in late 2010 and are now around their mid-2008 peak (Figure 3.1). Oil and energy prices also rose in recent months on the back of increased demand and concerns about supply disruptions. The spot price of a barrel of Brent crude oil reached $110 in April 2011, compared with an average of $34 a barrel over the past 30 years.

The significant volatility in commodity prices and the prospect that food and fuel prices may remain elevated for a sustained period are a significant challenge for monetary policymakers. One concern is that the recent rises in food and energy inflation may prove to be persistent, leading to expectations of rising inflation that could spill over into higher wage demands and underlying inflation.[1] Another concern is that attempting to stabilize inflation in the face of such high volatility could have significant economic costs. These concerns are most acute in economies where the share of food in the consumption basket is high and the effects of these shocks are largest.

How then should monetary policy respond to these risks? Standard advice, particularly in advanced economies, is to accommodate the first-round effects of food and energy price swings on the consumer price index (CPI) but not the second-round effects on other CPI components.[2] Because shocks to food and energy inflation are typically transitory, the standard advice amounts to a recommendation that central banks set and communicate their monetary policy in terms of underlying inflation. When commodity shocks are indeed largely transitory, this approach can deliver more stable headline CPI inflation over the medium term and lower output volatility than a framework that requires the central bank to stabilize headline inflation in the short term, which entails countering even the first-round effects of such shocks.

Central banks often operate in line with standard advice, but the details vary across countries. A number of central banks closely watch underly-

The authors of this chapter are John Simon (team leader), Daniel Leigh, Andrea Pescatori, Ali Alichi, Luis Catão, Ondra Kamenik, Heejin Kim, Douglas Laxton, Rafael Portillo, and Felipe Zanna. Shan Chen, Angela Espiritu, and Min Song provided research support.

[1]For example, recent studies suggest that oil prices may trend higher for many years to come on the back of scarce supplies and rising demand from emerging market economies such as India and China. For a further discussion of these risks, see the October 2008 and April 2011 issues of the *World Economic Outlook* and Helbling and Roach (2011).

[2]The rationale for accommodating first-round effects rather than attempting to prevent them is that such an approach reduces output fluctuations.

Figure 3.1. World Commodity Prices, 2000–11

(In real terms, as deflated by U.S. consumer price index)

Food and fuel prices have risen dramatically since 2000. Food and fuel prices peaked in 2008 at levels 80 percent and 250 percent above the levels in 2000. Current prices are 75 percent and 150 percent above 2000 levels, and there are concerns that structural forces will push prices higher over coming years.

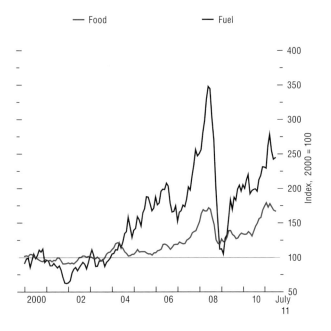

Sources: Haver Analytics; and IMF staff calculations.

ing inflation measures that down-weight or exclude certain volatile components, notably food and energy prices.[3] Some central banks set their price stability goals in terms of a core inflation measure.[4] Most others target headline inflation but define their targets over the medium term and thus down-weight the influence of transitory shocks, such as those to food and energy prices.[5] In this respect, the effect is similar to using an underlying inflation measure as the target.

Overall, a variety of measures of inflation are used either as targets or as guides. In what follows, underlying inflation is measured simply by headline

[3]For example, the Bank of Japan, the U.S. Federal Reserve, and the Reserve Bank of Australia all pay close attention to measures of underlying inflation that are not directly affected by movements in commodity prices. In the case of the Bank of Japan, a closely watched indicator of price stability is the year-over-year rate of change in the CPI, excluding fresh food. In the case of the Federal Reserve, food and energy components are excluded from the core personal consumption expenditure inflation measure used to describe the outlook for inflation in monetary policy reports. The Reserve Bank of Australia monitors a wide range of measures of underlying inflation, including trimmed mean and weighted median measures that down-weight volatile prices.

[4]For example, the Bank of Thailand currently defines its target in terms of a core inflation measure that excludes fresh food and energy prices. In the past, especially during periods of transition, some central banks, including the Reserve Bank of Australia, the Czech National Bank, and the Reserve Bank of New Zealand (RBNZ), defined their targets in terms of a measure of core inflation. More recently, having achieved low inflation, some of these central banks have moved to a headline measure in their formal targets. This evolution is discussed in a speech by the deputy governor of the RBNZ: "As inflation expectations have subsided, it has been possible to assume a degree more flexibility in the regime, and the current PTA [Policy Targets Agreement] reflects that. Rather than detailed calculations of the impact of specific shocks, as embodied in the old underlying inflation measure, the PTA now explicitly acknowledges that outcomes will occasionally fall outside the target range for a variety of reasons, even when the Bank is 'constantly and diligently' striving to deliver price stability" (Sherwin, 1999).

[5]The experience of the RBNZ, with its "hard-edged" targets, shows why such "flexible" medium-term targeting is the general practice. As stated by the deputy governor of the RBNZ: "While clearly a useful device for communicating the strength of the Bank's resolve to a wider public audience, the portrayal of the inflation target as hard-edged also carried risks given the lags and uncertainties in monetary policy decision making. A 'strict' approach to inflation targeting encouraged a search for precision in calculating 'core' or underlying inflation measures for accountability purposes and may have encouraged a shortening of policy horizons as the direct price effects of the exchange rate became more important to the achievement of the target outcomes" (Sherwin, 1999).

inflation, excluding food and energy inflation—also commonly referred to as "core inflation." The reason is that, in practice, food and energy prices are less indicative of medium-term inflation pressures than are the price changes of other goods and services. That said, using this simple "exclusion" measure as an indicator for underlying inflation raises some problems. Because it places zero weight on food and fuel prices, core inflation can be a poor measure of the cost of living. In addition, some argue that food and energy price inflation does contain useful information about underlying inflation and, therefore, hints at the likely evolution of inflation pressure over the medium term. These issues are discussed below.

Given the variety of approaches to the implementation of monetary policy, the range of inflation measures now in use, and the size of recent commodity price shocks, it is timely to reconsider the policy advice. Thus, this chapter addresses the following key questions:

- What are the effects of international commodity price swings on inflation across a variety of economies? What economic factors influence these effects?
- What is the appropriate monetary policy response to commodity price shocks? In particular, how does the approach of targeting underlying inflation rather than headline inflation perform in terms of delivering macroeconomic stability in different types of economies? Should central banks respond to persistent commodity price shocks any differently than to one-time shocks?
- Finally, what are the implications for monetary policy in today's environment, with excess demand pressures in some emerging and developing economies and economic slack in advanced economies?

These are the main findings of the chapter:

- Food price shocks tend to have larger effects on headline inflation in emerging and developing economies than in advanced economies. On a related note, because medium-term inflation expectations are weakly anchored in many emerging and developing economies, food price shocks have larger effects on inflation expectations in these economies.

- The measure of inflation used to define a central bank's target matters because of its effect on the central bank's credibility. In economies with low initial monetary policy credibility and high food shares in the consumption basket, focusing on underlying inflation—that is, a measure that reflects the changes in inflation that are likely to be sustained over the medium term—rather than on headline inflation, makes it easier to build credibility. The reason is that it is harder to hit headline inflation targets when commodity prices are volatile. Higher credibility, in turn, leads to better-anchored inflation expectations and lower volatility of both output and headline inflation.
- The desirability of setting and communicating monetary policy based on a measure of underlying inflation depends on the relative importance of headline inflation and output to a country's welfare. A headline framework can lower the volatility of headline inflation, but at the cost of significantly higher volatility in output (and hence in household income).
- Finally, in economies where central bank credibility is still limited and the share of food in consumption is high (as in a number of emerging and developing economies), a food price shock is likely to have even larger second-round effects and require a more aggressive policy response when excess demand pressures are high and inflation is running above target. This assumes that the economic costs rise as the gap increases between actual inflation and the target. In contrast, in economies where the central bank's credibility is strong, where food accounts for a low share in consumption baskets, and where there is substantial economic slack (as in major advanced economies today), the monetary policy tightening required to stabilize inflation is more gradual.

The first section of this chapter establishes some stylized facts about the effects of international commodity price swings on inflation in different types of economies. The following section considers how the monetary policy responses most appropriate for dealing with these shocks might differ across economies. The analysis uses simulations from a small open economy model that focuses on the difference in economic stability between a monetary policy framework based on underlying inflation (proxied by core inflation in the model) and one based on headline inflation.[6] The chapter then draws some policy conclusions and explores some practical considerations related to the definition of underlying inflation.

Commodity Price Swings and Inflation

This section examines the size and nature of the inflationary effects of international commodity price swings in different economies. It starts by reviewing recent developments in international commodity prices and then considers the various channels likely to affect how much international price movements pass through to domestic price movements. Finally, it looks at the overall pass-through from food prices to headline inflation. This discussion serves to explain the challenges commodity price shocks present for monetary policymakers and to identify what key characteristics of economies influence the size of these challenges. These characteristics become the building blocks for the model presented in the following section.

Swings in International Commodity Prices

Figure 3.1 shows that food and fuel prices have been rising since 2000. World food prices are about 80 percent higher in real terms than in January 2000, and oil prices are 175 percent higher. On the other hand, from a longer perspective, food prices hit a historical low in 2000 (Figure 3.2) after declining for decades.[7] Clearly, the potential range of swings in commodity prices is large.

Another key characteristic of international food and energy price movements is that it is difficult to predict their direction and persistence. Figure 3.3 compares real food prices with forecasts of food prices based on futures market prices over the past

Figure 3.2. World Commodity Prices, 1957–2011

(In real terms, as deflated by U.S. consumer price index)

In a long-term historical context, 2000 was a low point for both food and fuel prices. Current fuel prices are at historical highs (at least in real U.S. dollar terms), but food prices are at or below levels that prevailed before the mid-1990s.

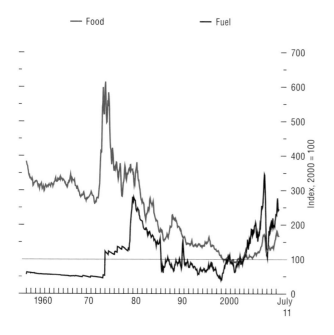

Sources: Haver Analytics; and IMF staff calculations.

---

[6]Numerous studies focus on the relative forecasting power of core versus headline inflation for future headline inflation (see, for example, Cogley, 2002; and OECD, 2005). However, because central banks tend to forecast inflation based on a wide range of economic indicators and modeling techniques rather than solely on headline or core inflation, this line of analysis is not pursued here.

[7]See Southgate (2007) for a discussion of the reasons behind the price declines.

decade. As prices started fluctuating substantially around 2005, the forecasts became more inaccurate and, most dramatically, missed the turning points in 2008 and 2009.[8]

From International to Domestic Commodity Prices

We now examine the pass-through from international commodity prices to domestic commodity prices. In particular, we estimate the effect of a 1 percent increase in international food prices (expressed in local currency) on domestic food prices.[9] Figure 3.4 shows the estimation results, which suggest that pass-through tends to be larger in emerging and developing economies than in advanced economies.[10] However, the size of the pass-through is relatively small. The median long-term pass-through of a 1 percent food price shock to domestic food prices is 0.18 percent in advanced economies and 0.34 percent in emerging and developing economies. There is even less pass-through—and little difference between advanced and emerging market economies—from oil prices to transportation prices.[11]

A number of factors help explain this incomplete pass-through. There is a significant local component in the production of food, including retail and distribution margins, excise taxes, and customs duties. Food and fuel subsidies may limit the degree of pass-through. In addition, there is generally significant domestic production of food, making domestic agricultural and weather conditions more influential than global market developments. Moreover, world

---

[8]In general, futures markets do not decisively beat a random walk forecast of commodity prices, as discussed by Roach (2011). For further discussion of the difficulties of forecasting commodity prices, see Groen and Pesenti (2011).

[9]See Appendix 3.1 for the countries included in the sample and Appendix 3.2 for details on the pass-through analysis.

[10]Throughout this chapter, advanced economies and emerging and developing economies are defined according to the classification in the Statistical Appendix. This classification does not separate emerging market economies from developing economies, but Appendix 3.1 shows the division between advanced and emerging and developing economies.

[11]We examine the pass-through of international oil prices to transportation prices rather than to domestic fuel prices, because only limited data are available for domestic fuel prices. The median pass-through of oil to transportation is 0.13 for advanced economies and 0.17 for emerging and developing economies.

Figure 3.3. Food Price Forecasts

The history of forecasts demonstrates the difficulty of determining whether any given price movement is likely to be permanent or temporary. This is particularly evident in the performance of forecasts over the period of increased volatility during the past five years.

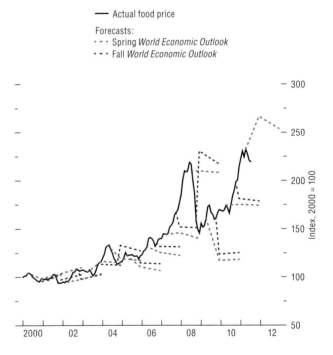

Source: IMF staff estimates.

Figure 3.4. Pass-through from World Inflation to Domestic Inflation

The pass-through of international food inflation to domestic food inflation is higher in emerging and developing economies than in advanced economies, and both are on average generally higher than the pass-through from crude oil inflation to domestic transportation inflation.

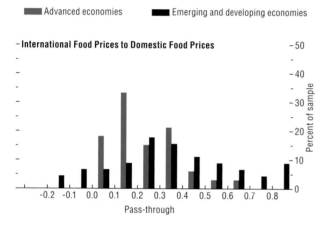

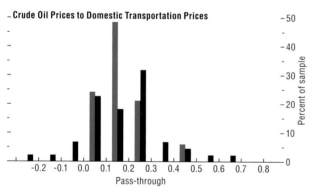

Sources: Haver Analytics; and IMF staff calculations.
Note: The pass-through from international to domestic inflation is estimated using country-by-country bivariate regressions. The pass-through is calculated as the sum of coefficients on the current value and 12 lags of the international variable divided by 1 minus the sum of coefficients on the 12 lags of the domestic variable.

commodity price indices do not necessarily reflect the consumption bundle in any given country. The world index includes, for example, wheat, barley, and rice in proportion to their value in international trade, but domestic consumption patterns vary across countries.

Focusing on more tightly defined consumer product categories, such as bread and bakery products, can help shed more light on the extent of pass-through when compositional effects are mitigated. Based on data for economies for which this more exact breakdown is available, Tables 3.1 and 3.2 show the pass-through of world crude oil prices to gasoline prices and the pass-through of world wheat prices to flour and bread. The higher pass-through for fuel is evident; however, even for such closely related food products as wheat, flour, and bread, the rate of pass-through is low.

Within the detailed pass-through results is evidence of price subsidies for certain commodities. For example, there is virtually no correlation between the gasoline price in Brazil and the world price, which reflects both the government's ownership of the largest national oil producer and the highly developed ethanol market. Similarly, government subsidies explain the lack of correlation between Indian flour and bread prices and world wheat prices. Subsidies generally transform a monetary policy challenge into a fiscal policy challenge. But because this chapter focuses on monetary policy and because such subsidies are generally outside the control of the monetary authorities, price subsidies are taken as a given.

One final note is that the results reveal a wide variation in effects across economies. The wide range in pass-through coefficients helps explain why, as Figure 3.5 shows, real domestic food price increases since 2000 have ranged from –15 percent to 70 percent despite the 80 percent increase in the real U.S. dollar world food price index over the same period. One reason real food prices have fallen over this period in some countries (for example, Bulgaria, Czech Republic, Ireland, Slovak Republic) is that their exchange rates appreciated against the U.S. dollar. Exchange rate effects can significantly influence how commodity price shocks affect a country, and Boxes 3.1 and 3.2 include further discussion of this.

Table 3.1. Gasoline Pass-through from Oil Prices

	Long-Term Pass-through
United States	0.65
India	0.56
Canada	0.49
France	0.46
South Africa	0.44
Russia	0.41
Japan	0.40
Italy	0.35
EU-27	0.34
United Kingdom	0.30
Germany	0.30
Korea	0.30
Mexico	0.06
Brazil	0.01
Average (median)	0.38

Source: IMF staff calculations.

EU-27: Austria, Belgium, Bulgaria, Cyprus, Czech Republic, Denmark, Estonia, Finland, France, Germany, Greece, Hungary, Ireland, Italy, Latvia, Lithuania, Luxembourg, Malta, Netherlands, Poland, Portugal, Romania, Slovak Republic, Slovenia, Spain, Sweden, and United Kingdom.

For transportation prices, the effects of world oil prices are similarly diverse.

Influences on Pass-through from Domestic Commodity Prices to Overall Inflation

Two key factors are used to gauge the effect of domestic food and energy prices on overall CPI inflation: the share of these components in the consumption basket and the anchoring of inflation expectations. The higher the food share, the

Table 3.2. Flour and Bread Pass-through from Wheat Prices

	Long-Term Pass-through	
	Flour	Bread
South Africa		0.33
Brazil	0.32	0.28
Mexico	0.41	0.19
Canada	0.48	0.19
Russia	0.17	0.16
United States	0.22	0.15
Japan		0.13
Germany		0.11
Italy	0.26	0.10
India	−0.05	0.00
Average (median)	0.26	0.16

Source: IMF staff calculations.

higher the direct effect on headline inflation. To the extent that food prices affect wage demands, higher pass-through to nonfood price inflation might be expected when the food share is higher. In countries with a poor track record of controlling inflation, food and fuel price shocks might also raise expectations of larger inflation in the future and might thereby raise pass-through when these expectations are reflected in prices.

Food share

The share of food in the CPI consumption basket is typically higher in emerging and developing economies than in advanced economies. For advanced economies in our sample, the median food share is 17 percent, whereas in emerging and developing economies, the median is 31 percent (Figure 3.6). Such a high food share implies that food price shocks will have a strong direct effect on headline inflation in these economies. These direct effects are shown in Figure 3.7: in 2008, food prices contributed about 5 percentage points to headline inflation in emerging and developing economies on average but only about 1 percentage point to advanced economy inflation. More recently, the contribution exceeded 2 percentage points for emerging and developing economies and about 0.5 percentage point for advanced economies. These averages also mask significant variations among economies—in some, food prices raised headline inflation by about 10 percentage points in 2008 and 5 percentage points in recent months. The contribution of transportation to headline inflation was more limited than that of food during 2003–08, possibly reflecting the minimal effect of world oil prices on transportation prices and the smaller share of fuel in consumer baskets.[12]

Inflation expectations

The overall effect of a food price shock on inflation, and the required policy response, are likely

[12]This analysis includes very few low-income countries (LICs). Box 3.1 investigates the experience of such countries in sub-Saharan Africa during the food price surge of 2007–08. Overall, it finds that the contribution of food prices to headline CPI inflation in LICs was similar to that of emerging and developing economies as reported here.

to depend on how well inflation expectations are anchored. If monetary policy credibility is low, then medium-term inflation expectations are likely to be revised upward in response to incoming inflation news. By contrast, if the private sector believes that the central bank will stabilize inflation, then medium-term inflation expectations should respond little to incoming inflation news, thus requiring smaller adjustments in monetary policy.

The extent to which inflation expectations are anchored is estimated using the response of medium-term inflation expectations to an unexpected increase in inflation in the current period by means of statistical analysis. In particular, we estimate the average response of expectations of future inflation to an unexpected 1 standard deviation increase in inflation in the current year.[13] The inflation expectation data are based on surveys of professional forecasters conducted in 20 advanced and 18 emerging and developing economies over the past two decades, and the statistical approach is based on that of Levin, Natalucci, and Piger (2004) and the October 2008 *World Economic Outlook*. We also explore how the response differs between advanced and emerging and developing economies and across different monetary policy regimes.

A key result is that expectations are generally less well anchored in emerging and developing economies than in advanced economies. On average, in emerging and developing economies, a 1 standard deviation shock to current-year inflation expectations, equal to 1.8 percentage points, has a substantial effect on medium-term inflation expectations. As Figure 3.8 illustrates, even as far as five years into the future, inflation is still expected to rise by 0.3 percentage point in response to such a shock. By contrast, in advanced economies, a 1 standard deviation shock to current-year inflation expectations, equal to 0.6 percentage point, has a negligible effect on medium-term inflation expectations (0.04 percentage point), suggesting a higher degree of policy credibility.[14]

---

[13]See Appendix 3.2 for details on estimates of inflation expectations.

[14]These results imply that medium-term expectations change 2.5 times more in emerging and developing economies than

Figure 3.5. Variability of Real Domestic Prices

Domestic food and transportation prices have generally risen far less than world food and oil prices since 2000, with a wide range of country experiences. These divergences reflect the fact that domestic food and transportation baskets are different from the world commodity price indices and also reflect incomplete pass-through from commodity prices to domestic consumption items.

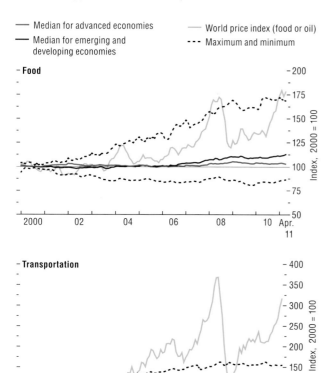

Sources: Haver Analytics; and IMF staff calculations.

Not all emerging and developing economies, however, have weakly anchored inflation expectations. Inflation expectations appear to be well anchored in emerging and developing economies in which the central bank has an explicit inflation target (see Figure 3.8). In particular, in emerging and developing economies that use an inflation-targeting framework, expectations of inflation two or more years in the future respond little to current-year inflation surprises.[15] In these economies, after a 1 standard deviation shock equal to 1.3 percentage points, inflation expectations five years out rise by only 0.07 percentage point, which is statistically indistinguishable from the response estimated for advanced economies. By contrast, where there is no inflation-targeting framework, inflation expectations as far as five years out rise by 0.5 percentage point following a 1 standard deviation surprise in current-year inflation.[16] However, as discussed in the October 2008 issue of the *World Economic Outlook,* the apparent benefits of inflation targeting may reflect the general quality of domestic monetary management and institutions in economies that adopt such a framework rather than the particular benefits of inflation targeting.

---

in advanced economies following a given inflation surprise—(0.3/1.8) divided by (0.04/0.6).

[15]For the purposes of the analysis, an inflation-targeting framework is identified based on the definition in Roger (2010), which includes four main elements: (1) an explicit central bank mandate to pursue price stability as the primary objective of monetary policy and a high degree of operational autonomy; (2) explicit quantitative targets for inflation; (3) central bank accountability for performance in achieving the inflation objective, mainly through high-transparency requirements for policy strategy and implementation; and (4) a policy approach based on a forward-looking assessment of inflation pressures, taking into account a wide array of information.

[16]Most of these economies have pegged exchange rates, which reduces their ability to respond to shocks to domestic inflation. However, additional analysis suggests that inflation expectations are just as weakly anchored in emerging and developing economies that do not have an inflation-targeting framework and have floating exchange rates (according to the de facto classification compiled by Ilzetzki, Reinhart, and Rogoff, 2008). Thus, the association between inflation targeting and the anchoring of expectations is not driven by the exchange rate regime.

Figure 3.6. Share of Food in the Consumption Basket

Emerging and developing economies tend to have a much higher share of food in their consumption baskets. The median CPI weight in advanced economies is 17 percent, whereas the median weight for emerging and developing economies is 31 percent.

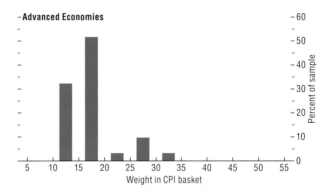

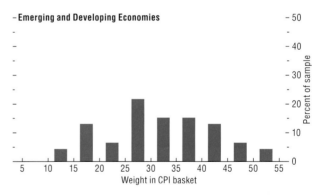

Source: Haver Analytics.
Note: CPI = consumer price index.

From Food Prices to Headline Inflation

Given the preceding discussion, pass-through from food to headline inflation might be expected to be higher where the share of food in consumption is larger and inflation expectations are less well anchored. This is indeed what we find. An estimation of the effect of food prices on headline inflation is shown in Figure 3.9.[17] The figure also includes, for reference, the median pass-through from international food prices to domestic food prices as calculated earlier in Figure 3.4.

The pass-through is much higher in emerging and developing economies, where the food share is typically higher and inflation expectations are less well anchored than in advanced economies. When combined with the fact that the pass-through from international to domestic food prices is higher in emerging market economies, it highlights that the effects of commodity prices on those economies are much larger than for advanced economies.

Overall, the preceding discussion has highlighted the following key characteristics of the data, which will inform the model-based analysis in the next section:

- Distinguishing between one-time and persistent commodity price shocks is difficult.
- Food has a high share in the consumption baskets of emerging and developing economies.
- Inflation expectations are well anchored in advanced economies and in inflation-targeting emerging and developing economies.
- Inflation expectations are less well anchored in some emerging and developing economies without inflation-targeting regimes.
- The pass-through from food prices to headline inflation is higher on average in emerging and developing economies than in advanced economies.

Monetary Policy and Food Price Shocks: A Simulation-Based Perspective

This section explores the appropriate monetary policy response to international food price shocks using a macroeconomic model that focuses on the role of

---

Figure 3.7. Contribution of Food and Transportation to Headline Inflation

Rising food prices raised overall inflation more in emerging and developing economies than in advanced economies. There is little evidence of transportation prices adding appreciably to headline inflation.

—— Advanced economies ——— Emerging and developing economies

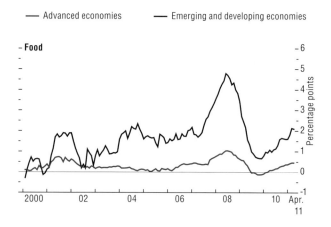

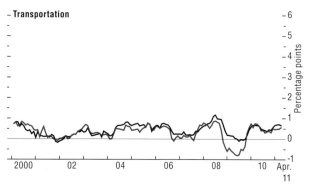

Sources: Haver Analytics; and IMF staff calculations.

---

[17]These parameters are imprecisely estimated, and there is a wide dispersion among individual country results. Consequently, only the median is reported.

monetary policy credibility and the food share in consumption baskets. For simplicity, energy price shocks
are not included. The model assesses the implications
of defining the central bank's inflation goal in terms of
headline inflation versus a measure of underlying inflation. This measure is not directly affected by temporary
food price shocks and here is called "core inflation."[18]

Monetary Policy Credibility and Food Price Shocks

The analysis focuses on a small open economy that
takes international commodity prices as given. The
structure of the model is relatively standard and in
line with the recent "New Keynesian" macroeconomic
literature. It consists of three equations: an aggregate
supply schedule (expectations-augmented Phillips
curve); an intertemporal aggregate demand (IS) equation; and an exchange rate–real interest rate parity
equation.[19] Within this three-equation bloc the model
shares results commonly found in the New Keynesian
literature. In particular, regardless of the food share
in the consumption basket, the central bank is fairly
well able to simultaneously stabilize both core inflation
and the output gap—although at the cost of a volatile
nominal interest rate.

A distinguishing feature of the model is the
introduction of an endogenous credibility formation
process, as in Alichi and others (2009).[20] The cred-

---

[18]As implied above, within the context of this model, there is
no distinction between core inflation and underlying inflation. The
key feature of the food component is that it is subject to exogenous
shocks that are largely beyond the control of domestic policymakers
and that the core measure is not directly affected by these shocks.
In practice, this food component might apply more to items such
as fresh fruit and vegetables than to restaurant meals and other
prepared meals, which largely reflect more slowly moving rental
and labor costs. The core measure could also be constructed as a
trimmed mean rather than an exclusion-based measure. Such practical matters are discussed in the final section of this chapter.

[19]The Phillips curve links current core inflation to past and
expected core inflation, the output gap, and the real exchange
rate change. The IS equation relates output gap growth to the
real interest rate and the real exchange rate. Finally, the uncovered
interest parity links exchange rate depreciation to the domestic
and world interest rate differential.

[20]The monetary policy literature is divided over the credibility
problem: the monetary authority either is fully credible, and the
central bank is able to manage the private sector's expectations, or
it is not credible at all. The latter case corresponds to "discretion,"
which means that the central bank conducts policy while taking
the private sector's expectations as given (see Woodford, 2003). The
approach here seeks a middle ground between those two extremes.

Figure 3.8. Response of Inflation Expectations to Inflation Surprises

Inflation surprises generally have larger effects on medium-term inflation
expectations in emerging and developing economies than in advanced economies.
However, in emerging and developing economies with an inflation-targeting
framework, inflation expectations are well anchored.

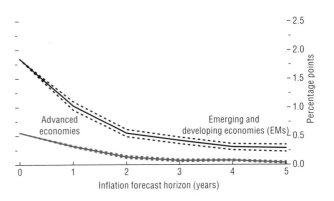

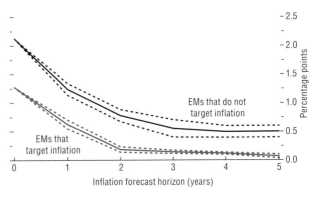

Sources: Consensus Economics; and IMF staff estimates.
Note: This figure shows expectations of inflation in the current year and one to five years
ahead as percentage point responses to a 1 standard deviation shock to current-year
inflation and the estimated effect of a 1 standard deviation unexpected change in domestic
consumer price index inflation based on private sector inflation expectations surveyed by
Consensus Economics, 1990–2010 spring and fall vintages. Unexpected change occurs in
year $t = 0$. Solid line indicates point estimates; dashed lines indicate 1 standard error
bands.

Figure 3.9. Pass-through from International to Domestic Food Price Inflation

The pass-through from international food price inflation to domestic food price inflation and from domestic food price inflation to headline inflation is higher in emerging and developing economies than in advanced economies.

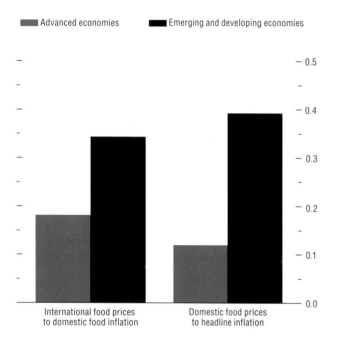

Source: IMF staff calculations.
Note: Estimates of pass-through from international to domestic food price inflation are from Figure 3.4. Estimates of the pass-through from domestic food prices to headline inflation are obtained by regressing headline inflation on lags of itself and current and lagged values of domestic food price inflation. To control for endogeneity, domestic food price inflation is instrumented by inflation in the international food price index expressed in domestic currency. The reported result is the median of country-by-country regressions.

ibility of monetary policy depends on the evolving track record of inflation relative to a long-term target. More precisely, it is assumed that a low-inflation target is announced once and for all by the central bank and is thereafter held constant. The central bank builds credibility over time by consistently attaining an inflation rate close to the targeted rate. The idea is that, in the long term, if monetary policy consistently holds inflation to the target rate, private sector inflation expectations become anchored to the inflation target.[21] Therefore, higher inflation volatility can complicate the task of establishing credibility, because it generally results in missing the target. To make the model more realistic, inflation that is above the target is assumed to imply a higher loss of credibility than inflation that is below the target; moreover, when inflation is way off target (a big miss), the effects are assumed to be disproportionately larger than for a small miss.

How does credibility affect the rest of the economy? An imperfect level of credibility substantially amplifies the trade-off between outlook and inflation that central banks face. In the model we assume that this amplification can happen in at least three different ways: (1) inflation expectations become more backward-looking and less well anchored (which increases inflation's persistence and makes it more difficult to stabilize inflation once it is off target);[22] (2) inflation expectations gain an upward bias; and (3) the pass-through from food to core inflation rises. This last channel captures the idea that cost-push inflation pressures stemming from the wage-bargaining process are stronger when central bank credibility is low. In other words, the lower the credibility, the higher the second-round effects. Most important, this introduces a clear trade-off between stabilizing core inflation and stabilizing the output gap. With full credibility, second-round effects disappear and inflation expectations are

[21]However, the credibility stock is also assumed to gradually rise over time, capturing the transitional process of building credibility typical of many economies. Starting from a relatively low initial credibility stock allows us to study how this convergence process can be hampered by commodity price shocks.

[22]The inflation bias and its importance when there is a lack of central bank credibility have been documented in various studies, such as Pasaogullari and Tsonev (2008), who examine the experience of the United Kingdom in the 1980s and 1990s.

entirely forward-looking, implying that even a highly persistent increase in food prices has little effect on expectations. By contrast, if credibility is low, even a one-time rise in food prices can de-anchor inflation expectations and induce strong second-round effects on core inflation. Restraining inflation then requires substantial monetary policy tightening (see Alichi and others, 2009).

The analysis also distinguishes between three stylized economy types. The key features that distinguish these economies are the degree of policy credibility and the share of food in households' consumption baskets. In the first economy, the share of food in the CPI is assumed to be 30 percent—in line with the average for emerging and developing economies—and the degree of policy credibility is low. In the second, the share of food in the CPI is still high, but the degree of policy credibility is also high. Finally, in the third economy, the share of food in the CPI is low (set at 10 percent), and the degree of policy credibility is high.[23] These can be considered, respectively, as an emerging and developing economy, a high-credibility emerging and developing economy, and a high-credibility advanced economy, but the emphasis is on the food share and credibility rather than on the stage of development.

For a given credibility level, the pass-through from food prices to core inflation is proportional to the food share. This implies that a high-food-share economy faces stronger second-round effects (and, hence, a worse policy trade-off) than one where the food share is low. In addition, to capture the fact that the wage-bargaining process is more affected by changes in food inflation in emerging market economies, the weight on relative food price inflation in driving inflation dynamics is assumed to be relatively high.

The model determines the optimal monetary policy response—through changes in the short-term interest rate—given the central bank's policy objectives. These relate to the variances of inflation,

the output gap, and changes in short-term interest rates. The model postulates that the central bank sets interest rates to minimize variability along all three dimensions.[24] With food price shocks, a policy trade-off arises because substantial movements in the policy rate may be required to stabilize inflation and the output gap. Moreover, second-round effects—in the Phillips curve, from domestic food inflation to core inflation—generate a policy trade-off between the output gap and core inflation. The central bank's policy preferences determine how it trades off gains from reducing inflation against the costs of lower output and higher interest rate volatility.

Food Price Shocks with Core or Headline Inflation Targets

We consider two policy frameworks: one in which the target of monetary policy and the credibility formation process are based on headline inflation, and one in which they are based on core inflation. Each framework has two elements: the measure of inflation targeted by the central bank and the measure of inflation the private sector uses to evaluate the central bank's track record relative to the target—its credibility. Under a headline framework, the public evaluates the performance of the central bank based on how close headline inflation is to the target. Under a core framework, the public evaluates the performance of the central bank based on how close underlying inflation is to the target. The choice of the framework has important consequences for conducting monetary policy and the resilience of the policy framework to various shocks. For example, keeping core inflation at the target would imply no loss of credibility under the core framework, even if headline inflation were to rise above core inflation. Missing the headline inflation target in the headline

---

[23]A 10 percent food share was chosen rather than the 17 percent estimated for the advanced economies in the empirical section to accentuate the differences between the two groups. There is also, logically, a fourth kind of economy to consider: one with a low food share in the CPI and a low degree of credibility. As a practical matter, the evidence from the previous section suggests that this kind of economy is rare, and it is excluded.

[24]Formally, the central bank minimizes a loss function consisting of the weighted sum of the squared deviations of inflation from target, the squared output gap, and the square of the change in the short-term nominal interest rate. The weights in the loss function reflect the central bank's preferences regarding the stabilization of these three variables. In the baseline, the weights on inflation and output stabilization are equal (set to 1) and four times larger than the weight on interest rate stabilization (set to 0.25). We also test the robustness of the results to alternative weights, as discussed in the text.

framework comes with a loss of credibility and thus a worsening output-inflation trade-off.

Through its effect on credibility, the choice of the framework eventually may affect the way expectations are formed.[25] More precisely, a low level of credibility implies that private sector expectations are barely managed by the monetary authority. At the extreme of no credibility, monetary policy has no effect on private sector expectations. At the other extreme, policy announcements by a perfectly credible monetary authority have a substantial effect on private sector expectations.

The next paragraphs compare how these two frameworks perform in the three different types of economies following a shock to international food prices.

Stylized emerging and developing economy

We first consider a high-food-share (30 percent), low-credibility economy that is hit by a one-time international food price shock.[26] To abstract from cyclical factors, inflation is set initially at its target level, and the output gap is set to zero. We relax these assumptions later. The shock is assumed to raise international food inflation by 5 percentage points. The simulation is conducted twice, first assuming that the policy framework is defined in terms of headline inflation and then assuming it is defined in terms of core inflation.

Under the headline framework, the central bank loses policy credibility in the short term because the shock's direct effect raises headline inflation above the target (Figure 3.10). In response, to stabilize headline inflation, the central bank tightens policy, thus raising real interest rates and causing a real

appreciation of the currency.[27] This policy tightening directly reduces the domestic price of imported food by raising the value of the domestic currency, and also restrains inflation by causing an output contraction. In addition, with the initial loss of policy credibility, inflation expectations become de-anchored and more backward-looking. Restoring policy credibility and reducing inflation expectations then require a sustained output slump with headline inflation a little below normal (inflation undershooting).

By contrast, under the core framework, the output cost of keeping core inflation close to its target is lower. In the short term, headline inflation rises by about the same amount as in the headline framework. However, with the central bank's mandate specified in terms of core inflation—which rises by less than headline inflation on impact—policy credibility is much less affected. The effects of this are significant. The enhanced policy credibility keeps inflation expectations better anchored and implies less need for policy tightening and output contraction. Consequently, both core and headline inflation are more stable under the core framework than under the headline framework. When combined with the smaller output loss, this implies that the core framework delivers superior macroeconomic stability. Nonetheless, if the central bank also cares about output gap stabilization, it must accept some second-round effects on core inflation.

The striking finding that targeting core inflation can deliver more stability in terms of both output and headline inflation than targeting headline inflation is robust to alternative weighting of policy priorities between inflation and output stabilization. This result is illustrated in Figure 3.11, which shows the policy frontier with respect to output gap and headline inflation volatility.[28] The core framework shifts the frontier toward zero. This implies that, over certain ranges, it is possible to simultaneously

---

[25]There are elements of this idea in the Central Bank of Egypt's (CBE's) recent decision to publish a core inflation measure. As the CBE *Annual Report* 2009/2010 explains (p. A), "By timely communicating the core inflation measure, the CBE aims to improve understanding of inflation dynamics. This is expected to reduce the pass-through of temporary price shocks to inflation expectations and, in turn, minimize the variability in inflation." Similarly, the RBNZ has stated, "…the initial move to inflation targets arose from a wish to influence inflationary expectations by stating clearly the Government's commitments" (Sherwin, 1999).

[26]International commodity prices have historically been well modeled as random walks, with changes that are unpredictable and not systematically followed by further changes in the same direction.

[27]The result—the real exchange rate appreciates in response to a rise in the price of imports (food)—is similar to the case of the "worst sufferer" economy modeled by Catão and Chang (2010), in which a rise in food or other commodity prices entails a terms-of-trade deterioration and a concomitant real exchange rate appreciation. See Box 3.2 for a further discussion of the implications of commodity price shocks for the comovement of the terms of trade and the real exchange rate in different types of economies.

[28]See Figure 3.11 for details on the policy frontier calculations.

achieve lower headline inflation volatility and lower output volatility by adopting a core framework.

A key element underlying the better performance of the core framework is that the temporary shock to headline inflation is not taken as a signal of central bank failure, and thus credibility and inflation expectations are not negatively affected. Focusing on core inflation here protects the central bank's credibility from the effects of international commodity price shocks that are, broadly speaking, beyond the control of domestic policymakers.[29]

The headline framework can deliver the lowest levels of headline inflation volatility—at the cost of significantly higher output volatility. In an economy in which headline inflation is much more important than output in determining overall welfare, it may be optimal to choose a headline framework.[30] We return to the implications of these findings, particularly for countries with a high food share in consumption, in the final section of this chapter.

Stylized emerging and developing economy with high policy credibility

The case of an economy with a high food share but also high policy credibility illustrates the benefits of high credibility for emerging and developing economies. As the analysis above suggests, some emerging and developing economies have better-anchored inflation expectations than others.

As Figure 3.12 shows, in this case, with better-anchored inflation expectations, the degree of monetary policy tightening needed is smaller than in the previous case. Moreover, high credibility substantially reduces second-round effects, which is particularly important for economies with a high

---

[29]This would be equally applicable to a country that is self-sufficient in food. In this case, however, food prices would be subject to domestic weather shocks rather than international food price shocks. The conclusions are the same: a central bank will be better able to preserve its credibility in the face of food price shocks if that credibility is built on core rather than headline inflation.

[30]Numerous studies in the literature assume equal weights placed on inflation and output in the loss function, including Gilchrist and Saito (2006). By contrast, in Figure 3.11, a weight on inflation that is approximately six times as large as that placed on output is required for the headline inflation framework to be preferable to the core inflation framework.

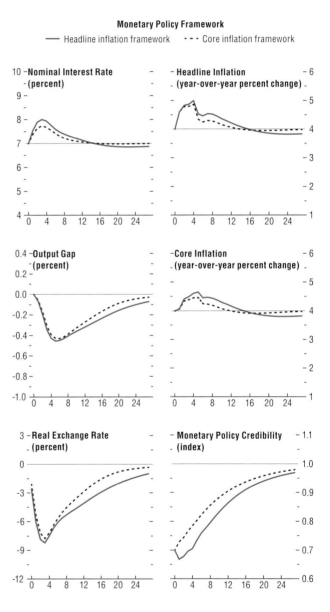

Figure 3.10. Response to a Food Price Shock in a Stylized Emerging and Developing Economy

In emerging and developing economies with a high food share in the consumption basket and low monetary policy credibility, targeting core inflation after a one-time food price increase helps to stabilize both output and headline inflation.

Source: IMF staff estimates.
Note: The time period is quarters. The food price shock occurs at $t = 0$.

Figure 3.11. Inflation-Output Policy Frontier

In emerging and developing economies with a high food share and low monetary policy credibility, targeting core inflation after a one-time food inflation shock helps to stabilize both output and headline inflation. Only when the relative weight on inflation is very high is it preferable to target headline inflation.

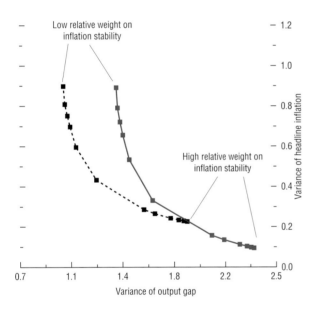

Monetary Policy Framework

■─■ Headline inflation framework   ■-■ Core inflation framework

Source: IMF staff estimates.
Note: The policy frontier is traced out by varying the weights attached to the three target variables in the central bank's loss function—namely, variances in inflation, the output gap, and policy rate changes. In particular, we normalize the weight on the variance of the output gap to 1 and fix the weight on the policy rate at 0.25. The points on the frontier are then computed by changing the weight on inflation variance from zero to 500. In this model these weights correspond to a society's preference for output volatility or inflation volatility.

food share.[31] Overall, higher credibility contributes to more stable economic outcomes, because expectations are better-anchored and policy responses to shocks can be more measured—reducing the resultant output fluctuations.

The core inflation framework still achieves greater output stabilization than the headline framework. As with the first simulation, the policy frontier shifts toward zero (although both frontiers are closer to zero as a result of the higher level of credibility).

In both cases, optimal policy requires that some second-round effects be allowed. Core inflation rises slightly above the target under both frameworks, but it then undershoots under the headline framework because the real exchange rate, after the initial appreciation, takes longer to normalize.

Stylized advanced economy

Finally, we consider how the results change for an economy with a low food share—set at 10 percent of the CPI rather than 30 percent as in the previous simulations—as well as higher initial policy credibility (as introduced in the second simulation).

Figure 3.13 shows that, for this type of economy, the difference between the two frameworks in terms of macroeconomic stability following food price shocks is negligible. In particular, with the small food share and with well-anchored inflation expectations, the effect of the international food shock is far smaller than in the other simulations.

Persistent Shocks

The above analysis considers the response to food price shocks under the assumption that they are known to be one-time occurrences. However, as discussed in the introduction, there are concerns that shocks may be becoming more persistent. This section therefore explores the effect of a larger, more persistent food price shock.[32] Figure 3.14 shows the response of a high-food-share, low-credibility

[31]Recall that the pass-through from food inflation to core inflation is proportional to the food share and the credibility gap.

[32]The initial size of the shock is the same as for the one-time shocks considered above. However, for this experiment, prices continue to increase after the initial shock, although at a declining rate. More formally, we consider a shock with an autoregressive parameter of 0.5, such that the first period increase is 5 percent-

economy to a persistent international food price shock and shows that the response is stronger than to the one-time shock. With a persistent shock, the central bank anticipates further food price increases down the road and increases the interest rate by more to minimize a potential loss of credibility. This, in turn, mitigates the effect of expected future pass-through from food to core inflation, dampening the surge of expected inflation. This interaction between credibility losses and second-round effects is less relevant when the shock is known to be purely temporary: with no expectation of further food price shocks, pass-through from food to core inflation is not relevant. This logic also can be seen in the reaction of the credibility index. In the case of a temporary shock, credibility is allowed to drop in the first period, given that no further inflation pressures are expected. In the case of persistent shocks, the central bank is more concerned about losing credibility because of the difficulty of regaining it in the face of continued inflation pressure from food prices. That is, if one anticipates further price shocks in the future, it is more important to preserve credibility than if no further price shocks are expected.

Commodity Price Shocks and Cyclical Conditions

How does the appropriate monetary policy response to a persistent food price shock differ for advanced economies with substantial economic slack and for emerging and developing economies with excess demand pressures and relatively low initial real interest rates?[33]

In Figure 3.15, the contrast between the two types of economies is dramatic. The different outcomes are driven mainly by two elements: the change in inflation for a given change in the output gap is increasing with the size of the output gap (that is, the slope of the Phillips curve is increasing in the output gap), and the additional loss of credibility is higher the greater the miss. Hence, in the emerging and developing model economy, policy credibility

age points, the second period increase is 2.5 percentage points, the third period increase is 1.25 percentage points, and so on.

[33]For the purposes of this exercise, we assume central banks are using a headline framework, but the main conclusions are similar for a core framework.

Figure 3.12. Response to a Food Price Shock in a Stylized High-Credibility Emerging and Developing Economy

In economies with a high food share in consumption and high monetary policy credibility, less monetary policy tightening is needed after a one-time food price shock. Targeting core inflation still achieves greater output stabilization, but there is now a slightly greater increase in headline inflation in the short term.

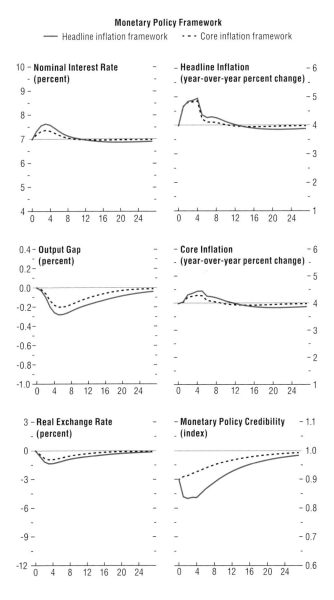

Source: IMF staff estimates.
Note: The time period is quarters. The food price shock occurs at $t = 0$.

Figure 3.13. Response to a Food Price Shock in a Stylized Advanced Economy

In economies with a small food share in consumption and with well-anchored inflation expectations, the impact of the international one-time food price shock is far smaller than in emerging and developing economies. The difference between targeting core and headline inflation in terms of delivering macroeconomic stability is also smaller.

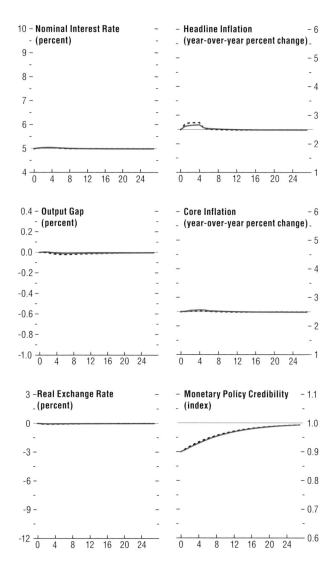

Monetary Policy Framework

—— Headline inflation framework   - - - Core inflation framework

Source: IMF staff estimates.
Note: The time period is quarters. The food price shock occurs at $t = 0$.

is already negatively affected by preexisting excess demand pressures and above-target inflation. The persistent food price shock exacerbates this credibility loss. A rapid rise in interest rates to well above normal is then required to restore policy credibility and re-anchor inflation expectations. By contrast, for the advanced model economy, the disinflationary effect of economic slack dominates the small inflationary effect of the food price shock. With medium-term expectations well anchored and thus small pass-through to core inflation, the required policy adjustment involves only a gradual withdrawal of monetary policy stimulus.

Policy Implications for Responding to Commodity Price Shocks

This section outlines some key policy implications of the chapter's analysis and some practical considerations about how to measure underlying inflation.

First, changes in commodity prices are likely to have a stronger and longer-lasting effect on inflation in emerging and developing economies than in advanced economies. There are three main reasons for this: in emerging and developing economies (1) the pass-through from international commodity prices is higher, (2) food and energy consumption shares tend to be higher, and (3) medium-term inflation expectations are less well anchored.

Second, the simulations show that central banks in economies with low credibility and high food shares in consumption may be able to better preserve and build monetary policy credibility by setting and communicating monetary policy in terms of underlying inflation (taken to be core inflation in our model) rather than headline inflation. Basing the policy objective on a measure of inflation that is inherently more stable and less subject to large and unpredictable international commodity price shocks is thus preferable. The higher policy credibility in turn allows the central bank to stabilize inflation (both headline and core) with less monetary policy tightening and a smaller associated output loss.

For these economies, the choice between focusing on core or headline inflation depends on the relative welfare gains from stabilizing headline inflation versus stabilizing output. It is sometimes suggested that, with high food shares in the consumption basket, the economic costs of volatility in food prices and headline inflation are high, and that it is therefore more appropriate to tie monetary policy closely to headline inflation targets. However, lowering the volatility of headline inflation means increasing the volatility of output and unemployment, and the economic costs of unemployment can also be very high in these economies. Although assessing the social and economic factors involved in ranking such priorities is beyond the scope of this chapter, the analysis does illustrate that there are significant trade-offs involved.

Setting and communicating monetary policy in terms of underlying inflation are likely to require significant effort on the part of the central bank. The importance of effective communication is evident in the sustained and ultimately successful efforts of the initial cohort of inflation-targeting central banks in this regard. The central banks in Australia, Canada, and New Zealand established their inflation-targeting frameworks in terms of a core inflation measure or with a prominent short-term role for core inflation and undertook sustained efforts to explain what they were doing to the public.[34] When inflation was successfully brought down and the policy was highly credible, these central banks moved to targeting headline inflation.[35]

In the absence of an effective communication strategy, however, simply changing the operating target to a measure of underlying inflation, such as core inflation, could be counterproductive. For example, policy credibility could suffer and economic outcomes could deteriorate if the central bank's performance continued to be evaluated based on the volatility of headline inflation when it is tar-

---

[34]For example, in the case of Australia, in 1999 Glenn Stevens, the assistant governor (and now governor) of the Reserve Bank of Australia observed that "One important presentational change that we did make was a progressive upgrading of the quality and quantity of our published material on the economy. Financial markets and the media began to take much more notice of the quarterly pieces we put out. The extent of this change has been quite substantial. In early 1992, these documents were typically 4 or 5 pages in length. By the middle of 1994, they had grown to 15–16 pages. In more recent years, *Semi-Annual Statements* have on occasion approached 50 pages, and exceeded 20,000 words" (Stevens, 1999).

[35]Recall the discussion of this in footnote 4.

Figure 3.14. One-Time versus Persistent Food Price Shocks

In economies with low monetary policy credibility and a high food share, the central bank facing a persistent shock increases the interest rate by more (relative to a one-time shock) to minimize losses in credibility.

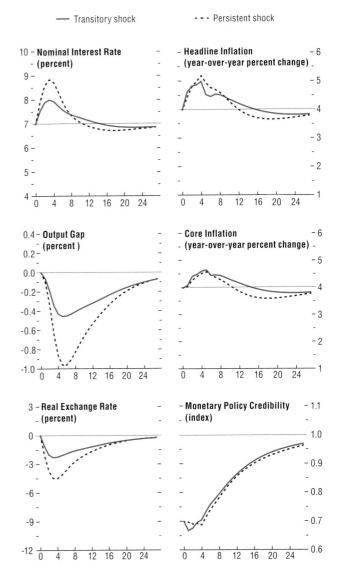

Source: IMF staff estimates.
Note: The time period is quarters. The food price shock occurs at *t* = 0.

Figure 3.15. Response to a Food Price Shock amid Current Cyclical Conditions

In emerging and developing economies with a high food share in consumption, low monetary policy credibility, and initial inflation already above target, aggressive monetary policy tightening is required after a food price shock (right column). By contrast, in advanced economies with well-anchored inflation expectations and economic slack, a gradual unwinding of monetary policy stimulus is required (left column).

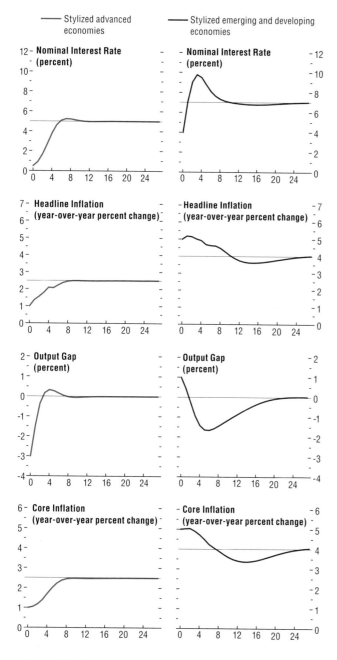

Source: IMF staff estimates.
Note: The time period is quarters. The food price shock occurs at $t = 0$.

geting core inflation. Any policy transition must be built on a firm foundation that includes effectively demonstrating the relevance of the chosen measure of underlying inflation.

Another important element in establishing a regime is the precise definition of the inflation target. As noted, a common criticism of exclusion-based core inflation measures is that they ignore the effects of food and fuel prices, which can undermine the credibility of the target in the eyes of the public. Additional credibility problems can arise if the average rate of inflation varies depending on which measure is used. In that respect, one of the key findings of this analysis is that the target measure of inflation should be resilient to transitory shocks from commodity prices, but an exclusion-based measure of inflation is not the only such target. For example, trimmed-mean or median measures of inflation do not automatically exclude food and fuel prices but still provide a less volatile and more robust measure of overall inflation trends than headline measures.[36] Such measures have tended to have the same average rates of inflation as headline measures over the long term.[37]

In practice, there is no perfect measure of underlying inflation, and different measures may be appropriate depending on the country and circumstances. Many central banks have chosen to target a headline inflation forecast and clarify what that forecast assumes for food and fuel prices. At least with respect to commodity price shocks, this is akin to targeting a measure of underlying inflation. The use of forecasts also allows for more flexibility than does a framework tied closely to current inflation, because the central bank can monitor a wide range of indicators of underlying inflation and place varying weights on these indicators as circumstances change. One drawback to using forecasts is that it is

[36]See Bryan and Cecchetti (1993) for a discussion of these measures.

[37]See Brischetto and Richards (2007) for a discussion of the long-term performance of trimmed-mean measures in Australia, the euro area, Japan, and the United States. It is possible to calculate asymmetric trims if the long-term averages do diverge (see, for example, Roger, 1997). However, as Brischetto and Richards argue, asymmetric trims may be harder to explain to the public and this may complicate the establishment of a targeting regime based upon them.

difficult to monitor the central bank's performance, because tomorrow never comes, which only increases the importance of a strong communications policy. (Other aspects of forecast targeting, such as the optimal time horizon, must also be carefully considered, but these are beyond the scope of this chapter.)[38]

[38]A related question regards the appropriate level for the inflation target when there are permanent shifts in the relative prices of commodities such as food and fuel. In such cases, targeting headline inflation implies a different long-term level for core inflation, and vice versa. If, for some reason, annual growth of 2 percent in the CPI index were deemed appropriate, the central bank could communicate an equivalent target for underlying inflation. However, a discussion of the appropriate level for an inflation target is beyond the scope of this chapter.

Finally, the simulations related to the current global environment underscore the policy advice implied by the cyclical positions alone. In emerging and developing economies with excess demand pressures, inflation already above target, and a high share of food in consumption baskets, tighter monetary conditions can help mitigate the negative effects of potential future food price shocks and the associated loss of monetary policy credibility. In contrast, in advanced economies with substantial economic slack, well-anchored inflation expectations, and a low share of food in consumption, there is ample room for monetary policy to accommodate any future commodity price shocks with little loss of credibility.

Appendix 3.1. Economies in the Data Set

Advanced Economies	Emerging and Developing Economies
Australia	Albania
Austria	Argentina
Belgium	Bahrain
Canada	Bosnia and Herzegovina
Czech Republic	Botswana
Denmark	Brazil
Estonia	Bulgaria
Finland	Chile
France	Colombia
Germany	Croatia
Greece	Ecuador
Hong Kong SAR	Egypt
Iceland	Hungary
Ireland	India
Israel	Jordan
Italy	Kazakhstan
Japan	Kuwait
Korea	Latvia
Netherlands	Lebanon
New Zealand	Lithuania
Norway	Former Yugoslav Republic of Macedonia
Portugal	Macao SAR
Singapore	Malaysia
Slovak Republic	Mauritius
Slovenia	Mexico
Spain	Montenegro
Sweden	Nigeria
Switzerland	Oman
Taiwan Province of China	Pakistan
United Kingdom	Peru
United States	Philippines
	Poland
	Qatar
	Romania
	Russia
	Saudi Arabia
	Serbia
	South Africa
	Thailand
	Tunisia
	Turkey
	Uganda
	Ukraine
	United Arab Emirates
	Uruguay
	Venezuela
	West Bank and Gaza

Appendix 3.2. Technical Appendix

Simulation Model Details

Headline inflation π_t^H is the weighted average of domestic food inflation π_t^F and core inflation π_t.

$$\pi_t^H = (1 - \omega_F)\pi_t + \omega_F\pi_t^F. \tag{3.1}$$

The parameter ω_F represents the share of food in the consumption basket.

A Phillips curve relates current core inflation to past and expected core inflation, previous period output gap x_{t-1}, the change in the real exchange rate change, ΔRER, and a term related to second-round effects from food to core inflation:

$$\pi_t = \alpha\pi_{w,t} + (1 - \alpha)\pi_{b,t-1} + g(x_{t-1}) + \beta_e\Delta RER_t \\ + (1 + \delta - S_t)\omega_F(\pi_{t-1}^F - \pi_{t-1}). \tag{3.2}$$

The function $g(x)$ is increasing and convex in its argument, S is the credibility stock bounded between zero and 1, and α and δ are parameters.[39] The variables π_w and π_b represent the forward- and backward-looking terms of the Phillips curve, which are defined as follows:

$$\pi_{w,t} = S_t\pi_{b,t+4} + (1 - S_t)(\pi_{b,t-1} + bias_t) \tag{3.3}$$

$$\pi_{b,t} = \sum_{i=0}^{4} \frac{\pi_{t-1}}{4}. \tag{3.4}$$

The lower the current credibility stock, S_t, the higher the importance of past inflation and the inflation bias term (*bias*) associated with imperfect credibility. The current stock of credibility has the following law of motion:

$$S_t = \vartheta S_{t-1} + (1 - \vartheta)\sigma_t \tag{3.5}$$

$$\sigma_t = \frac{(m_{b,t} - \pi_t^{tg})^2}{(m_{b,t} - \pi_t^{tg})^2 + (m_{l,t} - \pi_t^{tg})^2}. \tag{3.6}$$

The credibility signal σ_t is bounded between zero and 1, and the parameter ϑ ($0 < \vartheta < 1$) governs the rate at which credibility converges to σ_t. The variables m_b and m_l represent the inflation rates prevailing in the high- and low-inflation regimes, as perceived by the private sector. The variable π_t^{tg}

---

[39]The parameter δ is set to zero and 0.25 for the high- and low-credibility cases, respectively.

represents the inflation measure for which the central bank is held accountable. The closer π_t^{tg} is to the high-inflation level, the greater the loss in credibility. The perceived inflation rates prevailing in the high- and low-inflation regimes are as follows:

$$m_{h,t} = \alpha_h \pi_{t-1}^{tg} + (1 - \alpha_h)\pi^{high} \qquad (3.7)$$

$$m_{l,t} = \alpha_l \pi_{t-1}^{tg} + (1 - \alpha_l)\pi^{low} \quad . \qquad (3.8)$$

We interpret π^{low} as the (constant) target chosen by the central bank, and we assume $\pi^{high} \gg \pi^{low}$ such that we can focus on cases where $\pi_t^{tg} \le m_{h,t}$ at all times. The lowest level of credibility occurs when $m_{h,t} = \pi_t^{tg}$, implying that credibility, S_t, declines to zero at rate ϑ.

The choice of the framework boils down to the choice of π_t^{tg}. In the case of the core framework, we have $\pi_t^{tg} = \sum_{i=0}^{4} \frac{\pi_{t-1}}{4}$, while in the case of the headline framework we have $\pi_t^{tg} = \sum_{i=0}^{4} \frac{\pi_{t-1}^{H}}{4}$.

The output gap is governed by an intertemporal aggregate demand (IS) equation that links the output gap to the previous period real rate, r_{t-1}, and the current real exchange rate, RER. An uncovered interest parity equation relates the nominal policy rate, R_t, to the expected depreciation of the nominal exchange rate, e_t. All φs are positive parameters. Asterisks indicate values for the rest of the world.

$$x_t = \varphi_1 x_{t-1} + \varphi_2 E_t x_{t+1} - \varphi_r(r_{t-1} - r)$$
$$+ \varphi_e(RER_t - RER), \qquad (3.9)$$

$$R_t = R_t^* + \varphi_u(E_t e_{t+1} - e_t). \qquad (3.10)$$

Finally, other equations that close the model are the definitions of the inflation bias, the real exchange rate, and the real rate, which is

$$r_t = R_t - E_t \pi_{t+1}^{H}. \qquad (3.11)$$

The domestic food price is

$$\pi_t^F = 0.6\pi_t + 0.4(\pi_t^{*F} + \Delta e_t), \qquad (3.12)$$

where π_t^{*F} is the international food-inflation process, which is taken as exogenous:

$$\pi_t^{*F} = \rho \pi_{t-1}^{*F} + \varepsilon_t. \qquad (3.13)$$

In the calibration, we set the persistence parameter, ρ, equal to zero and 0.5 for temporary and persistent shocks, respectively.

Analysis of Pass-through from International Food Prices to Domestic Food Prices

The pass-through analysis is based on a country-by-country regression of monthly domestic food price inflation on current and 12 lags of monthly international commodity price inflation (converted to domestic currency), controlling for 12 lags of domestic food price inflation. The economies included in the database are listed in Appendix 3.1. The regression is run on the inflation rates because, despite long-term trends in the price levels, there is no evidence of a long-term relationship between the world food price index and domestic CPI food baskets. (Likely reasons for this are discussed in the section "From International to Domestic Commodity Prices.") In particular, the estimated equation is as follows:

$$\pi_t^{dom} = \sum_{j=1}^{12} \beta_j \pi_{t-j}^{dom} + \sum_{k=0}^{12} \gamma_k \pi_{t-k}^{int} + \varepsilon_{i,t}, \qquad (3.14)$$

where π_t^{dom} denotes domestic food inflation in month t, and π_{t-k}^{int} denotes international food inflation in month t. The long-term pass-through coefficient is computed as the sum of the coefficients on international food price inflation (γ_k) divided by 1 minus the sum of the coefficients on lagged domestic food inflation (β_j). An analogous equation is estimated to investigate the pass-through from international oil prices to domestic transportation prices. The sample includes 31 advanced economies and 47 emerging and developing economies over the period 2000–11. The long-term coefficients are generally statistically significant.

Analysis of Inflation Expectations

The change in future inflation expectations is the dependent variable on the left side of equation 3.15, and the explanatory variable on the right side is the unexpected change in current-year inflation, defined as the revision of expectations for inflation in year

t made between spring and fall of year t. Thus, the equation estimated is

$$\Delta E_{it}\pi_{i,t+N} = \alpha + \beta\Delta E_{it}\pi_{it} + \mu_i + \lambda_t + \nu_{i,t}, \quad (3.15)$$

where the subscript i denotes the ith country, the subscript t denotes the tth year, and $\Delta E_{it}\pi_{i,t+N}$ denotes the revision of expectations for inflation in year $t+N$. The approach includes a full set of country dummies (μ_i) and a full set of time dummies (λ_t) to take account of global shocks such as oil prices and the global business cycle. The estimation results are similar without controlling for global shocks, suggesting that inflation expectations are anchored roughly equally following global and domestic inflation shocks. The data on inflation expectations come from *Consensus Economics* and are based on surveys of professional forecasters published twice yearly in the spring (March/April) and fall (September/Octo-ber) from 1990 to 2010. An alternative measure of inflation expectations is based on the difference in yields between conventional and inflation-linked bonds (see, for example, Söderlind and Svensson, 1997). However, such yield-based estimates are not widely available for the economies considered in this chapter.

Additional analysis suggests that the response of medium-term expectations is similar for positive and negative inflation surprises. In particular, allowing positive and negative inflation surprises to have different effects by estimating an augmented equation,

$$\Delta E_{it}\pi_{i,t+N} = \alpha + \beta\Delta E_{it}\pi_{it} + \gamma\Delta Positive_{it} + \mu_i + \lambda_t + \nu_{i,t}, \quad (3.16)$$

where the term $\gamma\Delta Positive_{it}$ denotes a *positive* inflation surprise, yields an estimate of coefficient γ that is statistically indistinguishable from zero.

Box 3.1. Inflation in Sub-Saharan Africa during the 2008 Commodity Price Surge

This box focuses on the experience of 31 sub-Saharan African (SSA) economies during the food and fuel price surge of 2008 to highlight potential challenges for policymakers when facing such shocks. We start by considering these economies' broad macroeconomic environment and inflation experience during this period. Drawing on *IMF Staff Reports,* we then examine broad policy responses that help explain the experience of these economies during this price surge. Finally, we summarize the experience of the median SSA economy.

Although in most economies inflation increased during this period, experience varied widely and largely reflected differences in the policy mix rather than the effects of the food price shock itself. These results point to the importance of the policy stance in maintaining stable inflation in low-income countries facing external shocks. We also find that, although food inflation increased considerably for the median African country—accounting for most of the increase in headline inflation—domestic food prices were partially shielded from international prices due to sizable real currency appreciation, differences in food baskets, and the incomplete tradability of food. Spillovers from food and fuel to nonfood, nonfuel inflation were also somewhat limited, suggesting moderate second-round effects.

Structure of Sub-Saharan Economies

The majority of SSA economies have low income levels. The median gross national annual income in our sample was $950 per capita during 2001–05, much less than the median country in the world ($5,200). Because households in these economies tend to be poor, they spend a larger fraction of their income on food—about 50 percent—than do households in middle- and high-income countries (about 30 and 15 percent, respectively). There are, however, considerable variations in both income per capita and the share of expenditure allocated to food (Figure 3.1.1), with some countries (Botswana, Gabon, South Africa) in the middle-income category.

Economic performance in SSA economies is particularly vulnerable to changes in the external

The main authors of this box are Rafael Portillo and Felipe Zanna.

Figure 3.1.1. Income and Food Share in Sub-Saharan Africa

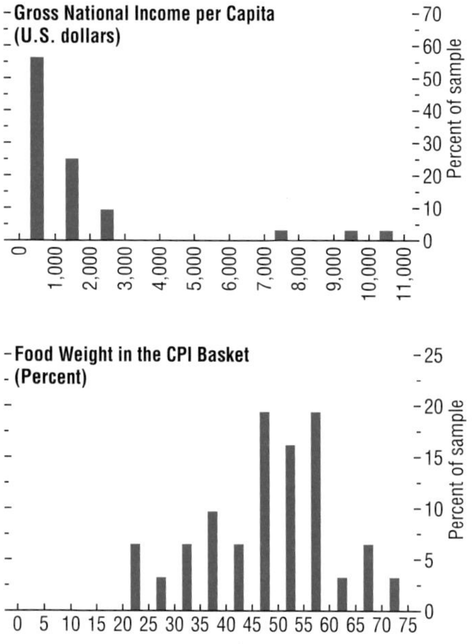

Sources: Haver Analytics; and IMF staff calculations.
Note: CPI = consumer price index.

environment. The region's trade consists primarily of commodities, with many economies specializing in one or two commodities. As net importers of food and fuel, all economies are exposed to large fluctuations in their terms of trade. In addition, access to international capital markets is limited, although countries such as Nigeria, South Africa, and Zambia experience large movements in private capital flows. In addition, most countries rely on official flows, such as grants and concessional loans, and remittances to finance sizable current account deficits.

Although SSA economies have often been subject to episodes of high inflation associated with economic and political instability, the region generally succeeded in stabilizing and reducing inflation during the first half of the 2000s. During this period, fiscal dominance—subordination of monetary policy to fiscal needs—subsided and growth accelerated. The median inflation rate in the region stood at 6

Box 3.1 *(continued)*

Figure 3.1.2. Changes in Inflation in Sub-Saharan Africa, 2007–08

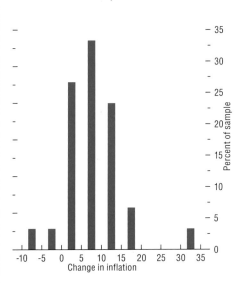

Sources: Haver Analytics; and IMF staff calculations.

percent by mid-2007, compared with 15 percent in 2000. Low inflation was achieved using a variety of monetary and exchange rate policies. About one-third of SSA economies (half our sample) operate hard pegs, of which most are in the CFA franc area. The rest have flexible exchange rate arrangements, ranging from soft pegs to fully floating arrangements. In the latter, central bank intervention in foreign exchange markets is common. Most countries with managed floats target monetary aggregates, although with considerable flexibility, and some can be considered to be practicing "inflation targeting light." In particular, although they target inflation, they do not have the institutional framework to formally adopt inflation targeting.[1]

---

[1]See Carare and Stone (2003). South Africa is a full-fledged inflation targeter, and Ghana is formally transitioning to inflation targeting.

Inflation during the 2008 Food Price Surge

Although inflation in SSA economies generally increased during the 2008 commodity price surge, there was a broad range of experience. Figure 3.1.2 illustrates this range using a histogram of the change in inflation in SSA economies between September 2007 and September 2008.

The variation in food and nonfood inflation was associated with a number of policy variables and economic features. In particular, as Table 3.1.1 shows, economies that reduced taxes on food or introduced export bans or quotas experienced smaller increases in food prices. The relationship between these policies and nonfood inflation was less clear. In addition, economies with lower income levels faced larger increases in food inflation, possibly because they could not afford the fiscal measures that would have offset the short-term effects of world food prices on domestic food prices.

The case of Madagascar illustrates the role of policy. Rice is the most important item in the food basket in Madagascar (15 percent of total consumption, and 55 to 70 percent of the daily caloric intake of households). As international prices increased in 2008, domestic prices—measured in U.S. dollars—stayed broadly constant (Figure 3.1.3). The government intervened actively in the rice market, imposing a suspension of rice exports in April and lowering value-added taxes on rice in the second half of the year, at an estimated budgetary cost of 0.3 percent of GDP.[2] In addition, the gap between domestic production and consumption in 2008 was closed by means of imports at preferential prices.

IMF Staff Reports shed light on these factors. These reports suggest that the policy responses and outcomes fall into three broad categories:

- Economies where increases in food and fuel inflation account for most of the inflation dynamics: Economies in this group include most of the CFA franc area countries that are not oil exporters (Benin, Burkina Faso, Cape Verde, Central African Republic, Comoros, Guinea-Bissau, Mali, Togo) as well as some with managed floats (Uganda, Mozambique). In these countries

---

[2]See IMF (2008).

Box 3.1 *(continued)*

Table 3.1.1. Variations in Inflation: Sub-Saharan Africa

Index of Measures Implemented	Correlation with Food Inflation	Changes in Macroeconomic Variables	Correlation with Food Inflation
Reduction in Taxes	−0.32	Government spending (% of GDP)	−0.29
Reduction in Import Tariffs	0.07	Base money growth	−0.05
Subsidies	−0.09	Broad money growth	0.06
Transfers	0.09	Credit growth	0.45
Export Bans/Quotas	−0.34	Current account (% of GDP)	−0.12
Price Controls	−0.03	Reserves accumulation	0.11
Structural Features		**Fuel prices**	0.13
Food Weight	−0.15		
Degree of Openness	−0.12		
Gross National Income per Capita	−0.53		

Source: IMF staff calculations.

nonfood, nonfuel inflation did not increase, partly because inflation expectations were better anchored. (Uganda has a track record of low inflation, while historically fixed parity with the euro has kept inflation low in the CFA franc area.) In some CFA franc countries, monetary policy tightened endogenously as these countries faced pressures on the balance of payments— partly due to their status as food importers—and lost reserves during this period. Note that, in spite of the solid anchor, CFA franc countries experienced very large increases in food and fuel inflation, consistent with large pass-through of international prices to domestic prices. The policy response in Uganda and Mozambique was different, however: money targets were relaxed and interest rates stayed broadly constant.

- Economies with expansionary macroeconomic policies: These economies experienced high or accelerating inflation during both 2007 and 2008, partly because of rising food inflation but also because of aggregate demand pressures and a loose policy mix. In some cases (Angola, Gabon, Nigeria), the aggregate demand pressures reflected an expansionary fiscal policy driven by higher oil revenues. In others (Kenya, Nigeria, Rwanda, Tanzania), the aggregate demand expansion reflected a combination of higher aid-financed government spending with unsterilized accumulation of reserves.[3] Many of these economies had higher public wage bills. With the exception of

[3]This policy combination is often referred to as "spending but not absorbing" the aid (see Berg and others, 2010).

Figure 3.1.3. Rice Price, Madagascar
(U.S. dollars a kilogram)

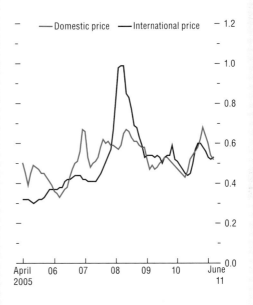

Source: IMF staff calculations.

Angola and, to a lesser extent, Nigeria, fuel prices were also increasing, suggesting possible fuel-driven inflation pressures.

- Economies that monetize debt: These are the countries with the highest inflation increases (about 20 to 30 percent), reflecting generalized price pressures—that is, very large increases in both food and nonfood prices. Unlike the previous group, the inflationary spike resulted from the complete subordination of monetary policy to

Box 3.1 *(continued)*

fiscal needs during this period. The Democratic Republic of Congo and Ethiopia fall into this category.

In sum, the cross-country experience suggests that, although all economies faced the same international commodity price shock, the policy stance helped shape the specific outcomes.

Inflation in the Median SSA Economy

Having discussed the variation across economies, we now summarize the experience of the median SSA economy during the 2008 commodity price surge. Given the large weight of food in consumer expenditures, a hefty increase in domestic food prices was to be expected in low-income countries (first-round effects). Nonfood inflation could also be expected to rise sharply due to higher fuel prices and potential spillovers from food to nonfood prices (second-round effects).

The experience of the median SSA economy provides evidence of first-round effects. In particular, as Table 3.1.2 shows, by September 2008—the month prices increased the most—food inflation had increased by 9.4 percentage points (from 6.4 percent to 15.8 percent) relative to the previous year. The increase, although large, was considerably smaller than the increase over the same period in the inflation rate in U.S. dollars of an index of internationally traded food commodities (29.3 percent). Two factors account for this large discrepancy. First, the median SSA economy experienced a nominal exchange rate appreciation of 9.3 percentage points against the U.S. dollar. This reduced, by one-third, the local currency equivalent of international food

inflation—that is, "imported" food inflation. Second, because baskets are different and the law of one price does not hold perfectly for all commodities, slightly less than half the increase in imported food inflation was passed through to domestic food prices. As discussed above in the case of Madagascar, government intervention is one reason for incomplete pass-through in this region.[4]

Table 3.1.2 also looks at changes in the domestic relative price of food for the median African economy—that is, it adjusts for headline inflation. We observe a broadly similar pattern, except that pass-through from international prices is now smaller. Just as the nominal appreciation helped dampen the effect on domestic food inflation, the real appreciation in 2008 also helped reduce the effect on the domestic relative price of food. Note that the real appreciation is consistent both with an improved external environment and with recent work on the macroeconomic adjustment to imported food prices—which emphasizes appreciation of the CPI-based real exchange rate in countries where the share of food in consumption is large.[5]

As Table 3.1.3 indicates, most of the increase in inflation observed during this period is the result of higher food prices. However, nonfood prices also increased by 2.9 percentage points. To assess whether the increase in nonfood prices reflects fuel prices or second-round effects of higher food prices, we estimate the direct and indirect effects of higher fuel prices on nonfood prices. The direct effect is given by the share of fuel in nonfood consumption expenditure—which we calibrate at 3 to 4 percent—whereas the indirect effect is given by the share of fuel in nonfood production—which we calibrate at 5 to 6 percent.[6] Because fuel prices in the median economy increased by 20 percent during this period, our calibration suggests that nonfood prices should have increased by 1.6 to 2 percentage points, which accounts for most of the 2.9 percentage point

Table 3.1.2. Food Inflation Dynamics

(percentage points, median sub-Saharan African economy, 2007–08)

	September 2007	September 2008
Domestic Inflation	6.4	15.8
International Inflation	7.3	36.6
Nominal Exchange Rate Depreciation	–6.0	–15.3
Imported Inflation	1.3	21.3
Change in Domestic Relative Price	0.2	3.7
Change in International Relative Price	4.6	31.6
Real Exchange Rate Depreciation	–5.4	–18.9
Change in Imported Relative Price	–0.7	12.7

Source: IMF staff calculations.

[4]Relative to 2008, the spike in commodity prices that started in 2010 and peaked in April 2011 appears, thus far, to have had a smaller effect on inflation.

[5]See Catão and Chang (2010).

[6]The calibration is based on the input-output tables for Uganda and the share of fuel in production in economies that do not produce oil.

Box 3.1 *(continued)*

Table 3.1.3. Inflation Dynamics
(percentage points, median sub-Saharan African economy, 2007–08)

	September 2007	September 2008
Food Inflation	6.4	15.8
Nonfood Inflation	4.9	7.8
Headline Inflation	6.2	12.1

Source: IMF staff calculations.
Note: median food weight = 0.51.

increase observed during this period. In sum, there appears to be little evidence of large second-round effects from food inflation to nonfood inflation.

An analysis by exchange rate regime finds a similar pattern but with interesting differences. Starting from a low base in mid-2007 (1.7 percent inflation), economies with hard pegs experienced larger increases in inflation (10 percent), mostly on account of food. Managed floats, on the other hand, experienced smaller increases in inflation (6 per-

cent), but starting from a higher base (8 percent). Note that the increase in inflation in hard pegs occurred despite a larger nominal appreciation vis-à-vis the U.S. dollar (9 percent versus 3.4 percent in managed floats), because these economies' exchange rates are fixed to the euro. The larger increase in inflation therefore reflects a larger pass-through of international prices.

What accounts for the relative stability of non-food inflation? As Table 3.1.4 indicates, the macroeconomic environment was broadly neutral during this period. There was a small increase in government spending. On the monetary front, there was a small increase in the growth rate of monetary aggregates; money targets were missed in eight countries for which there are data; and nominal interest rates stayed constant—all of which is broadly consistent with an accommodation of first-round effects.

Table 3.1.4. Macroeconomic Environment: Sub-Saharan Africa
(percent unless noted otherwise)

Macroeconomic Variables	Government Spending (% of GDP)	Base Money Growth	Broad Money Growth	Credit Growth	Current Account (% of GDP)	Reserves Accumulation (% of GDP)	Policy Rates
Median Change	0.3	1.0	1.0	3.8	−2.2	−0.9	0.6

Source: IMF staff calculations.

Box 3.2. Food Price Swings and Monetary Policy in Open Economies

This box examines the trade-offs facing monetary policymakers in small open economies following swings in world food inflation. The discussion focuses on emerging and developing economies where the share of food in the consumption basket is not only sizable in absolute terms but also is larger than that of the country's main trading partners. This implies that rises in global food inflation tend to increase domestic inflation as well as appreciate the real exchange rate. As monetary policymakers formulate their response to these developments, they need to keep in mind the important trade-offs between stabilizing inflation, consumption, and output.[1]

This box argues that these trade-offs depend on three main factors: first, whether the country is a net food exporter or importer; second, whether the country is more or less financially integrated with the rest of the world; and third, whether the country has some market power in its export markets. The conclusion is that monetary policy trade-offs are particularly acute for net food importers, but much less so if they are highly integrated with world capital markets or have some market power in their export markets.

Food Exporters

Net food exporters, facing a rise in world food prices, will also experience a terms-of-trade improvement. This tends to raise output and consumption. Given the high food consumption share, consumer price index (CPI) inflation will also rise and by more than in trading partners, thus inducing a real exchange rate appreciation. Therefore, the terms of trade and the real effective exchange rate will tend to move in the same direction (Figure 3.2.1). In this case, the central bank can help stabilize both inflation and the output gap by tightening monetary policy. This is because monetary policy tightening

This box was prepared by Luis Catão and is based largely on Catão and Chang (2010).

[1]The analysis assumes that monetary policy can influence real economic activity and the real exchange rate due to price and wage rigidities. Theoretically, if prices and wages were fully flexible, goods and factor markets integrated and fully competitive, and capital markets frictionless, monetary policy intervention would have no real effects.

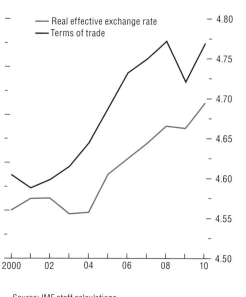

Figure 3.2.1. Net Commodity Exporters, 2000–10
(Percent)

Source: IMF staff calculations.

induces nominal exchange rate appreciation, helping stabilize both food prices in domestic currency and domestic food output.[2] If, however, there are significant real wage rigidities, wage costs may rise in tandem with (or even overreact to) food price inflation, putting pressure on costs, and trade-offs between output and inflation stabilization will arise.[3]

Food Importers

By contrast, for net food importers facing a rise in world food prices, stabilizing the domestic inflation rate poses a starker trade-off. Take, for example, the case of a country that exports tourism services and imports most of its food—the latter being an important input for the production of its

[2]Such a circumstance, in which the inflation and output stabilization objectives do not conflict with each other, has been labeled "divine coincidence" by Blanchard and Galí (2007).

[3]It has been argued, however, that such real wage rigidities are less prevalent in emerging and developing economies than in advanced economies.

Box 3.2 *(continued)*

services. Here, a rise in world food prices entails a worsening of the terms of trade and pushes up costs, thereby reducing disposable income and adversely affecting domestic output and consumption. At the same time, given the high food consumption share, the world food price rise implies higher CPI inflation. Unlike in the case of net food exporters, the terms of trade and the real exchange rate will tend to move in opposite directions, as illustrated in Figure 3.2.2. Monetary tightening aimed at stabilizing inflation will tend to appreciate the nominal exchange rate. Although this may help reduce domestic cost pressures, it will also tend to further appreciate the real exchange rate, decreasing competitiveness and dampening output beyond the deterioration in the country's terms of trade. Overall, in these economies, there is no divine coincidence, and policymakers must face the trade-off between stabilizing inflation and economic activity.[4]

At the same time, for net food importers, the negative effects on economic activity from monetary policy tightening in response to food price increases can be mitigated by three factors: the positive effect of the ensuing currency appreciation on output by dampening imported input costs, a "terms-of-trade externality" effect resulting from the same nominal appreciation, and international financial integration.

The first cost-reducing effect is straightforward.

The second is more subtle: a rise in interest rates and the ensuing currency appreciation can improve an economy's terms of trade if it has strong market power in its export markets. An example of this would be an economy that produces a relatively unique service, such as tourism, for which foreign demand is relatively insensitive to the price. Here, as a consequence of the nominal appreciation induced by monetary policy tightening, the foreign currency price of the economy's exports rises, implying a positive effect on the terms of trade (terms-of-trade externality), which will cushion the initial fall in output and consumption.

[4]These economies also correspond to the "worst sufferer" case modeled in Catão and Chang (2010).

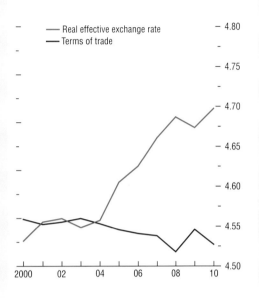

Figure 3.2.2. Net Commodity Importers, 2000–10
(Percent)

Source: IMF staff calculations.

The third factor is the degree of capital market integration: the more able the economy is to borrow abroad to smooth the shock, the less the fall in domestic consumption, and so the smaller the effect of monetary policy tightening on consumption and, ultimately, on domestic demand. Conversely, the greater the international capital market imperfections facing this economy, and the smaller its market power over what it produces and exports, the stronger the case for some accommodation of the food price shock. This prevents an overly tight monetary policy from exacerbating the adverse effects of the food price shock on the terms of trade and hence on output.[5] One way to achieve this in practice is to place a higher weight on the output gap in the monetary policy reaction function in these types of economies.

[5]See Frankel (2011) for a discussion of alternative monetary policy rules for small open economies with incomplete capital markets.

References

Alichi, Ali, Huigang Chen, Kevin Clinton, Charles Freedman, Marianne Johnson, Ondra Kamenik, Turgut Kisinbay, and Douglas Laxton, 2009, "Inflation Targeting under Imperfect Policy Credibility," IMF Working Paper 09/94 (Washington: International Monetary Fund).

Barro, Robert J., and David B. Gordon, 1983, "Rules, Discretion and Reputation in a Model of Monetary Policy," *Journal of Monetary Economics,* Vol. 12 (July), pp. 101–21.

Berg, Andrew, Tokhir Mirzoev, Rafael Portillo, and Luis-Felipe Zanna, 2010, "The Short-Run Macroeconomics of Aid Flows: Understanding the Interaction of Fiscal and Reserve Policy," IMF Working Paper 10/65 (Washington: International Monetary Fund).

Blanchard, Olivier, and Jordi Galí, 2007, "Real Wage Rigidities and the New Keynesian Model," *Journal of Money, Credit and Banking*, Vol. 39 (s1), pp. 35–65.

Brischetto, Andrea, and Anthony Richards, 2007, "The Performance of Timed Mean Measures of Underlying Inflation," presented at the Conference on Price Measurement for Monetary Policy, May 24–25, jointly sponsored by the Federal Reserve Banks of Cleveland and Dallas. http://dallasfed.org/news/research/2007/07price_brischetto.pdf.

Bryan, Michael F., and Stephen G. Cecchetti, 1993, "Measuring Core Inflation," NBER Working Paper No. 4303 (Cambridge, Massachusetts: National Bureau of Economic Research). http://ssrn.com/abstract=246875.

Carare, Alina, and Mark Stone, 2003, "Inflation Targeting Regimes," IMF Working Paper 03/9 (Washington: International Monetary Fund).

Catão, Luis, and Roberto Chang, 2010, "World Food Prices and Monetary Policy," NBER Working Paper No. 16563 (Cambridge, Massachusetts: National Bureau of Economic Research).

Central Bank of Egypt, *Annual Report* 2009/2010 (Cairo), p. A, footnote 40.

Cogley, Timothy, 2002, "A Simple Adaptive Measure of Core Inflation," *Journal of Money, Credit and Banking,* Vol. 34 (February), pp. 94–113.

Frankel, Jeffrey, 2011, "A Comparison of Monetary Anchor Options, Including Product Price Targeting for Commodity-Exporters in Latin America," *Economia* (May 7).

Gilbert, Christopher, 2010, "How to Understand High Food Prices," *Journal of Agricultural Economics,* No. 61, pp. 31–60.

Gilchrist, Simon, and Masashi Saito, 2006, "Expectations, Asset Prices, and Monetary Policy: The Role of Learning," NBER Working Paper No. 12442 (Cambridge, Massachusetts: National Bureau of Economic Research).

Groen, Jan J.J., and Paolo A. Pesenti, 2011, "Commodity Prices, Commodity Currencies, and Global Economic Developments," in *Commodity Prices and Markets, East Asia Seminar on Economics*, Vol. 20 (Chicago: University of Chicago Press), pp. 15–42.

Helbling and Roach, 2011, "Rising Prices on the Menu," *Finance and Development*, Vol. 48, No. 1 (March).

Ilzetzki, Ethan O., Carmen M. Reinhart, and Kenneth S. Rogoff, 2008, "Exchange Rate Arrangements into the 21st Century: Will the Anchor Currency Hold?" (unpublished; Cambridge, Massachusetts: Harvard University).

International Monetary Fund, 2008, "Republic of Madagascar—Fourth Review Under the Three-Year Arrangement Under the Poverty Reduction and Growth Facility and Requests for Waiver of Performance Criteria, Modification of Performance Criteria, and Augmentation of Access" (Washington).

Levin, Andrew T., Fabio M. Natalucci, and Jeremy M. Piger, 2004, "The Macroeconomic Effects of Inflation Targeting," *Federal Reserve Bank of St. Louis Review*, Vol. 86 (July/August), pp. 51–80.

Organization for Economic Cooperation and Development, 2005, "Measuring and Assessing Underlying Inflation," *OECD Economic Outlook* (June), pp. 270–90.

Pasaogullari, Mehmet, and Simeon Tsonev, 2008, "The Term Structure of Inflation Compensation in the Nominal Yield Curve," Job Market Paper (unpublished; New York: Columbia University). www.csef.it/seminarpdf/Pasaogullari.pdf.

Roach, Shaun, 2011, "Do Commodity Futures Help Predict Spot Prices?" (unpublished; Washington: International Monetary Fund).

Roger, Scott, 1997, "A Robust Measure of Core Inflation in New Zealand, 1949–96," Reserve Bank of New Zealand Discussion Paper No. G97/7 (Wellington: Reserve Bank of New Zealand). www.rbnz.govt.nz/research/discusspapers/g97_7.pdf.

———, 2010, "Inflation Targeting Turns 20," *Finance and Development*, Vol. 47, No. 1 (March).

Sherwin, Murray, 1999, "Inflation Targeting: 10 Years On," speech to the New Zealand Association of Economists Conference, Rotrua (July 1). www.rbnz.govt.nz/speeches/0077458.html.

Söderlind, Paul, and Lars Svensson, 1997, "New Techniques to Extract Market Expectations from Financial Instruments," *Journal of Monetary Economics*, Vol. 40, No. 2, pp. 383–429.

Southgate, Douglas, 2007, "Population Growth, Increases in Agricultural Production and Trends in Food Prices," *Electronic Journal of Sustainable Development*, Vol. 1, No. 3.

Stevens, Glenn, 1999, "Six Years of Inflation Targeting," Address by Mr. G.R. Stevens, Assistant Governor, Reserve Bank of Australia, to the Economic Society of Australia, Sydney (April 20). www.rba.gov.au/publications/bulletin/1999/may/pdf/bu-0599-2.pdf.

Walsh, James P., 2011, "Reconsidering the Role of Food Prices in Inflation," IMF Working Paper 11/71 (Washington: International Monetary Fund).

Woodford, Michael, 2003, *Interest and Prices* (Princeton, New Jersey: Princeton University Press).

SEPARATED AT BIRTH? THE TWIN BUDGET AND TRADE BALANCES

How do changes in taxes and government spending affect an economy's external balance? Based on a historical analysis of documented fiscal policy changes and on model simulations, this chapter finds that the current account responds substantially to fiscal policy—a fiscal consolidation of 1 percent of GDP typically improves an economy's current account balance by over a half percent of GDP. This comes about not only through lower imports due to a decline in domestic demand but also from a rise in exports due to a weakening currency. When the nominal exchange rate is fixed or the scope for monetary stimulus is limited, the current account adjusts by as much, but the adjustment is more painful: economic activity contracts more and the real exchange rate depreciates through domestic wage and price compression. When economies tighten fiscal policies simultaneously, what matters for the current account is how much an economy consolidates relative to others. Looking ahead, the differing magnitudes of fiscal adjustment plans across the world will help lower imbalances within the euro area and reduce emerging Asia's external surpluses. The relative lack of permanent consolidation measures in the United States suggests that fiscal policy will contribute little to lessening the U.S. external deficit.

Fiscal adjustment will be one of the primary forces shaping the contours of the postcrisis global economy. Large deficits and weak output growth in the aftermath of the Great Recession have substantially increased public debt levels in many of the advanced economies, highlighting their underlying debt sustainability problems. In response to this challenge, fiscal consolidation plans in the G7 advanced economies are large—averaging close to 4 percent of GDP between 2010 and 2016—and are quite varied, ranging from about 2½ percent of GDP in Germany to over 7 percent of GDP in the United Kingdom. In emerging and developing economies, which were not as adversely affected by

the crisis and are recovering faster, governments are planning to consolidate over the coming years in order to rebuild fiscal room and, in some cases, to head off overheating pressures.

Chapter 3 of the October 2010 *World Economic Outlook* looked at the implications of fiscal consolidation for output and came to some sobering conclusions. It found that fiscal consolidation typically reduces output and raises unemployment in the short term. In addition, consolidation is likely to be more painful if it occurs simultaneously across many economies and if monetary policy is not in a position to offset the negative effects on economic activity.

This chapter continues this research agenda, this time focusing on a different question: What implications will fiscal adjustment in various economies have for their external balances? In economies with twin fiscal and external deficits, such as the United States and some economies in the euro area, policymakers may be hoping that fiscal consolidation that addresses public debt sustainability concerns will also help bring down large external deficits. On the other hand, economies with large external surpluses, such as China, Germany, and Japan, may be concerned that fiscal consolidation will exacerbate their surpluses.

We attempt to shed light on this issue by addressing the following questions:

- How much does public sector adjustment affect external adjustment? This is closely related to the famous twin deficits hypothesis—the notion that a change in an economy's fiscal balance leads to a change in the same direction in its current account balance.[1]
- In what ways does fiscal adjustment influence the process of external adjustment? Is it simply a

The main authors of this chapter are Abdul Abiad (team leader), John Bluedorn, Jaime Guajardo, Michael Kumhof, and Daniel Leigh, with support from Murad Omoev, Katherine Pan, and Andy Salazar. This chapter draws heavily on a background paper by Bluedorn and Leigh (2011).

[1]The twin deficits hypothesis was invoked to help interpret the coincident large fiscal and current account deficits that characterized the United States during the 1980s. Henceforth, the term is used to refer to the potential link between fiscal and external balances, even though the analysis is not limited to deficit episodes.

matter of reduced public sector demand resulting in lower imports, or is there more to it? What happens to exports, the real exchange rate, and private saving and investment?

- How does the global environment—including characteristics that are particularly relevant at present, such as low global interest rates and synchronized fiscal adjustment across economies—shape the link between fiscal and external adjustment? How much will the fiscal adjustment currently planned and under way in various economies affect the constellation of current accounts around the world, and within regions such as the euro area?

A standard prediction of many textbook models is that fiscal consolidation leads to greater national saving and thus improves the current account. A number of empirical studies, however, find only a small effect from fiscal policy on the current account. In the literature survey by Abbas and others (2011), a majority of studies find that a 1 percent of GDP fiscal consolidation improves the current account balance by 0.1 to 0.4 percent of GDP.[2]

Because fiscal and current account balances move for many reasons, the key challenge for any empirical analysis is to identify the causal effect of fiscal policy on the current account. Two main problems complicate this task. First, both the fiscal balance and the current account balance respond to common factors, such as business cycle fluctuations. Second, governments may adjust fiscal policy in response to economic developments that affect the external balance, raising concerns about reverse causality. To deal with these pitfalls, one needs to isolate movements in the fiscal balance that are not responses to current account changes or to common factors. Then, any relationship between such fiscal changes and the external balance will represent the causal effect of fiscal policy on the current account. A conventional approach to isolating such fiscal policy changes is to identify them using a statistical concept, such as the change in the cyclically adjusted budget balance. As

this chapter explains, this is an imperfect measure of actual policy actions. Furthermore, such methods can bias the results against finding evidence of a twin deficits link.

We use an alternative approach to address these problems. Specifically, we examine historical documents to identify fiscal policy changes that are explicitly not a response either to business cycle fluctuations or to the current account. Our starting point is the data set of action-based fiscal consolidations in advanced economies over the past 30 years, developed for Chapter 3 of the October 2010 *World Economic Outlook*, which we update to include fiscal expansions. We then use this data set for a statistical analysis of the short- and medium-term effects of fiscal policy on the current account. This is complemented by simulations using the IMF's Global Integrated Monetary and Fiscal Model (GIMF) that allow us to explore issues that rarely arose in the past, such as the effect of the globally synchronized fiscal consolidation in progress today.

The main findings of the chapter are the following:

- Fiscal policy has a substantial and long-lasting effect on external balances. A fiscal consolidation of 1 percent of GDP results in an improvement in the current account of over a half percent of GDP within two years—an effect larger than found in most other studies using conventional approaches—and this persists into the medium term.
- The improvement in the current account following a fiscal consolidation comes not only through lower import volumes resulting from a decline in domestic demand but also from an increase in export volumes as a result of a weaker domestic currency.
- The current account adjustment is just as large when the nominal exchange rate is fixed or when monetary policy is constrained, but it is more painful—there is a sharper contraction in economic activity, and real exchange rate depreciation over the medium term occurs through a compression of domestic wages and prices, a process sometimes referred to as "internal devaluation."
- Fiscal consolidations synchronized across a number of economies shrink any improvements in the current accounts because everyone's cur-

---

[2]Studies finding estimates in this range include Alesina, Gruen, and Jones (1991); Bernheim (1988); Bussière, Fratzscher, and Müller (2010); Chinn and Ito (2007); Chinn and Prasad (2003); Gagnon (2011); Gruber and Kamin (2007); Lee and others (2008); and Summers (1986).

rent account cannot rise at the same time. What matters is how much consolidation an economy undertakes relative to other economies.

- Looking ahead, the differing magnitudes of fiscal adjustment plans will help lower imbalances within the euro area and reduce emerging Asia's external surplus. The relative lack of more permanent consolidation measures in the United States suggests that fiscal policy as currently planned will contribute little to bringing down the U.S. external deficit.

The first section of this chapter provides an empirical assessment of the link between fiscal and external adjustment using a historical database of fiscal policy changes. The second section conducts model-based simulations to address additional issues, such as the effect of fiscal policy when monetary policy is constrained and the impact when many economies simultaneously undertake fiscal consolidation. It also quantifies the contributions of planned fiscal adjustments in various economies to current account adjustment around the world. The last section draws some policy implications.

Estimating the Strength of the Twin Deficits Link

This section estimates the effect of fiscal policy on the current account. We start by explaining how we identify changes in fiscal policy from the historical record and how this approach differs from conventional approaches. We then report the estimated effects on the current account and compare the results with those based on a more conventional approach. Finally, we explore the channels through which fiscal adjustment affects external balances.

Identifying Fiscal Policy Changes

At the heart of virtually all empirical studies that estimate the effect of fiscal policy on the current account balance lies a key challenge: identifying deliberate fiscal policy changes. Fluctuations in economic activity would improve the budget balance without any change in policy and would also affect the current account. Therefore, using the change in the overall fiscal balance to measure changes in fiscal policy, as some studies do, would lead to biased

estimates of the effect of fiscal policy on the current account.[3]

A common approach to this challenge is to use the cyclically adjusted primary balance (CAPB) as a measure of the fiscal stance.[4] Cyclical adjustment offers an intuitive way of dealing with the fact that tax revenue and government spending move automatically with the business cycle. The hope is that cyclically adjusted changes in fiscal variables reflect policymakers' decisions to change taxes and spending. However, as discussed in Chapter 3 of the October 2010 *World Economic Outlook*, the conventional approach of using cyclically adjusted fiscal data is far from perfect. Three issues with cyclical adjustment arise that complicate tests of the twin deficits hypothesis:

- Even after cyclical adjustment, the CAPB typically includes nonpolicy factors, which may be correlated with other developments affecting economic activity and the current account.[5] For example, an asset price boom improves the CAPB by increasing capital gains and cyclically adjusted tax revenues. Such was the case in Ireland before the recent crisis. Because these booms raise domestic demand and imports, worsening the current account balance, they tend to generate a negative correlation between the CAPB and the current account, biasing the estimated effect of fiscal policy downward. Other nonpolicy factors can move the CAPB and current account balance in the same direction. For example, a positive terms-of-trade shock could raise cyclically adjusted revenues while improving the current account balance, leading to an upward bias.

- Even if the CAPB contained only discretionary fiscal policy changes, some of these could still be responses to cyclical developments. To the extent

---

[3]Of the 21 studies surveyed in Abbas and others (2011), 13 use the overall fiscal balance as the explanatory variable.

[4]The CAPB is calculated by taking the actual primary balance—noninterest revenue minus noninterest spending—and subtracting the estimated effect of business cycle fluctuations on the fiscal accounts.

[5]For a discussion of how cyclically adjusted fiscal data contain nonpolicy factors correlated with economic activity, see, for example, Guajardo, Leigh, and Pescatori (2011); Romer and Romer (2010); Milesi-Ferretti (2009); Morris and Schuknecht (2007); and Wolswijk (2007).

that domestic booms in economic activity tend to coincide with a worsening current account balance, countercyclical fiscal policies would be associated with a falling current account balance, biasing the estimated effect downward. An example is Denmark in 1986, where the government cut spending and raised taxes to reduce the risk of the economy overheating.

- The CAPB may contain fiscal policy changes that respond directly to external developments. In an economy with rapid import growth and a rising current account deficit, the government might raise taxes or cut government spending in order to restrain domestic demand and help unwind the current account imbalance. Such a discretionary fiscal policy response to developments affecting the current account would be a case of reverse causality and would again tend to generate a negative correlation between the CAPB and the current account, biasing the estimated effect downward. France in 1983 provides such an example, where fiscal policy tightening was motivated by a desire to reduce the current account deficit.

Other approaches also have been used to reduce the endogeneity of the fiscal measure. For example, some studies focus exclusively on government spending to avoid the strong influence of the economic cycle on government revenues. However, to the extent that at least some discretionary changes in government purchases may be motivated by a response to the business cycle, the problem persists.[6]

The Historical Approach to Identifying Fiscal Policy Changes

To address the hazards highlighted above, this chapter uses an alternative approach based on identifying changes in fiscal policy directly from the historical record. This historical approach is similar to that of Romer and Romer (2010) but has been expanded to include multiple economies and to go beyond the tax changes they examine. The starting point is the data set of action-based fiscal consolidations compiled for the October 2010 *World Economic Outlook* and subsequently revised in Devries and others (2011). Based on an analysis of contemporaneous historical records, this data set identifies fiscal consolidations that were not motivated by cyclical or external considerations. The documents used to produce the data set include IMF *Staff Reports* and *Recent Economic Developments*, Organization for Economic Cooperation and Development *Economic Surveys*, central bank reports, and budget documents, among others. Because there is no reason to expect the link between fiscal and external balances to be limited to consolidations, we have enlarged the data set to include fiscal expansions as well.

Based on this approach, we identify tax and spending changes motivated either by a desire to reduce the budget deficit or by some other noncyclical objective, such as higher potential output growth, increased social fairness, limiting the size of government, or external military actions. These types of policy changes are less likely to be systematically correlated with other developments affecting the current account in the short term and are thus valid for estimating the effects of fiscal policy on the current account. Austria in 1996 provides an example of a fiscal policy tightening motivated by budget deficit reduction. Specifically, the authorities cut government spending and raised taxes to meet the budget deficit criteria for European Monetary Union (EMU) accession, based on the 1992 Maastricht Treaty, and not because there was a risk of economic overheating or a desire to improve the current account balance.[7] Canada in 1998 provides an example of fiscal policy easing motivated by long-term considerations rather than cyclical concerns. In particular, tax cuts were part of comprehensive tax reform designed to reduce marginal income tax rates to improve long-term growth, and the additional

---

[6]Furthermore, taking this approach means neglecting the impact of policy changes on the revenue side, which is also of interest to policymakers. Moreover, changes in government spending are often accompanied by changes in taxes and thus cannot be used in isolation to estimate the impact on the current account balance.

[7]As the 1997 *IMF Staff Report* explains (p. 4), "With first-round participation in EMU the top economic priority since EU membership in 1995, the federal government agreed with the social partners and the lower levels of government on a phased two-year consolidation package to reduce the structural deficit."

government spending was motivated primarily by a desire to enhance education and health care.

Although the historical approach addresses the aforementioned problems associated with the conventional approach, both the conventional approach and our approach remain subject to some additional criticisms. In particular, if policymakers postpone fiscal consolidation until the economy recovers, then fiscal consolidations will be associated with favorable economic developments using both the conventional approach and our approach. On the other hand, if fiscal consolidation accelerates in downturns to stay on a desired deficit-reduction track, then the identified fiscal consolidations will be associated with unfavorable economic outcomes using both the conventional approach and our approach. Thus, the overall direction of these potential biases is unclear. Furthermore, to the extent that cyclical motivations behind the timing of policy are reflected in the record, the historical approach will identify and exclude them, minimizing any bias.[8]

For the 17 economies covered over the 1978–2009 period (a total of 544 country-year observations), we identify 291 fiscal policy changes that were not motivated by cyclical or external considerations.[9] Almost two-thirds of the actions are fiscal consolidations. Figure 4.1 shows the incidence of our action-based fiscal consolidations and expansions by year across the economies in the sample. The average fiscal policy change is a fiscal consolidation of 0.4 percent of GDP, and the range of actions runs from a fiscal consolidation of 4.7 percent of GDP to a fiscal expansion of 3.5 percent of GDP.

Figure 4.1. Incidence of Action-Based Fiscal Policy Changes by Year
(Frequency count)

There were 291 fiscal policy changes identified over the past 30 years in advanced economies, of which almost two-thirds were consolidations. The average fiscal policy change is a fiscal consolidation of 0.4 percent of GDP.

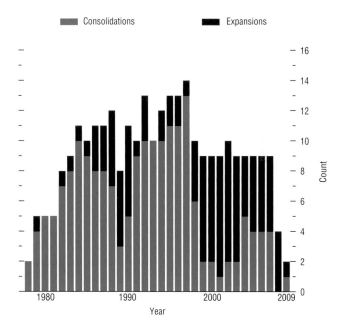

Source: IMF staff calculations.

[8]Both conventional approaches and our historical approach record changes in fiscal policy when they are implemented rather than when they are announced, which ignores the role of anticipation effects highlighted by Ramey (2011). However, as Beetsma, Giuliodori and Klaassen (2008) point out, the role of anticipation effects is likely to be smaller at the annual frequency used here than at the quarterly frequency used by Ramey (2011) and Romer and Romer (2010).

[9]The economies covered include Australia, Austria, Belgium, Canada, Denmark, Finland, France, Germany, Ireland, Italy, Japan, the Netherlands, Portugal, Spain, Sweden, the United Kingdom, and the United States.

Estimated Effects of Fiscal Policy on the Current Account

With these action-based fiscal policy changes in hand, we use straightforward statistical techniques to estimate the effect of fiscal policy on the current account. The methodology is similar to that of Cerra and Saxena (2008) and Romer and Romer (2010), among others. Specifically, we regress changes in the current-account-to-GDP ratio on its lagged values (to capture the normal dynamics of the current account) as well as on contemporaneous and lagged values of our action-based fiscal policy measure, also measured relative to GDP.[10] Including lags allows for fiscal policy changes to work on the current account with a delay. The specification also includes a full set of time fixed effects to account for common shocks, such as shifts in oil prices, and economy-specific fixed effects to account for differences in economies' normal external positions.

Because we want to estimate the *overall* effect of fiscal policy changes on the current account, we do not include possible transmission channels for fiscal policy, such as the exchange rate or the monetary policy rate, as additional explanatory variables in the model. As a general rule, we rely on the exogeneity of the fiscal policy changes identified through the historical approach to deliver unbiased estimates of the causal effect of fiscal policy. This exogeneity allows us to have a minimal specification.[11]

The regression results suggest that fiscal policy changes have effects on the current account that are both large and long-lasting. Figure 4.2 shows that a 1 percent of GDP fiscal consolidation raises the current-account-to-GDP ratio by 0.6 percentage point within two years. After five years, the increase in the current account balance remains over a half percent

of GDP.[12] The finding of a large and long-lasting twin deficits link also survives a variety of robustness tests, including different estimation approaches, alternative specifications, dropping outliers, and distinguishing between types of fiscal policy changes, as reported in Appendix 4.2.

By contrast, using the conventional CAPB-based approach suggests that fiscal consolidation has a much smaller effect.[13] In this case, a fiscal consolidation of 1 percent of GDP raises the current-account-to-GDP ratio by only 0.1 percentage point within two years, with the effect fading over time. This result is broadly consistent with estimates in the literature for advanced economies, suggesting that the bias associated with the conventional approach may be substantial.

Channels for External Adjustment

Having established a strong link between fiscal and external current account balances, this section looks at the ways in which fiscal policy affects the current account. Is it simply a matter of fiscal consolidation reducing domestic demand and imports, or is there more to it? We start by reviewing the effect of fiscal policy on economic activity, thus updating the results presented in Chapter 3 of the October 2010 *World Economic Outlook* using our expanded data set. We then look at the responses of saving and investment, imports and exports, and exchange rates and interest rates. To explore these channels, we use the same statistical model used for the current account, but with these other variables of interest as the dependent variable. We also repeat the analysis for some of the variables using the more conventional CAPB-based approach to shed light on why the estimated effect on the current account is larger using our approach.

---

[10]See Appendix 4.1 for a description of the data sources and construction, and Appendix 4.2 for further details on the estimation methodology and additional robustness tests.

[11]The estimated responses are cumulated to recover the response of the level of the current-account-to-GDP ratio to a permanent 1 percent of GDP fiscal policy change. The figures that follow illustrate the effects of a fiscal consolidation; the effects of a fiscal expansion would be the reverse. In a robustness check in Appendix 4.2, we show that fiscal consolidations and expansions have roughly symmetric effects on the current account. We cannot reject that their magnitudes are identical.

[12]The magnitude of this effect is close to that found by Kumhof and Laxton (2009) in simulations using a calibrated non-Ricardian open economy dynamic stochastic general equilibrium model featuring finitely lived households.

[13]The cyclically adjusted data come from Alesina and Ardagna (2010). We are grateful to the authors for sharing their data.

Economic activity

Fiscal consolidation typically has a contractionary effect on economic activity (Figure 4.3, blue lines).[14] In particular, a fiscal consolidation equal to 1 percent of GDP reduces real output by 0.6 percent of GDP within two years, with a partial recovery over the next few years. Domestic demand contracts by more than 1 percent within two years; this contraction in domestic demand is likely to improve the current account balance through lower import demand and domestic investment.

By contrast, using the conventional CAPB-based approach suggests that fiscal consolidation is typically painless, with output and domestic demand expanding in the short term (Figure 4.3, red lines). In particular, a 1 percent of GDP fiscal consolidation raises output by 0.3 percent within two years, while domestic demand expands by 0.5 percent. However, this result likely reflects the endogenous nature of the CAPB-based measure of the fiscal policy stance, as discussed above.[15] For example, a boom in the stock market improves the CAPB by increasing capital gains and cyclically adjusted tax revenues. Such developments are also likely to be reflected in higher consumption and investment. It is therefore not surprising that the conventional approach finds little evidence of contractionary effects on economic activity.

Saving and investment

Fiscal consolidation improves the current account balance by both lowering investment and raising national saving. As Figure 4.4 shows, a 1 percent of GDP fiscal consolidation tends to raise national saving by 0.35 percent of GDP within three years. Meanwhile, the investment-to-GDP ratio drops by 0.3 percentage point within two years, with a slight rebound thereafter.

---

[14]These results are consistent with those reported in the October 2010 *World Economic Outlook*, based on the earlier data set of 15 countries and without the additional fiscal expansions motivated by noncyclical objectives included in this chapter.

[15]For additional discussion of the differences between the action-based and conventional approaches and the effect of fiscal policy on economic activity, see Guajardo, Leigh, and Pescatori (2011).

Figure 4.2. Effects on the Current Account of a 1 Percent of GDP Fiscal Consolidation
(Percent of GDP)

When fiscal policy changes are identified directly from historical records, the estimated effect on the current account is large and long-lasting. By contrast, estimates obtained using a conventional approach suggest fiscal policy has little effect on the current account.

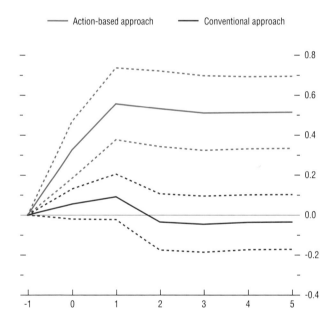

Approach to Identifying Fiscal Policy Changes

——— Action-based approach ——— Conventional approach

Source: IMF staff calculations.

Note: X-axis units are years, where *t* = 0 denotes the year of consolidation. Dashed lines indicate the 90 percent confidence interval around the point estimate. The conventional approach shown here uses changes in the cyclically adjusted primary balance as the measure of change in fiscal policy. The results are broadly similar if the actual change in the overall fiscal balance is used instead. The effect of a fiscal expansion would be the reverse of the response to a consolidation.

Figure 4.3. Effects on Economic Activity of a 1 Percent of GDP Fiscal Consolidation

(Percent)

Fiscal consolidation typically has contractionary effects on output and domestic demand according to our action-based approach. By contrast, using a conventional approach suggests that the opposite is true.

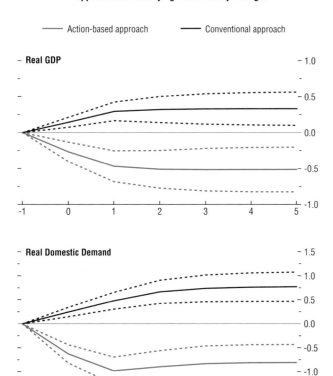

Approach for Identifying Fiscal Policy Changes

—— Action-based approach   —— Conventional approach

Source: IMF staff calculations.

Note: X-axis units are years, where *t* = 0 denotes the year of consolidation. Dashed lines indicate the 90 percent confidence interval around the point estimate. The conventional approach shown here uses changes in the cyclically adjusted primary balance as the measure of change in fiscal policy. The results are broadly similar if the actual change in the overall fiscal balance is used instead. The effect of a fiscal expansion would be the reverse of the response to a consolidation.

As seen in the bottom panel of Figure 4.4, under the CAPB-based approach, investment actually increases in the short term, largely offsetting the increase in national saving associated with fiscal consolidation. Specifically, a 1 percent of GDP fiscal consolidation based on the CAPB is associated with a rise in the investment-to-GDP ratio of 0.3 percentage point within three years. In the short term, the increase in investment is smaller than the rise in national saving, which climbs by 0.4 percentage point within two years—explaining the small improvement in the current account balance. However, this surge in investment likely reflects the endogenous nature of the CAPB-based measure of the fiscal policy stance, as discussed above. It is therefore not surprising that the CAPB-based approach finds little evidence of a twin deficits link.[16]

The stark difference between the estimated effects on investment across the action-based versus the CAPB-based fiscal changes highlights the importance of the fiscal policy identification choice. Henceforth, we focus only on the results using the action-based approach to fiscal policy identification.

Separating the public and private components of saving and investment, we find that public saving rises by 0.6 percent of GDP, whereas public investment declines by about 0.2 percent of GDP (Figure 4.5, top panel). Thus, fiscal policy changes enacted to deliver 1 percent of GDP in fiscal consolidation improve the overall balance by about 0.8 percent of GDP. The improvement in the fiscal balance is not one-for-one for a number of reasons. First, the fiscal consolidation has a detrimental effect on economic activity, with automatic stabilizers offsetting at least part of the budgetary savings. Second, discretionary countercyclical stimulus is sometimes implemented, again offsetting part of the potential gains.[17]

---

[16]The large difference between the responses to the action-based and CAPB-based fiscal changes also applies to the response of the real exchange rate, which *appreciates* in response to a CAPB-based fiscal consolidation but *depreciates* in response to an action-based fiscal consolidation, as discussed below.

[17]An example is Germany in 1982, where the government embarked on consolidation, but economic developments over the course of the year led to the introduction of some countercyclical expansionary measures, reducing the saving achieved from the consolidation package.

The response of private saving and investment to fiscal policy changes is relatively muted. There is a small decline in private saving (Figure 4.5, bottom panel) that only partially offsets the rise in public saving. As a result, national saving rises significantly.[18] Turning to investment, private investment falls in the short term, possibly in response to the weaker economic activity that results from fiscal consolidation. However, this decline in private investment is temporary. By the second year after consolidation, the private-investment-to-GDP ratio rebounds to its level prior to consolidation. Thus, it is the improvement in the public saving-investment gap that drives the improvement in the current account.

Exports, imports, and relative prices

Although the current account improves in response to fiscal consolidation, it might not be viewed favorably if it is simply due to a decline in imports coming from the domestic demand contraction. To see whether this is the case, we examine the behavior of exports and imports of goods and services in response to changes in fiscal policy. As it turns out, the improvement in the current account comes about through *both* higher exports and lower imports. In response to a fiscal consolidation of 1 percent of GDP, export volumes rise by just under 1 percent in the short term, while import volumes fall just over 1 percent (Figure 4.6).[19] Over the medium term, the effect on exports attenuates until it is about a half percent, while that on imports remains above 1 percent.

What is behind this rise in exports and fall in imports? As Figure 4.7 illustrates, an important factor is a shift in the real exchange rate (top-left panel). The real exchange rate depreciates by 1 percent within one year and remains depreciated over the next few years. In the short term, the real depreciation is driven entirely by nominal depreciation (top-right panel). Over the medium term, the real value of the currency stays low because domestic

---

[18]This provides evidence against Ricardian equivalence, which posits that an increase in government saving is fully offset by a fall in private saving in response to lower anticipated future taxes.

[19]When expressed in *percent of GDP*, the improvement in the current account is driven primarily by the rise in exports.

Figure 4.4. Effects on Saving and Investment of a 1 Percent of GDP Fiscal Consolidation

(Percent of GDP)

The current account adjustment in response to fiscal consolidation occurs through both an increase in saving and a fall in investment. Conventional approaches to measuring fiscal policy changes find a rise in investment following a consolidation, which offsets the rise in saving and reduces the effect on the current account.

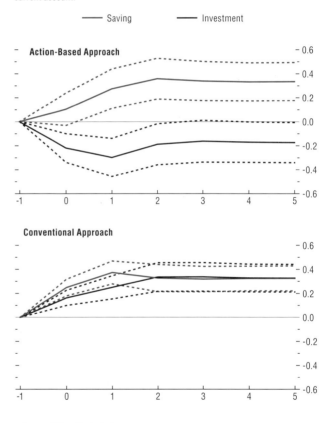

Source: IMF staff calculations.
Note: X-axis units are years, where *t* = 0 denotes the year of consolidation. Dashed lines indicate the 90 percent confidence interval around the point estimate. The conventional approach shown here uses changes in the cyclically adjusted primary balance as the measure of change in fiscal policy. The results are broadly similar if the actual change in the overall fiscal balance is used instead. Fiscal policy changes are action-based. The effect of a fiscal expansion would be the reverse of the response to a consolidation.

Figure 4.5. Effects on the Composition of Saving and Investment of a 1 Percent of GDP Fiscal Consolidation
(Percent of GDP)

Fiscal consolidation is associated with a rise in public saving and a fall in public investment. The response of private saving and investment to fiscal policy changes is relatively muted.

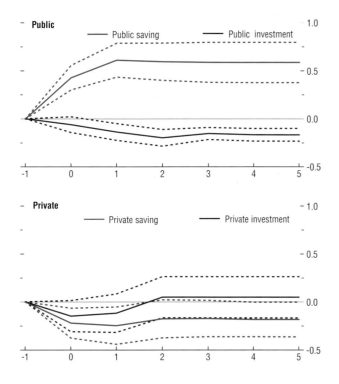

Source: IMF staff calculations.
Note: X-axis units are years, where *t* = 0 denotes the year of consolidation. Dashed lines indicate the 90 percent confidence interval around the point estimate. Fiscal policy changes are action-based. The effect of a fiscal expansion would be the reverse of the response to a consolidation.

relative prices decline (middle-left panel).[20] This is evident in the decline of the domestic price vis-à-vis trading partners and especially in the decline of unit labor costs (middle-right panel). This shift in relative prices likely supports the rise in export volumes following a fiscal consolidation. Interestingly, the estimated responses of exports and imports are broadly consistent with those implied by the estimated shift in the real exchange rate and standard trade elasticities.[21] One factor that might contribute to a weaker currency is the fall in interest rates (bottom panels). Both the short-term policy rate and the long-term rate (measured here by 10-year government bond yields) decline by about 10 basis points. This is similar to the interest rate responses seen in a standard dynamic general equilibrium model (Clinton and others, 2010).

What Happens When Monetary Policy and Exchange Rates Are Constrained?

The evidence presented above suggests that a key mechanism underlying the twin deficits link is a real depreciation of the exchange rate. Usually, this occurs mainly through a fall in the nominal value of the currency. But how does the current account respond to fiscal policy changes if the nominal exchange rate cannot respond and monetary policy is constrained? Is the result a smaller current account response?

To shed light on how the twin deficits link changes when the nominal exchange rate and monetary policy are constrained, we compare the behavior of the current account under pegged and nonpegged exchange rate regimes.[22] For pegged exchange rate regimes,

[20]The relative price is defined as the ratio between the consumer price index (CPI)-based real effective exchange rate and the nominal effective exchange rate. It captures the difference between domestic prices and trade-weighted average prices in trading partners.

[21]For example, Bayoumi and Faruqee (1998, p. 32) report that, within two years, a 1 percent real depreciation should raise exports by 0.7 percent and reduce imports by 0.9 percent, all else equal. In our sample, the estimated impact of fiscal consolidation is a real depreciation of 1 percent. The conventional elasticities would thus imply an impact on exports and imports of 0.7 percent and –0.9 percent, respectively, close to our estimated effects.

[22]See Appendix 4.1 for a description of the exchange rate regime indicator.

without exiting the peg, neither changes in monetary policy in response to economy-specific developments nor nominal exchange rate depreciation is possible. The results suggest that the effect of fiscal consolidation on the current account remains large even for economies with pegged exchange rate regimes (Figure 4.8, top panel). The estimated effect of a 1 percent of GDP fiscal consolidation on the current account within two years is a half percent of GDP for the pegged exchange rate sample, which levels off to slightly less than a half percent of GDP in subsequent years.

If monetary policy is constrained and the nominal exchange rate cannot adjust, how is the external adjustment accomplished? The remaining panels in Figure 4.8 show that in the pegged exchange rate subsample, fiscal consolidation results in a more pronounced and persistent compression of domestic prices. This leads to a depreciation of the real exchange rate, even without any nominal depreciation. Such cost compression, sometimes referred to as "internal devaluation," is also visible in the larger decline in unit labor costs. The compression of domestic prices vis-à-vis trading partners helps support the current account improvement over the medium term.

Insights from Model-Based Simulations

The previous section analyzed historical episodes of fiscal consolidation to assess the effects of fiscal policy on external balances. However, historical analysis can draw only on patterns that have been seen before; it cannot fully address issues that are relevant today but that rarely arose in the past, such as the zero lower bound on nominal interest rates. Therefore, to complement the empirical analysis, this section examines the twin deficits link in the controlled "laboratory" setting of the Global Integrated Monetary and Fiscal Model (GIMF), a dynamic general equilibrium model designed to simulate the effects of fiscal and monetary policy changes.[23]

---

[23]For a description of the theoretical structure of the GIMF, see Appendix 4.3 and Kumhof and others (2010). Kumhof and Laxton (2009) and Clinton and others (2010) examine the effects of fiscal consolidation on external balances using the GIMF. As those papers report, GIMF simulations produce results for the effect of fiscal policy on the current account that are in line with those reported in the previous section of this chapter.

Figure 4.6. Effects on Export and Import Volumes of a 1 Percent of GDP Fiscal Consolidation

(Percent)

Import volumes fall and export volumes rise following a fiscal consolidation.

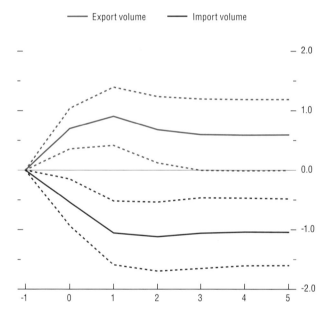

Source: IMF staff calculations.
Note: X-axis units are years, where *t* = 0 denotes the year of consolidation. Dashed lines indicate the 90 percent confidence interval around the point estimate. Fiscal policy changes are action-based. The effect of a fiscal expansion would be the reverse of the response to a consolidation.

Figure 4.7. Effects on Exchange Rates, Prices, and Interest Rates of a 1 Percent of GDP Fiscal Consolidation

Behind the rise in net exports is a shift in the real exchange rate, driven by nominal depreciation and a decline in domestic relative prices. Interest rates tend to decline.

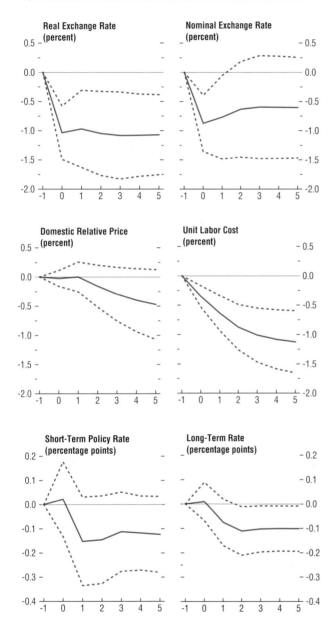

Source: IMF staff calculations.

Note: X-axis units are years, where $t = 0$ denotes the year of consolidation. Dashed lines indicate the 90 percent confidence interval around the point estimate. The nominal and real exchange rates are indices of trade-weighted bilateral exchange rates (effective exchange rates). The domestic relative price is the difference between home and foreign price levels. Fiscal policy changes are action-based. The effect of a fiscal expansion would be the reverse of the response to a consolidation.

In particular, we explore the following questions:

- How do the effects of fiscal consolidation change when nominal interest rates are near zero and can fall no further?
- How do the effects change when many economies simultaneously undertake fiscal consolidations of comparable magnitudes?
- How much will the varied fiscal adjustments being undertaken and planned in various economies affect the constellation of current accounts around the world and within regions such as the euro area?

External Adjustment When Monetary Policy Is Constrained

Since the onset of the Great Recession, short-term interest rates in the largest advanced economies have been near zero. Yet, of the historical episodes considered above, only those of Japan since the 1990s occurred in an environment of near-zero interest rates. In the other episodes, interest rate cuts were possible and typically followed fiscal consolidation.

Therefore, to illustrate the effects of fiscal consolidation on external balances when interest rates are near zero and can fall no further, we use model simulations. In particular, we examine what happens when a small open economy, which we calibrate to fit the main features of Canada, implements fiscal consolidation with and without constrained monetary policy. The consolidation considered here is a reduction in the deficit equivalent to 1 percent of GDP, composed entirely of spending cuts.[24]

The results suggest the following:

- When the interest rate is free to move, the improvement of the current account in response to consolidation is about a half percent of GDP after two years (Figure 4.9, top panel, blue line).[25] This response is similar to the estimates from the empirical analysis in the previous section. Furthermore, the mechanisms at work in the model are

[24]Specifically, three-quarters of the spending cuts fall on government consumption, with the rest falling on government investment. As seen in Appendix 4.3, the effects on the current account are similar when the adjustment is implemented using different fiscal instruments.

[25]In the model, when monetary policy is unconstrained, it follows a Taylor rule to set interest rates.

consistent with what was shown in the preceding section. Fiscal consolidation reduces economic activity, which improves the current account through lower imports. Monetary policy easing in response to this negative demand shock spurs depreciation of the exchange rate. This boosts exports, further improving the current account.

- When interest rates cannot move, the response of the current account to a fiscal consolidation is still of the same magnitude, just slightly higher than a half percent of GDP (Figure 4.9, top panel, red line). Here, the simulation assumes that interest rates are fixed for two years.[26] The inability of the central bank during this period to offset the slump induced by the cut in government spending results in a sharper fall in aggregate demand and inflation than when monetary policy is unconstrained. The resulting fall in economic activity and domestic relative prices results in an "internal devaluation" that boosts net exports and the current account.[27] Thus, the model simulation corroborates the finding of the empirical analysis that external balances adjust just as much even when monetary policy is constrained.

Simultaneous and Uniform Global Fiscal Consolidation

How do the effects of fiscal consolidation on the current account change when many economies consolidate at the same time? This question is relevant today, because many economies have set fiscal consolidation in motion.

To address this issue, the simulations compare a situation in which only Canada cuts its fiscal deficit

[26]When the option of cutting interest rates is removed for a long time—in the GIMF, three or more years—the model generates unstable macroeconomic dynamics, which complicates the computation of simulation results. For simplicity, the analysis ignores the possibility of the central bank responding to the consolidation by using unconventional monetary tools, such as quantitative or qualitative easing. To the extent that such policies would be used to support output in response to the consolidation, the simulations reported here may overstate the impact of the zero interest rate lower bound.

[27]Similarly, as additional simulations suggest, when the nominal exchange rate is fixed and the response of monetary policy to domestic developments is thus constrained, aggregate demand and domestic relative prices fall more than when the exchange rate is flexible. However, the current account adjustment is of the same size.

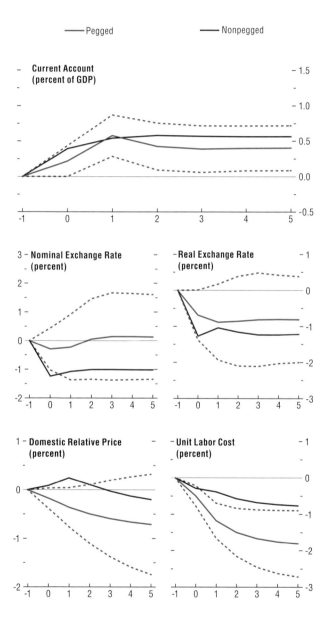

Figure 4.8. Effects of a 1 Percent of GDP Fiscal Consolidation under Pegged and Nonpegged Exchange Rate Regimes

Under a pegged exchange rate, the current account adjustment is just as large, but it is accompanied by a greater reduction of relative prices and unit labor costs.

Source: IMF staff calculations.
Note: X-axis units are years, where $t = 0$ denotes the year of consolidation. Dashed lines indicate the 90 percent confidence interval around the point estimate. Fiscal policy changes are action-based. The effect of a fiscal expansion would be the reverse of the response to a consolidation.

Figure 4.9. Effects of a 1 Percent of GDP Fiscal Consolidation under Constrained Monetary Policy: GIMF Simulations

When the scope for monetary easing is constrained, the current account adjustment is just as large. In the short term, it is associated with a larger fall in economic activity and smaller real exchange rate depreciation.

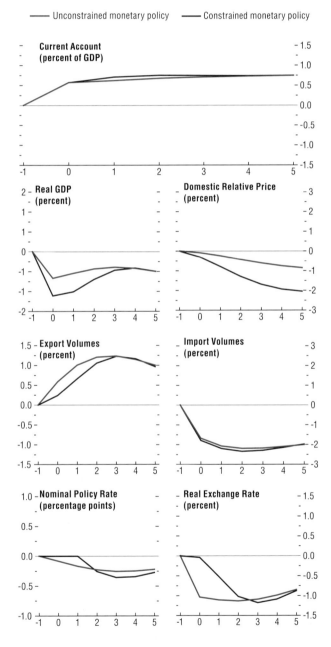

Source: IMF staff calculations.
Note: X-axis units are years, where *t* = 0 denotes the year of a 1 percent of GDP fiscal consolidation. The responses in the figures are model simulations for Canada from the IMF's Global Integrated Monetary and Fiscal Model (GIMF).

with one in which the entire world does so simultaneously (global fiscal consolidation) by the same amount. We again use Canada to illustrate the case of an economy small enough to have only minimal spillover effects on the rest of the world but open enough that fiscal contraction in the rest of the world has significant effects on its external balance and output.[28]

As before, the adjustment involves reducing the deficit-to-GDP ratio by 1 percentage point across all economies, with the adjustment composed entirely of spending cuts. Three-quarters of the spending cuts fall on government consumption, and the rest falls on government investment. We assume that monetary policy cannot respond in both Canada and the rest of the world for two years, to more closely resemble current conditions in which interest rates in many advanced economies are near the zero lower bound.[29]

In stark contrast to the situation where only Canada consolidates, a synchronized global consolidation equal in size does not improve Canada's external balance (Figure 4.10, top panel, red line). Canada's exports decline as global demand falls because of the synchronized fiscal consolidation, and unlike in the case of unilateral consolidation, there is no boost from the exchange rate.[30] This finding of no improvement in the external balance should not be surprising. Because the sum of all current accounts in the world must be zero according to the balance-of-payments identity, it is impossible for all economies' current account balances to improve at the same time. Fiscal consolidation does not automatically result in an improved current account—what matters is how much consolidation an economy undertakes relative to other economies.

[28]In 2009, Canada's GDP was 1.9 percent of global GDP on a purchasing-power-parity basis, and the sum of its exports and imports represented 71 percent of domestic GDP.
[29]Eighty percent of Canada's trade is with the United States and Europe, and so the assumption of constrained monetary policy for the rest of the world is more reasonable than allowing interest rates to move freely.
[30]Canada's real exchange rate appreciates because there are fewer liquidity-constrained households in Canada compared with the rest of the world. Liquidity-constrained households cannot borrow, and so fiscal consolidation results in a larger fall in consumption and domestic prices—and hence a real depreciation—in the rest of the world or, equivalently, a real appreciation in Canada.

Current Fiscal Adjustment Plans and Their Implications for External Balances

The fiscal adjustments currently planned by various economies over the coming years are, of course, not uniform in size or timing. The United Kingdom has embarked on an ambitious fiscal consolidation path, with policies aimed at improving the structural primary balance by more than 7 percent of GDP over the next six years. By contrast, some emerging and developing economies envision much smaller or even negative changes in their structural primary balance over the same period, as exit from stimulus is offset by increased fiscal spending on infrastructure investment or on strengthening social safety nets. What are the implications of these fiscal adjustments for the global constellation of current accounts?

To examine this question, we utilize a six-region version of the GIMF. The six regions are the United States, Japan, Germany, the euro area excluding Germany, emerging Asia, and the rest of the world.[31] Across these regions, the size of the planned fiscal adjustment between 2010 and 2016 ranges from a high of 4.6 percent of GDP in the United States to a low of 1.6 percent of GDP in emerging Asia (Figure 4.11, top-left panel). One important difference across the regions, however, is how much of the improvement in the structural primary balance in the coming years is the result of new permanent consolidation measures and how much is due to the expiration of temporary stimulus measures implemented in the wake of the crisis. For example, almost two-thirds of the projected improvement in the U.S. fiscal position is from letting temporary stimulus measures expire; about 1.7 percent of GDP of the improvement is due to new, permanent fiscal consolidation measures.[32] In contrast, most of

---

[31]The emerging Asia region includes China, Hong Kong SAR, India, Indonesia, Korea, Malaysia, the Philippines, Singapore, and Thailand. The rest of the world region includes both advanced economies, such as Australia, New Zealand, and the United Kingdom, and emerging and developing economies, excluding emerging Asia.

[32]Fiscal consolidation plans for the United States are based on the president's budget proposal of February 2011. The budget plan passed August 2 outlines measures that generate a deficit reduction of roughly the same order of magnitude. But because the second stage of the plan still needs to be decided by a bipartisan commission in Congress, there is much uncertainty regarding the exact size and timing of the new plan.

Figure 4.10. Effects of a Synchronized Global 1 Percent of GDP Fiscal Consolidation: GIMF Simulations

If all economies engage in synchronized fiscal consolidations of the same size, then there is little effect on the current account, and the short-term output contraction is larger. This is because it is not possible to have simultaneous real depreciation and current account improvement in all economies.

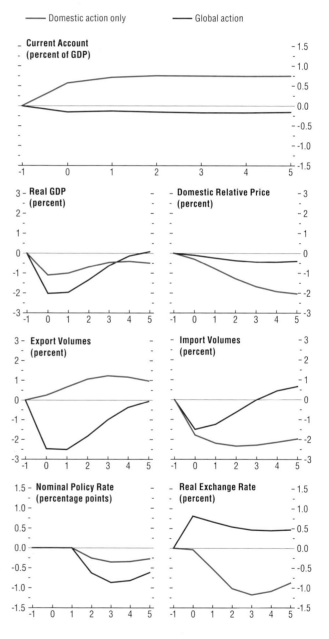

Source: IMF staff calculations.
Note: X-axis units are years, where *t* = 0 denotes the year of a 1 percent of GDP fiscal consolidation undertaken either by the domestic economy alone or by all economies together. The responses in the figures are model simulations for Canada from the IMF's Global Integrated Monetary and Fiscal Model (GIMF). Monetary policy is assumed to be constrained, with rates fixed for two years.

Figure 4.11. Planned Fiscal Adjustment and Its Current Account Impact: GIMF Simulations

(Percent of GDP)

The differing magnitudes of fiscal adjustment plans across economies imply lower imbalances within the euro area, smaller external surpluses in emerging Asia, and a larger U.S. current account deficit.

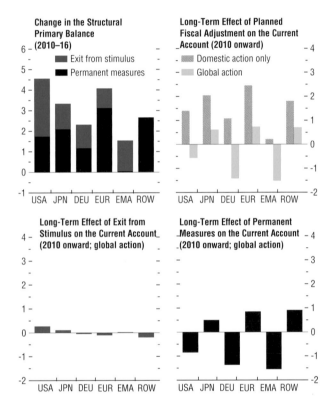

Source: IMF staff calculations.

Note: The current account impacts are model simulations from the IMF's Global Integrated Monetary and Fiscal Model, using the planned fiscal adjustment for each region, which show the long-term effect of the planned fiscal adjustment on the current account relative to 2010. When the long-term effects are weighted by their region's share of world GDP, they sum to zero, as required by the global balance-of-payments identity. The shares of each region in world GDP are Germany (6%); emerging Asia (13%); euro area (16%); Japan (8%); rest of the World (32%); United States (25%). The stylized compositions of the fiscal instruments used within each region are United States (30% government consumption, 40% labor taxes, 20% targeted transfers, 10% general transfers); euro area (40% government consumption, 30% labor taxes, 20% targeted transfers, 10% general transfers); all other regions (35% government consumption, 35% labor taxes, 20% targeted transfers, 10% general transfers). DEU: Germany; EMA: emerging Asia; EUR: euro area excluding Germany; JPN: Japan; ROW: rest of the world; USA: United States.

the improvement in the fiscal position of the euro area excluding Germany is due to permanent fiscal measures. It is these more permanent fiscal policy measures that have a substantial long-term effect on external balances (Clinton and others, 2010).[33]

We perform two experiments—unilateral consolidation and global consolidation.[34] First, we determine the long-term effect of fiscal adjustment on current accounts if each region undertakes its fiscal adjustment from now until 2016 as planned, but other regions do not.[35] As shown by the light blue bars in the top-right panel of Figure 4.11, unilateral consolidation by any region would improve its external balance as compared with its 2010 level, in line with the analysis above. The relative magnitudes of the improvement in the current account are roughly proportional to the height of the red bars—representing the size of permanent fiscal measures—in the top-left panel. This is because, as stated above, the permanent measures have a long-term effect on the external balance, whereas exit from temporary stimulus has a much smaller, short-term effect on the current account.

If all economies consolidate simultaneously, the *relative* amount of permanent fiscal measures determines how a region's current account responds. As shown by the yellow bars in the top-right panel of Figure 4.11, the relatively large scale of permanent fiscal consolidation being undertaken by the euro

---

[33]The reason for this is that permanent fiscal consolidation significantly reduces the stock of domestic public debt over time. A temporary stimulus, however, has little impact on the stock of domestic public debt, and thus only a very small effect on portfolio rebalancing and on the current account.

[34]Note that these simulations are not a prediction of where current accounts are headed in the coming years—they focus *only* on the impact of fiscal adjustment on the current account. Many other factors that affect the behavior of private saving and investment over the coming years—including growth differentials, inflation and interest rate developments, structural reforms, and so on—will also affect the current account. As a result, the projected change in the current account will differ from what these simulations suggest.

[35]More specifically, six simulations are run (one for each region) in which the region of interest undertakes its planned permanent fiscal measures and exit from stimulus (the red and blue bars in the top-left panel of Figure 4.11), while none of the other regions undertake any fiscal measures. All fiscal plans are assumed to be expected and fully credible.

area excluding Germany would improve that region's current account by about 0.7 percent of GDP; the smaller scale of fiscal adjustment by Germany would reduce its current account surplus by 1.4 percent of GDP. Thus, the varying size of planned fiscal adjustments contributes to a lowering of external imbalances within the euro area as a whole. In emerging Asia, not only is the improvement in the structural balance smaller than in other regions, but much of it results from letting stimulus measures expire. Consequently, planned fiscal adjustment would contribute to reducing that region's large external surplus. Finally, because the bulk of the large fiscal adjustment in the United States is due to the expiration of temporary fiscal stimulus and not because of new, permanent fiscal measures, the planned fiscal adjustment around the world is not likely to help narrow the U.S. current account deficit. In fact, it may widen.

Summary and Implications for the Outlook

We conclude this chapter with a brief summary of the results and a discussion of possible policy implications. First, as policymakers formulate their fiscal plans to achieve various goals—which at present are focused on securing fiscal sustainability, rebuilding fiscal room, or containing overheating pressures—the fact that fiscal adjustments have large effects on external balances is something they will need to keep in mind. For some economies, such as the United States and some euro area economies, the results suggest that fiscal consolidation of the right magnitude can help reduce twin fiscal and external deficits. For other economies, such as Germany, Japan, and China, there could be a trade-off between budget deficit reduction and a desire to reduce external surpluses.

Second, external adjustment is not driven solely by the fall in domestic demand from fiscal consolidation. The contractionary effect of fiscal consolidation

is now well established, with consequent effects on import demand, and this is something policymakers cannot ignore—fiscal consolidation hurts. But the current account also improves because exports get a boost from the real exchange rate depreciation that tends to accompany fiscal consolidation.

Third, the painful aspects of external adjustment are amplified if an economy's monetary policy or exchange rate is constrained. When policy rates cannot decline—because they are already at or close to zero or because they are outside the domestic monetary authority's realm of control—policymakers should expect a long and rough road ahead. In such cases, external adjustment still occurs, but it takes place through a sharper contraction in economic activity because monetary policy cannot soften the blow. This results in a greater decline in imports. The real exchange rate still depreciates, but it occurs through greater compression of domestic wages and prices. This is the kind of adjustment awaiting some of the euro area economies.

When many economies consolidate at the same time, what matters for the current account is how much consolidation an economy undertakes relative to others. Taking current fiscal plans as an example, some economies—including the United Kingdom, some members of the euro area, and other advanced economies such as Canada and Australia—are expected to have much larger fiscal adjustments based on permanent measures. As a result, fiscal adjustment in these economies is expected to contribute positively to their external balances. Germany and emerging Asia are also consolidating, but by a lesser amount. This should contribute to a lowering of their external surpluses. However, the relatively small size of permanent fiscal measures currently envisioned for the United States suggests that fiscal consolidation there will do little to reduce the U.S. external deficit.

Appendix 4.1. Data Construction and Sources

The data sources used in the analysis are listed in Table 4.1. We draw primarily on the databases of the World Economic Outlook (WEO) and the Organization for Economic Cooperation and Development Economic Outlook (OECD-EO).

The current account, exports, imports, public saving, investment, and public investment are all taken relative to GDP for the analysis, using the corresponding source database's measure of GDP. For example, this means that the current-account-to-GDP ratio is calculated by taking the ratio of the WEO current account measure (which is in U.S. dollars) to the WEO GDP measure in U.S. dollars. In the case of variables from the OECD-EO, such as public saving, we divide by the appropriate OECD-EO GDP measure. Real variables

(export volumes, import volumes, real GDP) are taken as natural logarithms. Price, cost, and exchange rate indices are also taken as natural logarithms. Interest rates are in percentage points.

To ensure that the national accounting identity holds, we calculate overall national saving, private saving, and private investment, all relative to GDP, as residuals using the following identities:

$$CA = S - I$$
$$S = S_{PUB} + S_{PRIV}$$
$$I = I_{PUB} + I_{PRIV}, \tag{4.1}$$

where CA denotes current account to GDP, S denotes saving to GDP, and I denotes investment to GDP. Both saving and investment are then broken down into their public and private components. We

Table 4.1. Data Sources

Variable Description	Variable Code	Source
Current Account	BCA	World Economic Outlook (WEO) Database[1]
Domestic Demand	TDDV	Organization for Economic Cooperation and Development Economic Outlook (OECD-EO) Database[2]
Export Price Index	PEXP	WEO Database
Export Volume	NX_R	WEO Database
Exports of Goods and Services	NX	WEO Database
GDP (local currency)	GDP	OECD-EO Database
GDP (local currency)	NGDP	WEO Database
GDP (real local currency)	NGDP_R	WEO Database
GDP (U.S. dollars)	NGDPD	WEO Database
GDP Price Index	PGDP	WEO Database
Import Price Index	PIMP	WEO Database
Import Volume	NM_R	WEO Database
Imports of Goods and Services	NM	WEO Database
Local Currency/U.S. Dollar Exchange Rate	ENDA	WEO Database
Long-Term Bond Rate	Various Series[3]	Datastream and Haver Analytics
National Investment	NI	WEO Database
Nominal Effective Exchange Rate	ENEER	IMF Information Notice System (IMF-INS) Database[4]
Overall Fiscal Balance	NLG	OECD-EO Database
Public Investment	CAPOG	OECD-EO Database
Public Saving	SAVG	OECD-EO Database
Real Effective Exchange Rate	EREER	IMF-INS Database
Short-Term Policy Rate	Various Series[3]	Datastream
Unit Labor Cost	ULC	OECD-EO Database
CAPB-Based Fiscal Changes[5]		Alesina and Ardagna (2010)
Coarse Exchange Rate Regime Classification		Ilzetzki, Reinhart, and Rogoff (2008)
Public Debt to GDP		Abbas and others (2010)

[1]April 2011, published version.

[2]Economic Outlook No. 89, June 2011, OLIS version.

[3]See appendix text for details on the interest rate series used.

[4]The series is extended back from its start to 1978 using inhouse calculations. See Appendix 4.1 text for details.

[5]CAPB = cyclically adjusted primary balance.

calculate overall saving as the difference between the current account and investment, private saving as the difference between overall saving and public saving, and private investment as the difference between investment and public investment.

There are some gaps in the OECD-EO data for some of the economies in the 1970s and 1980s. To address this, we splice the relevant series relative to GDP with the corresponding series relative to GDP, taken from an earlier vintage of the OECD-EO data.[36] This affects only two economies: Germany and Ireland. For Germany, we splice it with data from the former Federal Republic of Germany during 1978–90, taken from the former economies section of OECD-EO number 89. For Ireland, we splice it with data from 1978–89, taken from OECD-EO number 60 (December 1996, Public Version).

The short-term policy rate series for the economies in the sample come from Datastream: AUPRATE (Australia), OEPRATE (Austria), BGPRATE (Belgium), CNPRATE (Canada), DKPRATE (Denmark), FNPRATE (Finland), FRPRATE (France), BDPRATE (Germany), IRPRATE (Ireland), ITPRATE (Italy), JPPRATE (Japan), NLPRATE (Netherlands), PTPRATE (Portugal), ESPRATE (Spain), SDPRATE (Sweden), UKPRATE (United Kingdom), and USPRATE (United States).

The long-term government bond yield series are from Datastream and Haver Analytics. These are the Datastream series: CNGBOND (Canada), JPG-BOND (Japan), and NLGBOND (Netherlands). These are the Haver Analytics series: N193G10E@G10 (Australia), C122IB@IFS (Austria), C124IB@IFS (Belgium), N172RG10@G10 (Finland), C132IB@IFS (France), N134RG10@G10 (Germany), C178IB@IFS (Ireland), C136IB@IFS (Italy), C182IB@IFS (Portugal), N184RG10@G10 (Spain), C144IB@IFS (Sweden), N112RG10@G10 (United Kingdom), and N111RG10@G10 (United States). For Denmark, we splice two series from Haver Analytics to achieve greater time coverage (N128G10E@G10 and C128IB@IFS). For their period of overlap, the two series are very similar.

[36]We do this only after confirming that there is no break introduced into the series by this procedure.

The nominal and real effective exchange rate series are from the IMF Information Notice System (IMF-INS) database, which starts in the early 1980s. We extend these series back to 1978 for each economy, applying the methodology used to construct the IMF-INS effective exchange rates (see Lee and others, 2008, for full details).

The exchange rate regime indicator is constructed from the database in Ilzetzki, Reinhart, and Rogoff (2008), which is an update of Reinhart and Rogoff (2004). We use their coarse classification at the annual frequency to construct a binary exchange rate regime indicator, distinguishing between pegged and nonpegged regimes. The pegged regime corresponds to their classification of "peg"; the nonpegged regime (the complement of the pegged regime) is the union of their crawling peg, managed float, and freely floating categories. We extend the indicator over 2008–09 by carrying the 2007 value forward.

See the main text for a description of how the action-based fiscal policy changes are identified.

Appendix 4.2. Statistical Methodology, Robustness Checks, and Selected Additional Results on Export and Import Responses

This appendix provides further details about the statistical methods used and the robustness of the regression results. It first describes the baseline regression model and estimation strategy. It then continues with a discussion and summary of a variety of robustness checks for the core results. The appendix concludes with a set of selected additional results on the export and import responses.

Model Specification and Estimation

The baseline specification is a cross-section and time fixed effects panel data model:

$$\Delta Y_{i,t} = \mu_i + \lambda_t + \sum_{s=1}^{2} \beta_s \Delta Y_{i,t-s} + \sum_{s=0}^{2} \gamma_s \Delta F_{i,t-s} + \varepsilon_{i,t} \quad (4.2)$$

where subscript i indexes economies, subscript t indexes years, and ΔY is the change in the dependent variable of interest. The term ΔF is the estimated size of our action-based fiscal consolidation or expansion in percent of GDP. The term μ_i denotes an economy fixed effect, λ_t denotes a year fixed effect, and $\varepsilon_{i,t}$ is a mean-zero error term. β and γ denote the coefficients on the lagged dependent variable and the fiscal policy change, respectively, with s indexing the lag of the corresponding variable. The baseline regression's lag order of 2 is selected based on a review of the information criteria and serial correlation properties associated with various lag lengths.

Because we want an estimate of the overall effect of fiscal policy changes on the dependent variable of interest, we do not include any mediating variables or possible transmission channels for fiscal policy as additional explanatory variables. The inclusion of mediating variables would net out any effect of fiscal policy that works through the mediating variables, leading to a distorted picture of the overall effect. Moreover, if the additional explanatory variables are endogenous, their presence in the model would further contaminate the estimated effect of fiscal policy. These considerations lead us to adopt a conservative and simple specification, relying on the research design underlying our identified fiscal policy changes to ensure their exogeneity. This allows us to recover an unbiased estimate of the effect of fiscal policy with a minimal specification.

The equation is estimated in changes because nonstationarity tests indicate that a unit root in the level of the current-account-to-GDP ratio (the key variable of interest) over 1978–2009 cannot be rejected for 16 of the 17 economies in the sample. In order to ensure comparability of the estimation method and to address nonstationarity issues, the same specification in changes is also used for the other dependent variables of interest. The estimated responses of the changes are then cumulated to recover the response of the level of the dependent variable to a permanent 1 percent of GDP fiscal consolidation. The standard errors of the impulse responses are calculated using the delta method.

Robustness Checks

The baseline results of the effect of a fiscal policy change on the current-account-to-GDP ratio were subjected to a variety of robustness checks, including the following:

1. Estimation by two-stage least squares (TSLS): We also estimated the model under the assumption that the action-based fiscal policy change can act as an instrument for the fiscal policy change based on the CAPB.

2. Transformation of the fiscal policy change measure into deviations from the in-sample trade-weighted partner average fiscal policy change: To confirm that the relative size and sign of the fiscal policy change is what matters for the current account rather than the absolute size and sign, we constructed for each economy the trade-weighted average of its in-sample trading partners' fiscal policy changes, which was then subtracted from each economy's fiscal policy change to derive its relative change.

3. A static panel model: The lagged dependent variables were dropped from the set of explanatory variables, and five years of lags of the action-based fiscal policy changes were added to the model. The cumulated impulse response at a given horizon is then simply the sum of the coefficients on the fiscal policy change and its lags up to the given horizon.

4. Estimation by difference generalized method of moments (GMM): Because the time dimension relative to the cross-section dimension of the sample is large (32 versus 17), any dynamic panel bias arising from the correlation of the cross-section fixed effect and the lagged dependent variables should be comparatively small. To ensure that this was the case, we also estimated the model using Arellano and Bond's (1991) difference GMM procedure.[37]

5. A larger set of lags: The lags of the dependent variable and the fiscal policy changes in the dynamic model were increased to four (the baseline is two).

[37]To avoid the weak instruments problem associated with instrument proliferation in dynamic models, the instrument set was restricted to the second through fourth lags of the lagged dependent variables (in addition to the exogenous variables). The estimated model passes both the Sargan overidentification and difference-in-Sargan tests, with p-values over 10 percent. The model also passes the Arellano-Bond test for no serial correlation in the first differences of order 2.

6. Dropping outliers: Cook's distance statistic was calculated for all observations in the baseline model for the current account. Observations whose Cook's distance statistic exceeded the threshold of $\frac{4}{N}$, where N is the number of observations underlying the regression, were then dropped and the model reestimated. This procedure flagged 27 of the 493 observations appearing in the baseline model as outliers.

7. Trimming extreme values of the action-based fiscal policy changes: The top and bottom 5 percent of the fiscal policy changes were set to zero and the model was reestimated.

8. Comparison of the effects of fiscal expansions versus consolidations.

9. Comparison of the effects of primarily tax-based versus spending-based fiscal policy changes.

The responses of the current account to a 1 percent of GDP action-based fiscal consolidation under the first seven robustness checks are shown in Figure 4.12. At the five-year horizon, the responses range from about 0.45 (when policy changes are expressed as deviations from trade-weighted partner averages) to about 0.7 (when extreme values of the fiscal policy changes are set to zero). Apart from the TSLS estimates, the overall shapes of the responses are remarkably similar across robustness checks. The TSLS estimates show a much stronger initial response of about 0.7 on impact and 0.8 in the year after a fiscal consolidation. This then settles down at the lower level of about 0.7 in the second year. Confidence bands around the estimates (not shown) indicate a roughly similar pattern of statistical significance as seen in the baseline.[38]

Figure 4.13 shows the responses to fiscal policy changes when different types of fiscal policy changes are allowed to have different effects. As noted, we considered two cases: fiscal expansions versus consolidations, and primarily tax-based versus spending-based fiscal policy changes. The top panel shows the responses to fiscal policy changes that are allowed to differ according to whether they are expansions or consolidations. Not surprisingly, the response to fis-

---

[38]As a further robustness check, we also estimated the model over the set of samples where we drop one economy at a time. All the estimated responses looked similar to the baseline, indicating that no single economy is driving the results.

Figure 4.12. Robustness: Effects on the Current Account of a 1 Percent of GDP Fiscal Consolidation

(Percent of GDP)

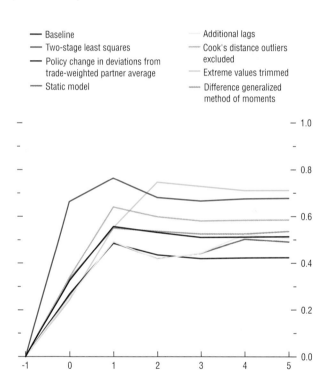

Source: IMF staff calculations.
Note: X-axis units are years, where $t = 0$ denotes the year of consolidation. See Appendix 4.2 text for full details on the robustness checks. Fiscal policy changes are action-based. The effect of a fiscal expansion would be the reverse of the response to a consolidation.

Figure 4.13. Effects on the Current Account of a 1 Percent of GDP Fiscal Policy Change

(Percent of GDP)

Fiscal consolidations and expansions have roughly symmetric effects on the current account. Tax-based fiscal policy changes have a larger effect on the current account than spending-based changes, although the difference is not statistically significant.

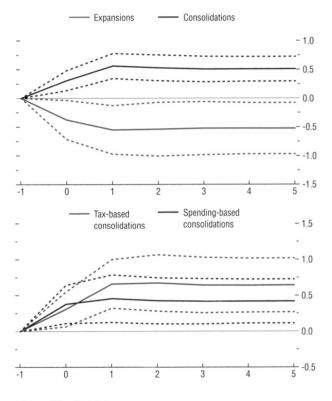

Source: IMF staff calculations.

Note: X-axis units are years, where *t* = 0 denotes the year of consolidation. Dashed lines indicate the 90 percent confidence interval around the point estimate. Fiscal policy changes are action-based. The effect of a fiscal expansion would be the reverse of the response to a consolidation.

cal expansions is of opposite sign to that for consolidations. The effects of expansions and consolidations are roughly symmetric. At the five-year horizon, it is 0.5 for consolidations and the same magnitude but of opposite sign for expansions. Both responses are statistically significant.

The bottom panel shows the responses to a fiscal consolidation that is either primarily tax-based or spending-based. A tax-based consolidation has a larger effect on the current account (about 0.7 at the five-year horizon) than does a spending-based consolidation (about 0.4 at the five-year horizon). Although both responses are significantly different from zero from the time the consolidation is implemented onward, a test of the difference between the tax-based versus spending-based fiscal change fails to reject equality.

Overall, the baseline results appear to be extremely robust.

Appendix 4.3. Global Integrated Monetary and Fiscal Model (GIMF)

This appendix gives an overview of the structure of the model that underlies the chapter's simulation results, followed by a simulation of the effects of different fiscal instruments on the current account. For more details on the model's structure, see Kumhof and others (2010). For further analysis of the twin deficits link using the GIMF, see Kumhof and Laxton (2009) and Clinton and others (2010).

Main Features of the GIMF

The GIMF is a multiregion dynamic structural general equilibrium (DSGE) model with optimizing behavior by households and firms and full intertemporal stock-flow accounting. Friction in the form of sticky prices and wages, real adjustment costs, liquidity-constrained households, along with finite planning horizons of households, gives the model certain key properties—notably, an important role for monetary and fiscal policy in economic stabilization.

The assumption of finite horizons separates the GIMF from standard monetary DSGE models and allows it to have well-defined steady states in which economies can be long-term debtors and creditors. This allows users to study the transition from one steady state to another where fiscal policy and private saving behavior play a critical role in both the dynamic adjustment to and characteristics of the new steady state.

Asset markets are incomplete in the model. Government debt is only held domestically, as noncontingent one-period nominal bonds denominated in domestic currency. The only assets traded internationally are noncontingent one-period nominal bonds denominated in U.S. dollars, which can be issued by the U.S. government and by private agents in any region. Firms are also only owned domestically. Equity is not traded in domestic financial markets; instead, households receive lump-sum dividend payments.

Firms employ capital and labor to produce tradable and nontradable goods. There is a financial sector as found in Bernanke, Gertler, and Gilchrist (1999), which incorporates a procyclical financial accelerator, with the cost of external finance facing firms rising with their indebtedness.

The GIMF encompasses the entire world economy, explicitly modeling all the bilateral trade flows and their relative prices for each region, including exchange rates. The standard production version comprises six regions. The international linkages in the model allow the analysis of policy spillovers at the regional and global levels.

Household sector

There are two types of households, both of which consume goods and supply labor. First, there are overlapping-generation households that optimize their borrowing and saving decisions over a 20-year planning horizon. Second, there are liquidity-constrained households, which do not save and have no access to credit. Both types of households pay direct taxes on labor income, indirect taxes on consumption spending, and a lump-sum tax.

Production sector

Firms that produce tradable and nontradable goods are managed in accordance with the preferences of their owners, who are finitely lived households. Therefore, firms also have finite planning horizons. The main substantive implication of this assumption is the presence of a substantial equity premium driven by impatience. Firms are subject to nominal rigidities in price setting as well as real adjustment costs in labor hiring and investment. They pay capital income taxes to governments and wages and dividends to households.

Financial sector

The current version of the GIMF contains a limited menu of financial assets. Government debt consists of one-period nominal bonds denominated in domestic currency. Banks offer households one-period fixed-term deposits, which is their source of funds for loans to firms. These financial assets, as well as ownership of firms, are not tradable across borders. Optimizing households may, however, issue or purchase tradable U.S.-dollar-denominated obligations.

Uncovered interest parity does not hold, due to the presence of country risk premiums. The premiums create deviations, both in the short and the long term, between interest rates in different regions, even after adjustment for expected exchange rate changes.

International dimensions and spillovers

All bilateral trade flows are explicitly modeled, as are the relative prices for each region, including exchange rates. These flows include exports and imports of intermediate and final goods. They are calibrated in the steady state to match flows observed in the recent data. International linkages are driven by the global saving and investment decision, a by-product of consumers' finite horizons. This leads to uniquely defined current account balances and net foreign asset positions for each region. Because asset markets are incomplete, net foreign asset positions are represented by noncontingent one-period nominal bonds denominated in U.S. dollars.

Along with uncovered interest parity, and long-term movements in the world real interest rate, the magnitude of the international trade linkages is the main determinant of spillover effects from shocks in one region onto other regions in the world.

Fiscal and monetary policy

Fiscal policy is conducted using a variety of fiscal instruments related to spending and taxation. Government spending may take the form of consumption or investment expenditure or lump-sum transfers, either

Figure 4.14. Fiscal Instruments and Their Effects on the Current Account

(Percent of GDP)

The response of the current account is similar for most fiscal instruments, ranging between 0.4 and 0.6 percent of GDP in year *t* = 1, and between 0.7 and 0.8 percent in the medium term. The current account response is somewhat smaller, both in the short and medium term, when fiscal consolidation is based on labor income taxes, and somewhat larger in the medium term, when fiscal consolidation is based on capital income taxes.

— Capital income taxes —— Targeted transfers
— Labor taxes   —— Government consumption
— Consumption taxes   —— Government investment
— General transfers

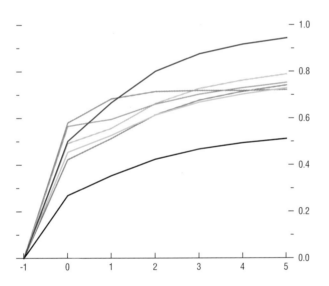

Source: IMF staff calculations.
Note: X-axis units are years, where *t* = 0 denotes the year of a 1 percent of GDP fiscal consolidation in the domestic economy. The responses in the figure are model simulations for Canada from the IMF Global Integrated Monetary and Fiscal Model (GIMF). Monetary policy is unconstrained in all cases.

to all households or targeted to liquidity-constrained households. Revenue accrues from the taxes on labor income and capital, consumption taxes, and the lump-sum tax, mentioned above. Government investment spending augments public infrastructure, which depreciates at a constant rate over time.

When conducting monetary policy, the central bank uses an inflation-forecast-based interest rate rule. The central bank varies the gap between the actual policy rate and the long-term equilibrium rate to achieve a stable target rate of inflation over time.

Fiscal Instruments and Their Effects on the Current Account

Does the impact of fiscal policy on the current account differ depending on which fiscal instrument is used? To answer this question we examine what happens when a small open economy with unconstrained monetary policy, which we calibrate to fit the main features of Canada, implements fiscal consolidation using different instruments. In particular, we examine the effects of a 1 percent of GDP fiscal consolidation on the current account when this consolidation is implemented using each of the following fiscal instruments, one at a time: labor income taxes, capital income taxes, consumption taxes, government consumption, government investment, general transfers, and targeted transfers.[39]

As shown in Figure 4.14, the response of the current account balance to a fiscal consolidation of 1 percent of GDP is large regardless of the instrument. For most of these instruments, the current account improvement ranges between 0.4 and 0.6 percent of GDP during the first year, with the exception of labor income taxes, for which the improvement in the current account is about 0.3 percent of GDP. Over the medium term, the improvement in the current account balances ranges between 0.7 and 0.8 percent of GDP for most instruments, with the exception of labor income taxes, with an improvement in the current account balance of 0.5 percent of GDP, and capital income taxes, with an improvement in the current account balance of 0.9 percent of GDP.

[39]These transfers are targeted to the liquidity-constrained households.

References

Abbas, S.M. Ali, Nazim Belhocine, Asmaa A. Elganainy, and Mark A. Horton, 2010, "A Historical Public Debt Database," IMF Working Paper 10/245 (Washington: International Monetary Fund). www.imf.org/external/pubs/cat/longres.aspx?sk=24332.0.

Abbas, S.M. Ali, Jacques Bouhga-Hagbe, Antonio Fatás, Paolo Mauro, and Ricardo C. Velloso, 2011, "Fiscal Policy and the Current Account" (unpublished; Washington: International Monetary Fund). www.imf.org/external/np/seminars/eng/2010/eui/pdf/ABH.pdf.

Alesina, Alberto, and Silvia Ardagna, 2010, "Large Changes in Fiscal Policy: Taxes Versus Spending," *Tax Policy and the Economy*, Vol. 24, ed. by Jeffrey R. Brown (Cambridge, Massachusetts: National Bureau of Economic Research), pp. 35–68.

Alesina, Alberto, David W.R. Gruen, and Matthew T. Jones, 1991, "Fiscal Adjustment, the Real Exchange Rate and Australia's External Imbalance," *Australian Economic Review*, Vol. 24, No. 3, pp. 38–51.

Arellano, Manuel, and Stephen Bond, 1991, "Some Tests of Specification for Panel Data: Monte Carlo Evidence and an Application to Employment Equations," *Review of Economic Studies*, Vol. 58, pp. 277–97.

Bayoumi, Tamim, and Hamid Faruqee, 1998, "A Calibrated Model of the Underlying Current Account," in *Exchange Rate Assessment: Extensions of the Macroeconomic Balance Approach*, IMF Occasional Paper No. 167, ed. by Peter Isard and Hamid Faruqee (Washington: International Monetary Fund).

Beetsma, Roel, Massimo Giuliodori, and Franc Klaassen, 2008, "The Effects of Public Spending Shocks on Trade Balances and Budget Deficits in the European Union," *Journal of the European Economic Association*, Vol. 6, No. 2–3, pp. 414–23.

Bernanke, Ben, Mark Gertler, and Simon Gilchrist, 1999, "The Financial Accelerator in a Quantitative Business Cycle Framework," in *Handbook of Macroeconomics*, Vol. 1C, ed. by J.B. Taylor and M. Woodford (Amsterdam: North-Holland).

Bernheim, B. Douglas, 1988, "Budget Deficits and the Balance of Trade," in *Tax Policy and the Economy*, Vol. 2, ed. by Lawrence Summers (Cambridge, Massachusetts: MIT Press), pp. 1–31.

Bluedorn, John C., and Daniel Leigh, 2011, "Revisiting the Twin Deficits Hypothesis: The Effect of Fiscal Consolidation on the Current Account" (unpublished; Washington: International Monetary Fund). www.imf.org/external/np/seminars/eng/2010/eui/pdf/BL.pdf.

Bussière, Matthieu, Marcel Fratzscher, and Gernot J. Müller, 2010, "Productivity Shocks, Budget Deficits and the Current Account," *Journal of International Money and Finance,* Vol. 29, No. 8, pp. 1562–79.

Cerra, Valerie, and Sweta Chaman Saxena, 2008, "Growth Dynamics: The Myth of Economic Recovery," *American Economic Review*, Vol. 98, No. 1, pp. 439–57.

Chinn, Menzie D., and Hiro Ito, 2007, "Current Account Balances, Financial Development and Institutions: Assaying the World 'Saving Glut,'" *Journal of International Money and Finance,* Vol. 26, pp. 546–69.

Chinn, Menzie D., and Eswar S. Prasad, 2003, "Medium-Term Determinants of Current Accounts in Industrial and Developing Countries: An Empirical Exploration," *Journal of International Economics,* Vol. 59, No. 1, pp. 47–76.

Clinton, Kevin, Michael Kumhof, Douglas Laxton, and Susanna Mursula, 2010, "Budget Consolidation: Short-Term Pain and Long-Term Gain," IMF Working Paper 10/163 (Washington: International Monetary Fund).

Devries, Pete, Jaime Guajardo, Daniel Leigh, and Andrea Pescatori, 2011, "A New Action-Based Dataset of Fiscal Consolidation in OECD Countries," IMF Working Paper 11/128 (Washington: International Monetary Fund).

Gagnon, Joseph, 2011, "Current Account Imbalances and Coming Back," Working Paper No. 11-1 (Washington: Peterson Institute for International Economics).

Gruber, Joseph W., and Steve B. Kamin, 2007, "Explaining the Global Pattern of Current Account Imbalances," *Journal of International Money and Finance,* Vol. 26, pp. 500–22.

Guajardo, Jaime, Daniel Leigh, and Andrea Pescatori, 2011, "Expansionary Austerity: New International Evidence," IMF Working Paper 11/158 (Washington: International Monetary Fund).

Ilzetzki, Ethan, Carmen M. Reinhart, and Kenneth S. Rogoff, 2008, "The Country Chronologies and Background Material to Exchange Rate Arrangements in the 21st Century: Which Anchor Will Hold?" (unpublished; College Park: University of Maryland). http://terpconnect.umd.edu/~creinhar/Papers/ERA-Country%20chronologies.pdf.

Kumhof, Michael, and Douglas Laxton, 2009, "Fiscal Deficits and Current Account Deficits," IMF Working Paper 09/237 (Washington: International Monetary Fund).

Kumhof, Michael, Douglas Laxton, Dirk Muir, and Susanna Mursula, 2010, "The Global Integrated Monetary and Fiscal Model (GIMF)—Theoretical Structure," IMF Working Paper 10/34 (Washington: International Monetary Fund).

Lee, Jaewoo, Gian Maria Milesi-Ferretti, Jonathan Ostry, Alessandro Prati, and Luca Antonio Ricci, 2008, *Exchange Rate Assessments: CGER Methodologies,* IMF

Occasional Paper No. 261 (Washington: International Monetary Fund).

Milesi-Ferretti, Gian Maria, 2009, "The Financial Crisis and Its International Transmission: Some Tentative Lessons" (unpublished; Washington: International Monetary Fund).

Morris, Richard, and Ludger Schuknecht, 2007, "Structural Balances and Revenue Windfalls: The Role of Asset Prices Revisited," European Central Bank Working Paper Series No. 737 (Frankfurt).

Ramey, Valerie A., 2011, "Identifying Government Spending Shocks: It's All in the Timing," *Quarterly Journal of Economics,* Vol. 126, No. 1, pp. 1–50.

Reinhart, Carmen M., and Kenneth S. Rogoff, 2004, "The Modern History of Exchange Rate Arrangements: A Reinterpretation," *Quarterly Journal of Economics*, Vol. 119, No. 1 (February), pp. 1–48.

Romer, Christina D., and David H. Romer, 2010, "The Macroeconomic Effects of Tax Changes: Estimates Based on a New Measure of Fiscal Shocks," *American Economic Review,* Vol. 100, No. 3, pp. 763–801.

Summers, Lawrence H., 1986, "Debt Problems and Macroeconomic Policies," NBER Working Paper No. 2061 (Cambridge, Massachusetts: National Bureau of Economic Research).

Wolswijk, Guido, 2007, "Short- and Long-Run Tax Elasticities—the Case of the Netherlands," European Central Bank Working Paper Series No. 763 (Frankfurt).

The following remarks by the Acting Chair were made at the conclusion of the Executive Board's discussion of the World Economic Outlook on August 31, 2011

Executive Directors observed that global economic activity has weakened and become more uneven across countries, financial volatility has risen, and downside risks have increased sharply. These developments are largely symptomatic of limited progress by key advanced economies in eliminating sovereign and financial sector imbalances to facilitate a shift from public to private demand. Meanwhile, rebalancing from external to domestic demand in key emerging market economies still has a long way to go. The global recovery has been further impeded by unexpected shocks, including supply disruptions from the earthquake and tsunami in Japan, the surge in oil prices, and political unrest in the Middle East and North Africa region. While the impact of these shocks will gradually fade, the fundamental real and financial weaknesses will remain in the absence of decisive and increasingly urgent policy responses.

Directors noted that, in most advanced economies with crisis legacies—such as overleveraged household and financial sectors and overstretched public balances—real GDP growth and employment are anemic, and ongoing fiscal withdrawal will continue to weigh on demand. In others, activity is more robust. In emerging market and developing economies, growth remains strong but will likely moderate from last year given lackluster activity in the major advanced economies and greater financial tensions. Overheating pressures have been building until recently, amid strong growth in credit and asset prices, widening current account imbalances, and resilient capital flows. Meanwhile, many developing and low-income countries remain vulnerable to high and volatile levels of food and fuel prices.

Directors stressed that the foremost priority for key advanced economies is to address sovereign and banking sector fragilities, which pose significant downside risks to the global outlook. In the euro area, it is imperative to repair and reform financial markets and institutions, further boost bank capital where needed, and implement the commitments made at the July 2011 EU Summit. Over the medium term, stronger euro area governance and progress toward a more integrated economic union remain important priorities. In the United States and Japan, political commitment to a well-paced, credible fiscal consolidation plan is an urgent priority, and renewed action to revive the U.S. housing market is also crucial. In general, fiscal policies need to strike the right balance between restoring medium-term public debt sustainability and limiting short-term deleterious effects on growth, taking care to maintain the credibility of fiscal policies. The policy response will vary by country but will likely require consolidation through entitlement and tax reforms and accelerated structural reforms to boost jobs, competitiveness, and potential output. Fiscal plans that credibly achieve medium-term fiscal sustainability could provide the needed policy room to support the near-term recovery, reducing reliance on monetary policy and its spillover effects.

Directors generally agreed that, given the tepid recovery in key advanced economies and growing downside risks, monetary policy should continue to be highly accommodative for the foreseeable future. A number of Directors saw limited scope for additional monetary support, including through unconventional measures, noting risks of distorting incentives and resource allocation. Directors stressed the need for continued progress in financial sector supervision and macroprudential policies to contain risks of excessive leverage emanating from a prolonged period of low interest rates.

Directors stressed that emerging market and developing economies should continue to strengthen fiscal positions to address fiscal risks and rebuild policy room, fend off excessive reliance on capital inflows, and alleviate the burden on monetary policy. At the same time, fiscal consolidation should protect infrastructure and social spending, thereby sustaining medium-term growth prospects and protecting the poor. Economies with strong public sector balance sheets could postpone adjustment if external downside risks threaten to materialize.

Directors noted that the monetary policy needs differ across emerging market and developing economies. The monetary tightening phase should continue in countries with increasing signs of overheating risks. In other economies, given the unusual uncertainty in the global environment, policymakers could consider a cautious approach to slowing the pace of monetary tightening while being watchful of financial stability risks, including from a potential reversal in capital flows.

Directors underscored the importance of maintaining vigilance against potential financial risks in light of past or continued capital flows and strong credit growth in some emerging market economies. Further efforts are necessary to enhance financial sector regulation, including by widening the perimeter of supervision to include nonbank intermediation and use of macroprudential measures to limit risk taking. In economies with persistently large current account surpluses, greater exchange rate flexibility—complemented with structural reforms—is key to dampening inflation pressures, fostering a balanced expansion, and facilitating global rebalancing over the medium term.

Directors emphasized that the escalation of global uncertainty even after three years since the onset of the global crisis is a reminder that the fundamental problems that caused the crisis remain largely unaddressed, while new risks have built up. The policy room to respond to potential exigencies has further narrowed. A renewed spirit of international policy cooperation is needed to advance internal and global demand rebalancing in a more meaningful way, as well as to resist trade protectionism. Without this, strong global growth and financial stability will remain elusive for years to come.

STATISTICAL APPENDIX

The Statistical Appendix presents historical data as well as projections. It comprises five sections: Assumptions, What's New, Data and Conventions, Classification of Countries, and Statistical Tables.

The assumptions underlying the estimates and projections for 2011–12 and the medium-term scenario for 2013–16 are summarized in the first section. The second section presents a brief description of changes to the database and statistical tables. The third section provides a general description of the data and of the conventions used for calculating country group composites. The classification of countries in the various groups presented in the *World Economic Outlook* (WEO) is summarized in the fourth section.

The last, and main, section comprises the statistical tables. (Statistical Appendix A is included here; Statistical Appendix B is available online.) Data in these tables have been compiled on the basis of information available through early September 2011. The figures for 2011 and beyond are shown with the same degree of precision as the historical figures solely for convenience; because they are projections, the same degree of accuracy is not to be inferred.

Assumptions

Real effective *exchange rates* for the advanced economies are assumed to remain constant at their average levels during the period July 18–August 15, 2011. For 2011 and 2012, these assumptions imply average U.S. dollar/SDR conversion rates of 1.589 and 1.593, U.S. dollar/euro conversion rates of 1.413 and 1.412, and yen/U.S. dollar conversion rates of 80.2 and 78.0, respectively.

It is assumed that the *price of oil* will average $103.20 a barrel in 2011 and $100.00 a barrel in 2012.

Established *policies* of national authorities are assumed to be maintained. The more specific policy

assumptions underlying the projections for selected economies are described in Box A1.

With regard to *interest rates,* it is assumed that the London interbank offered rate (LIBOR) on six-month U.S. dollar deposits will average 0.4 percent in 2011 and 0.5 percent in 2012, that three-month euro deposits will average 1.3 percent in 2011 and 1.2 percent in 2012, and that six-month yen deposits will average 0.5 percent in 2011 and 0.3 percent in 2012.

With respect to *introduction of the euro,* on December 31, 1998, the Council of the European Union decided that, effective January 1, 1999, the irrevocably fixed conversion rates between the euro and currencies of the member countries adopting the euro are as follows. (See Box 5.4 of the October 1998 *World Economic Outlook* for details on the conversion rates.)

1 euro	=	13.7603	Austrian schillings
	=	40.3399	Belgian francs
	=	0.585274	Cyprus pound[1]
	=	1.95583	Deutsche mark
	=	15.6466	Estonian krooni[2]
	=	5.94573	Finnish markkaa
	=	6.55957	French francs
	=	340.750	Greek drachma[3]
	=	0.787564	Irish pound
	=	1,936.27	Italian lire
	=	40.3399	Luxembourg francs
	=	0.42930	Maltese lira[4]
	=	2.20371	Netherlands guilders
	=	200.482	Portuguese escudos
	=	30.1260	Slovak koruna[5]
	=	239.640	Slovenian tolars[6]
	=	166.386	Spanish pesetas

[1]Established on January 1, 2008.
[2]Established on January 1, 2011.
[3]Established on January 1, 2001.
[4]Established on January 1, 2008.
[5]Established on January 1, 2009.
[6]Established on January 1, 2007.

What's New

- Data for Estonia are now included in the euro area aggregates and for advanced economies.
- As in the April 2011 *World Economic Outlook,* WEO aggregated data exclude Libya for the projection years due to the uncertain political situation.
- Starting with the September 2011 *World Economic Outlook,* Guyana and Suriname are classified as members of the South America region and Belize as a member of the Central America region. Previously, they were members of the Caribbean region.
- For Sudan, the projections for 2011 and later exclude South Sudan.

Data and Conventions

Data and projections for 184 economies form the statistical basis for the *World Economic Outlook* (the WEO database). The data are maintained jointly by the IMF's Research Department and regional departments, with the latter regularly updating country projections based on consistent global assumptions.

Although national statistical agencies are the ultimate providers of historical data and definitions, international organizations are also involved in statistical issues, with the objective of harmonizing methodologies for the compilation of national statistics, including analytical frameworks, concepts, definitions, classifications, and valuation procedures used in the production of economic statistics. The WEO database reflects information from both national source agencies and international organizations.

Most countries' macroeconomic data presented in the *World Economic Outlook* conform broadly to the 1993 version of the *System of National Accounts* (SNA). The IMF's sector statistical standards—the *Balance of Payments Manual, Fifth Edition* (BPM5), the *Monetary and Financial Statistics Manual* (MFSM 2000), and the *Government Finance Statistics Manual 2001* (GFSM 2001)—have all been aligned with the 1993 SNA. These standards reflect the IMF's special interest in countries' external positions, financial sector stability, and public sector fiscal positions. The process of adapting country data to the new standards begins in earnest when the manuals are released. However, full concordance with the manuals is ultimately dependent on the provision by national statistical compilers of revised country data; hence, the *World Economic Outlook* estimates are only partially adapted to these manuals. Nonetheless, for many countries the impact of conversion to the updated standards will be small on major balances and aggregates. Many other countries have partially adopted the latest standards and will continue implementation over a period of years.

Consistent with the recommendations of the 1993 SNA, several countries have phased out their traditional *fixed-base-year* method of calculating real macroeconomic variable levels and growth by switching to a *chain-weighted* method of computing aggregate growth. The chain-weighted method frequently updates the weights of price and volume indicators. It allows countries to measure GDP growth more accurately by reducing or eliminating the downward biases in volume series built on index numbers that average volume components using weights from a year in the moderately distant past.

Composite data for country groups in the *World Economic Outlook* are either sums or weighted averages of data for individual countries. Unless noted otherwise, multiyear averages of growth rates are expressed as compound annual rates of change.[7] Arithmetically weighted averages are used for all data for the emerging and developing economies group except inflation and money growth, for which geometric averages are used. The following conventions apply.

- Country group composites for exchange rates, interest rates, and growth rates of monetary aggregates are weighted by GDP converted to U.S. dollars at market exchange rates (averaged over the preceding three years) as a share of group GDP.
- Composites for other data relating to the domestic economy, whether growth rates or ratios, are weighted by GDP valued at purchasing power parity (PPP) as a share of total world or group GDP.[8]

[7]Averages for real GDP and its components, employment, per capita GDP, inflation, factor productivity, trade, and commodity prices, are calculated based on the compound annual rate of change, except for the unemployment rate, which is based on the simple arithmetic average.

[8]See Box A2 of the April 2004 *World Economic Outlook* for a summary of the revised PPP-based weights and Annex IV of the May 1993 *World Economic Outlook*. See also Anne-Marie Gulde

- Composites for data relating to the domestic economy for the euro area (17 member countries throughout the entire period unless noted otherwise) are aggregates of national source data using GDP weights. Annual data are not adjusted for calendar-day effects. For data prior to 1999, data aggregations apply 1995 European currency unit exchange rates.
- Composites for fiscal data are sums of individual country data after conversion to U.S. dollars at the average market exchange rates in the years indicated.
- Composite unemployment rates and employment growth are weighted by labor force as a share of group labor force.
- Composites relating to the external economy are sums of individual country data after conversion to U.S. dollars at the average market exchange rates in the years indicated for balance of payments data and at end-of-year market exchange rates for debt denominated in currencies other than U.S. dollars. Composites of changes in foreign trade volumes and prices, however, are arithmetic averages of percent changes for individual countries weighted by the U.S. dollar value of exports or imports as a share of total world or group exports or imports (in the preceding year).
- Unless noted otherwise, group composites are computed if 90 percent or more of the share of group weights is represented.

Classification of Countries

Summary of the Country Classification

The country classification in the *World Economic Outlook* divides the world into two major groups: advanced economies, and emerging and developing economies.[9] This classification is not based on strict

---

and Marianne Schulze-Ghattas, "Purchasing Power Parity Based Weights for the *World Economic Outlook*," in *Staff Studies for the World Economic Outlook* (International Monetary Fund, December 1993), pp. 106–23.

[9]As used here, the terms "country" and "economy" do not always refer to a territorial entity that is a state as understood by international law and practice. Some territorial entities included here are not states, although their statistical data are maintained on a separate and independent basis.

criteria, economic or otherwise, and it has evolved over time. The objective is to facilitate analysis by providing a reasonably meaningful method for organizing data. Table A provides an overview of the country classification, showing the number of countries in each group by region and summarizing some key indicators of their relative size (GDP valued by PPP, total exports of goods and services, and population).

Some countries remain outside the country classification and therefore are not included in the analysis. Anguilla, Cuba, the Democratic People's Republic of Korea, Montserrat, and South Sudan are examples of countries that are not IMF members, and their economies therefore are not monitored by the IMF. San Marino is omitted from the group of advanced economies for lack of a fully developed database. Likewise, the Marshall Islands, the Federated States of Micronesia, Palau, and Somalia are omitted from the emerging and developing economies group composites because of data limitations.

General Features and Composition of Groups in the *World Economic Outlook* Classification
Advanced Economies

The 34 advanced economies are listed in Table B. The seven largest in terms of GDP—the United States, Japan, Germany, France, Italy, the United Kingdom, and Canada—constitute the subgroup of *major advanced economies,* often referred to as the Group of Seven (G7). The members of the *euro area* and the *newly industrialized Asian economies* are also distinguished as subgroups. Composite data shown in the tables for the euro area cover the current members for all years, even though the membership has increased over time.

Table C lists the member countries of the European Union, not all of which are classified as advanced economies in the *World Economic Outlook.*

Emerging and Developing Economies

The group of emerging and developing economies (150) includes all those that are not classified as advanced economies.

The *regional breakdowns* of emerging and developing economies are *central and eastern Europe (CEE),*

Commonwealth of Independent States (CIS), developing Asia, Latin America and the Caribbean (LAC), Middle East and North Africa (MENA), and sub-Saharan Africa (SSA).

Emerging and developing economies are also classified according to *analytical criteria.* The analytical criteria reflect the composition of export earnings and other income from abroad; a distinction between net creditor and net debtor economies; and, for the net debtors, financial criteria based on external financing sources and experience with external debt servicing. The detailed composition of emerging and developing economies in the regional and analytical groups is shown in Tables D and E.

The analytical criterion by *source of export earnings* distinguishes between categories: *fuel* (Standard International Trade Classification—SITC 3) and *nonfuel* and then focuses on *nonfuel primary products* (SITCs 0, 1, 2, 4, and 68). Economies are categorized into one of these groups when their main source of export earnings exceeds 50 percent of total exports on average between 2005 and 2009.

The financial criteria focus on *net creditor economies, net debtor economies,* and *heavily indebted poor countries* (HIPCs). Economies are categorized as net debtors when their current account balance accumulations from 1972 (or earliest data available) to 2009 are negative. Net debtor economies are further differentiated on the basis of two additional financial criteria: *official external financing* and *experience with debt servicing.*[10] Net debtors are placed in the official external financing category when 65 percent or more of their total debt, on average between 2005 and 2009, is financed by official creditors.

The HIPC group comprises the countries that are or have been considered by the IMF and the World Bank for participation in their debt initiative known as the HIPC Initiative, which aims to reduce the external debt burdens of all the eligible HIPCs to a "sustainable" level in a reasonably short period of time.[11] Many of these countries have already benefited from debt relief and have graduated from the initiative.

[10]During 2005–09, 44 economies incurred external payments arrears or entered into official or commercial bank debt-rescheduling agreements. This group is referred to as *economies with arrears and/or rescheduling during 2005–09.*

[11]See David Andrews, Anthony R. Boote, Syed S. Rizavi, and Sukwinder Singh, *Debt Relief for Low-Income Countries: The Enhanced HIPC Initiative,* IMF Pamphlet Series No. 51 (Washington: International Monetary Fund, November 1999).

Table A. Classification by *World Economic Outlook* Groups and Their Shares in Aggregate GDP, Exports of Goods and Services, and Population, 2010[1]

(Percent of total for group or world)

	Number of Economies	GDP Advanced Economies	GDP World	Exports of Goods and Services Advanced Economies	Exports of Goods and Services World	Population Advanced Economies	Population World
Advanced Economies	**34**	**100.0**	**52.1**	**100.0**	**63.6**	**100.0**	**15.0**
United States		37.5	19.5	15.4	9.8	30.4	4.6
Euro Area	17	28.0	14.6	41.1	26.1	32.3	4.8
Germany		7.6	4.0	12.6	8.0	8.0	1.2
France		5.5	2.9	5.6	3.5	6.2	0.9
Italy		4.6	2.4	4.6	2.9	5.9	0.9
Spain		3.5	1.8	3.2	2.0	4.5	0.7
Japan		11.2	5.8	7.3	4.6	12.5	1.9
United Kingdom		5.6	2.9	5.6	3.5	6.1	0.9
Canada		3.4	1.8	3.9	2.5	3.3	0.5
Other Advanced Economies	13	14.3	7.5	26.8	17.1	15.4	2.3
Memorandum							
Major Advanced Economies	7	75.4	39.3	54.9	34.9	72.5	10.9
Newly Industrialized Asian Economies	4	7.5	3.9	15.4	9.8	8.3	1.2

	Number of Economies	GDP Emerging and Developing Economies	GDP World	Exports of Goods and Services Emerging and Developing Economies	Exports of Goods and Services World	Population Emerging and Developing Economies	Population World
Emerging and Developing Economies	**150**	**100.0**	**47.9**	**100.0**	**36.4**	**100.0**	**85.0**
Regional Groups							
Central and Eastern Europe	14	7.2	3.5	9.4	3.4	3.0	2.6
Commonwealth of Independent States[2]	13	8.9	4.3	9.9	3.6	4.9	4.2
Russia		6.3	3.0	6.5	2.4	2.5	2.1
Developing Asia	27	50.3	24.1	43.8	15.9	61.4	52.2
China		28.4	13.6	25.7	9.3	23.2	19.7
India		11.4	5.5	5.2	1.9	20.6	17.5
Excluding China and India	25	10.5	5.1	12.9	4.7	17.6	15.0
Latin America and the Caribbean	32	18.0	8.6	14.6	5.3	9.8	8.3
Brazil		6.1	2.9	3.4	1.2	3.3	2.8
Mexico		4.4	2.1	4.6	1.7	1.9	1.6
Middle East and North Africa	20	10.5	5.0	17.0	6.2	7.1	6.0
Sub-Saharan Africa	44	5.1	2.4	5.4	2.0	13.8	11.7
Excluding Nigeria and South Africa	42	2.6	1.2	2.8	1.0	10.2	8.7
Analytical Groups							
By Source of Export Earnings							
Fuel	27	18.0	8.6	26.6	9.7	11.6	9.8
Nonfuel	123	82.0	39.3	73.4	26.7	88.4	75.2
Of Which, Primary Products	20	2.3	1.1	2.6	1.0	4.8	4.1
By External Financing Source							
Net Debtor Economies	121	50.5	24.2	43.1	15.7	61.8	52.5
Of Which, Official Financing	28	2.5	1.2	1.8	0.6	9.7	8.2
Net Debtor Economies by Debt-Servicing Experience							
Economies with Arrears and/or Rescheduling during 2005–09	44	4.9	2.4	4.4	1.6	9.6	8.2
Other Net Debtor Economies	77	45.5	21.8	38.7	14.1	52.1	44.3
Other Groups							
Heavily Indebted Poor Countries	39	2.4	1.2	1.9	0.7	10.7	9.1

[1]The GDP shares are based on the purchasing-power-parity valuation of economies' GDP. The number of countries comprising each group reflects those for which data are included in the group aggregates.

[2]Georgia and Mongolia, which are not members of the Commonwealth of Independent States, are included in this group for reasons of geography and similarities in economic structure.

Table B. Advanced Economies by Subgroup

Major Currency Areas

United States
Euro Area
Japan

Euro Area

Austria	Germany	Netherlands
Belgium	Greece	Portugal
Cyprus	Ireland	Slovak Republic
Estonia	Italy	Slovenia
Finland	Luxembourg	Spain
France	Malta	

Newly Industrialized Asian Economies

Hong Kong SAR[1]	Singapore
Korea	Taiwan Province of China

Major Advanced Economies

Canada	Italy	United States
France	Japan	
Germany	United Kingdom	

Other Advanced Economies

Australia	Israel	Sweden
Czech Republic	Korea	Switzerland
Denmark	New Zealand	Taiwan Province of China
Hong Kong SAR[1]	Norway	
Iceland	Singapore	

[1]On July 1, 1997, Hong Kong was returned to China and became a Special Administrative Region of China.

Table C. European Union

Austria	Germany	Netherlands
Belgium	Greece	Poland
Bulgaria	Hungary	Portugal
Cyprus	Ireland	Romania
Czech Republic	Italy	Slovak Republic
Denmark	Latvia	Slovenia
Estonia	Lithuania	Spain
Finland	Luxembourg	Sweden
France	Malta	United Kingdom

Table D. Emerging and Developing Economies by Region and Main Source of Export Earnings

	Fuel	Nonfuel Primary Products
Commonwealth of Independent States[1]		
	Azerbaijan	Mongolia
	Kazakhstan	Uzbekistan
	Russia	
	Turkmenistan	
Developing Asia		
	Brunei Darussalam	Papua New Guinea
	Timor-Leste	Solomon Islands
Latin America and the Caribbean		
	Ecuador	Chile
	Trinidad and Tobago	Guyana
	Venezuela	Peru
		Suriname
Middle East and North Africa		
	Algeria	Mauritania
	Bahrain	
	Islamic Republic of Iran	
	Iraq	
	Kuwait	
	Libya	
	Oman	
	Qatar	
	Saudi Arabia	
	Sudan	
	United Arab Emirates	
	Republic of Yemen	
Sub-Saharan Africa		
	Angola	Burkina Faso
	Chad	Burundi
	Republic of Congo	Democratic Republic of Congo
	Equatorial Guinea	Guinea
	Gabon	Guinea-Bissau
	Nigeria	Malawi
		Mali
		Mozambique
		Sierra Leone
		Zambia
		Zimbabwe

[1]Mongolia, which is not a member of the Commonwealth of Independent States, is included in this group for reasons of geography and similarities in economic structure.

Table E. Emerging and Developing Economies by Region, Net External Position, and Status as Heavily Indebted Poor Countries

	Net External Position		Heavily Indebted Poor Countries[2]		Net External Position		Heavily Indebted Poor Countries[2]
	Net Creditor	Net Debtor[1]			Net Creditor	Net Debtor[1]	
Central and Eastern Europe				Kiribati	*		
Albania		*		Lao People's Democratic Republic		*	
Bosnia and Herzegovina		*		Malaysia	*		
Bulgaria		*		Maldives		*	
Croatia		*		Myanmar		*	
Hungary		*		Nepal		•	
Kosovo		*		Pakistan		*	
Latvia		*		Papua New Guinea	*		
Lithuania		*		Philippines		*	
Former Yugoslav Republic of Macedonia		*		Samoa		•	
Montenegro		*		Solomon Islands		*	
Poland		*		Sri Lanka		*	
Romania		*		Thailand		*	
Serbia		*		Timor-Leste	*		
Turkey		*		Tonga		*	
Commonwealth of Independent States[3]				Tuvalu		•	
				Vanuatu		*	
Armenia		*		Vietnam		*	
Azerbaijan	*			**Latin America and the Caribbean**			
Belarus		*					
Georgia		*		Antigua and Barbuda		*	
Kazakhstan		*		Argentina		*	
Kyrgyz Republic		•	*	The Bahamas		*	
Moldova		*		Barbados		*	
Mongolia		•		Belize		*	
Russia	*			Bolivia	*		•
Tajikistan		*		Brazil		*	
Turkmenistan	*			Chile		*	
Ukraine		*		Colombia		*	
Uzbekistan	*			Costa Rica		*	
Developing Asia				Dominica		*	
Islamic Republic of Afghanistan		•	•	Dominican Republic		*	
Bangladesh		•		Ecuador		•	
Bhutan		*		El Salvador		*	
Brunei Darussalam	*			Grenada		*	
Cambodia		*		Guatemala		*	
China	*			Guyana		•	•
Republic of Fiji		*		Haiti		•	•
India		*		Honduras		*	•
Indonesia	*			Jamaica		*	
				Mexico		*	

Table E *(concluded)*

	Net External Position		Heavily Indebted Poor Countries[2]		Net External Position		Heavily Indebted Poor Countries[2]
	Net Creditor	Net Debtor[1]			Net Creditor	Net Debtor[1]	
Nicaragua		*	•	Cameroon		*	•
Panama		*		Cape Verde		*	
Paraguay		*		Central African Republic		•	•
Peru		*		Chad		*	*
St. Kitts and Nevis		*		Comoros		•	*
St. Lucia		*		Democratic Republic of Congo		•	•
St. Vincent and the Grenadines		•		Republic of Congo		•	•
Suriname		•		Côte d'Ivoire		*	*
Trinidad and Tobago	*			Equatorial Guinea		*	
Uruguay		*		Eritrea		•	•
Venezuela	*			Ethiopia		•	•
Middle East and North Africa				Gabon	*		
				The Gambia		•	•
Algeria	*			Ghana		•	•
Bahrain	*			Guinea		*	*
Djibouti		*		Guinea-Bissau		*	•
Egypt		*		Kenya		*	
Islamic Republic of Iran	*			Lesotho		*	
Iraq	*			Liberia		*	•
Jordan		*		Madagascar		•	•
Kuwait	*			Malawi		*	•
Lebanon		*		Mali		•	•
Libya	*			Mauritius		*	
Mauritania		*	•	Mozambique		*	•
Morocco		*		Namibia	*		
Oman	*			Niger		*	•
Qatar	*			Nigeria	*		
Saudi Arabia	*			Rwanda		•	•
Sudan		*	*	São Tomé and Príncipe		*	•
Syrian Arab Republic	•			Senegal		*	•
Tunisia		*		Seychelles		*	
United Arab Emirates	*			Sierra Leone		*	•
Republic of Yemen		*		South Africa		*	
Sub-Saharan Africa				Swaziland		*	
Angola	*			Tanzania		*	•
Benin		*	•	Togo		•	•
Botswana	*			Uganda		*	•
Burkina Faso		•	•	Zambia		*	•
Burundi		•	•	Zimbabwe		•	

[1]Dot instead of star indicates that the net debtor's main external finance source is official financing.

[2]Dot instead of star indicates that the country has reached the completion point.

[3]Georgia and Mongolia, which are not members of the Commonwealth of Independent States, are included in this group for reasons of geography and similarities in economic structure.

Box A1. Economic Policy Assumptions Underlying the Projections for Selected Economies

Fiscal Policy Assumptions

The short-term fiscal policy assumptions used in the *World Economic Outlook* (WEO) are based on officially announced budgets, adjusted for differences between the national authorities and the IMF staff regarding macroeconomic assumptions and projected fiscal outturns. The medium-term fiscal projections incorporate policy measures that are judged likely to be implemented. In cases in which the IMF staff has insufficient information to assess the authorities' budget intentions and prospects for policy implementation, an unchanged structural primary balance is assumed unless indicated otherwise. Specific assumptions used in some of the advanced economies follow. (See also Tables B5, B6, B7, and B9 in the online section of the Statistical Appendix for data on fiscal net lending/borrowing and structural balances.)[1]

Argentina: The 2011 forecasts are based on the 2010 outturn and IMF staff assumptions. For the outer years, the IMF staff assumes unchanged policies.

Australia: Fiscal projections are based IMF staff projections and the 2011–12 budget.

Austria: Projections assume compliance with the expenditure ceilings of the federal financial framework law for 2012–15.

Belgium: IMF staff projections for 2011 and beyond are based on unchanged policies. The 2011 projections, however, include some of the measures

included in the 2011 federal budget. For local governments, unchanged policies imply the continuation of their electoral cycle.

Brazil: The 2011 forecast is based on the budget law, the spending reduction package announced by the authorities earlier this year, and IMF staff assumptions. For 2012 and outer years, the IMF staff assumes adherence to the announced primary target and further increase in public investment in line with the authorities' intentions.

Canada: Projections use the baseline forecasts in the latest Budget 2011—A Low-Tax Plan for Jobs and Growth, tabled on June 6, 2011. The IMF staff makes some adjustments to this forecast for differences in macroeconomic projections. The IMF staff forecast also incorporates the most recent data releases from Finance Canada (Update of Economic and Fiscal Projections, October 2010) and Statistics Canada, including federal, provincial, and territorial budgetary outturns through the end of the first quarter of 2011.

China: For 2010, the government is assumed to continue and complete the stimulus program it announced in late 2008, and so there is no significant fiscal impulse. The withdrawal of the stimulus is assumed to start in 2011, resulting in a negative fiscal impulse of about 1 percent of GDP (reflecting both higher revenue and lower spending).

Denmark: Projections for 2010–11 are aligned with the latest official budget estimates and the underlying economic projections, adjusted where appropriate for the IMF staff's macroeconomic assumptions. For 2012–16, the projections incorporate key features of the medium-term fiscal plan as embodied in the authorities' 2009 Convergence Program submitted to the European Union.

France: Estimates for the general government in 2010 reflect the actual outturn. Projections for 2011 and beyond reflect the authorities' 2011–14 multi-year budget, adjusted for differences in assumptions on macro and financial variables, and revenue projections.

Germany: The estimates for 2010 are preliminary estimates from the Federal Statistical Office of Germany. The IMF staff's projections for 2011 and beyond reflect the authorities' adopted core federal

---

[1] The output gap is actual minus potential output, as a percent of potential output. Structural balances are expressed as a percent of potential output. The structural balance is the actual net lending/borrowing minus the effects of cyclical output from potential output, corrected for one-time and other factors, such as asset and commodity prices and output composition effects. Changes in the structural balance consequently include effects of temporary fiscal measures, the impact of fluctuations in interest rates and debt-service costs, and other noncyclical fluctuations in net lending/borrowing. The computations of structural balances are based on IMF staff estimates of potential GDP and revenue and expenditure elasticities. (See the October 1993 *World Economic Outlook*, Annex I.) Net debt is defined as gross debt minus financial assets of the general government, which include assets held by the social security insurance system. Estimates of the output gap and of the structural balance are subject to significant margins of uncertainty.

Box A1 *(continued)*

government budget plan adjusted for the differences in the IMF staff's macroeconomic framework and staff assumptions about fiscal developments in state and local governments, the social insurance system, and special funds. The estimate of gross debt as of December 31, 2010, includes portfolios of impaired assets and noncore business transferred to institutions that are winding up.

Greece: Macroeconomic and fiscal projections for 2011 and the medium term are consistent with the policies agreed between IMF staff and the authorities in the context of the Stand-By Arrangement. Fiscal projections assume a strong front-loaded fiscal adjustment, which already started in 2010, but will be followed by further measures during 2011–15 in line with the Medium Term Fiscal Strategy. Growth is expected to bottom out in late 2010 and gradually rebound after that, coming into positive territory in 2012. Outflows of deposits are expected to continue through 2012, and credit to contract as banks deleverage. The data include fiscal data revisions for 2006–09. These revisions rectify a number of shortfalls with earlier statistics. First, government-controlled enterprises whose sales cover less than 50 percent of production costs have been reclassified into the general government sector, in line with Eurostat guidelines. A total of 17 such enterprises or entities were identified and included, including a number of large loss-making entities. The inclusion implies that the debt of these entities (7¼ percent of GDP) is now included in headline general government debt data and that their annual losses increase the annual deficit (to the extent their called guarantees were not already reflected). Second, the revisions reflect better information on arrears (including tax refund arrears, arrears on lump sum payments to retiring civil servant pensioners, and arrears to health sector suppliers), as well as corrections of social security balances on account of corrected imputed interest payments, double counting of revenues, and other inaccuracies. Finally, new information on swaps also became available and further helps explain the upward revision in debt data.

Hong Kong SAR: Projections are based on the authorities' medium-term fiscal projections.

Hungary: Fiscal projections include IMF staff projections of the macro framework and of the impact of existing legislated measures, as well as fiscal policy plans as announced by end of the first week of September 2011.

India: Historical data are based on budgetary execution data. Projections are based on available information on the authorities' fiscal plans, with adjustments for IMF staff assumptions. Subnational data are incorporated with a lag of up to two years; general government data are thus finalized well after central government data. IMF presentation differs from Indian national accounts data, particularly regarding divestment and license auction proceeds, net versus gross recording of revenues in certain minor categories, and some public sector lending.

Indonesia: The 2010 central government deficit was lower than expected (0.6 percent of GDP), reflecting underspending, particularly for public investment. The 2011 central government deficit is estimated at 1.3 percent of GDP, lower than the revised budget estimate of 2.1 percent of GDP. Higher oil prices will have a negative budgetary impact in the absence of fuel subsidy reform, but this effect is likely to be offset by underspending, in particular on public investment, given significant budgeted increases. Fiscal projections for 2012–16 are built around key policy reforms needed to support economic growth—namely, enhancing budget implementation to ensure fiscal policy effectiveness, reducing energy subsidies through gradual administrative price increases, and continuous revenue mobilization efforts to create room for infrastructure development.

Ireland: Fiscal projections are based on the 2011 budget and the medium-term adjustment envisaged in the December 2010 EU/IMF–supported program, as modified by the May 2011 Jobs Initiative, which include a total of €15 billion in consolidation measures during 2011–14. The fiscal projections are adjusted for differences between the macroeconomic projections of the IMF staff and those of the Irish authorities. A preliminary adjustment is also made for the reduction in interest rates on EU financing agreed July 21 by the European Council. (See the Alternative Scenario in Annex I of the IMF

Box A1 *(continued)*

staff report for Ireland's Third Review under the Extended Arrangement.)

Italy: Fiscal projections incorporate the impact of the July 2010 fiscal adjustment measures for 2011–13 and the July–August 2011 fiscal adjustment package for 2011–14. (The August package is based on the government's decree approved August 13, 2011.) The estimates for 2010 are the preliminary outturn data from the Italian National Institute of Statistics (Istat). The IMF staff projections are based on the authorities' estimates of the policy scenario (as derived, in part, by the IMF staff), including the above-mentioned medium-term fiscal consolidation packages and adjusted mainly for differences in macroeconomic assumptions and for less optimistic assumptions concerning the impact of revenue administration measures. After 2014, a constant cyclically adjusted primary balance net of one-time items is assumed, with the primary surplus remaining below 5 percent of GDP.

Japan: The projections assume fiscal measures already announced by the government and gross reconstruction spending of about 1 percent of GDP each in 2011 and 2012 (total of 2 percent of GDP). The medium-term projections assume that expenditure and revenue of the general government are adjusted in line with current underlying demographic and economic trends (excluding fiscal stimulus and reconstruction spending).

Korea: Fiscal projections assume that fiscal policies will be implemented in 2011 as announced by the government. Projections of expenditure for 2011 are about 3 percent lower than the budget, taking into account the authorities' historically conservative budget assumptions. Revenue projections reflect the IMF staff's macroeconomic assumptions, adjusted for discretionary revenue-raising measures included in the 2009 and 2010 tax revision plans. The medium-term projections assume that the government will continue with its consolidation plans and balance the budget (excluding social security funds) by 2013; the government's medium-term goal is to achieve balance by 2013–14.

Mexico: Fiscal projections are based on (1) the IMF staff's macroeconomic projections; (2) the modified balanced budget rule under the Fis-

cal Responsibility Legislation, including the use of the exceptional clause; and (3) the authorities' projections for spending, including for pensions and health care, and for wage restraint. For 2012, projections assume compliance with the balanced budget rule.

Netherlands: Fiscal projections for the period 2011–16 are based on the Bureau for Economic Policy Analysis budget projections, after adjusting for differences in macroeconomic assumptions. For 2016, the projection assumes that fiscal consolidation continues at the same pace as for 2015.

New Zealand: Fiscal projections are based on the authorities' 2010 budget and IMF staff estimates. The New Zealand fiscal accounts switched to generally accepted accounting principles beginning in fiscal year 2006/07, with no comparable historical data.

Portugal: 2011 and medium-term fiscal projections reflect the authorities' commitments under the EU/IMF–supported program.

Russia: Projections for 2011–13 are based on the non-oil deficit in percent of GDP implied by the approved 2011–13 medium-term budget, the 2011 supplemental budget, an assumed second supplemental budget for 2011, and IMF staff revenue projections. The IMF staff assumes an unchanged non-oil federal government balance in percent of GDP during 2013–16.

Saudi Arabia: The authorities base their budget on a conservative assumption for oil prices—the 2011 budget is based on a price of $54 a barrel—with adjustments to expenditure allocations considered in the event that revenues exceed budgeted amounts. IMF staff projections of oil revenues are based on WEO baseline oil prices discounted by 5 percent, reflecting the higher sulfur content in Saudi crude oil. Regarding non-oil revenues, customs receipts are assumed to grow in line with imports, investment income in line with the London interbank offered rate (LIBOR), and fees and charges as a function of non-oil GDP. On the expenditure side, wages are assumed to rise at a natural rate of increase in the medium term, with adjustments for recently announced changes in the wage structure. In 2013 and 2016, 13th-month pay is awarded based on the

Box A1 *(continued)*

lunar calendar. Transfers are projected to increase in 2011 primarily due to a one-time transfer to specialized credit institutions and a two-month salary bonus. Interest payments are projected to decline in line with the authorities' policy of reducing the outstanding stock of public debt. Capital spending in 2011 is projected to be about 25 percent higher than in the budget approved in December 2010 and in line with the priorities established in the authorities' Ninth Development Plan. Recently announced capital spending on housing is assumed to start in 2012 and continue over the medium term.

Singapore: For fiscal year 2011/12, projections are based on budget numbers. For the remainder of the projection period, the IMF staff assumes unchanged policies.

South Africa: Fiscal projections are based on the authorities' 2011 budget and policy intentions stated in the Budget Review, published February 23, 2011.

Spain: The 2010 numbers are the authorities' estimated outturns for the general government for the year. For 2011 and beyond, the projections are based on the 2011 budget, new measures implemented during the course of 2011, and the authorities' medium-term plan, adjusted for the IMF staff's macroeconomic projections.

Sweden: Fiscal projections for 2011 are in line with the authorities' projections. The impact of cyclical developments on the fiscal accounts is calculated using the Organization for Economic Cooperation and Development's latest semi-elasticity.

Switzerland: Projections for 2010–16 are based on IMF staff calculations, which incorporate measures to restore balance in the federal accounts and strengthen social security finances.

Turkey: Fiscal projections assume that the authorities' 2011–13 Medium-Term Program (MTP) budget balance targets will be exceeded by saving amnesty-related revenue and saving the portion of revenue overperformance that exceeds MTP projections.

United Kingdom: Fiscal projections are based on the authorities' 2011 budget announced in March 2011 and the Economic and Fiscal Outlook by the Office for Budget Responsibility published along

with the budget. These projections incorporate the announced medium-term consolidation plans from 2011 onward. The projections are adjusted for differences in forecasts of macroeconomic and financial variables.

United States: Fiscal projections are based on the president's fiscal year 2012 budget proposal adjusted for final fiscal year 2011 appropriations and the IMF staff's assessment of likely future policies adopted by Congress. Compared with the president's budget, the IMF staff assumes more front-loaded discretionary spending cuts, a further extension of emergency unemployment benefits and the payroll tax cut, and delayed action on the proposed revenue-raising measures. No explicit adjustment has been made for the provisions contained in the August Budget Control Act to the extent that the president's budget proposal already contained significant deficit-reduction measures. The fiscal projections are adjusted to reflect the IMF staff's forecasts of key macroeconomic and financial variables and different accounting treatment of the financial sector support, and are converted to the general government basis.

Monetary Policy Assumptions

Monetary policy assumptions are based on the established policy framework in each country. In most cases, this implies a nonaccommodative stance over the business cycle: official interest rates will increase when economic indicators suggest that inflation will rise above its acceptable rate or range; they will decrease when indicators suggest that prospective inflation will not exceed the acceptable rate or range, that prospective output growth is below its potential rate, and that the margin of slack in the economy is significant. On this basis, the LIBOR on six-month U.S. dollar deposits is assumed to average 0.4 percent in 2011 and 0.5 percent in 2012 (see Table 1.1). The rate on three-month euro deposits is assumed to average 1.3 percent in 2011 and 1.2 percent in 2012. The rate on six-month Japanese yen deposits is assumed to average 0.5 percent in 2011 and 0.3 percent in 2012.

Australia: A monetary tightening of 25 to 50 basis points is built into the baseline. This is in line

Box A1 *(concluded)*

with surveys, but not with market expectations as reflected in overnight indexed swap rates.

Brazil: Monetary policy assumptions are broadly in line with market expectations and consistent with inflation gradually converging to the middle of the target range by December 31, 2012.

Canada: Monetary policy assumptions are in line with market expectations.

China: Monetary tightening built into the baseline is consistent with the authorities' forecast of 16 percent year-over-year growth for M2 in 2011.

Denmark: The monetary policy is to maintain the peg to the euro.

Euro area: Monetary policy assumptions for euro area member countries are in line with market expectations.

India: The policy (interest) rate assumption is based on the average of market forecasts.

Indonesia: Monetary policy is expected to be tightened in 2012, through a combination of reserve requirement increases and policy rate hikes. Medium-term monetary policy is assumed to be consistent with the central bank's inflation target.

Japan: The current monetary policy conditions are held for the projection period, and no further tightening or loosening is assumed.

Korea: Monetary policy assumptions incorporate further monetary tightening of 25 basis points for the remainder of 2011. This is in line with market expectations derived from interest rate forwards and swaps. For 2012, the policy rate is forecast to converge to 4 percent, the neutral rate for Korea estimated from a structural model, by the end of

the year. This will require two rate hikes of 25 basis points each during the year.

Mexico: Monetary assumptions are consistent with reaching the inflation target.

Russia: Monetary projections assume unchanged policies, as indicated in recent statements by the Central Bank of Russia. Specifically, policy rates are assumed to remain at the current levels, with limited interventions in the foreign exchange markets.

Saudi Arabia: Monetary policy projections assume the continuation of the exchange rate peg to the U.S. dollar.

South Africa: Monetary projections are based on the assumption that the authorities follow an estimated policy reaction function.

Switzerland: Monetary policy variables reflect historical data from the national authorities and the market.

Turkey: Monetary projections assume no further tightening of the policy rate over the near term.

United Kingdom: Monetary projections assume unchanged policy rates through December 31, 2012. This assumption is consistent with current market expectations.

United States: Given the outlook for sluggish growth and inflation, the IMF staff expects the federal funds target to remain at near-zero levels until early 2014. This assumption is broadly consistent with the Federal Reserve Open Market Committee's statement in early August that economic conditions are likely to warrant exceptionally low levels for the federal funds rate at least through mid-2013.

List of Tables

Output

Inflation

Financial Policies

Foreign Trade

Current Account Transactions

Balance of Payments and External Financing

Flow of Funds

Medium-Term Baseline Scenario

Table A1. Summary of World Output[1]
(Annual percent change)

	Average 1993–2002	2003	2004	2005	2006	2007	2008	2009	2010	Projections 2011	Projections 2012	Projections 2016
World	**3.3**	**3.6**	**4.9**	**4.6**	**5.3**	**5.4**	**2.8**	**−0.7**	**5.1**	**4.0**	**4.0**	**4.9**
Advanced Economies	**2.8**	**1.9**	**3.1**	**2.7**	**3.1**	**2.8**	**0.1**	**−3.7**	**3.1**	**1.6**	**1.9**	**2.7**
United States	3.4	2.5	3.5	3.1	2.7	1.9	−0.3	−3.5	3.0	1.5	1.8	3.4
Euro Area	2.1	0.7	2.2	1.7	3.2	3.0	0.4	−4.3	1.8	1.6	1.1	1.7
Japan	0.8	1.4	2.7	1.9	2.0	2.4	−1.2	−6.3	4.0	−0.5	2.3	1.3
Other Advanced Economies[2]	3.8	2.6	4.1	3.4	3.9	4.0	1.1	−2.3	4.3	2.8	3.0	3.2
Emerging and Developing Economies	**4.1**	**6.2**	**7.5**	**7.3**	**8.2**	**8.9**	**6.0**	**2.8**	**7.3**	**6.4**	**6.1**	**6.7**
Regional Groups												
Central and Eastern Europe	3.2	4.8	7.3	5.8	6.4	5.5	3.1	−3.6	4.5	4.3	2.7	3.9
Commonwealth of Independent States[3]	−1.2	7.7	8.1	6.7	8.9	8.9	5.3	−6.4	4.6	4.6	4.4	4.2
Developing Asia	7.1	8.1	8.5	9.5	10.3	11.5	7.7	7.2	9.5	8.2	8.0	8.6
Latin America and the Caribbean	2.7	2.1	6.0	4.6	5.6	5.8	4.3	−1.7	6.1	4.5	4.0	3.9
Middle East and North Africa	3.3	7.3	5.9	5.4	6.0	6.7	4.6	2.6	4.4	4.0	3.6	5.1
Sub-Saharan Africa	3.7	4.9	7.1	6.2	6.4	7.1	5.6	2.8	5.4	5.2	5.8	5.1
Memorandum												
European Union	2.4	1.5	2.6	2.2	3.6	3.3	0.7	−4.2	1.8	1.7	1.4	2.1
Analytical Groups												
By Source of Export Earnings												
Fuel	1.3	7.3	7.9	6.7	7.6	8.0	5.0	−1.5	4.3	4.7	4.4	4.3
Nonfuel	4.9	6.0	7.4	7.4	8.4	9.1	6.3	3.8	8.0	6.8	6.4	7.2
Of Which, Primary Products	3.9	4.1	5.5	6.1	6.2	6.7	6.6	1.5	7.1	6.4	6.0	5.7
By External Financing Source												
Net Debtor Economies	3.5	4.5	6.5	6.0	6.7	6.8	4.6	0.8	6.8	5.1	4.8	5.5
Of Which, Official Financing	3.5	3.3	6.3	6.4	6.1	5.8	6.3	5.1	5.5	5.7	5.3	5.9
Net Debtor Economies by Debt-Servicing Experience												
Economies with Arrears and/or Rescheduling during 2005–09	2.4	6.1	7.5	7.8	7.6	7.7	5.9	2.1	6.6	5.8	4.5	4.9
Memorandum												
Median Growth Rate												
Advanced Economies	3.2	2.2	4.0	3.1	4.0	4.1	0.9	−3.5	2.5	2.1	2.0	2.4
Emerging and Developing Economies	3.8	5.0	5.3	5.4	5.6	6.3	5.2	1.8	4.3	4.6	4.5	4.5
Output per Capita												
Advanced Economies	2.0	1.2	2.4	1.9	2.4	2.0	−0.6	−4.3	2.5	1.0	1.3	2.1
Emerging and Developing Economies	2.7	5.0	6.3	6.3	7.1	7.7	4.9	1.6	6.2	5.4	5.1	5.8
World Growth Rate Based on Market Exchange	**2.8**	**2.7**	**3.9**	**3.5**	**4.0**	**4.0**	**1.5**	**−2.3**	**4.0**	**3.0**	**3.2**	**4.0**
Value of World Output (billions of U.S. dollars)												
At Market Exchange Rates	30,110	37,393	42,084	45,525	49,308	55,680	61,191	57,722	62,911	70,012	73,741	91,575
At Purchasing Power Parities	37,216	48,780	52,636	56,699	61,546	66,679	69,968	70,036	74,385	78,853	82,828	103,489

[1]Real GDP.
[2]In this table, Other Advanced Economies means advanced economies excluding the United States, Euro Area countries, and Japan.
[3]Georgia and Mongolia, which are not members of the Commonwealth of Independent States, are included in this group for reasons of geography and similarities in economic structure.

Table A2. Advanced Economies: Real GDP and Total Domestic Demand[1]

(Annual percent change)

	Average 1993–2002	2003	2004	2005	2006	2007	2008	2009	2010	Projections 2011	Projections 2012	Projections 2016	Fourth Quarter[2] 2010:Q4	Fourth Quarter[2] Projections 2011:Q4	Fourth Quarter[2] Projections 2012:Q4
Real GDP															
Advanced Economies	**2.8**	**1.9**	**3.1**	**2.7**	**3.1**	**2.8**	**0.1**	**−3.7**	**3.1**	**1.6**	**1.9**	**2.7**	**2.9**	**1.4**	**2.2**
United States	3.4	2.5	3.5	3.1	2.7	1.9	−0.3	−3.5	3.0	1.5	1.8	3.4	3.1	1.1	2.0
Euro Area	2.1	0.7	2.2	1.7	3.2	3.0	0.4	−4.3	1.8	1.6	1.1	1.7	2.0	1.1	1.6
Germany	1.4	−0.4	0.7	0.8	3.9	3.4	0.8	−5.1	3.6	2.7	1.3	1.3	3.8	1.6	2.0
France	2.0	0.9	2.3	1.9	2.7	2.2	−0.2	−2.6	1.4	1.7	1.4	2.1	1.4	1.4	1.7
Italy	1.6	0.0	1.5	0.7	2.0	1.5	−1.3	−5.2	1.3	0.6	0.3	1.2	1.5	0.4	0.4
Spain	3.2	3.1	3.3	3.6	4.0	3.6	0.9	−3.7	−0.1	0.8	1.1	1.8	0.6	0.7	1.7
Netherlands	3.0	0.3	2.0	2.2	3.5	3.9	1.8	−3.5	1.6	1.6	1.3	1.8	1.9	1.0	2.0
Belgium	2.3	0.8	3.1	2.0	2.7	2.8	0.8	−2.7	2.1	2.4	1.5	1.8	2.1	1.9	2.1
Austria	2.2	0.8	2.5	2.5	3.6	3.7	2.2	−3.9	2.1	3.3	1.6	1.8	3.3	2.1	2.0
Greece	2.7	5.9	4.4	2.3	5.2	4.3	1.0	−2.3	−4.4	−5.0	−2.0	3.3	−7.4	−3.1	−1.1
Portugal	2.7	−0.9	1.6	0.8	1.4	2.4	0.0	−2.5	1.3	−2.2	−1.8	2.0	1.0	−4.0	1.0
Finland	3.5	2.0	4.1	2.9	4.4	5.3	1.0	−8.2	3.6	3.5	2.2	2.0	5.5	2.1	2.5
Ireland	7.3	4.2	4.5	5.3	5.3	5.2	−3.0	−7.0	−0.4	0.4	1.5	3.3	0.0	1.4	2.3
Slovak Republic	. . .	4.8	5.1	6.7	8.5	10.5	5.8	−4.8	4.0	3.3	3.3	4.2	3.3	2.9	3.9
Slovenia	4.1	2.9	4.4	4.0	5.8	6.8	3.7	−8.1	1.2	1.9	2.0	2.0	2.5	2.1	1.9
Luxembourg	4.7	1.5	4.4	5.4	5.0	6.6	1.4	−3.6	3.5	3.6	2.7	3.1	5.7	2.2	3.1
Estonia	. . .	7.6	7.2	9.4	10.6	6.9	−5.1	−13.9	3.1	6.5	4.0	3.8	6.8	3.9	4.8
Cyprus	4.1	1.9	4.2	3.9	4.1	5.1	3.6	−1.7	1.0	0.0	1.0	2.7	2.5	−3.1	4.2
Malta	. . .	−0.3	1.8	4.2	1.9	4.6	5.4	−3.3	3.1	2.4	2.2	2.3	3.6	4.3	2.0
Japan	0.8	1.4	2.7	1.9	2.0	2.4	−1.2	−6.3	4.0	−0.5	2.3	1.3	2.5	0.5	2.0
United Kingdom	3.1	2.8	3.0	2.2	2.8	2.7	−0.1	−4.9	1.4	1.1	1.6	2.7	1.5	1.5	1.7
Canada	3.5	1.9	3.1	3.0	2.8	2.2	0.7	−2.8	3.2	2.1	1.9	2.2	3.3	1.4	2.5
Korea[3]	6.1	2.8	4.6	4.0	5.2	5.1	2.3	0.3	6.2	3.9	4.4	4.0	4.7	4.5	4.3
Australia	4.0	3.3	3.8	3.1	2.6	4.6	2.6	1.4	2.7	1.8	3.3	3.3	2.7	2.6	2.5
Taiwan Province of China	5.0	3.7	6.2	4.7	5.4	6.0	0.7	−1.9	10.9	5.2	5.0	4.9	6.0	5.7	6.0
Sweden	2.8	2.3	4.2	3.2	4.3	3.3	−0.6	−5.3	5.7	4.4	3.8	2.5	7.6	2.6	4.8
Switzerland	1.3	−0.2	2.5	2.6	3.6	3.6	2.1	−1.9	2.7	2.1	1.4	1.8	2.9	1.7	1.4
Hong Kong SAR	3.0	3.0	8.5	7.1	7.0	6.4	2.3	−2.7	7.0	6.0	4.3	4.3	6.3	5.9	2.2
Singapore	6.1	4.6	9.2	7.4	8.7	8.8	1.5	−0.8	14.5	5.3	4.3	4.0	12.0	6.3	5.3
Czech Republic	. . .	3.6	4.5	6.3	6.8	6.1	2.5	−4.1	2.3	2.0	1.8	3.2	2.7	1.5	2.5
Norway	3.4	1.0	3.9	2.7	2.3	2.7	0.7	−1.7	0.3	1.7	2.5	2.1	1.2	1.6	2.8
Israel	4.5	1.5	4.8	4.9	5.6	5.5	4.0	0.8	4.8	4.8	3.6	3.6	5.9	3.5	4.3
Denmark	2.4	0.4	2.3	2.4	3.4	1.6	−1.1	−5.2	1.7	1.5	1.5	1.9	2.6	1.4	2.2
New Zealand	3.8	4.2	4.5	3.3	1.0	2.8	−0.1	−2.0	1.7	2.0	3.8	2.3	1.1	2.5	4.4
Iceland	3.3	2.4	7.7	7.5	4.6	6.0	1.4	−6.9	−3.5	2.5	2.5	3.0	0.0	3.7	1.4
Memorandum															
Major Advanced Economies	2.5	1.8	2.8	2.4	2.7	2.2	−0.3	−4.2	2.9	1.3	1.7	2.6	2.8	1.1	1.9
Newly Industrialized Asian Economies	5.4	3.2	5.9	4.8	5.8	5.9	1.8	−0.7	8.4	4.7	4.5	4.3	6.0	5.2	4.7
Real Total Domestic Demand															
Advanced Economies	**2.8**	**2.2**	**3.2**	**2.7**	**2.8**	**2.3**	**−0.3**	**−4.0**	**2.9**	**1.4**	**1.5**	**2.8**	**2.9**	**1.5**	**1.4**
United States	3.8	2.9	3.9	3.2	2.6	1.2	−1.5	−4.4	3.4	1.3	1.0	3.8	3.6	0.6	1.5
Euro Area	. . .	1.4	1.9	1.8	3.0	2.8	0.4	−3.7	1.1	1.0	0.6	1.5	1.6	0.5	1.2
Germany	0.9	0.5	0.0	−0.2	2.7	1.9	1.3	−2.6	2.4	2.1	0.9	1.1	3.4	1.6	1.2
France	1.9	1.5	2.6	2.6	2.7	3.1	0.1	−2.4	1.3	1.9	1.4	2.2	1.2	1.2	2.1
Italy	1.3	0.8	1.3	0.9	2.0	1.3	−1.4	−3.9	1.6	0.7	0.0	1.1	2.2	0.1	0.3
Spain	3.1	3.8	4.8	5.1	5.2	4.1	−0.6	−6.0	−1.1	−0.9	0.5	1.6	−0.6	−0.5	1.3
Japan	0.8	0.8	1.9	1.7	1.2	1.3	−1.4	−4.8	2.2	0.4	2.1	1.0	2.0	1.4	1.3
United Kingdom	3.3	2.9	3.5	2.1	2.5	3.1	−0.7	−5.5	2.7	−0.4	0.9	2.6	2.9	−0.6	1.3
Canada	2.9	4.5	4.1	5.0	4.4	3.9	2.8	−2.8	5.2	3.4	2.3	1.8	4.3	3.1	2.5
Other Advanced Economies[4]	3.9	2.0	4.6	3.3	4.0	4.7	1.6	−2.7	5.6	3.9	3.9	3.7	4.3	6.0	1.7
Memorandum															
Major Advanced Economies	2.6	2.1	2.9	2.4	2.4	1.7	−0.8	−4.1	2.9	1.2	1.2	2.7	3.1	0.9	1.4
Newly Industrialized Asian Economies	4.7	0.8	4.8	2.9	4.2	4.3	1.7	−2.9	7.3	4.5	4.5	4.4	4.4	8.4	1.0

[1]In this and other tables, when countries are not listed alphabetically, they are ordered on the basis of economic size.
[2]From the fourth quarter of the preceding year.
[3]The 2011 annual GDP growth forecast is as of September 5, 2011. The recent revision of the second quarter GDP data would imply a revision of the 2011 annual GDP growth forecast to 4 percent.
[4]In this table, Other Advanced Economies means advanced economies excluding the G7 (Canada, France, Germany, Italy, Japan, United Kingdom, United States) and Euro Area countries.

Table A3. Advanced Economies: Components of Real GDP
(Annual percent change)

	Averages		2003	2004	2005	2006	2007	2008	2009	2010	Projections	
	1993–2002	2003–12									2011	2012
Private Consumer Expenditure												
Advanced Economies	**2.9**	**1.5**	**2.0**	**2.7**	**2.7**	**2.6**	**2.4**	**0.1**	**−1.4**	**1.9**	**1.3**	**1.3**
United States	3.8	1.7	2.8	3.3	3.4	2.9	2.3	−0.6	−1.9	2.0	1.8	1.0
Euro Area	...	0.9	1.2	1.5	1.8	2.1	1.6	0.3	−1.2	0.8	0.3	0.6
Germany	1.2	0.4	0.3	0.4	0.2	1.5	−0.2	0.6	−0.1	0.6	0.5	0.5
France	1.9	1.4	1.7	1.6	2.4	2.4	2.3	0.2	0.2	1.3	0.6	1.0
Italy	1.3	0.5	1.0	0.7	1.1	1.2	1.1	−0.8	−1.8	1.0	0.7	0.6
Spain	2.8	1.7	2.9	4.2	4.2	3.8	3.7	−0.6	−4.2	1.2	0.8	1.4
Japan	1.2	0.6	0.4	1.6	1.3	1.5	1.6	−0.7	−1.9	1.8	−0.7	1.0
United Kingdom	3.6	1.1	3.0	3.1	2.2	1.8	2.2	0.4	−3.2	0.7	−0.5	1.5
Canada	3.1	2.9	3.0	3.3	3.7	4.2	4.6	3.0	0.4	3.3	1.8	1.8
Other Advanced Economies[1]	4.2	2.9	1.8	3.7	3.5	3.6	4.7	1.2	0.3	3.5	3.6	3.6
Memorandum												
Major Advanced Economies	2.8	1.3	2.0	2.4	2.5	2.4	2.0	−0.2	−1.5	1.7	1.0	1.0
Newly Industrialized Asian Economies	5.5	3.1	0.6	3.0	3.9	3.8	4.7	1.0	0.4	4.2	4.6	4.7
Public Consumption												
Advanced Economies	**2.0**	**1.4**	**2.2**	**1.8**	**1.3**	**1.7**	**1.9**	**2.2**	**2.5**	**1.2**	**0.0**	**−0.5**
United States	1.7	0.8	2.2	1.4	0.6	1.0	1.3	2.2	2.0	0.9	−1.2	−1.8
Euro Area	...	1.5	1.7	1.6	1.6	2.2	2.2	2.3	2.5	0.5	0.1	−0.1
Germany	1.4	1.1	0.3	−0.6	0.3	0.9	1.4	3.1	3.3	1.7	0.5	0.5
France	1.3	1.4	1.9	2.1	1.3	1.5	1.5	1.2	2.3	1.2	0.5	0.2
Italy	0.5	0.8	1.9	2.2	1.9	0.5	0.9	0.5	1.0	−0.6	0.3	−1.1
Spain	3.1	3.3	4.8	6.3	5.5	4.6	5.5	5.8	3.2	−0.7	−1.2	−0.8
Japan	2.9	1.6	2.3	1.9	1.6	0.4	1.5	0.5	3.0	2.2	1.1	1.5
United Kingdom	1.6	1.4	3.4	3.0	2.0	1.4	1.3	1.6	1.0	1.0	0.7	−1.2
Canada	1.1	2.4	3.1	2.0	1.4	3.0	2.7	4.4	3.6	2.4	1.0	0.1
Other Advanced Economies[1]	2.9	2.4	2.4	1.9	2.1	3.2	3.1	3.0	3.5	2.7	1.6	1.1
Memorandum												
Major Advanced Economies	1.7	1.1	2.1	1.6	1.0	1.0	1.4	1.9	2.2	1.2	−0.2	−0.8
Newly Industrialized Asian Economies	3.8	2.9	2.2	2.4	2.4	3.9	4.0	3.3	4.5	3.4	1.8	1.5
Gross Fixed Capital Formation												
Advanced Economies	**3.4**	**0.9**	**2.1**	**4.5**	**4.3**	**4.0**	**2.2**	**−2.8**	**−12.5**	**2.2**	**2.7**	**3.8**
United States	5.6	0.3	3.3	6.3	5.3	2.5	−1.4	−5.1	−15.2	2.0	2.7	4.7
Euro Area	...	0.6	1.1	2.3	3.1	5.5	4.7	−0.9	−12.1	−0.8	2.6	1.8
Germany	0.1	1.6	−1.2	−0.2	0.8	8.2	4.7	1.7	−11.4	5.5	6.9	2.5
France	2.0	1.6	2.2	3.0	4.4	4.2	6.3	0.2	−8.9	−1.3	3.2	3.3
Italy	1.9	−0.5	−1.2	2.3	0.8	2.9	1.7	−3.8	−11.9	2.5	1.4	1.3
Spain	4.4	−0.7	5.9	5.1	7.0	7.2	4.5	−4.8	−16.0	−7.6	−5.1	−0.9
Japan	−1.2	−0.7	−0.5	1.4	3.1	0.5	−1.2	−3.6	−11.7	−0.2	2.3	3.6
United Kingdom	4.5	0.3	1.1	5.1	2.4	6.4	7.8	−5.0	−15.4	3.7	−2.5	1.9
Canada	4.2	4.2	6.2	7.8	9.3	7.1	3.5	2.0	−13.0	10.0	7.0	3.9
Other Advanced Economies[1]	4.3	3.8	2.7	6.2	4.6	5.7	6.7	−0.2	−5.9	7.7	5.2	6.4
Memorandum												
Major Advanced Economies	3.2	0.5	1.9	4.4	4.2	3.4	0.9	−3.4	−13.5	2.3	2.8	3.8
Newly Industrialized Asian Economies	4.1	3.2	1.9	6.2	2.2	3.9	4.6	−3.0	−4.3	11.5	4.4	5.6

Table A3. Advanced Economies: Components of Real GDP (concluded)

	Averages		2003	2004	2005	2006	2007	2008	2009	2010	Projections	
	1993–2002	2003–12									2011	2012
Final Domestic Demand												
Advanced Economies	**2.8**	**1.4**	**2.1**	**2.9**	**2.8**	**2.7**	**2.3**	**−0.1**	**−2.9**	**1.8**	**1.3**	**1.5**
United States	3.8	1.3	2.8	3.5	3.3	2.5	1.4	−1.0	−3.6	1.8	1.5	1.1
Euro Area	. . .	1.0	1.3	1.7	2.0	2.8	2.4	0.5	−2.8	0.4	0.7	0.7
Germany	1.1	0.8	0.0	0.1	0.3	2.6	1.1	1.3	−1.7	1.7	1.7	0.9
France	1.8	1.4	1.9	2.0	2.5	2.5	2.9	0.4	−1.1	0.8	1.1	1.2
Italy	1.3	0.3	0.7	1.4	1.2	1.4	1.2	−1.2	−3.4	0.9	0.7	0.4
Spain	3.2	1.4	4.0	4.8	5.2	4.9	4.2	−0.7	−6.0	−1.2	−0.9	0.5
Japan	0.8	0.5	0.5	1.6	1.9	1.1	1.0	−1.1	−3.4	1.5	0.2	1.7
United Kingdom	3.3	1.1	2.8	3.4	2.2	2.5	2.9	−0.3	−4.3	1.2	−0.5	1.0
Canada	2.8	3.0	3.7	3.9	4.4	4.6	4.0	3.0	−2.1	4.5	2.8	1.9
Other Advanced Economies[1]	3.9	3.0	2.1	3.9	3.4	4.0	4.9	1.2	−0.7	4.2	3.6	3.9
Memorandum												
Major Advanced Economies	2.6	1.1	2.0	2.7	2.6	2.3	1.7	−0.4	−3.2	1.7	1.1	1.1
Newly Industrialized Asian												
Economies	4.8	3.1	1.2	3.7	3.2	3.9	4.7	0.4	−0.1	5.6	4.1	4.5
Stock Building[2]												
Advanced Economies	**0.0**	**0.0**	**0.1**	**0.3**	**−0.1**	**0.1**	**0.0**	**−0.2**	**−1.1**	**1.1**	**0.1**	**0.1**
United States	0.0	0.0	0.1	0.4	−0.1	0.1	−0.2	−0.5	−0.9	1.6	−0.1	0.0
Euro Area	. . .	0.1	0.1	0.2	−0.2	0.2	0.4	−0.1	−0.8	0.6	0.3	−0.1
Germany	−0.1	0.1	0.4	−0.1	−0.4	0.1	0.8	0.0	−0.8	0.6	0.4	0.0
France	0.1	0.1	−0.4	0.6	0.1	0.2	0.2	−0.3	−1.3	0.5	0.9	0.1
Italy	0.0	0.0	0.1	−0.1	−0.3	0.5	0.1	−0.2	−0.6	0.9	−0.1	0.0
Spain	−0.1	0.0	−0.1	0.0	−0.1	0.3	−0.1	0.1	0.0	0.1	0.0	0.0
Japan	0.0	0.0	0.2	0.3	−0.1	0.2	0.3	−0.2	−1.5	0.6	0.2	0.4
United Kingdom	0.1	0.0	0.2	0.1	0.0	0.0	0.1	−0.5	−1.2	1.5	0.2	0.0
Canada	0.1	0.1	0.7	0.1	0.5	−0.2	−0.1	−0.2	−0.8	0.6	0.5	0.4
Other Advanced Economies[1]	0.0	0.0	−0.1	0.6	−0.1	0.0	−0.1	0.3	−1.8	1.1	0.3	0.1
Memorandum												
Major Advanced Economies	0.0	0.0	0.1	0.3	−0.1	0.1	0.0	−0.4	−1.0	1.2	0.1	0.1
Newly Industrialized Asian												
Economies	−0.1	0.0	−0.2	0.8	−0.2	0.2	−0.3	1.0	−2.6	1.4	0.3	0.0
Foreign Balance[2]												
Advanced Economies	**−0.1**	**0.2**	**−0.3**	**−0.1**	**−0.1**	**0.2**	**0.5**	**0.5**	**0.4**	**0.2**	**0.2**	**0.5**
United States	−0.5	0.2	−0.5	−0.7	−0.3	−0.1	0.6	1.2	1.2	−0.5	0.2	0.7
Euro Area	. . .	0.1	−0.6	0.3	−0.1	0.2	0.2	0.1	−0.6	0.7	0.6	0.5
Germany	0.4	0.3	−0.8	1.1	0.8	1.1	1.5	−0.1	−2.8	1.4	0.6	0.4
France	0.1	−0.3	−0.6	−0.2	−0.7	0.0	−0.9	−0.3	−0.2	0.1	−0.3	0.0
Italy	0.3	−0.2	−0.8	0.2	−0.3	0.0	0.2	0.1	−1.3	−0.5	−0.1	0.5
Spain	−0.1	0.1	−0.8	−1.7	−1.7	−1.4	−0.8	1.5	2.7	1.0	1.7	0.6
Japan	0.1	0.4	0.7	0.8	0.3	0.8	1.1	0.2	−1.5	1.8	−0.8	0.2
United Kingdom	−0.3	0.1	−0.1	−0.7	0.0	0.2	−0.5	0.7	0.9	−1.1	1.4	0.6
Canada	0.6	−1.3	−2.3	−0.8	−1.6	−1.4	−1.5	−2.1	0.2	−2.2	−1.3	−0.4
Other Advanced Economies[1]	0.3	0.7	0.6	0.4	1.0	0.9	0.8	0.2	1.5	0.6	0.3	0.2
Memorandum												
Major Advanced Economies	−0.2	0.1	−0.4	−0.2	−0.2	0.2	0.5	0.6	0.1	0.0	0.0	0.5
Newly Industrialized Asian												
Economies	0.4	1.5	2.0	1.3	2.1	1.9	2.2	0.5	1.8	1.8	1.0	0.6

[1]In this table, Other Advanced Economies means advanced economies excluding the G7 (Canada, France, Germany, Italy, Japan, United Kingdom, United States) and Euro Area countries.
[2]Changes expressed as percent of GDP in the preceding period.

Table A4. Emerging and Developing Economies: Real GDP[1]

(Annual percent change)

	Average 1993–2002	2003	2004	2005	2006	2007	2008	2009	2010	Projections 2011	2012	2016
Central and Eastern Europe[2]	**3.2**	**4.8**	**7.3**	**5.8**	**6.4**	**5.5**	**3.1**	**−3.6**	**4.5**	**4.3**	**2.7**	**3.9**
Albania	6.7	5.8	5.7	5.8	5.4	5.9	7.5	3.3	3.5	2.5	3.5	4.0
Bosnia and Herzegovina	. . .	3.9	6.3	3.9	6.0	6.2	5.7	−2.9	0.7	2.2	3.0	4.5
Bulgaria	−1.2	5.5	6.7	6.4	6.5	6.4	6.2	−5.5	0.2	2.5	3.0	4.0
Croatia	2.9	5.4	4.1	4.3	4.9	5.1	2.2	−6.0	−1.2	0.8	1.8	3.0
Hungary	3.1	4.0	4.5	3.2	3.6	0.8	0.8	−6.7	1.2	1.8	1.7	3.2
Kosovo	. . .	5.4	2.6	3.8	3.4	6.3	6.9	2.9	4.0	5.3	5.0	4.5
Latvia	2.9	7.2	8.7	10.6	12.2	10.0	−4.2	−18.0	−0.3	4.0	3.0	4.0
Lithuania	. . .	10.2	7.4	7.8	7.8	9.8	2.9	−14.7	1.3	6.0	3.4	3.8
Former Yugoslav Republic of Macedonia	0.0	2.8	4.6	4.4	5.0	6.1	5.0	−0.9	1.8	3.0	3.7	4.0
Montenegro	. . .	2.5	4.4	4.2	8.6	10.7	6.9	−5.7	1.1	2.0	3.5	3.8
Poland	4.6	3.9	5.3	3.6	6.2	6.8	5.1	1.6	3.8	3.8	3.0	3.6
Romania	1.7	5.2	8.5	4.2	7.9	6.3	7.3	−7.1	−1.3	1.5	3.5	4.1
Serbia	. . .	2.5	9.3	5.4	3.6	5.4	3.8	−3.5	1.0	2.0	3.0	5.0
Turkey	3.0	5.3	9.4	8.4	6.9	4.7	0.7	−4.8	8.9	6.6	2.2	4.3
Commonwealth of Independent States[2,3]	**−1.2**	**7.7**	**8.1**	**6.7**	**8.9**	**8.9**	**5.3**	**−6.4**	**4.6**	**4.6**	**4.4**	**4.2**
Russia	−0.9	7.3	7.2	6.4	8.2	8.5	5.2	−7.8	4.0	4.3	4.1	3.8
Excluding Russia	−2.0	9.1	10.7	7.7	10.7	9.9	5.5	−3.0	6.0	5.3	5.1	5.1
Armenia	4.4	14.0	10.5	13.9	13.2	13.7	6.9	−14.1	2.1	4.6	4.3	4.0
Azerbaijan	−1.4	10.5	10.2	26.4	34.5	25.0	10.8	9.3	5.0	0.2	7.1	2.3
Belarus	0.8	7.0	11.4	9.4	10.0	8.6	10.2	0.2	7.6	5.0	1.2	5.0
Georgia	. . .	11.1	5.9	9.6	9.4	12.3	2.4	−3.8	6.4	5.5	5.2	5.0
Kazakhstan	0.3	9.3	9.6	9.7	10.7	8.9	3.2	1.2	7.3	6.5	5.6	6.4
Kyrgyz Republic	−0.9	7.0	7.0	−0.2	3.1	8.5	7.6	2.9	−1.4	7.0	6.0	5.0
Moldova	−3.8	6.6	7.4	7.5	4.8	3.0	7.8	−6.0	6.9	7.0	4.5	5.0
Mongolia	2.7	7.0	10.6	7.3	18.8	10.2	8.9	−1.3	6.4	11.5	11.8	15.6
Tajikistan	−1.7	10.2	10.6	6.7	7.0	7.8	7.9	3.9	6.5	6.0	6.0	5.0
Turkmenistan	1.6	17.1	14.7	13.0	11.0	11.1	14.7	6.1	9.2	9.9	7.2	6.8
Ukraine	−4.9	9.6	12.0	2.9	7.5	7.5	1.9	−14.5	4.2	4.7	4.8	4.0
Uzbekistan	1.9	4.2	7.4	7.0	7.5	9.5	9.0	8.1	8.5	7.1	7.0	6.0

Table A4. Emerging and Developing Economies: Real GDP[1] *(continued)*

	Average 1993–2002	2003	2004	2005	2006	2007	2008	2009	2010	Projections 2011	2012	2016
Developing Asia	**7.1**	**8.1**	**8.5**	**9.5**	**10.3**	**11.5**	**7.7**	**7.2**	**9.5**	**8.2**	**8.0**	**8.6**
Islamic Republic of Afghanistan	...	8.4	1.1	11.2	5.6	13.7	3.6	20.9	8.2	7.1	7.2	9.5
Bangladesh	5.0	5.8	6.1	6.3	6.5	6.3	6.0	5.9	6.4	6.3	6.1	7.2
Bhutan	6.2	7.7	5.9	7.1	6.8	17.9	4.7	6.7	8.3	8.1	8.5	13.2
Brunei Darussalam	2.1	2.9	0.5	0.4	4.4	0.2	−1.9	−1.8	2.6	2.8	2.2	3.3
Cambodia	7.0	8.5	10.3	13.3	10.8	10.2	6.7	−2.0	6.0	6.7	6.5	7.7
China	9.8	10.0	10.1	11.3	12.7	14.2	9.6	9.2	10.3	9.5	9.0	9.5
Republic of Fiji	2.8	1.0	5.5	2.5	1.9	−0.9	1.0	−1.3	0.3	1.5	1.8	1.5
India	5.8	6.9	7.6	9.0	9.5	10.0	6.2	6.8	10.1	7.8	7.5	8.1
Indonesia	3.4	4.8	5.0	5.7	5.5	6.3	6.0	4.6	6.1	6.4	6.3	7.0
Kiribati	4.4	2.3	2.2	3.9	1.9	0.4	−1.1	−0.7	1.8	3.0	3.5	2.0
Lao People's Democratic Republic	6.1	6.2	7.0	6.8	8.6	7.8	7.8	7.6	7.9	8.3	8.4	7.4
Malaysia	5.8	5.8	6.8	5.3	5.8	6.5	4.8	−1.6	7.2	5.2	5.1	5.0
Maldives	7.1	16.3	10.4	−8.7	19.6	10.4	10.9	−7.5	7.1	6.5	4.6	3.5
Myanmar	8.6	13.8	13.6	13.6	13.1	12.0	3.6	5.1	5.5	5.5	5.5	5.7
Nepal	4.5	3.9	4.7	3.5	3.4	3.4	6.1	4.4	4.6	3.5	3.8	3.9
Pakistan	3.6	4.7	7.5	9.0	5.8	6.8	3.7	1.7	3.8	2.6	3.8	5.0
Papua New Guinea	2.5	4.4	0.6	3.9	2.3	7.2	6.6	5.5	7.0	9.0	5.5	5.0
Philippines	3.6	5.0	6.7	4.8	5.2	6.6	4.2	1.1	7.6	4.7	4.9	5.0
Samoa	4.2	3.8	4.2	7.0	2.1	2.3	4.9	−5.1	−0.2	2.0	2.1	2.8
Solomon Islands	−0.4	6.5	4.9	5.4	6.9	10.7	7.3	−1.2	6.5	5.6	6.1	5.3
Sri Lanka	4.5	5.9	5.4	6.2	7.7	6.8	6.0	3.5	8.0	7.0	6.5	6.5
Thailand	3.6	7.1	6.3	4.6	5.1	5.0	2.6	−2.4	7.8	3.5	4.8	5.0
Timor-Leste	...	0.1	4.2	6.2	−5.8	9.1	11.0	12.9	6.0	7.3	8.6	7.9
Tonga	1.9	1.8	0.0	−0.4	−0.4	0.9	1.3	−0.3	0.3	1.4	1.7	1.8
Tuvalu	...	−3.3	−1.4	−4.0	2.9	5.5	7.6	−1.7	−0.5	1.0	1.4	1.4
Vanuatu	1.7	3.7	4.5	5.2	7.4	6.5	6.2	3.5	2.2	3.8	4.2	4.0
Vietnam	7.5	7.3	7.8	8.4	8.2	8.5	6.3	5.3	6.8	5.8	6.3	7.5

Table A4. Emerging and Developing Economies: Real GDP[1] *(continued)*

	Average 1993–2002	2003	2004	2005	2006	2007	2008	2009	2010	Projections 2011	2012	2016
Latin America and the Caribbean	**2.7**	**2.1**	**6.0**	**4.6**	**5.6**	**5.8**	**4.3**	**−1.7**	**6.1**	**4.5**	**4.0**	**3.9**
Antigua and Barbuda	2.9	5.7	4.1	7.9	12.9	8.3	2.2	−9.6	−4.1	2.0	2.5	4.6
Argentina[4]	0.6	9.0	8.9	9.2	8.5	8.6	6.8	0.8	9.2	8.0	4.6	4.0
The Bahamas	4.4	−1.3	0.9	3.4	2.5	1.4	−1.3	−5.4	1.0	2.0	2.5	2.7
Barbados	1.8	2.0	4.8	3.9	3.6	3.8	−0.2	−4.7	0.3	1.8	2.2	3.5
Belize	4.7	9.3	4.6	3.0	4.7	1.2	3.8	0.0	2.7	2.5	2.8	2.5
Bolivia	3.5	2.7	4.2	4.4	4.8	4.6	6.1	3.4	4.1	5.0	4.5	4.5
Brazil	2.9	1.1	5.7	3.2	4.0	6.1	5.2	−0.6	7.5	3.8	3.6	4.2
Chile	5.0	4.0	6.0	5.6	4.6	4.6	3.7	−1.7	5.2	6.5	4.7	4.5
Colombia	2.5	3.9	5.3	4.7	6.7	6.9	3.5	1.5	4.3	4.9	4.5	4.5
Costa Rica	4.5	6.4	4.3	5.9	8.8	7.9	2.7	−1.3	4.2	4.0	4.1	4.5
Dominica	1.4	6.2	0.8	−1.7	3.6	3.9	7.8	−0.7	0.3	0.9	1.5	1.9
Dominican Republic	5.7	−0.3	1.3	9.3	10.7	8.5	5.3	3.5	7.8	4.5	5.5	6.0
Ecuador	2.2	3.3	8.8	5.7	4.8	2.0	7.2	0.4	3.6	5.8	3.8	2.7
El Salvador	3.9	2.3	1.9	3.6	3.9	3.8	1.3	−3.1	1.4	2.0	2.5	4.0
Grenada	4.2	8.5	−0.4	13.4	−4.7	6.1	2.2	−7.6	−1.4	0.0	1.0	3.0
Guatemala	3.5	2.5	3.2	3.3	5.4	6.3	3.3	0.5	2.8	2.8	3.0	3.5
Guyana	3.9	−0.7	1.6	−1.9	5.1	7.0	2.0	3.3	4.4	5.3	6.0	3.0
Haiti	0.3	0.4	−3.5	1.8	2.2	3.3	0.8	2.9	−5.4	6.1	7.5	5.5
Honduras	3.0	4.5	6.2	6.1	6.6	6.2	4.1	−2.1	2.8	3.5	3.5	4.0
Jamaica	0.6	3.5	1.4	1.1	3.0	1.4	−0.9	−3.0	−1.2	1.5	1.7	3.0
Mexico	2.7	1.4	4.0	3.2	5.2	3.2	1.2	−6.2	5.4	3.8	3.6	3.2
Nicaragua	3.9	2.5	5.3	4.3	4.2	3.6	2.8	−1.5	4.5	4.0	3.3	4.0
Panama	4.0	4.2	7.5	7.2	8.5	12.1	10.1	3.2	7.5	7.4	7.2	5.0
Paraguay	1.4	3.8	4.1	2.9	4.3	6.8	5.8	−3.8	15.0	6.4	5.0	4.0
Peru	4.3	4.0	5.0	6.8	7.7	8.9	9.8	0.9	8.8	6.2	5.6	6.0
St. Kitts and Nevis	4.2	−2.2	6.4	7.4	2.3	9.3	5.7	−4.4	−1.5	1.5	1.8	3.5
St. Lucia	1.0	4.8	6.0	−2.6	7.4	1.5	5.8	−1.3	4.4	2.0	2.6	2.4
St. Vincent and the Grenadines	3.0	7.2	4.6	3.0	6.0	3.1	−0.6	−2.3	−1.8	−0.4	2.0	3.5
Suriname	1.1	6.3	8.5	4.5	3.8	5.1	4.7	3.1	4.4	5.0	5.0	5.4
Trinidad and Tobago	5.6	14.4	7.9	6.2	13.2	4.8	2.4	−3.5	−0.6	1.1	2.6	2.7
Uruguay	0.7	2.3	4.6	6.8	4.3	7.3	8.6	2.6	8.5	6.0	4.2	4.0
Venezuela	0.0	−7.8	18.3	10.3	9.9	8.8	5.3	−3.2	−1.5	2.8	3.6	1.8
Middle East and North Africa	**3.3**	**7.3**	**5.9**	**5.4**	**6.0**	**6.7**	**4.6**	**2.6**	**4.4**	**4.0**	**3.6**	**5.1**
Algeria	2.3	6.9	5.2	5.1	2.0	3.0	2.4	2.4	3.3	2.9	3.3	4.0
Bahrain	4.8	7.2	5.6	7.9	6.7	8.4	6.3	3.1	4.1	1.5	3.6	4.2
Djibouti	−0.8	3.2	3.0	3.2	4.8	5.1	5.8	5.0	3.5	4.8	5.1	5.8
Egypt	4.8	3.2	4.1	4.5	6.8	7.1	7.2	4.7	5.1	1.2	1.8	6.5
Islamic Republic of Iran	3.2	7.2	5.1	4.7	5.8	10.8	0.6	3.5	3.2	2.5	3.4	4.6
Iraq	. . .	. . .	. . .	−0.7	6.2	1.5	9.5	4.2	0.8	9.6	12.6	9.8
Jordan	4.3	4.2	8.6	8.1	8.1	8.2	7.2	5.5	2.3	2.5	2.9	5.0
Kuwait	4.8	17.4	11.2	10.4	5.3	4.5	5.0	−5.2	3.4	5.7	4.5	4.7
Lebanon	4.0	3.2	7.5	1.0	0.6	7.5	9.3	8.5	7.5	1.5	3.5	4.0
Libya[5]	−1.6	13.0	4.4	10.3	6.7	7.5	2.3	−2.3	4.2	. . .	. . .	. . .
Mauritania	2.9	5.6	5.2	5.4	11.4	1.0	3.5	−1.2	5.2	5.1	5.7	5.5
Morocco	3.2	6.3	4.8	3.0	7.8	2.7	5.6	4.9	3.7	4.6	4.6	5.9
Oman	3.8	0.3	3.4	4.0	5.5	6.7	12.9	1.1	4.1	4.4	3.6	3.6
Qatar	7.4	6.3	17.7	7.5	26.2	18.0	17.7	12.0	16.6	18.7	6.0	4.9
Saudi Arabia	1.4	7.7	5.3	5.6	3.2	2.0	4.2	0.1	4.1	6.5	3.6	4.2
Sudan[6]	5.4	7.4	3.6	7.9	9.4	10.2	3.7	4.6	6.5	−0.2	−0.4	5.5
Syrian Arab Republic	3.4	−2.0	6.9	6.2	5.0	5.7	4.5	6.0	3.2	−2.0	1.5	5.0
Tunisia	4.2	5.5	6.0	4.0	5.7	6.3	4.5	3.1	3.1	0.0	3.9	7.0
United Arab Emirates	4.5	16.4	10.1	8.6	8.8	6.5	5.3	−3.2	3.2	3.3	3.8	4.2
Republic of Yemen	5.0	3.7	4.0	5.6	3.2	3.3	3.6	3.9	8.0	−2.5	−0.5	4.8

Table A4. Emerging and Developing Economies: Real GDP[1] *(concluded)*

	Average 1993–2002	2003	2004	2005	2006	2007	2008	2009	2010	Projections 2011	2012	2016
Sub-Saharan Africa	**3.7**	**4.9**	**7.1**	**6.2**	**6.4**	**7.1**	**5.6**	**2.8**	**5.4**	**5.2**	**5.8**	**5.1**
Angola	3.5	3.3	11.2	20.6	20.7	22.6	13.8	2.4	3.4	3.7	10.8	6.0
Benin	4.9	4.0	3.1	2.9	3.8	4.6	5.0	2.7	2.6	3.8	4.3	5.0
Botswana	6.3	6.3	6.0	1.6	5.1	4.8	3.0	−4.9	7.2	6.2	5.3	4.7
Burkina Faso	5.5	7.8	4.5	8.7	5.5	3.6	5.2	3.2	7.9	4.9	5.6	6.4
Burundi	−1.7	−1.2	4.8	0.9	5.1	3.6	4.5	3.5	3.9	4.2	4.8	5.0
Cameroon[7]	2.9	4.0	3.7	2.3	3.2	3.4	2.6	2.0	3.2	3.8	4.5	4.5
Cape Verde	7.5	4.7	4.3	6.5	10.1	8.6	6.2	3.7	5.4	5.6	6.4	4.5
Central African Republic	1.5	−7.1	1.0	2.4	3.8	3.7	2.0	1.7	3.3	4.1	5.0	5.7
Chad	3.5	14.7	33.6	7.9	0.2	0.2	1.7	−1.2	13.0	2.5	6.9	3.5
Comoros	1.6	2.5	−0.2	4.2	1.2	0.5	1.0	1.8	2.1	2.2	3.5	4.0
Democratic Republic of Congo	−3.6	5.8	6.6	7.8	5.6	6.3	6.2	2.8	7.2	6.5	6.0	6.2
Republic of Congo	1.8	0.8	3.5	7.8	6.2	−1.6	5.6	7.5	8.8	5.0	7.0	3.1
Côte d'Ivoire	3.2	−1.7	1.6	1.9	0.7	1.6	2.3	3.8	2.4	−5.8	8.5	5.2
Equatorial Guinea	36.7	14.0	38.0	9.7	1.3	21.4	10.7	5.7	−0.8	7.1	4.0	−3.4
Eritrea	5.1	−2.7	1.5	2.6	−1.0	1.4	−9.8	3.9	2.2	8.2	6.3	1.8
Ethiopia	5.6	−2.1	11.7	12.6	11.5	11.8	11.2	10.0	8.0	7.5	5.5	6.5
Gabon	1.6	2.5	1.4	3.0	1.2	5.6	2.3	−1.4	5.7	5.6	3.3	3.2
The Gambia	3.8	6.9	7.0	0.3	3.4	6.0	6.3	6.7	6.1	5.5	5.5	5.5
Ghana	4.5	5.1	5.3	6.0	6.1	6.5	8.4	4.0	7.7	13.5	7.3	4.4
Guinea	4.4	1.2	2.3	3.0	2.5	1.8	4.9	−0.3	1.9	4.0	4.2	6.8
Guinea-Bissau	0.4	0.4	2.8	4.3	2.1	3.2	3.2	3.0	3.5	4.8	4.7	4.7
Kenya	2.2	2.8	4.6	6.0	6.3	7.0	1.5	2.6	5.6	5.3	6.1	6.6
Lesotho	3.5	4.1	2.4	3.0	4.7	4.5	4.2	3.1	3.6	5.1	5.1	4.9
Liberia	...	−31.3	2.6	5.3	7.8	9.4	7.1	4.6	5.6	6.9	9.4	4.6
Madagascar	1.5	9.8	5.3	4.6	5.0	6.2	7.1	−3.7	0.6	1.0	4.7	5.1
Malawi	3.0	5.5	5.5	2.6	2.1	9.5	8.3	9.0	6.5	4.6	4.2	3.6
Mali	4.5	7.6	2.3	6.1	5.3	4.3	5.0	4.5	5.8	5.3	5.5	5.1
Mauritius	4.8	4.3	5.5	1.5	4.9	5.8	5.5	3.0	4.2	4.2	4.1	4.5
Mozambique	8.5	6.5	7.9	8.4	8.7	7.3	6.8	6.3	6.8	7.2	7.5	7.8
Namibia	3.0	4.3	12.3	2.5	7.1	5.4	4.3	−0.7	4.8	3.6	4.2	4.3
Niger	2.8	7.1	−0.8	8.4	5.8	3.1	9.6	−0.9	8.0	5.5	12.5	6.6
Nigeria	4.7	10.3	10.6	5.4	6.2	7.0	6.0	7.0	8.7	6.9	6.6	6.0
Rwanda	2.2	2.2	7.4	9.4	9.2	5.5	11.2	4.1	7.5	7.0	6.8	6.5
São Tomé and Príncipe	2.7	5.4	6.6	5.7	6.7	6.0	5.8	4.0	4.5	5.0	6.0	4.4
Senegal	3.2	6.7	5.9	5.6	2.4	5.0	3.2	2.2	4.2	4.0	4.5	5.4
Seychelles	3.4	−5.9	−2.9	6.7	6.4	9.6	−1.3	0.7	6.2	5.0	4.4	4.1
Sierra Leone	−1.9	9.5	7.4	7.2	7.3	6.4	5.5	3.2	5.0	5.1	51.4	3.8
South Africa	2.8	2.9	4.6	5.3	5.6	5.6	3.6	−1.7	2.8	3.4	3.6	3.6
Swaziland	2.7	3.9	2.3	2.2	2.9	2.8	3.1	1.2	2.0	−2.1	0.6	2.4
Tanzania	4.0	6.9	7.8	7.4	7.0	6.9	7.3	6.7	6.4	6.1	6.1	6.9
Togo	1.0	5.0	2.1	1.2	4.1	2.3	2.4	3.2	3.7	3.8	4.4	4.4
Uganda	7.2	6.5	6.8	6.3	10.8	8.4	8.7	7.2	5.2	6.4	5.5	7.0
Zambia	0.5	5.1	5.4	5.3	6.2	6.2	5.7	6.4	7.6	6.7	6.7	7.3
Zimbabwe[8]	...	−17.2	−6.9	−2.2	−3.5	−3.7	−17.7	6.0	9.0	6.0	3.1	3.0

[1]For many countries, figures for recent years are IMF staff estimates. Data for some countries are for fiscal years.

[2]Data for some countries refer to real net material product (NMP) or are estimates based on NMP. For many countries, figures for recent years are IMF staff estimates. The figures should be interpreted only as indicative of broad orders of magnitude because reliable, comparable data are not generally available. In particular, the growth of output of new private enterprises of the informal economy is not fully reflected in the recent figures.

[3]Georgia and Mongolia, which are not members of the Commonwealth of Independent States, are included in this group for reasons of geography and similarities in economic structure.

[4]Figures are based on the official GDP data. The authorities have committed to improve the quality of Argentina's official GDP, so as to bring it into compliance with their obligations under the IMF's Articles of Agreement. Until the quality of data reporting has improved, IMF staff will also use alternative measures of GDP growth for macroeconomic surveillance, including estimates by private analysts, which have been, on average, significantly lower than official GDP growth from 2008 onward.

[5]Libya's projections are excluded due to the uncertain political situation.

[6]Projections for 2011 and later exclude South Sudan.

[7]The percent changes in 2002 are calculated over a period of 18 months, reflecting a change in the fiscal year cycle (from July–June to January–December).

[8]The Zimbabwe dollar ceased circulating in early 2009. Data are based on IMF staff estimates of price and exchange rate developments in U.S. dollars. IMF staff estimates of U.S. dollar values may differ from authorities' estimates. Real GDP is in constant 2009 prices.

Table A5. Summary of Inflation
(Percent)

	Average 1993–2002	2003	2004	2005	2006	2007	2008	2009	2010	Projections 2011	2012	2016
GDP Deflators												
Advanced Economies	**1.8**	**1.7**	**2.1**	**2.1**	**2.1**	**2.3**	**2.0**	**0.8**	**1.0**	**1.9**	**1.3**	**1.6**
United States	1.9	2.1	2.8	3.3	3.2	2.9	2.2	1.1	1.2	2.1	1.1	1.5
Euro Area	1.9	2.2	1.9	2.0	1.9	2.4	2.0	0.9	0.8	1.4	1.4	1.7
Japan	−0.6	−1.6	−1.1	−1.2	−0.9	−0.7	−1.0	−0.4	−2.1	−1.5	−0.5	0.5
Other Advanced Economies[1]	2.4	2.1	2.4	1.9	2.2	2.7	2.9	0.8	2.4	3.5	2.3	2.2
Consumer Prices												
Advanced Economies	**2.2**	**1.9**	**2.0**	**2.3**	**2.4**	**2.2**	**3.4**	**0.1**	**1.6**	**2.6**	**1.4**	**1.8**
United States	2.5	2.3	2.7	3.4	3.2	2.9	3.8	−0.3	1.6	3.0	1.2	1.7
Euro Area[2]	2.1	2.1	2.2	2.2	2.2	2.1	3.3	0.3	1.6	2.5	1.5	1.9
Japan	0.2	−0.3	0.0	−0.3	0.3	0.0	1.4	−1.4	−0.7	−0.4	−0.5	0.8
Other Advanced Economies[1]	2.4	1.8	1.8	2.1	2.1	2.1	3.8	1.5	2.4	3.5	2.6	2.2
Emerging and Developing Economies	**28.6**	**6.6**	**5.9**	**5.8**	**5.6**	**6.5**	**9.2**	**5.2**	**6.1**	**7.5**	**5.9**	**4.3**
Regional Groups												
Central and Eastern Europe	44.9	10.9	6.6	5.9	5.9	6.0	8.1	4.7	5.3	5.2	4.5	3.6
Commonwealth of Independent States[3]	108.2	12.3	10.4	12.1	9.4	9.7	15.6	11.2	7.2	10.3	8.7	6.4
Developing Asia	6.8	2.6	4.1	3.7	4.2	5.4	7.4	3.1	5.7	7.0	5.1	3.5
Latin America and the Caribbean	39.2	10.4	6.6	6.3	5.3	5.4	7.9	6.0	6.0	6.7	6.0	5.3
Middle East and North Africa	8.9	5.5	6.5	6.4	7.5	10.1	13.5	6.6	6.8	9.9	7.6	5.1
Sub-Saharan Africa	22.9	10.8	7.6	8.9	6.9	6.9	11.7	10.6	7.5	8.4	8.3	5.8
Memorandum												
European Union	5.0	2.2	2.3	2.3	2.3	2.4	3.7	0.9	2.0	3.0	1.8	2.0
Analytical Groups												
By Source of Export Earnings												
Fuel	48.4	11.3	9.7	10.0	9.0	10.1	15.0	9.4	8.2	10.6	8.4	6.5
Nonfuel	23.6	5.5	5.0	4.8	4.7	5.6	7.9	4.3	5.6	6.8	5.4	3.9
Of Which, Primary Products	27.0	5.0	3.8	5.2	5.2	5.1	9.1	5.2	4.0	5.5	4.9	4.1
By External Financing Source												
Net Debtor Economies	30.6	7.4	5.6	5.9	5.8	6.0	9.0	7.2	7.1	7.8	6.8	4.5
Of Which, Official Financing	21.1	8.5	6.3	7.6	7.5	7.8	12.9	9.3	6.5	9.0	8.9	5.5
Net Debtor Economies by Debt-Servicing Experience												
Economies with Arrears and/or Rescheduling during 2005–09	24.1	12.0	7.9	8.1	8.7	8.2	11.4	6.6	8.0	11.7	10.6	6.9
Memorandum												
Median Inflation Rate												
Advanced Economies	2.4	2.1	2.1	2.2	2.3	2.1	3.9	0.7	2.0	3.1	2.1	2.0
Emerging and Developing Economies	8.2	4.3	4.4	6.0	6.0	6.3	10.3	3.8	4.4	6.2	5.0	4.0

[1]In this table, Other Advanced Economies means advanced economies excluding the United States, Euro Area countries, and Japan.
[2]Based on Eurostat's harmonized index of consumer prices.
[3]Georgia and Mongolia, which are not members of the Commonwealth of Independent States, are included in this group for reasons of geography and similarities in economic structure.

Table A6. Advanced Economies: Consumer Prices

(Annual percent change)

	Average 1993–2002	2003	2004	2005	2006	2007	2008	2009	2010	Projections 2011	Projections 2012	Projections 2016	End of Period[1] 2010	End of Period[1] Projections 2011	End of Period[1] Projections 2012
Consumer Prices															
Advanced Economies	**2.2**	**1.9**	**2.0**	**2.3**	**2.4**	**2.2**	**3.4**	**0.1**	**1.6**	**2.6**	**1.4**	**1.8**	**2.0**	**2.3**	**1.3**
United States	2.5	2.3	2.7	3.4	3.2	2.9	3.8	−0.3	1.6	3.0	1.2	1.7	1.7	2.5	0.9
Euro Area[2]	2.1	2.1	2.2	2.2	2.2	2.1	3.3	0.3	1.6	2.5	1.5	1.9	2.2	2.3	1.5
Germany	1.7	1.0	1.8	1.9	1.8	2.3	2.8	0.2	1.2	2.2	1.3	2.0	1.9	2.2	1.3
France	1.6	2.2	2.3	1.9	1.9	1.6	3.2	0.1	1.7	2.1	1.4	1.9	1.7	2.1	1.4
Italy	3.1	2.8	2.3	2.2	2.2	2.0	3.5	0.8	1.6	2.6	1.6	2.0	2.1	2.6	1.6
Spain	3.3	3.1	3.1	3.4	3.6	2.8	4.1	−0.2	2.0	2.9	1.5	1.8	2.9	2.0	1.4
Netherlands	2.5	2.2	1.4	1.5	1.7	1.6	2.2	1.0	0.9	2.5	2.0	1.8	1.8	2.3	2.0
Belgium	1.8	1.5	1.9	2.5	2.3	1.8	4.5	0.0	2.3	3.2	2.0	2.0	3.4	2.5	2.0
Austria	1.8	1.3	2.0	2.1	1.7	2.2	3.2	0.4	1.7	3.2	2.2	1.9	2.2	2.6	1.9
Greece	6.4	3.4	3.0	3.5	3.3	3.0	4.2	1.3	4.7	2.9	1.0	1.0	5.1	2.1	0.6
Portugal	3.5	3.3	2.5	2.1	3.0	2.4	2.7	−0.9	1.4	3.4	2.1	1.6	2.2	3.2	2.1
Finland	1.7	1.3	0.1	0.8	1.3	1.6	3.9	1.6	1.7	3.1	2.0	2.0	2.8	2.2	2.2
Ireland	2.8	4.0	2.3	2.2	2.7	2.9	3.1	−1.7	−1.6	1.1	0.6	1.8	−0.2	1.3	1.0
Slovak Republic	. . .	8.4	7.5	2.8	4.3	1.9	3.9	0.9	0.7	3.6	1.8	2.8	1.3	2.7	2.9
Slovenia	12.1	5.6	3.6	2.5	2.5	3.6	5.7	0.9	1.8	1.8	2.1	2.1	1.9	2.1	2.3
Luxembourg	2.0	2.0	2.2	2.5	2.7	2.3	3.4	0.4	2.3	3.6	1.4	1.9	2.8	3.9	1.5
Estonia	. . .	1.3	3.0	4.1	4.4	6.6	10.4	−0.1	2.9	5.1	3.5	2.5	5.4	4.6	3.3
Cyprus	3.1	4.0	1.9	2.0	2.2	2.2	4.4	0.2	2.6	4.0	2.4	2.1	1.9	4.5	1.9
Malta	3.2	1.9	2.7	2.5	2.6	0.7	4.7	1.8	2.0	2.6	2.3	2.5	4.0	1.6	2.3
Japan	0.2	−0.3	0.0	−0.3	0.3	0.0	1.4	−1.4	−0.7	−0.4	−0.5	0.8	−0.4	−0.3	−0.2
United Kingdom[2]	1.8	1.4	1.3	2.0	2.3	2.3	3.6	2.1	3.3	4.5	2.4	2.0	3.4	4.5	2.0
Canada	1.8	2.7	1.8	2.2	2.0	2.1	2.4	0.3	1.8	2.9	2.1	2.0	2.2	2.6	2.0
Korea	4.2	3.5	3.6	2.8	2.2	2.5	4.7	2.8	3.0	4.5	3.5	3.0	3.5	4.1	3.0
Australia	2.5	2.8	2.3	2.7	3.5	2.3	4.4	1.8	2.8	3.5	3.3	2.6	2.7	3.7	3.8
Taiwan Province of China	1.7	−0.3	1.6	2.3	0.6	1.8	3.5	−0.9	1.0	1.8	1.8	2.0	7.6	2.3	1.8
Sweden	1.7	2.3	1.0	0.8	1.5	1.7	3.3	2.0	1.9	3.0	2.5	2.0	2.1	2.9	2.2
Switzerland	1.1	0.6	0.8	1.2	1.1	0.7	2.4	−0.5	0.7	0.7	0.9	1.0	0.7	0.7	0.9
Hong Kong SAR	2.8	−2.6	−0.4	0.9	2.0	2.0	4.3	0.6	2.3	5.5	4.5	3.0	3.1	4.0	4.5
Singapore	1.2	0.5	1.7	0.5	1.0	2.1	6.6	0.6	2.8	3.7	2.9	2.0	4.0	1.8	5.1
Czech Republic	. . .	0.1	2.8	1.8	2.5	2.9	6.3	1.0	1.5	1.8	2.0	2.0	2.3	1.6	2.2
Norway	2.2	2.5	0.5	1.5	2.3	0.7	3.8	2.2	2.4	1.7	2.2	2.5	2.8	2.0	2.4
Israel	7.1	0.7	−0.4	1.3	2.1	0.5	4.6	3.3	2.7	3.4	1.6	2.0	2.6	2.2	2.0
Denmark	2.1	2.1	1.2	1.8	1.9	1.7	3.4	1.3	2.3	3.2	2.4	1.9	2.9	2.7	2.8
New Zealand	1.9	1.7	2.3	3.0	3.4	2.4	4.0	2.1	2.3	4.4	2.7	2.1	4.0	0.8	5.0
Iceland	3.3	2.1	3.2	4.0	6.8	5.0	12.4	12.0	5.4	4.2	4.5	2.5	2.4	6.2	2.9
Memorandum															
Major Advanced Economies	1.9	1.7	2.0	2.3	2.4	2.2	3.2	−0.1	1.4	2.4	1.1	1.7	1.6	2.2	1.0
Newly Industrialized Asian Economies	3.1	1.5	2.4	2.2	1.6	2.2	4.5	1.3	2.3	3.7	3.1	2.6	4.7	3.3	3.0

[1]December–December changes. Several countries report Q4–Q4 changes.
[2]Based on Eurostat's harmonized index of consumer prices.

Table A7. Emerging and Developing Economies: Consumer Prices[1]

(Annual percent change)

	Average 1993–2002	2003	2004	2005	2006	2007	2008	2009	2010	Projections 2011	Projections 2012	Projections 2016	End of Period[2] 2010	End of Period[2] Projections 2011	End of Period[2] Projections 2012
Central and Eastern Europe[3]	**44.9**	**10.9**	**6.6**	**5.9**	**5.9**	**6.0**	**8.1**	**4.7**	**5.3**	**5.2**	**4.5**	**3.6**	**5.2**	**5.5**	**3.9**
Albania	17.0	2.3	2.9	2.4	2.4	2.9	3.4	2.2	3.6	3.9	3.5	3.0	3.4	3.5	2.9
Bosnia and Herzegovina	...	0.5	0.3	3.6	6.1	1.5	7.4	−0.4	2.1	4.0	2.5	2.7	3.1	4.0	2.5
Bulgaria	71.2	2.3	6.1	6.0	7.4	7.6	12.0	2.5	3.0	3.8	2.9	3.0	4.4	3.1	2.8
Croatia	45.9	1.8	2.0	3.3	3.2	2.9	6.1	2.4	1.0	3.2	2.4	3.0	1.9	3.6	2.7
Hungary	15.8	4.4	6.8	3.6	3.9	7.9	6.1	4.2	4.9	3.7	3.0	3.0	4.7	3.5	3.0
Kosovo	...	0.3	−1.1	−1.4	0.6	4.4	9.4	−2.4	3.5	8.3	2.6	1.7	6.6	6.2	1.9
Latvia	17.8	2.9	6.2	6.9	6.6	10.1	15.3	3.3	−1.2	4.2	2.3	2.2	2.4	3.7	1.8
Lithuania	...	−1.1	1.2	2.7	3.8	5.8	11.1	4.2	1.2	4.2	2.6	2.2	3.6	3.2	2.5
Former Yugoslav Republic of Macedonia	30.1	1.2	−0.4	0.5	3.2	2.3	8.4	−0.8	1.5	4.4	2.0	2.0	3.0	3.7	2.0
Montenegro	...	7.5	3.1	3.4	3.0	4.2	8.5	3.4	0.5	3.1	2.0	2.0	0.7	3.0	1.8
Poland	16.2	0.8	3.5	2.1	1.0	2.5	4.2	3.5	2.6	4.0	2.8	2.5	3.1	3.5	2.5
Romania	71.4	15.4	11.9	9.0	6.6	4.8	7.8	5.6	6.1	6.4	4.3	3.0	8.0	5.0	3.8
Serbia	...	2.9	10.6	17.3	12.7	6.5	12.4	8.1	6.2	11.3	4.3	4.0	10.3	7.9	3.5
Turkey	72.1	25.3	8.6	8.2	9.6	8.8	10.4	6.3	8.6	6.0	6.9	5.0	6.4	8.0	5.7
Commonwealth of Independent States[3],[4]	**108.2**	**12.3**	**10.4**	**12.1**	**9.4**	**9.7**	**15.6**	**11.2**	**7.2**	**10.3**	**8.7**	**6.4**	**8.9**	**10.2**	**7.9**
Russia	95.3	13.7	10.9	12.7	9.7	9.0	14.1	11.7	6.9	8.9	7.3	6.5	8.8	7.5	7.1
Excluding Russia	147.1	8.7	9.1	10.7	8.9	11.5	19.5	10.1	8.0	13.6	12.2	6.1	9.2	16.8	9.9
Armenia	147.8	4.7	7.0	0.6	3.0	4.6	9.0	3.5	7.3	8.8	3.3	4.0	8.5	5.7	4.1
Azerbaijan	108.2	2.2	6.7	9.7	8.4	16.6	20.8	1.5	5.7	9.3	10.3	5.4	7.9	11.2	9.5
Belarus	247.2	28.4	18.1	10.3	7.0	8.4	14.8	13.0	7.7	41.0	35.5	6.2	9.9	65.3	20.0
Georgia	...	4.8	5.7	8.3	9.2	9.2	10.0	1.7	7.1	9.6	5.0	5.0	11.2	7.0	5.0
Kazakhstan	111.7	6.6	7.1	7.9	8.6	10.8	17.2	7.4	7.4	8.9	7.9	6.0	8.0	9.5	7.5
Kyrgyz Republic	65.2	3.1	4.1	4.3	5.6	10.2	24.5	6.8	7.8	19.1	9.4	6.0	18.9	13.0	8.0
Moldova	65.7	11.7	12.4	11.9	12.7	12.4	12.7	0.0	7.4	7.9	7.8	5.0	8.1	9.5	6.0
Mongolia	40.8	5.1	7.9	12.5	4.5	8.2	26.8	6.3	10.2	10.2	14.3	7.6	14.3	15.1	9.3
Tajikistan	182.0	16.4	7.2	7.3	10.0	13.2	20.4	6.5	6.5	13.6	10.0	5.0	9.8	14.0	8.5
Turkmenistan	246.3	5.6	5.9	10.7	8.2	6.3	14.5	−2.7	4.4	6.1	7.2	6.0	4.8	7.5	7.0
Ukraine	149.3	5.2	9.0	13.5	9.1	12.8	25.2	15.9	9.4	9.3	9.1	5.0	9.1	10.7	8.5
Uzbekistan	128.0	11.6	6.6	10.0	14.2	12.3	12.7	14.1	9.4	13.1	11.8	11.0	12.1	12.7	11.0

Table A7. Emerging and Developing Economies: Consumer Prices[1] *(continued)*

	Average 1993–2002	2003	2004	2005	2006	2007	2008	2009	2010	Projections 2011	Projections 2012	Projections 2016	End of Period[2] 2010	End of Period[2] Projections 2011	End of Period[2] Projections 2012
Developing Asia	**6.8**	**2.6**	**4.1**	**3.7**	**4.2**	**5.4**	**7.4**	**3.1**	**5.7**	**7.0**	**5.1**	**3.5**	**6.2**	**6.3**	**4.9**
Islamic Republic of Afghanistan	...	24.1	13.2	12.3	5.1	13.0	26.8	−12.2	7.7	8.4	3.2	5.0	16.6	2.0	5.0
Bangladesh	4.9	5.4	6.1	7.0	6.8	9.1	8.9	5.4	8.1	10.1	7.4	5.6	8.3	9.0	7.1
Bhutan	7.0	2.1	4.6	5.3	5.0	5.2	8.3	8.6	7.0	6.5	5.0	4.0	9.1	5.8	4.7
Brunei Darussalam	1.5	0.3	0.9	1.1	0.2	1.0	2.1	1.0	0.4	1.8	1.2	1.2	0.9	1.8	1.2
Cambodia	13.6	1.0	3.9	6.3	6.1	7.7	25.0	−0.7	4.0	6.4	5.6	3.0	3.1	8.2	4.1
China	6.2	1.2	3.9	1.8	1.5	4.8	5.9	−0.7	3.3	5.5	3.3	3.0	4.7	5.1	3.0
Republic of Fiji	3.2	2.8	2.3	2.5	4.8	7.7	3.7	5.5	8.4	5.5	5.0	5.0	7.5	5.0	5.0
India	7.3	3.7	3.9	4.0	6.3	6.4	8.3	10.9	12.0	10.6	8.6	4.1	9.5	8.9	8.5
Indonesia	13.8	6.8	6.1	10.5	13.1	6.0	9.8	4.8	5.1	5.7	6.5	4.5	7.0	5.0	6.4
Kiribati	3.0	1.9	−0.9	−0.3	−1.5	4.2	11.0	8.8	−2.8	7.7	5.0	2.5	−1.4	8.0	4.0
Lao People's Democratic Republic	28.5	15.5	10.5	7.2	6.8	4.5	7.6	0.0	6.0	8.7	6.7	3.9	5.8	9.7	6.0
Malaysia	3.0	1.1	1.4	2.9	3.6	2.0	5.4	0.6	1.7	3.2	2.5	2.3	2.1	3.2	2.5
Maldives	4.3	−2.8	6.3	2.5	3.5	7.4	12.3	4.0	4.7	12.1	8.4	3.0	5.1	15.0	3.5
Myanmar	27.9	24.9	3.8	10.7	26.3	32.9	22.5	8.2	8.2	6.7	3.7	4.0	8.9	5.2	4.2
Nepal	6.9	4.7	4.0	4.5	8.0	6.2	6.7	12.6	9.6	9.5	8.0	6.0	9.0	9.4	8.1
Pakistan	8.0	3.1	4.6	9.3	7.9	7.8	12.0	20.8	11.7	13.9	14.0	8.0	12.7	13.1	12.0
Papua New Guinea	10.5	14.7	2.1	1.8	2.4	0.9	10.8	6.9	6.0	8.4	8.7	6.8	7.8	9.5	8.0
Philippines	6.9	3.5	6.0	7.6	6.2	2.8	9.3	3.2	3.8	4.5	4.1	4.0	3.1	4.6	4.2
Samoa	3.8	4.3	7.8	7.8	3.2	4.5	6.2	14.4	−0.2	2.9	3.0	4.0	0.3	2.9	3.0
Solomon Islands	9.5	10.5	6.9	7.0	11.1	7.7	17.4	7.1	1.0	6.0	5.0	5.0	0.8	6.5	5.6
Sri Lanka	9.7	9.0	9.0	11.0	10.0	15.8	22.6	3.4	5.9	8.4	6.6	5.5	6.9	7.1	6.0
Thailand	3.8	1.8	2.8	4.5	4.6	2.2	5.5	−0.8	3.3	4.0	4.1	2.7	3.0	4.2	5.6
Timor-Leste	...	7.2	3.2	1.8	4.1	8.9	7.6	0.1	4.9	10.5	6.0	5.0	8.0	6.5	6.0
Tonga	4.2	11.5	10.6	8.3	6.0	7.5	7.3	3.4	4.0	5.9	4.8	6.0	6.6	5.8	3.9
Tuvalu	...	2.9	2.4	3.2	4.2	2.3	10.4	−0.3	−1.9	0.5	2.6	2.2	−1.8	0.5	2.6
Vanuatu	2.5	3.0	1.4	1.2	2.0	3.9	4.8	4.3	2.8	2.2	2.9	3.0	3.4	2.8	3.0
Vietnam	5.6	3.3	7.9	8.4	7.5	8.3	23.1	6.7	9.2	18.8	12.1	5.0	11.8	19.0	8.1

Table A7. Emerging and Developing Economies: Consumer Prices[1] (continued)

	Average 1993–2002	2003	2004	2005	2006	2007	2008	2009	2010	Projections 2011	Projections 2012	Projections 2016	End of Period[2] 2010	End of Period[2] Projections 2011	End of Period[2] Projections 2012
Latin America and the Caribbean	**39.2**	**10.4**	**6.6**	**6.3**	**5.3**	**5.4**	**7.9**	**6.0**	**6.0**	**6.7**	**6.0**	**5.3**	**6.6**	**6.5**	**5.6**
Antigua and Barbuda	2.3	2.0	2.0	2.1	1.8	1.4	5.3	−0.6	3.4	3.7	4.1	2.2	2.9	4.4	3.1
Argentina[5]	4.7	13.4	4.4	9.6	10.9	8.8	8.6	6.3	10.5	11.5	11.8	11.0	10.9	11.0	11.0
The Bahamas	1.7	3.0	1.2	2.0	1.8	2.5	4.4	2.1	1.0	2.5	2.0	2.0	1.6	4.0	1.5
Barbados	1.8	1.6	1.4	6.1	7.3	4.0	8.1	3.7	5.8	6.9	5.9	2.8	6.6	7.2	4.6
Belize	1.6	2.6	3.1	3.7	4.2	2.3	6.4	2.0	−0.2	2.1	3.3	2.5	0.0	4.2	2.5
Bolivia	6.0	3.3	4.4	5.4	4.3	8.7	14.0	3.3	2.5	9.8	4.8	4.0	7.2	6.9	4.7
Brazil	103.5	14.8	6.6	6.9	4.2	3.6	5.7	4.9	5.0	6.6	5.2	4.5	5.9	6.3	4.5
Chile	6.4	2.8	1.1	3.1	3.4	4.4	8.7	1.7	1.5	3.1	3.1	3.0	3.0	3.6	3.1
Colombia	15.7	7.1	5.9	5.0	4.3	5.5	7.0	4.2	2.3	3.3	2.9	2.8	3.2	3.1	3.1
Costa Rica	13.0	9.4	12.3	13.8	11.5	9.4	13.4	7.8	5.7	5.3	6.8	4.0	5.8	6.0	7.5
Dominica	1.2	1.6	2.4	1.6	2.6	3.2	6.4	0.0	3.3	4.2	1.9	2.0	2.3	3.8	2.3
Dominican Republic	7.3	27.4	51.5	4.2	7.6	6.1	10.6	1.4	6.3	8.3	6.2	4.0	6.2	7.0	5.5
Ecuador	37.0	7.9	2.7	2.1	3.3	2.3	8.4	5.2	3.6	4.4	4.9	3.0	3.3	5.4	4.8
El Salvador	6.3	2.1	4.5	4.7	4.0	4.6	7.3	0.4	1.2	4.6	4.9	2.8	2.1	7.0	3.0
Grenada	1.7	2.2	2.3	3.5	4.3	3.9	8.0	−0.3	3.4	4.2	3.2	2.0	4.2	3.1	2.4
Guatemala	8.7	5.6	7.6	9.1	6.6	6.8	11.4	1.9	3.9	6.3	5.4	4.0	5.4	7.0	5.5
Guyana	6.9	6.0	4.7	6.9	6.7	12.2	8.1	3.0	3.7	5.8	5.8	5.8	4.5	6.3	5.4
Haiti	18.6	26.7	28.3	16.8	14.2	9.0	14.4	3.4	4.1	7.3	8.0	3.4	4.7	9.6	8.7
Honduras	15.4	7.7	8.0	8.8	5.6	6.9	11.5	8.7	4.7	7.8	7.8	6.0	6.5	8.6	7.8
Jamaica	14.8	10.1	13.5	15.1	8.5	9.3	22.0	9.6	12.6	8.1	6.4	5.5	11.8	6.9	5.6
Mexico	15.6	4.6	4.7	4.0	3.6	4.0	5.1	5.3	4.2	3.4	3.1	3.0	4.4	3.3	3.0
Nicaragua	9.0	5.3	8.5	9.6	9.1	11.1	19.8	3.7	5.5	8.3	8.2	7.0	9.2	8.2	7.3
Panama	1.0	0.6	0.5	2.9	2.5	4.2	8.8	2.4	3.5	5.7	3.5	2.5	4.9	5.5	3.3
Paraguay	11.3	14.2	4.3	6.8	9.6	8.1	10.2	2.6	4.7	8.7	7.8	4.0	7.2	9.0	6.7
Peru	11.3	2.3	3.7	1.6	2.0	1.8	5.8	2.9	1.5	3.1	2.4	2.0	2.1	3.3	2.5
St. Kitts and Nevis	3.0	2.3	2.2	3.4	8.5	4.5	5.4	1.9	0.5	4.7	4.7	2.5	3.9	3.9	2.9
St. Lucia	2.5	1.0	1.5	3.9	3.6	2.8	5.5	−0.2	3.3	2.5	2.5	2.4	4.2	3.7	2.3
St. Vincent and the Grenadines	1.7	0.1	2.9	3.4	3.0	7.0	10.1	0.4	0.6	2.5	1.4	2.5	0.5	3.1	0.5
Suriname	73.5	23.0	9.1	9.9	11.3	6.4	14.6	−0.1	6.9	17.9	10.4	4.0	10.3	19.9	7.5
Trinidad and Tobago	5.1	3.8	3.7	6.9	8.3	7.9	12.0	7.0	10.5	9.6	5.7	5.0	13.4	5.8	5.5
Uruguay	21.7	19.4	9.2	4.7	6.4	8.1	7.9	7.1	6.7	7.7	6.5	6.0	6.9	7.2	6.0
Venezuela	39.9	31.1	21.7	16.0	13.7	18.7	30.4	27.1	28.2	25.8	24.2	22.5	27.2	24.5	24.0
Middle East and North Africa	**8.9**	**5.5**	**6.5**	**6.4**	**7.5**	**10.1**	**13.5**	**6.6**	**6.8**	**9.9**	**7.6**	**5.1**	**8.9**	**8.7**	**6.9**
Algeria	11.2	2.6	3.6	1.6	2.3	3.6	4.9	5.7	3.9	3.9	4.3	3.7	4.5	4.5	4.1
Bahrain	1.0	1.7	2.2	2.6	2.0	3.3	3.5	2.8	2.0	1.0	1.8	2.5	2.0	1.0	2.5
Djibouti	2.8	2.0	3.1	3.1	3.5	5.0	12.0	1.7	4.0	7.1	1.9	2.5	2.8	9.1	1.8
Egypt	5.9	3.2	8.1	8.8	4.2	11.0	11.7	16.2	11.7	11.1	11.3	8.5	10.7	11.8	11.0
Islamic Republic of Iran	22.1	15.6	15.3	10.4	11.9	18.4	25.4	10.8	12.4	22.5	12.5	7.0	19.9	15.0	11.0
Iraq	...	...	...	37.0	53.2	30.8	2.7	−2.2	2.4	5.0	5.0	4.0	3.3	5.0	5.0
Jordan	2.7	1.6	3.4	3.5	6.3	4.7	13.9	−0.7	5.0	5.4	5.6	4.1	6.1	4.9	4.8
Kuwait	1.7	1.0	1.3	4.1	3.1	5.5	10.6	4.0	4.1	6.2	3.4	3.1	4.1	6.2	3.4
Lebanon	6.3	1.3	1.7	−0.7	5.6	4.1	10.8	1.2	4.5	5.9	5.0	2.2	5.1	5.7	4.2
Libya[6]	1.7	−2.1	1.0	2.9	1.4	6.2	10.4	2.8	2.5	...	...	...	2.5	...	...
Mauritania	5.3	5.2	10.4	12.1	6.2	7.3	7.3	2.2	6.3	6.2	6.3	4.9	6.1	6.2	6.3
Morocco	2.9	1.2	1.5	1.0	3.3	2.0	3.9	1.0	1.0	1.5	2.7	2.6	2.2	2.0	2.7
Oman	−0.2	0.2	0.7	1.9	3.4	5.9	12.6	3.5	3.3	3.8	3.3	3.0	4.2	3.3	2.9
Qatar	2.2	2.3	6.8	8.8	11.8	13.8	15.0	−4.9	−2.4	2.3	4.1	4.0	0.4	2.3	4.1
Saudi Arabia	0.3	0.6	0.4	0.6	2.3	4.1	9.9	5.1	5.4	5.4	5.3	4.0	5.4	6.2	4.4
Sudan[7]	45.2	7.7	8.4	8.5	7.2	8.0	14.3	11.3	13.0	20.0	17.5	6.4	15.4	22.0	17.0
Syrian Arab Republic	3.9	5.8	4.4	7.2	10.4	4.7	15.2	2.8	4.4	6.0	5.0	5.0	6.3	6.0	5.0
Tunisia	3.6	2.7	3.6	2.0	4.1	3.4	4.9	3.5	4.4	3.5	4.0	3.5	4.1	3.5	4.0
United Arab Emirates	3.2	3.1	5.0	6.2	9.3	11.1	12.3	1.6	0.9	2.5	2.5	2.0	1.7	2.5	2.5
Republic of Yemen	27.3	10.8	12.5	9.9	10.8	7.9	19.0	3.7	11.2	19.0	18.0	6.9	12.5	25.5	10.5

Table A7. Emerging and Developing Economies: Consumer Prices[1] *(concluded)*

	Average 1993–2002	2003	2004	2005	2006	2007	2008	2009	2010	Projections 2011	Projections 2012	Projections 2016	End of Period[2] 2010	End of Period[2] Projections 2011	End of Period[2] Projections 2012
Sub-Saharan Africa	**22.9**	**10.8**	**7.6**	**8.9**	**6.9**	**6.9**	**11.7**	**10.6**	**7.5**	**8.4**	**8.3**	**5.8**	**6.9**	**9.4**	**6.8**
Angola	527.9	98.3	43.6	23.0	13.3	12.2	12.5	13.7	14.5	15.0	13.9	5.2	15.3	15.0	11.2
Benin	7.4	1.5	0.9	5.4	3.8	1.3	8.0	2.2	2.1	2.8	3.0	3.0	4.0	2.7	3.0
Botswana	9.2	9.2	7.0	8.6	11.6	7.1	12.6	8.1	6.9	7.8	6.2	4.9	7.4	7.2	5.2
Burkina Faso	5.1	2.0	–0.4	6.4	2.4	–0.2	10.7	2.6	–0.6	1.9	2.0	2.0	–0.3	2.0	2.0
Burundi	14.5	10.7	8.0	13.5	2.7	8.3	24.4	10.7	6.4	8.7	12.5	5.0	4.1	14.0	10.9
Cameroon[8]	5.7	0.6	0.3	2.0	4.9	1.1	5.3	3.0	1.3	2.6	2.5	2.5	2.6	2.6	2.5
Cape Verde	4.4	1.2	–1.9	0.4	4.8	4.4	6.8	1.0	2.1	5.0	4.9	2.0	3.4	6.1	4.3
Central African Republic	4.9	4.4	–2.2	2.9	6.7	0.9	9.3	3.5	1.5	2.8	2.6	2.0	2.3	3.7	2.1
Chad	6.2	–1.8	–4.8	3.7	8.1	–7.4	8.3	10.1	–2.1	2.0	5.0	3.0	–2.2	4.7	5.0
Comoros	4.8	3.7	4.5	3.0	3.4	4.5	4.8	4.8	2.7	5.8	3.3	3.0	3.2	5.0	1.7
Democratic Republic of Congo	546.2	12.8	4.0	21.4	13.2	16.7	18.0	46.2	23.5	14.8	12.5	7.7	9.8	16.4	8.5
Republic of Congo	7.1	1.7	3.7	2.5	4.7	2.6	6.0	4.3	5.0	5.9	5.2	3.1	5.4	5.0	4.2
Côte d'Ivoire	6.2	3.3	1.5	3.9	2.5	1.9	6.3	1.0	1.4	3.0	2.5	2.5	5.1	3.0	2.5
Equatorial Guinea	9.1	7.3	4.2	5.7	4.5	2.8	4.3	7.2	7.5	7.3	7.0	6.9	7.5	7.3	7.0
Eritrea	11.2	22.7	25.1	12.5	15.1	9.3	19.9	33.0	12.7	13.3	12.3	12.3	14.2	12.3	12.3
Ethiopia	1.9	15.1	8.6	6.8	12.3	15.8	25.3	36.4	2.8	18.1	31.2	9.9	7.3	38.1	15.0
Gabon	4.9	2.1	0.4	1.2	–1.4	5.0	5.3	1.9	1.4	2.3	3.4	3.0	0.7	3.5	3.2
The Gambia	3.8	17.0	14.3	5.0	2.1	5.4	4.5	4.6	5.0	5.9	5.5	5.0	5.8	6.0	5.0
Ghana	27.6	26.7	12.6	15.1	10.2	10.7	16.5	19.3	10.7	8.7	8.7	6.5	8.6	9.0	8.5
Guinea	4.6	11.0	17.5	31.4	34.7	22.9	18.4	4.7	15.5	20.6	13.8	4.0	20.8	18.4	10.0
Guinea-Bissau	18.5	–3.5	0.8	3.2	0.7	4.6	10.4	–1.6	1.1	4.6	2.0	2.0	5.7	2.7	2.0
Kenya	12.0	9.8	11.8	9.9	6.0	4.3	15.1	10.6	4.1	12.1	7.4	5.0	4.5	11.8	6.0
Lesotho	9.1	6.4	4.6	3.6	6.3	9.2	10.7	5.9	3.4	6.5	5.1	4.6	3.6	8.3	2.3
Liberia	...	10.3	3.6	6.9	7.2	13.7	17.5	7.4	7.3	8.8	1.6	5.0	6.6	6.1	2.2
Madagascar	16.2	–1.1	14.0	18.4	10.8	10.4	9.2	9.0	9.2	10.3	8.5	5.0	10.1	10.5	6.5
Malawi	32.4	9.6	11.4	15.5	13.9	8.0	8.7	8.4	7.4	8.6	11.5	8.4	6.3	11.4	9.4
Mali	5.1	–1.2	–3.1	6.4	1.5	1.5	9.1	2.2	1.3	2.8	2.3	2.4	1.9	2.4	2.8
Mauritius	7.1	3.9	4.7	4.9	8.7	8.6	9.7	2.5	2.9	6.7	5.3	4.4	6.1	5.8	4.4
Mozambique	23.4	13.5	12.6	6.4	13.2	8.2	10.3	3.3	12.7	10.8	7.2	5.6	16.6	8.0	5.6
Namibia	9.1	7.2	4.1	2.3	5.1	6.7	10.4	8.8	4.5	5.0	5.6	4.5	3.1	5.7	5.5
Niger	6.2	–1.8	0.4	7.8	0.1	0.1	10.5	1.1	0.9	4.0	2.0	2.0	2.7	3.4	2.0
Nigeria	26.0	14.0	15.0	17.9	8.2	5.4	11.6	12.5	13.7	10.6	9.0	8.5	11.7	9.5	8.5
Rwanda	13.8	7.4	12.0	9.1	8.8	9.1	15.4	10.3	2.3	3.9	6.5	5.0	0.2	7.5	5.5
São Tomé and Príncipe	29.4	9.8	13.3	17.2	23.1	18.6	32.0	17.0	13.3	11.4	7.4	3.0	12.9	10.0	5.0
Senegal	4.8	0.0	0.5	1.7	2.1	5.9	5.8	–1.7	1.2	3.6	2.5	2.1	4.3	2.7	2.3
Seychelles	2.4	3.3	3.9	0.6	–1.9	5.3	37.0	31.9	–2.4	2.6	4.6	2.6	0.4	5.2	3.5
Sierra Leone	17.0	7.5	14.2	12.0	9.5	11.6	14.8	9.2	17.8	18.0	11.0	5.4	18.4	16.0	11.0
South Africa	7.6	5.8	1.4	3.4	4.7	7.1	11.5	7.1	4.3	5.9	5.0	4.7	3.5	5.9	4.8
Swaziland	9.1	7.3	3.4	4.9	5.2	8.1	12.7	7.4	4.5	8.3	7.8	5.2	4.5	12.3	3.0
Tanzania	15.3	4.4	4.1	4.4	5.6	6.3	8.4	11.8	10.5	7.0	9.4	5.0	7.2	10.9	5.6
Togo	6.6	–0.9	0.4	6.8	2.2	0.9	8.7	1.9	3.2	4.0	2.8	2.0	6.9	4.5	1.4
Uganda	6.9	5.7	5.0	8.0	6.6	6.8	7.3	14.2	9.4	6.5	16.9	5.0	4.2	15.7	10.0
Zambia	41.0	21.4	18.0	18.3	9.0	10.7	12.4	13.4	8.5	9.1	7.5	5.0	7.9	8.9	6.0
Zimbabwe[9]	...	...	...	...	...	...	...	6.2	3.0	3.6	6.5	5.0	3.2	6.5	6.0

[1]In accordance with standard practice in the *World Economic Outlook*, movements in consumer prices are indicated as annual averages rather than as December–December changes during the year, as is the practice in some countries. For many countries, figures for recent years are IMF staff estimates. Data for some countries are for fiscal years.

[2]December–December changes. Several countries report Q4–Q4 changes.

[3]For many countries, inflation for the earlier years is measured on the basis of a retail price index. Consumer price index (CPI) inflation data with broader and more up-to-date coverage are typically used for more recent years.

[4]Georgia and Mongolia, which are not members of the Commonwealth of Independent States, are included in this group for reasons of geography and similarities in economic structure.

[5]Figures are based on the official CPI data. The authorities have committed to improve the quality of Argentina's official CPI, so as to bring it into compliance with their obligations under the IMF's Articles of Agreement. Until the quality of data reporting has improved, IMF staff will also use alternative measures of inflation for macroeconomic surveillance, including estimates by provincial statistical offices and private analysts, which have shown inflation considerably higher than the official inflation rate from 2007 onward.

[6]Libya's projections are excluded due to the uncertain political situation.

[7]Projections for 2011 and later exclude South Sudan.

[8]The percent changes in 2002 are calculated over a period of 18 months, reflecting a change in the fiscal year cycle (from July–June to January–December).

[9]The Zimbabwe dollar ceased circulating in early 2009. Data are based on IMF staff estimates of price and exchange rate developments in U.S. dollars. IMF staff estimates of U.S. dollar values may differ from authorities' estimates.

Table A8. Major Advanced Economies: General Government Fiscal Balances and Debt[1]

(Percent of GDP unless noted otherwise)

	Average 1995–2004	2005	2006	2007	2008	2009	2010	Projections 2011	2012	2016
Major Advanced Economies										
Net Lending/Borrowing	...	–3.4	–2.3	–2.1	–4.4	–9.9	–8.5	–7.9	–6.5	–4.2
Output Gap[2]	–0.1	–0.2	0.4	0.7	–1.0	–6.0	–4.4	–4.3	–4.0	–0.8
Structural Balance[2]	...	–3.1	–2.4	–2.2	–3.6	–5.8	–6.1	–5.5	–4.4	–3.7
United States										
Net Lending/Borrowing	...	–3.2	–2.0	–2.7	–6.5	–12.8	–10.3	–9.6	–7.9	–6.0
Output Gap[2]	0.2	0.0	0.3	0.0	–2.2	–7.1	–5.6	–5.6	–5.5	–1.3
Structural Balance[2]	...	–2.7	–2.0	–2.2	–4.5	–6.7	–7.0	–6.4	–5.0	–4.9
Net Debt	43.2	42.7	42.0	42.9	48.7	60.6	68.3	72.6	78.4	88.7
Gross Debt	62.3	61.7	61.1	62.3	71.6	85.2	94.4	100.0	105.0	115.4
Euro Area										
Net Lending/Borrowing	–2.6	–2.5	–1.4	–0.7	–2.0	–6.3	–6.0	–4.1	–3.1	–1.3
Output Gap[2]	–0.2	–0.3	1.2	2.4	1.3	–3.4	–2.5	–1.9	–1.7	0.0
Structural Balance[2]	–2.7	–2.7	–2.3	–2.1	–2.7	–4.4	–4.2	–3.0	–2.1	–1.2
Net Debt	55.3	55.7	54.3	52.0	53.9	62.1	65.9	68.6	70.1	68.6
Gross Debt	70.9	70.3	68.6	66.4	70.1	79.7	85.8	88.6	90.0	86.6
Germany[3]										
Net Lending/Borrowing	–3.2	–3.4	–1.6	0.3	0.1	–3.1	–3.3	–1.7	–1.1	0.4
Output Gap[2]	–0.6	–1.4	1.0	2.7	2.3	–3.7	–1.6	–0.3	–0.4	0.0
Structural Balance[2,4]	–2.5	–2.6	–2.3	–1.1	–0.7	–1.1	–2.3	–1.4	–0.9	0.4
Net Debt	43.7	53.5	53.0	50.2	49.7	56.4	57.6	57.2	57.0	55.3
Gross Debt	60.6	68.5	67.9	65.0	66.4	74.1	84.0	82.6	81.9	75.0
France										
Net Lending/Borrowing	–3.1	–3.0	–2.4	–2.8	–3.3	–7.6	–7.1	–5.9	–4.6	–1.4
Output Gap[2]	0.1	–0.2	0.5	0.7	–0.7	–4.2	–3.6	–3.0	–2.6	0.0
Structural Balance[2,4]	–3.0	–3.1	–2.5	–3.0	–2.9	–4.8	–4.6	–3.8	–2.8	–1.2
Net Debt	52.6	60.7	59.7	59.6	62.3	72.0	76.5	81.0	83.5	81.9
Gross Debt	59.3	66.7	64.0	64.2	68.2	79.0	82.3	86.8	89.4	87.7
Italy										
Net Lending/Borrowing	–3.6	–4.4	–3.3	–1.5	–2.7	–5.3	–4.5	–4.0	–2.4	–1.1
Output Gap[2]	0.0	–0.4	0.8	1.5	–0.5	–3.9	–3.2	–2.8	–2.5	0.0
Structural Balance[2,5]	–4.3	–4.5	–3.3	–2.5	–2.6	–3.9	–3.1	–2.6	–1.1	–1.2
Net Debt	97.1	89.3	89.8	87.3	89.2	97.1	99.4	100.4	100.7	94.8
Gross Debt	112.1	105.9	106.6	103.6	106.3	116.1	119.0	121.1	121.4	114.1
Japan										
Net Lending/Borrowing	–6.3	–4.8	–4.0	–2.4	–4.2	–10.3	–9.2	–10.3	–9.1	–7.3
Output Gap[2]	–1.0	–0.7	–0.2	0.6	–1.3	–7.8	–4.4	–5.2	–3.5	0.0
Structural Balance[2]	–5.9	–4.6	–3.9	–2.6	–3.7	–7.1	–7.4	–8.1	–7.6	–7.3
Net Debt	54.6	84.6	84.3	81.5	96.5	110.0	117.2	130.6	139.0	166.9
Gross Debt[6]	135.4	191.6	191.3	187.7	195.0	216.3	220.0	233.1	238.4	253.4
United Kingdom										
Net Lending/Borrowing	–1.8	–3.3	–2.6	–2.7	–4.9	–10.3	–10.2	–8.5	–7.0	–1.7
Output Gap[2]	–0.1	–0.3	0.3	1.0	0.7	–3.7	–2.6	–2.9	–3.2	–0.8
Structural Balance[2]	–1.7	–3.1	–2.8	–3.3	–5.9	–8.5	–8.0	–6.3	–4.7	–1.1
Net Debt	37.6	37.3	38.0	38.2	45.6	60.9	67.7	72.9	76.9	72.5
Gross Debt	42.8	42.1	43.1	43.9	52.0	68.3	75.5	80.8	84.8	80.4
Canada										
Net Lending/Borrowing	–0.2	1.5	1.6	1.6	0.1	–4.9	–5.6	–4.3	–3.2	0.3
Output Gap[2]	0.5	1.5	1.7	1.7	0.2	–4.0	–2.4	–2.1	–2.1	–0.4
Structural Balance[2]	–0.4	0.9	0.8	0.6	–0.5	–2.5	–4.0	–3.0	–1.9	0.5
Net Debt	52.9	31.0	26.3	22.9	22.3	28.3	32.2	34.9	36.8	33.3
Gross Debt	88.1	71.6	70.3	66.5	71.1	83.3	84.0	84.1	84.2	73.0

Note: The methodology and specific assumptions for each country are discussed in Box A1 in the Statistical Appendix. The country group composites for fiscal data are calculated as the sum of the U.S. dollar values for the relevant individual countries.

[1]Debt data refer to the end of the year. Debt data are not always comparable across countries.

[2]Percent of potential GDP.

[3]Beginning in 1995, the debt and debt-services obligations of the Treuhandstalt (and of various other agencies) were taken over by the general government. This debt is equivalent to 8 percent of GDP, and the associated debt service to 1/2 to 1 percent of GDP.

[4]Excludes sizable one-time receipts from the sale of assets, including licenses.

[5]Excludes one-time measures based on the authorities' data and, in the absence of the latter, receipts from the sale of assets.

[6]Includes equity shares.

Table A9. Summary of World Trade Volumes and Prices
(Annual percent change)

	Averages		2003	2004	2005	2006	2007	2008	2009	2010	Projections	
	1993–2002	2003–12	2003	2004	2005	2006	2007	2008	2009	2010	2011	2012
Trade in Goods and Services												
World Trade[1]												
Volume	6.5	5.8	6.1	11.2	8.0	9.1	7.7	3.0	−10.7	12.8	7.5	5.8
Price Deflator												
In U.S. Dollars	−1.1	5.2	9.6	9.1	5.1	5.3	7.8	10.9	−10.2	5.2	10.1	0.8
In SDRs	−0.3	3.0	1.4	3.2	5.4	5.8	3.7	7.4	−8.0	6.3	5.7	0.6
Volume of Trade												
Exports												
Advanced Economies	6.0	4.8	4.0	9.6	6.5	9.1	6.8	2.1	−11.9	12.3	6.2	5.2
Emerging and Developing Economies	8.3	8.6	11.7	15.4	12.0	10.6	10.2	4.7	−7.7	13.6	9.4	7.8
Imports												
Advanced Economies	6.3	4.2	4.8	9.7	6.7	7.9	5.2	0.6	−12.4	11.7	5.9	4.0
Emerging and Developing Economies	7.0	9.7	10.8	16.4	11.7	10.8	13.8	9.1	−8.0	14.9	11.1	8.1
Terms of Trade												
Advanced Economies	0.0	−0.3	0.9	−0.3	−1.5	−1.2	0.4	−1.9	2.4	−1.1	−0.4	−0.1
Emerging and Developing Economies	0.2	1.4	0.5	2.3	4.4	2.7	0.2	3.3	−4.7	3.0	2.9	−0.7
Trade in Goods												
World Trade[1]												
Volume	6.5	6.0	7.4	11.7	7.9	9.1	7.5	2.8	−12.0	14.1	8.4	5.8
Price Deflator												
In U.S. Dollars	−1.0	5.2	8.7	8.4	5.7	5.9	7.6	11.4	−11.4	6.6	10.2	0.8
In SDRs	−0.2	3.0	0.5	2.5	6.0	6.3	3.4	7.9	−9.2	7.8	5.8	0.6
World Trade Prices in U.S. Dollars[2]												
Manufactures	−1.4	4.0	13.1	5.4	2.7	2.6	6.4	6.9	−6.5	2.6	7.0	1.1
Oil	2.7	14.9	15.8	30.7	41.3	20.5	10.7	36.4	−36.3	27.9	30.6	−3.1
Nonfuel Primary Commodities	−0.9	9.2	5.9	15.2	6.1	23.2	14.1	7.5	−15.7	26.3	21.2	−4.7
Food	−1.5	7.7	6.3	14.0	−0.9	10.5	15.2	23.4	−14.7	11.5	22.1	−4.4
Beverages	1.3	9.2	4.8	−0.9	18.1	8.4	13.8	23.3	1.6	14.1	17.2	−5.2
Agricultural Raw Materials	0.2	4.4	0.6	4.1	0.5	8.8	5.0	−0.8	−17.0	33.2	26.1	−7.5
Metal	−1.2	15.6	11.8	34.6	22.4	56.2	17.4	−7.8	−19.2	48.2	18.6	−3.5
World Trade Prices in SDRs[2]												
Manufactures	−0.6	1.9	4.6	−0.3	2.9	3.0	2.3	3.5	−4.2	3.7	2.8	0.9
Oil	3.6	12.5	7.1	23.6	41.6	21.0	6.4	32.1	−34.8	29.3	25.4	−3.4
Nonfuel Primary Commodities	−0.1	6.9	−2.1	9.0	6.3	23.8	9.6	4.1	−13.6	27.7	16.4	−4.9
Food	−0.7	5.5	−1.7	7.8	−0.7	11.0	10.7	19.5	−12.6	12.7	17.3	−4.7
Beverages	2.1	6.9	−3.1	−6.3	18.3	8.8	9.4	19.4	4.1	15.4	12.6	−5.4
Agricultural Raw Materials	1.1	2.3	−7.0	−1.6	0.8	9.3	0.9	−3.9	−14.9	34.7	21.1	−7.7
Metal	−0.3	13.2	3.3	27.3	22.7	56.9	12.8	−10.7	−17.2	49.8	13.9	−3.8
World Trade Prices in Euros[2]												
Manufactures	1.8	−0.1	−5.5	−4.1	2.5	1.8	−2.5	−0.4	−1.2	7.7	0.5	1.2
Oil	6.1	10.4	−3.3	18.9	41.0	19.5	1.4	27.1	−32.7	34.3	22.6	−3.0
Nonfuel Primary Commodities	2.3	4.9	−11.6	4.8	5.9	22.3	4.5	0.1	−10.9	32.6	13.8	−4.6
Food	1.7	3.4	−11.2	3.7	−1.1	9.6	5.6	14.9	−9.8	17.0	14.7	−4.3
Beverages	4.6	4.9	−12.5	−9.9	17.8	7.5	4.2	14.8	7.3	19.8	10.1	−5.1
Agricultural Raw Materials	3.5	0.3	−16.0	−5.3	0.3	8.0	−3.8	−7.6	−12.3	39.9	18.4	−7.4
Metal	2.0	11.0	−6.7	22.4	22.2	55.0	7.5	−14.1	−14.6	55.5	11.4	−3.4

Table A9. Summary of World Trade Volumes and Prices *(concluded)*

| | Averages | | 2003 | 2004 | 2005 | 2006 | 2007 | 2008 | 2009 | 2010 | Projections | |
	1993–2002	2003–12									2011	2012
Trade in Goods												
Volume of Trade												
Exports												
Advanced Economies	5.8	4.9	5.3	10.0	6.1	9.1	6.4	1.9	−14.0	14.4	7.1	5.2
Emerging and Developing Economies	8.3	8.3	12.1	14.5	11.7	10.0	9.4	4.7	−8.0	13.5	9.6	7.6
Fuel Exporters	3.7	5.6	12.7	11.4	9.0	5.5	5.7	4.5	−7.0	5.1	6.6	4.1
Nonfuel Exporters	10.0	9.4	11.9	15.6	12.8	12.0	11.0	4.7	−8.5	16.9	10.8	9.1
Imports												
Advanced Economies	6.4	4.6	6.4	10.6	6.8	8.3	5.3	0.4	−13.6	13.5	6.9	4.0
Emerging and Developing Economies	7.1	9.6	12.0	16.8	11.6	10.4	13.3	8.4	−9.5	15.3	12.4	8.0
Fuel Exporters	2.3	9.9	10.7	15.4	15.5	12.1	23.1	14.5	−12.4	6.1	11.6	5.9
Nonfuel Exporters	8.5	9.6	12.2	17.1	10.8	10.0	11.2	6.9	−8.8	17.5	12.5	8.4
Price Deflators in SDRs												
Exports												
Advanced Economies	−0.6	2.1	1.1	1.1	3.3	3.9	3.0	4.6	−6.4	4.7	5.7	0.4
Emerging and Developing Economies	1.8	5.6	0.6	6.9	13.1	11.8	5.0	13.3	−13.4	13.9	7.7	0.3
Fuel Exporters	3.7	9.6	3.8	15.1	28.8	17.6	6.7	24.2	−25.6	23.4	17.2	−2.7
Nonfuel Exporters	1.2	4.0	−0.4	4.0	7.3	9.2	4.2	8.6	−7.4	10.1	4.1	1.5
Imports												
Advanced Economies	−0.7	2.3	0.1	1.8	5.1	5.3	2.5	7.2	−9.9	6.0	5.8	0.5
Emerging and Developing Economies	1.6	4.0	−0.3	4.0	7.7	8.4	4.7	10.1	−8.1	10.2	4.0	1.2
Fuel Exporters	1.8	4.2	0.1	4.0	8.7	8.1	4.2	8.5	−4.9	8.4	4.4	1.6
Nonfuel Exporters	1.5	4.0	−0.3	4.0	7.5	8.5	4.8	10.5	−8.9	10.7	3.9	1.2
Terms of Trade												
Advanced Economies	0.1	−0.2	1.1	−0.7	−1.7	−1.3	0.5	−2.4	3.8	−1.2	−0.1	−0.1
Emerging and Developing Economies	0.2	1.5	0.9	2.8	5.1	3.1	0.3	2.9	−5.7	3.3	3.6	−0.9
Regional Groups												
Central and Eastern Europe	0.4	−0.3	−0.9	1.1	−1.7	−1.4	1.7	−3.3	4.3	−1.1	−1.9	0.0
Commonwealth of Independent States[3]	1.7	5.7	8.5	12.0	14.6	8.9	2.3	13.8	−19.2	12.2	10.9	−1.8
Developing Asia	−0.5	−0.9	−0.6	−1.9	−1.3	−1.0	−1.9	−2.6	3.6	−4.4	−0.1	1.0
Latin America and the Caribbean	0.6	3.0	2.1	5.9	4.9	7.5	2.0	3.1	−9.4	11.0	5.8	−1.2
Middle East and North Africa	0.2	3.8	0.9	6.7	16.8	6.9	1.5	12.2	−16.4	8.1	9.9	−4.3
Sub-Saharan Africa	0.3	2.6	1.5	4.7	11.0	3.2	2.0	7.1	−16.6	20.1	3.4	−5.7
Analytical Groups												
By Source of Export Earnings												
Fuel Exporters	1.8	5.2	3.7	10.6	18.4	8.8	2.4	14.4	−21.8	13.9	12.2	−4.2
Nonfuel Exporters	−0.3	0.0	−0.1	0.0	−0.2	0.7	−0.5	−1.7	1.7	−0.5	0.3	0.4
Memorandum												
World Exports in Billions of U.S. Dollars												
Goods and Services	6,746	16,597	9,329	11,318	12,876	14,853	17,308	19,745	15,798	18,760	22,248	23,736
Goods	5,383	13,301	7,445	9,038	10,333	11,974	13,849	15,861	12,344	15,015	17,977	19,178
Average Oil Price[4]	2.7	14.9	15.8	30.7	41.3	20.5	10.7	36.4	−36.3	27.9	30.6	−3.1
In U.S. Dollars a Barrel	19.82	69.64	28.89	37.76	53.35	64.27	71.13	97.04	61.78	79.03	103.20	100.00
Export Unit Value of Manufactures[5]	−1.4	4.0	13.1	5.4	2.7	2.6	6.4	6.9	−6.5	2.6	7.0	1.1

[1]Average of annual percent change for world exports and imports.

[2]As represented, respectively, by the export unit value index for manufactures of the advanced economies and accounting for 83 percent of the advanced economies' trade (export of goods) weights; the average of U.K. Brent, Dubai, and West Texas Intermediate crude oil prices; and the average of world market prices for nonfuel primary commodities weighted by their 2002–04 shares in world commodity exports.

[3]Georgia and Mongolia, which are not members of the Commonwealth of Independent States, are included in this group for reasons of geography and similarities in economic structure.

[4]Percent change of average of U.K. Brent, Dubai, and West Texas Intermediate crude oil prices.

[5]Percent change for manufactures exported by the advanced economies.

Table A10. Summary of Balances on Current Account

	2003	2004	2005	2006	2007	2008	2009	2010	Projections 2011	Projections 2012	Projections 2016
				Billions of U.S. Dollars							
Advanced Economies	**−217.0**	**−216.8**	**−410.0**	**−451.6**	**−342.2**	**−491.3**	**−71.4**	**−91.0**	**−131.0**	**24.9**	**−127.3**
United States	−519.1	−628.5	−745.8	−800.6	−710.3	−677.1	−376.6	−470.9	−467.6	−329.3	−498.8
Euro Area[1,2]	37.1	112.2	38.8	36.4	20.2	−98.6	13.4	34.8	16.8	55.9	74.5
Japan	136.2	172.1	165.7	170.4	211.0	157.1	141.8	195.9	147.0	172.5	140.5
Other Advanced Economies[3]	128.7	127.4	131.3	142.1	136.9	127.4	150.0	149.2	172.8	125.8	156.4
Memorandum											
Newly Industrialized Asian Economies	84.3	86.9	82.8	99.4	130.9	87.8	128.6	131.5	138.6	145.5	156.4
Emerging and Developing Economies	**145.1**	**214.5**	**407.9**	**639.3**	**628.1**	**679.8**	**287.8**	**422.3**	**592.3**	**513.5**	**679.5**
Regional Groups											
Central and Eastern Europe	−32.4	−55.1	−61.1	−89.0	−137.8	−160.4	−50.0	−80.5	−119.4	−108.0	−158.9
Commonwealth of Independent States[4]	35.7	63.5	87.6	96.3	71.7	107.7	41.3	75.3	113.5	79.5	6.3
Developing Asia	85.2	90.8	137.6	268.8	400.3	412.7	291.4	313.2	363.1	411.8	773.1
Latin America and the Caribbean	9.3	21.4	36.1	50.2	14.9	−30.5	−24.2	−56.9	−78.7	−100.2	−160.7
Middle East and North Africa	59.5	101.5	211.5	282.2	265.8	349.2	49.9	183.5	306.9	238.8	249.6
Sub-Saharan Africa	−12.2	−7.7	−3.6	30.8	13.1	1.0	−20.7	−12.2	6.9	−8.4	−29.9
Memorandum											
European Union	12.4	59.2	−18.2	−55.7	−95.1	−186.4	−14.0	−23.4	−32.7	8.1	47.4
Analytical Groups											
By Source of Export Earnings											
Fuel	103.9	184.6	347.3	476.6	430.3	593.3	146.5	333.6	540.5	429.3	340.5
Nonfuel	41.2	29.9	60.6	162.7	197.8	86.5	141.3	88.7	51.8	84.2	339.0
Of Which, Primary Products	−4.4	−0.7	−1.6	9.4	6.7	−15.2	−3.6	−5.2	−11.7	−15.9	−9.1
By External Financing Source											
Net Debtor Economies	−31.6	−58.9	−98.4	−117.7	−215.4	−368.0	−183.5	−258.9	−339.9	−375.3	−534.5
Of Which, Official Financing	−6.0	−5.0	−5.8	−2.3	−4.3	−11.6	−9.8	−12.3	−16.9	−21.0	−18.8
Net Debtor Economies by Debt-Servicing Experience											
Economies with Arrears and/or Rescheduling during 2005–09	2.0	−6.5	−8.7	−5.5	−18.7	−33.7	−29.8	−37.6	−46.2	−51.4	−42.2
World[1]	**−71.9**	**−2.4**	**−2.1**	**187.7**	**285.8**	**188.4**	**216.4**	**331.3**	**461.3**	**538.4**	**552.1**

Table A10. Summary of Balances on Current Account *(concluded)*

	2003	2004	2005	2006	2007	2008	2009	2010	2011	2012	2016
									Projections		
					Percent of GDP						
Advanced Economies	**−0.7**	**−0.7**	**−1.2**	**−1.2**	**−0.9**	**−1.2**	**−0.2**	**−0.2**	**−0.3**	**0.1**	**−0.2**
United States	−4.7	−5.3	−5.9	−6.0	−5.1	−4.7	−2.7	−3.2	−3.1	−2.1	−2.7
Euro area[1,2]	0.4	1.1	0.4	0.3	0.2	−0.7	0.1	0.3	0.1	0.4	0.5
Japan	3.2	3.7	3.6	3.9	4.8	3.2	2.8	3.6	2.5	2.8	2.1
Other Advanced Economies[3]	2.2	1.9	1.8	1.8	1.5	1.4	1.8	1.6	1.6	1.1	1.2
Memorandum											
Newly Industrialized Asian Economies	7.0	6.5	5.5	6.0	7.2	5.1	8.0	7.0	6.4	6.1	5.0
Emerging and Developing Economies	**1.9**	**2.4**	**3.8**	**5.0**	**4.0**	**3.6**	**1.6**	**2.0**	**2.4**	**2.0**	**1.7**
Regional Groups											
Central and Eastern Europe	−4.1	−5.6	−5.2	−6.8	−8.4	−8.3	−3.1	−4.6	−6.2	−5.4	−5.9
Commonwealth of Independent States[4]	6.2	8.2	8.7	7.4	4.2	4.9	2.5	3.8	4.6	2.9	0.2
Developing Asia	2.8	2.6	3.4	5.6	6.6	5.6	3.7	3.3	3.3	3.4	4.2
Latin America and the Caribbean	0.5	1.0	1.4	1.6	0.4	−0.7	−0.6	−1.2	−1.4	−1.7	−2.2
Middle East and North Africa	6.5	9.5	16.0	18.0	14.2	15.0	2.4	7.7	11.2	9.0	6.3
Sub-Saharan Africa	−2.8	−1.4	−0.6	4.3	1.6	0.1	−2.3	−1.2	0.6	−0.6	−1.8
Memorandum											
European Union	0.1	0.4	−0.1	−0.4	−0.6	−1.0	−0.1	−0.1	−0.2	0.0	0.2
Analytical Groups											
By Source of Export Earnings											
Fuel	7.4	10.3	15.1	16.6	12.1	13.1	3.9	7.7	10.4	8.0	4.3
Nonfuel	0.7	0.4	0.7	1.6	1.6	0.6	1.0	0.5	0.3	0.4	1.1
Of Which, Primary Products	−2.2	−0.1	−0.6	2.9	1.8	−3.6	−0.9	−1.0	−2.0	−2.6	−1.1
By External Financing Source											
Net Debtor Economies	−0.7	−1.2	−1.6	−1.7	−2.6	−3.9	−2.1	−2.4	−2.8	−2.9	−3.1
Of Which, Official Financing	−3.2	−2.3	−2.5	−0.9	−1.4	−3.2	−2.6	−2.9	−3.6	−4.1	−2.7
Net Debtor Economies by Debt-Servicing Experience											
Net Debtor Economies with Arrears and/ or Rescheduling during 2005–09	0.7	−1.4	−1.7	−0.9	−2.6	−3.8	−3.5	−3.9	−4.2	−4.4	−2.8
World[1]	−0.2	0.0	0.0	0.4	0.5	0.3	0.4	0.5	0.7	0.8	0.6
Memorandum											
In Percent of Total World Current Account Transactions	−0.4	0.0	0.0	0.6	0.8	0.5	0.7	0.9	1.0	1.1	0.9
In Percent of World GDP	−0.2	0.0	0.0	0.4	0.5	0.3	0.4	0.5	0.7	0.8	0.6

[1]Reflects errors, omissions, and asymmetries in balance of payments statistics on current account, as well as the exclusion of data for international organizations and a limited number of countries. See "Classification of Countries" in the introduction to this Statistical Appendix.

[2]Calculated as the sum of the balances of individual Euro Area countries.

[3]In this table, Other Advanced Economies means advanced economies excluding the United States, Euro Area countries, and Japan.

[4]Georgia and Mongolia, which are not members of the Commonwealth of Independent States, are included in this group for reasons of geography and similarities in economic structure.

Table A11. Advanced Economies: Balance on Current Account
(Percent of GDP)

	2003	2004	2005	2006	2007	2008	2009	2010	Projections 2011	Projections 2012	Projections 2016
Advanced Economies	**−0.7**	**−0.7**	**−1.2**	**−1.2**	**−0.9**	**−1.2**	**−0.2**	**−0.2**	**−0.3**	**0.1**	**−0.2**
United States	−4.7	−5.3	−5.9	−6.0	−5.1	−4.7	−2.7	−3.2	−3.1	−2.1	−2.7
Euro Area[1]	0.4	1.1	0.4	0.3	0.2	−0.7	0.1	0.3	0.1	0.4	0.5
Germany	1.9	4.7	5.1	6.3	7.5	6.3	5.6	5.7	5.0	4.9	4.0
France	0.7	0.5	−0.5	−0.6	−1.0	−1.7	−1.5	−1.7	−2.7	−2.5	−2.5
Italy	−1.3	−0.9	−1.7	−2.6	−2.4	−2.9	−2.1	−3.3	−3.5	−3.0	−1.7
Spain	−3.5	−5.3	−7.4	−9.0	−10.0	−9.6	−5.2	−4.6	−3.8	−3.1	−2.2
Netherlands	5.6	7.8	7.6	9.7	6.7	4.4	4.9	7.1	7.5	7.7	5.8
Belgium	3.4	3.2	2.0	1.9	1.6	−1.8	0.0	1.0	0.6	0.9	2.4
Austria	1.7	2.2	2.2	2.8	3.5	4.9	3.1	2.7	2.8	2.7	2.7
Greece	−6.6	−5.9	−7.4	−11.2	−14.4	−14.7	−11.0	−10.5	−8.4	−6.7	−2.0
Portugal	−6.5	−8.4	−10.4	−10.7	−10.1	−12.6	−10.9	−9.9	−8.6	−6.4	−2.6
Finland	4.8	6.2	3.4	4.2	4.3	2.8	2.3	3.1	2.5	2.5	2.5
Ireland	0.0	−0.6	−3.5	−3.5	−5.3	−5.6	−2.9	0.5	1.8	1.9	1.0
Slovak Republic	−5.9	−7.8	−8.5	−7.8	−5.3	−6.6	−3.2	−3.5	−1.3	−1.1	−1.4
Slovenia	−0.8	−2.6	−1.7	−2.5	−4.8	−6.7	−1.3	−0.8	−1.7	−2.1	−2.1
Luxembourg	8.1	11.9	11.5	10.4	10.1	5.3	6.9	7.8	9.8	10.3	9.5
Estonia	−11.3	−11.3	−10.0	−15.3	−17.2	−9.7	4.5	3.6	2.4	2.3	−4.2
Cyprus	−2.3	−5.0	−5.9	−7.0	−11.7	−17.2	−7.5	−7.7	−7.2	−7.6	−7.2
Malta	−3.1	−5.9	−8.7	−9.8	−8.1	−7.4	−7.5	−4.8	−3.8	−4.8	−5.0
Japan	3.2	3.7	3.6	3.9	4.8	3.2	2.8	3.6	2.5	2.8	2.1
United Kingdom	−1.6	−2.1	−2.6	−3.4	−2.6	−1.6	−1.7	−3.2	−2.7	−2.3	−0.8
Canada	1.2	2.3	1.9	1.4	0.8	0.3	−3.0	−3.1	−3.3	−3.8	−2.1
Korea	2.4	4.5	2.2	1.5	2.1	0.3	3.9	2.8	1.5	1.4	1.0
Australia	−5.2	−6.0	−5.7	−5.3	−6.2	−4.5	−4.2	−2.7	−2.2	−4.7	−6.3
Taiwan Province of China	9.8	5.8	4.8	7.0	8.9	6.9	11.4	9.3	11.0	11.0	8.3
Sweden	7.0	6.6	6.8	8.4	9.2	8.7	7.0	6.3	5.8	5.3	4.7
Switzerland	13.3	13.4	14.1	14.9	8.9	2.3	11.4	15.8	12.5	10.9	9.9
Hong Kong SAR	10.4	9.5	11.4	12.1	12.3	13.7	8.6	6.2	5.4	5.5	7.7
Singapore	22.7	17.0	21.1	24.8	27.3	14.6	19.0	22.2	19.8	18.5	14.1
Czech Republic	−6.3	−5.3	−1.3	−2.5	−3.3	−0.6	−3.3	−3.7	−3.3	−3.4	−1.2
Norway	12.3	12.7	16.3	17.2	14.1	17.9	12.9	12.4	14.0	12.8	10.6
Israel	0.6	1.9	3.2	5.1	2.9	0.8	3.6	2.9	0.3	0.7	2.0
Denmark	3.7	3.3	4.1	3.1	1.4	2.4	3.8	5.1	6.4	6.4	6.1
New Zealand	−3.9	−5.7	−7.9	−8.2	−8.0	−8.7	−2.9	−4.1	−3.9	−5.6	−7.2
Iceland	−4.8	−9.8	−16.1	−25.7	−15.7	−28.3	−11.7	−10.2	1.9	3.2	−0.9
Memorandum											
Major Advanced Economies	−1.5	−1.4	−1.9	−2.0	−1.3	−1.4	−0.7	−1.0	−1.2	−0.7	−1.0
Euro Area[2]	0.3	0.8	0.1	−0.1	0.1	−1.5	−0.3	−0.4	0.1	0.4	0.5
Newly Industrialized Asian Economies	7.0	6.5	5.5	6.0	7.2	5.1	8.0	7.0	6.4	6.1	5.0

[1]Calculated as the sum of the balances of individual Euro Area countries.
[2]Corrected for reporting discrepancies in intra-area transactions.

Table A12. Emerging and Developing Economies: Balance on Current Account

(Percent of GDP)

	2003	2004	2005	2006	2007	2008	2009	2010	Projections 2011	2012	2016
Central and Eastern Europe	**−4.1**	**−5.6**	**−5.2**	**−6.8**	**−8.4**	**−8.3**	**−3.1**	**−4.6**	**−6.2**	**−5.4**	**−5.9**
Albania	−5.0	−4.0	−6.1	−5.6	−10.4	−15.1	−13.5	−11.8	−10.9	−9.8	−6.9
Bosnia and Herzegovina	−19.2	−16.2	−17.1	−8.0	−10.7	−14.3	−6.2	−5.6	−6.2	−5.6	−4.7
Bulgaria	−5.3	−6.4	−11.7	−17.6	−30.2	−23.2	−8.9	−1.0	1.6	0.6	−4.1
Croatia	−6.0	−4.1	−5.3	−6.6	−7.2	−8.8	−5.2	−1.1	−1.8	−2.7	−5.0
Hungary	−8.0	−8.4	−7.6	−7.6	−6.9	−7.4	0.4	2.1	2.0	1.5	−2.0
Kosovo	−8.1	−8.3	−7.4	−6.7	−8.3	−15.2	−17.1	−16.3	−25.0	−20.5	−15.8
Latvia	−8.1	−12.9	−12.5	−22.5	−22.3	−13.1	8.6	3.6	1.0	−0.5	−3.4
Lithuania	−6.9	−7.6	−7.1	−10.7	−14.6	−13.4	4.5	1.8	−1.9	−2.7	−4.7
Former Yugoslav Republic of Macedonia	−4.0	−8.2	−2.5	−0.9	−7.0	−12.8	−6.7	−2.8	−5.5	−6.6	−5.3
Montenegro	−6.7	−7.2	−8.5	−24.1	−39.5	−50.6	−30.3	−25.6	−24.5	−22.1	−8.9
Poland	−2.5	−5.2	−2.4	−3.8	−6.2	−6.6	−4.0	−4.5	−4.8	−5.1	−5.3
Romania	−5.8	−8.4	−8.6	−10.4	−13.4	−11.6	−4.2	−4.3	−4.5	−4.6	−4.6
Serbia	−7.3	−12.1	−8.7	−10.2	−16.1	−21.6	−7.1	−7.2	−7.7	−8.9	−5.6
Turkey	−2.5	−3.7	−4.6	−6.1	−5.9	−5.7	−2.3	−6.6	−10.3	−7.4	−7.5
Commonwealth of Independent States[1]	**6.2**	**8.2**	**8.7**	**7.4**	**4.2**	**4.9**	**2.5**	**3.8**	**4.6**	**2.9**	**0.2**
Russia	8.2	10.1	11.1	9.5	5.9	6.2	4.1	4.8	5.5	3.5	0.1
Excluding Russia	0.2	2.2	1.3	0.6	−1.3	0.8	−2.0	0.8	1.6	0.9	0.4
Armenia	−6.8	−0.5	−1.0	−1.8	−6.4	−11.8	−15.8	−13.9	−11.7	−10.7	−7.1
Azerbaijan	−27.8	−29.8	1.3	17.6	27.3	35.5	23.6	27.7	22.7	19.3	8.2
Belarus	−2.4	−5.3	1.4	−3.9	−6.7	−8.6	−13.0	−15.5	−13.4	−9.9	−8.9
Georgia	−9.6	−6.9	−11.1	−15.1	−19.7	−22.6	−11.2	−9.6	−10.8	−9.2	−5.9
Kazakhstan	−0.9	0.8	−1.8	−2.5	−8.1	4.7	−3.8	2.9	5.9	4.6	2.0
Kyrgyz Republic	1.7	4.9	2.8	−3.1	−0.2	−8.1	0.7	−7.2	−7.7	−7.6	−3.7
Moldova	−6.6	−1.8	−7.6	−11.4	−15.3	−16.3	−8.5	−8.3	−9.9	−10.3	−7.5
Mongolia	−7.1	1.3	1.3	6.5	6.3	−12.9	−9.0	−14.9	−15.0	−10.5	11.4
Tajikistan	−1.3	−3.9	−1.7	−2.8	−8.6	−7.6	−5.9	2.1	−3.6	−6.7	−4.4
Turkmenistan	2.7	0.6	5.1	15.7	15.5	16.5	−16.0	−11.7	−2.9	−2.6	10.1
Ukraine	5.8	10.6	2.9	−1.5	−3.7	−7.1	−1.5	−2.1	−3.9	−5.3	−4.0
Uzbekistan	5.8	7.2	7.7	9.1	7.3	8.7	2.2	6.7	8.0	7.4	3.6

Table A12. Emerging and Developing Economies: Balance on Current Account *(continued)*

	2003	2004	2005	2006	2007	2008	2009	2010	Projections 2011	Projections 2012	Projections 2016
Developing Asia	**2.8**	**2.6**	**3.4**	**5.6**	**6.6**	**5.6**	**3.7**	**3.3**	**3.3**	**3.4**	**4.2**
Islamic Republic of Afghanistan	−16.5	−4.7	−2.7	−5.7	0.9	−1.6	−2.6	2.7	−0.8	−4.4	−7.5
Bangladesh	0.3	−0.3	0.0	1.2	1.1	1.9	3.3	2.2	0.1	−0.8	−0.5
Bhutan	−22.1	−17.3	−28.7	−4.2	12.1	−2.2	−9.4	−4.6	−10.7	−16.0	−13.9
Brunei Darussalam	50.6	48.3	52.7	56.4	51.1	54.3	40.2	45.0	48.5	46.9	50.2
Cambodia	−3.6	−2.2	−3.8	−0.6	−2.5	−6.2	−5.2	−4.1	−9.3	−6.7	−1.4
China	2.8	3.6	5.9	8.6	10.1	9.1	5.2	5.2	5.2	5.6	7.2
Republic of Fiji	−6.4	−12.6	−9.3	−18.1	−14.2	−19.3	−8.4	−5.6	−10.3	−9.0	−8.1
India	1.5	0.1	−1.3	−1.0	−0.7	−2.0	−2.8	−2.6	−2.2	−2.2	−2.9
Indonesia	3.5	−0.2	−1.0	3.0	2.4	0.0	2.5	0.8	0.2	−0.4	−1.3
Kiribati	−15.0	−21.8	−41.7	−24.2	−29.4	−34.7	−29.8	−22.6	−31.7	−27.9	−24.2
Lao People's Democratic Republic	−13.1	−17.9	−18.1	−9.9	−15.7	−18.5	−21.0	−18.2	−19.4	−19.6	−17.5
Malaysia	12.0	12.1	15.0	16.4	15.9	17.7	16.5	11.5	11.3	10.8	8.4
Maldives	−3.2	−11.4	−27.5	−23.2	−28.5	−35.5	−20.3	−25.7	−22.3	−20.1	−21.8
Myanmar	−1.0	2.4	3.7	7.1	0.6	−2.2	−1.3	−1.4	−3.0	−4.2	4.8
Nepal	2.4	2.7	2.0	2.1	−0.1	2.7	4.2	−2.4	−0.9	−0.4	−1.1
Pakistan	4.9	1.8	−1.4	−3.9	−4.8	−8.5	−5.7	−2.2	0.2	−1.7	−3.3
Papua New Guinea	4.3	2.1	6.1	9.2	3.3	10.1	−8.0	−23.7	−21.2	−15.2	11.4
Philippines	0.3	1.8	1.9	4.4	4.8	2.1	5.6	4.2	1.7	1.3	1.6
Samoa	−8.3	−8.4	−9.6	−10.2	−15.9	−6.4	−3.1	−8.1	−12.7	−13.3	−6.8
Solomon Islands	6.3	16.3	−7.0	−9.3	−13.8	−19.3	−19.3	−28.5	−21.7	−21.4	−55.2
Sri Lanka	−0.4	−3.1	−2.5	−5.3	−4.3	−9.5	−0.5	−2.9	−3.1	−3.3	−3.1
Thailand	3.4	1.7	−4.3	1.1	6.3	0.8	8.3	4.6	4.8	2.5	0.0
Timor-Leste	−15.1	21.1	78.8	165.5	329.0	455.6	245.4	227.1	196.9	167.6	63.7
Tonga	0.7	0.4	−5.2	−8.1	−8.6	−11.7	−11.1	−9.4	−11.3	−11.2	−6.9
Tuvalu	32.8	−15.9	−2.6	14.2	13.3	0.3	−32.5	14.6	−15.2	−16.4	−19.1
Vanuatu	−5.9	−4.5	−8.7	−6.5	−7.0	−11.1	−8.2	−5.9	−5.9	−6.3	−6.3
Vietnam	−4.9	−3.5	−1.1	−0.3	−9.8	−11.9	−6.6	−3.8	−4.7	−3.8	−1.7

Table A12. Emerging and Developing Economies: Balance on Current Account *(continued)*

	2003	2004	2005	2006	2007	2008	2009	2010	Projections 2011	Projections 2012	Projections 2016
Latin America and the Caribbean	**0.5**	**1.0**	**1.4**	**1.6**	**0.4**	**−0.7**	**−0.6**	**−1.2**	**−1.4**	**−1.7**	**−2.2**
Antigua and Barbuda	−11.3	−12.8	−18.4	−27.3	−30.1	−26.6	−20.1	−12.5	−16.3	−16.0	−19.5
Argentina	6.3	1.7	2.6	3.2	2.4	1.5	2.1	0.8	−0.3	−0.9	−1.2
The Bahamas	−4.6	−2.4	−8.4	−17.7	−16.4	−14.9	−11.4	−11.7	−16.9	−18.5	−12.9
Barbados	−4.0	−8.3	−10.0	−6.4	−4.4	−10.5	−6.3	−8.7	−9.0	−7.7	−4.5
Belize	−18.2	−14.7	−13.6	−2.1	−4.1	−10.7	−6.2	−3.0	−3.1	−4.4	−6.8
Bolivia	1.0	3.8	6.5	11.3	12.0	12.0	4.7	4.6	4.2	3.9	2.7
Brazil	0.8	1.8	1.6	1.2	0.1	−1.7	−1.5	−2.3	−2.3	−2.5	−3.2
Chile	−1.1	2.2	1.2	4.9	4.5	−1.9	1.6	1.9	0.1	−1.5	−2.0
Colombia	−1.0	−0.8	−1.3	−1.9	−2.9	−2.9	−2.2	−3.1	−2.6	−2.5	−2.0
Costa Rica	−5.0	−4.3	−4.9	−4.5	−6.3	−9.3	−2.0	−4.0	−4.9	−5.1	−5.4
Dominica	−15.6	−16.0	−21.0	−12.9	−20.8	−25.6	−21.3	−21.6	−22.2	−20.9	−16.5
Dominican Republic	5.1	4.8	−1.4	−3.6	−5.3	−9.9	−5.0	−8.6	−8.1	−6.1	−5.1
Ecuador	−1.4	−1.6	1.0	4.4	3.6	2.5	−0.3	−3.3	−3.0	−3.1	−3.5
El Salvador	−4.7	−4.1	−3.6	−4.1	−6.1	−7.1	−1.5	−2.3	−3.8	−3.5	−3.1
Grenada	−17.7	−6.7	−20.9	−22.8	−29.8	−29.1	−24.5	−24.0	−25.4	−24.5	−20.3
Guatemala	−4.7	−4.9	−4.6	−5.0	−5.2	−4.3	0.0	−2.0	−3.3	−3.8	−4.3
Guyana	−5.8	−6.7	−10.1	−13.1	−11.1	−13.2	−9.2	−9.3	−12.9	−23.9	−10.5
Haiti	−1.5	−1.6	0.7	−1.5	−1.5	−4.4	−3.5	−2.4	−2.6	−5.9	−5.3
Honduras	−6.8	−7.7	−3.0	−3.7	−9.0	−15.4	−3.7	−6.2	−6.4	−6.2	−5.5
Jamaica	−7.6	−6.4	−9.5	−10.0	−16.5	−17.8	−10.9	−8.1	−8.3	−7.9	−3.2
Mexico	−1.0	−0.7	−0.6	−0.5	−0.9	−1.5	−0.7	−0.5	−1.0	−0.9	−0.9
Nicaragua	−16.1	−14.5	−14.3	−13.4	−17.8	−23.8	−12.2	−14.5	−16.0	−17.7	−10.3
Panama	−4.5	−7.5	−4.9	−3.1	−7.2	−11.9	−0.2	−11.2	−12.4	−11.9	−6.2
Paraguay	2.3	2.1	0.2	1.4	1.5	−1.9	−0.1	−2.8	−3.9	−3.7	−2.7
Peru	−1.5	0.0	1.4	3.1	1.4	−4.2	0.2	−1.5	−2.7	−2.8	−2.3
St. Kitts and Nevis	−29.1	−17.0	−15.7	−16.9	−19.3	−26.9	−26.6	−21.5	−23.1	−21.4	−16.8
St. Lucia	−14.6	−10.5	−17.0	−28.6	−32.4	−28.4	−12.7	−12.5	−17.2	−17.9	−14.9
St. Vincent and the Grenadines	−16.5	−19.6	−18.0	−19.3	−28.0	−32.9	−29.4	−31.1	−27.4	−25.2	−17.5
Suriname	−18.0	−10.3	−13.0	7.8	10.7	9.6	−1.1	1.0	0.4	−0.2	0.1
Trinidad and Tobago	8.7	12.4	22.5	39.6	24.8	31.3	8.2	18.8	20.3	20.3	15.6
Uruguay	−0.7	0.0	0.2	−2.0	−0.9	−4.7	0.6	−0.4	−1.6	−3.0	−1.6
Venezuela	14.1	13.8	17.7	14.8	8.8	12.0	2.6	4.9	7.3	5.8	2.8
Middle East and North Africa	**6.5**	**9.5**	**16.0**	**18.0**	**14.2**	**15.0**	**2.4**	**7.7**	**11.2**	**9.0**	**6.3**
Algeria	13.0	13.0	20.5	24.7	22.8	20.2	0.3	7.9	13.7	10.9	8.0
Bahrain	2.0	4.2	11.0	13.8	15.7	10.2	2.9	4.9	12.6	13.7	11.9
Djibouti	3.4	−1.3	−3.2	−11.5	−21.4	−24.3	−9.1	−4.8	−10.8	−11.6	−13.3
Egypt	2.4	4.3	3.2	1.6	2.1	0.5	−2.3	−2.0	−1.9	−2.2	−1.9
Islamic Republic of Iran	0.6	0.6	8.2	9.3	10.5	6.5	3.0	6.0	7.8	7.1	5.3
Iraq	. . .	. . .	6.2	19.0	12.5	19.2	−13.8	−3.2	−0.9	−1.2	6.8
Jordan	11.5	0.1	−18.0	−11.5	−16.8	−9.3	−3.3	−4.9	−6.7	−8.4	−4.9
Kuwait	19.7	26.2	37.2	44.6	36.8	40.5	23.6	27.8	33.5	30.4	28.7
Lebanon	−13.0	−15.3	−13.4	−5.3	−6.8	−9.2	−9.7	−10.9	−14.7	−13.8	−11.0
Libya[2]	8.4	21.1	38.3	51.0	43.2	38.9	15.9	14.4	. . .	. . .	. . .
Mauritania	−13.6	−34.6	−47.2	−1.3	−17.2	−14.8	−10.7	−8.7	−7.5	−7.5	−6.8
Morocco	3.2	1.7	1.8	2.2	−0.1	−5.2	−5.4	−4.3	−5.2	−4.0	−2.3
Oman	2.4	4.5	16.8	15.4	5.9	8.3	−1.3	8.8	14.5	12.9	7.5
Qatar	25.3	22.4	29.9	25.1	25.4	28.7	10.2	25.3	32.6	30.1	19.7
Saudi Arabia	13.1	20.8	28.5	27.8	24.3	27.8	5.6	14.9	20.6	14.2	6.8
Sudan[3]	−7.9	−6.6	−11.1	−15.5	−12.7	−9.4	−13.9	−6.7	−7.3	−7.6	−5.5
Syrian Arab Republic	−13.6	−3.1	−2.2	1.4	−0.2	−1.3	−3.6	−3.9	−6.1	−6.1	−5.0
Tunisia	−2.7	−2.4	−0.9	−1.8	−2.4	−3.8	−2.8	−4.8	−5.7	−5.5	−3.9
United Arab Emirates	5.2	5.6	11.6	15.3	6.0	7.4	3.0	7.0	10.3	9.2	7.1
Republic of Yemen	1.5	1.6	3.8	1.1	−7.0	−4.6	−10.2	−4.5	−5.3	−4.7	−3.0

Table A12. Emerging and Developing Economies: Balance on Current Account *(concluded)*

	2003	2004	2005	2006	2007	2008	2009	2010	Projections 2011	Projections 2012	Projections 2016
Sub-Saharan Africa	**−2.8**	**−1.4**	**−0.6**	**4.3**	**1.6**	**0.1**	**−2.3**	**−1.2**	**0.6**	**−0.6**	**−1.8**
Angola	−5.6	3.8	18.2	25.6	17.5	8.5	−10.0	8.9	12.0	7.3	1.2
Benin	−9.4	−7.0	−6.3	−5.3	−10.2	−8.1	−8.9	−6.9	−7.6	−7.1	−5.4
Botswana	5.7	3.5	15.2	17.2	15.0	6.9	−5.8	−4.9	−4.3	−1.7	2.0
Burkina Faso	−9.6	−11.0	−11.6	−9.1	−8.2	−11.2	−4.2	−3.5	−1.6	−5.2	−4.8
Burundi	−4.6	−8.4	−1.2	−14.5	−24.6	−15.0	−16.1	−13.4	−16.4	−17.0	−17.7
Cameroon	−1.8	−3.4	−3.4	1.6	1.4	−0.8	−3.8	−2.8	−3.8	−3.3	−3.0
Cape Verde	−11.1	−14.3	−3.5	−5.4	−14.7	−15.6	−15.2	−11.2	−12.9	−11.9	−7.3
Central African Republic	−2.2	−1.8	−6.5	−3.0	−6.2	−9.9	−8.1	−10.1	−9.9	−9.5	−7.1
Chad	−49.0	−17.1	1.2	−0.4	13.7	8.9	−10.3	−31.3	−18.9	−13.0	−5.8
Comoros	−3.2	−4.6	−7.3	−6.7	−6.2	−11.0	−9.0	−8.6	−13.7	−13.5	−7.2
Democratic Republic of Congo	0.8	−3.0	−13.3	−2.7	−1.1	−17.5	−10.5	−6.9	−5.8	−4.7	2.2
Republic of Congo	4.8	−5.7	3.7	3.6	−6.5	2.3	−7.4	5.1	7.4	9.7	−1.8
Côte d'Ivoire	2.1	1.6	0.2	2.8	−0.7	1.9	7.4	5.0	1.0	−0.4	−3.1
Equatorial Guinea	−33.3	−21.6	−6.2	7.7	4.3	9.1	−17.1	−24.2	−9.6	−10.5	−6.7
Eritrea	9.7	−0.7	0.3	−3.6	−6.1	−5.5	−7.6	−5.6	0.7	3.4	0.2
Ethiopia	−1.3	−1.4	−6.3	−9.1	−4.5	−5.6	−5.0	−4.4	−6.3	−8.6	−5.9
Gabon	9.5	11.2	22.9	15.6	17.2	24.1	6.1	10.5	14.8	12.3	3.7
The Gambia	−7.3	−7.0	−13.4	−10.2	−10.5	−13.4	−12.9	−15.5	−17.2	−14.2	−13.9
Ghana	−1.1	−2.4	−5.1	−6.2	−8.0	−10.8	−4.0	−7.0	−6.5	−4.9	−1.6
Guinea	−0.8	3.8	7.6	7.0	−10.3	−7.5	−11.4	−12.0	−19.8	−18.3	9.1
Guinea-Bissau	−0.5	1.4	−2.1	−5.6	−4.4	−4.9	−6.4	−6.7	−7.4	−8.8	−5.4
Kenya	−0.2	0.1	−1.5	−2.3	−4.0	−6.7	−5.8	−7.0	−8.9	−8.5	−4.6
Lesotho	3.0	10.6	3.3	1.9	9.0	5.9	−5.2	−17.7	−26.2	−11.1	1.2
Liberia	−24.4	−20.2	−37.4	−13.8	−28.7	−57.3	−38.3	−43.5	−35.8	−60.8	0.1
Madagascar	−6.0	−10.6	−11.6	−9.9	−12.7	−20.6	−21.1	−8.2	−8.2	−7.9	−7.3
Malawi	−11.7	−11.2	−14.7	−12.5	1.0	−9.7	−5.5	−1.2	−5.3	−3.1	0.1
Mali	−7.0	−7.9	−8.5	−4.1	−6.9	−12.7	−5.9	−7.5	−6.8	−5.9	−6.9
Mauritius	1.6	−1.8	−5.0	−9.1	−5.4	−10.1	−7.4	−8.2	−9.9	−8.0	−3.1
Mozambique	−17.5	−10.7	−11.6	−10.7	−9.7	−11.9	−12.2	−10.5	−11.8	−11.5	−10.6
Namibia	6.1	7.0	4.7	13.9	9.1	2.7	1.8	−1.3	−0.7	−3.3	−6.1
Niger	−7.5	−7.3	−8.9	−8.6	−8.2	−13.0	−25.0	−22.5	−26.7	−16.4	−2.3
Nigeria	−6.0	5.6	5.9	26.5	18.7	15.4	13.0	8.4	13.5	11.1	5.8
Rwanda	−2.5	1.8	1.0	−4.3	−2.2	−4.9	−7.3	−6.0	−5.2	−9.1	−4.2
São Tomé and Príncipe	−14.8	−19.1	−14.2	−29.7	−40.7	−38.5	−25.3	−26.7	−40.5	−36.9	−21.0
Senegal	−6.4	−6.9	−8.9	−9.2	−11.6	−14.2	−6.7	−5.9	−7.4	−7.2	−6.3
Seychelles	0.2	−5.5	−18.7	−13.2	−20.5	−48.9	−40.0	−31.6	−32.2	−18.9	−8.6
Sierra Leone	−4.8	−5.8	−7.1	−5.6	−5.5	−11.5	−8.4	−27.5	−49.2	−7.6	−12.3
South Africa	−1.0	−3.0	−3.5	−5.3	−7.0	−7.1	−4.1	−2.8	−2.8	−3.7	−5.5
Swaziland	4.9	3.1	−4.1	−7.4	−2.2	−8.2	−14.0	−18.5	−11.8	−9.0	−5.7
Tanzania	−0.2	−2.5	−3.8	−7.6	−10.0	−11.1	−10.2	−8.8	−8.8	−10.2	−6.0
Togo	−10.8	−10.0	−9.9	−8.4	−8.7	−6.8	−6.6	−7.2	−7.8	−7.7	−6.6
Uganda	−4.7	0.1	−1.4	−3.4	−3.1	−3.1	−7.8	−8.8	−4.0	−8.9	−4.4
Zambia	−14.3	−10.4	−8.5	−0.4	−6.5	−7.2	4.2	3.8	3.2	0.3	2.5
Zimbabwe[4]	. . .	. . .	−10.9	−8.6	−7.2	−23.2	−24.4	−23.3	−11.4	−13.8	−7.9

[1]Georgia and Mongolia, which are not members of the Commonwealth of Independent States, are included in this group for reasons of geography and similarities in economic structure.
[2]Libya's projections are excluded due to the uncertain political situation.
[3]Projections for 2011 and later exclude South Sudan.
[4]The Zimbabwe dollar ceased circulating in early 2009. Data are based on IMF staff estimates of price and exchange rate developments in U.S. dollars. IMF staff estimates of U.S. dollar values may differ from authorities' estimates.

Table A13. Emerging and Developing Economies: Net Financial Flows[1]

(Billions of U.S. dollars)

	Average 2000–02	2003	2004	2005	2006	2007	2008	2009	2010	Projections 2011	Projections 2012
Emerging and Developing Economies											
Private Financial Flows, Net	73.2	167.9	241.4	323.5	302.5	715.1	245.6	267.4	482.3	574.7	610.9
Private Direct Investment, Net	155.5	146.6	187.8	291.5	303.6	441.4	467.0	310.6	324.8	429.3	462.0
Private Portfolio Flows, Net	−34.4	−0.8	14.9	32.1	−45.2	81.1	−66.1	98.8	197.5	127.1	121.3
Other Private Financial Flows, Net	−47.9	22.1	38.7	−0.1	44.1	192.6	−155.3	−142.0	−40.1	18.4	27.7
Official Financial Flows, Net[2]	−14.1	−43.0	−66.0	−87.8	−159.1	−88.3	−94.8	134.1	96.4	−34.4	−50.3
Change in Reserves[3]	−109.2	−321.6	−410.7	−586.9	−747.8	−1,219.8	−734.9	−508.2	−892.2	−1,130.6	−1,061.4
Memorandum											
Current Account[4]	75.0	145.1	214.5	407.9	639.3	628.1	679.8	287.8	422.3	592.3	513.5
Central and Eastern Europe											
Private Financial Flows, Net	21.1	39.1	49.7	102.1	117.5	182.6	153.1	26.6	79.5	99.6	109.6
Private Direct Investment, Net	14.8	14.6	30.6	37.8	64.1	74.8	66.4	29.3	21.5	31.3	40.2
Private Portfolio Flows, Net	1.5	5.1	15.7	20.8	0.8	−4.1	−10.1	9.2	27.0	42.1	25.5
Other Private Financial Flows, Net	4.8	19.4	3.4	43.5	52.6	111.9	96.8	−11.9	30.9	26.3	43.9
Official Flows, Net[2]	4.8	4.9	9.6	3.3	5.2	−6.2	20.3	48.4	34.8	28.9	9.5
Change in Reserves[3]	−4.6	−10.9	−12.8	−43.6	−32.3	−36.7	−4.1	−29.0	−37.1	−22.5	−15.4
Commonwealth of Independent States[5]											
Private Financial Flows, Net	−4.6	20.9	5.6	29.1	51.7	129.2	−97.9	−62.7	−25.9	−18.9	4.4
Private Direct Investment, Net	4.1	5.4	13.2	11.7	21.3	28.3	50.6	16.7	7.6	29.6	30.5
Private Portfolio Flows, Net	1.3	2.0	4.7	3.9	4.9	19.5	−31.5	−9.5	10.4	7.6	11.1
Other Private Financial Flows, Net	−10.0	13.4	−12.3	13.5	25.4	81.4	−117.0	−69.8	−43.9	−56.1	−37.2
Official Flows, Net[2]	−4.3	−11.2	−10.1	−18.3	−25.4	−6.0	−19.0	42.5	0.3	4.8	6.3
Change in Reserves[3]	−16.7	−32.7	−54.9	−77.1	−127.9	−168.0	27.0	−7.9	−53.2	−97.0	−83.6
Developing Asia											
Private Financial Flows, Net	24.6	79.4	163.2	129.2	94.9	212.5	79.5	196.1	319.5	320.7	308.2
Private Direct Investment, Net	50.8	58.5	68.3	131.9	131.6	175.4	161.8	102.9	159.3	169.6	169.4
Private Portfolio Flows, Net	−13.6	22.1	39.2	16.6	−44.5	68.7	20.9	58.2	92.7	77.0	76.8
Other Private Financial Flows, Net	−12.6	−1.2	55.6	−19.4	7.7	−31.6	−103.1	35.0	67.5	74.1	62.0
Official Flows, Net[2]	−4.4	−16.2	−19.8	−3.5	2.5	0.7	−7.1	21.3	21.0	18.5	14.4
Change in Reserves[3]	−62.9	−188.7	−243.0	−277.5	−355.6	−621.7	−504.7	−452.4	−592.7	−712.0	−745.4
Latin America and the Caribbean											
Private Financial Flows, Net	38.1	17.0	15.1	45.2	38.0	108.9	66.3	34.4	99.3	160.4	128.7
Private Direct Investment, Net	64.4	37.9	50.9	56.8	32.7	91.3	98.0	68.8	73.2	128.8	139.9
Private Portfolio Flows, Net	−9.9	−12.5	−23.1	3.1	16.6	40.2	−12.0	35.5	70.8	34.2	25.4
Other Private Financial Flows, Net	−16.4	−8.4	−12.6	−14.7	−11.2	−22.6	−19.8	−69.8	−44.7	−2.6	−36.7
Official Flows, Net[2]	11.9	5.7	−9.0	−38.1	−53.9	−5.0	3.2	46.2	51.7	43.8	37.1
Change in Reserves[3]	−1.1	−32.5	−23.3	−36.0	−52.5	−133.9	−50.7	−49.3	−103.5	−120.2	−62.6
Middle East and North Africa											
Private Financial Flows, Net	−7.9	9.8	−2.9	−3.2	−9.6	63.5	31.1	62.1	10.5	−20.0	17.1
Private Direct Investment, Net	9.9	17.7	13.1	35.9	45.0	48.9	58.1	64.1	43.2	36.4	43.8
Private Portfolio Flows, Net	−10.2	−15.6	−23.6	−12.8	−29.9	−43.7	−3.9	10.0	3.2	−29.6	−17.8
Other Private Financial Flows, Net	−7.5	7.7	7.6	−26.3	−24.7	58.3	−23.1	−12.0	−35.9	−26.8	−8.9
Official Flows, Net[2]	−21.7	−27.0	−36.4	−27.1	−58.3	−76.3	−102.6	−44.2	−43.0	−144.1	−135.5
Change in Reserves[3]	−21.3	−57.0	−58.1	−129.7	−151.3	−231.0	−185.2	21.5	−102.8	−145.0	−122.1
Sub-Saharan Africa											
Private Financial Flows, Net	1.9	1.6	10.7	21.0	10.1	18.5	13.5	11.0	−0.7	32.9	43.0
Private Direct Investment, Net	11.5	12.5	11.7	17.4	8.9	22.8	32.1	28.9	19.9	33.6	38.1
Private Portfolio Flows, Net	−3.4	−2.1	2.0	0.4	7.0	0.5	−29.5	−4.4	−6.6	−4.2	0.3
Other Private Financial Flows, Net	−6.2	−8.7	−3.0	3.2	−5.8	−4.8	10.9	−13.4	−13.9	3.5	4.6
Official Flows, Net[2]	−0.3	0.7	−0.2	−4.0	−29.2	4.5	10.4	19.9	31.5	13.7	17.9
Change in Reserves[3]	−2.6	0.2	−18.6	−23.0	−28.2	−28.5	−17.3	8.9	−3.0	−33.8	−32.3
Memorandum											
Fuel Exporting Countries											
Private Financial Flows, Net	−21.4	17.3	−8.1	2.3	6.6	121.8	−145.4	−58.5	−88.2	−89.3	−35.8
Other Countries											
Private Financial Flows, Net	94.5	150.6	249.4	321.2	295.9	593.3	391.0	326.0	570.5	664.0	646.8

[1]Net financial flows comprise net direct investment, net portfolio investment, other net official and private financial flows, and changes in reserves.
[2]Excludes grants and includes transactions in external assets and liabilities of official agencies.
[3]A minus sign indicates an increase.
[4]The sum of the current account balance, net private financial flows, net official flows, and the change in reserves equals, with the opposite sign, the sum of the capital account and errors and omissions.
[5]Georgia and Mongolia, which are not members of the Commonwealth of Independent States, are included in this group for reasons of geography and similarities in economic structure.

Table A14. Emerging and Developing Economies: Private Financial Flows[1]

(Billions of U.S. dollars)

	Average 2000–02	2003	2004	2005	2006	2007	2008	2009	2010	Projections 2011	2012
Emerging and Developing Economies											
Private Financial Flows, Net	73.2	167.9	241.4	323.5	302.5	715.1	245.6	267.4	482.3	574.7	610.9
Assets	−112.3	−125.3	−265.5	−369.0	−740.4	−952.0	−572.7	−253.8	−558.2	−457.6	−526.3
Liabilities	184.5	291.7	506.4	691.4	1,042.1	1,665.5	815.3	522.0	1,039.5	1,030.5	1,135.2
Central and Eastern Europe											
Private Financial Flows, Net	21.1	39.1	49.7	102.1	117.5	182.6	153.1	26.6	79.5	99.6	109.6
Assets	−6.7	−10.2	−30.0	−17.8	−56.3	−44.3	−28.8	−11.6	−6.6	15.7	0.0
Liabilities	27.9	49.2	79.7	119.8	173.5	226.0	181.1	38.2	85.9	83.8	109.6
Commonwealth of Independent States[2]											
Private Financial Flows, Net	−4.6	20.9	5.6	29.1	51.7	129.2	−97.9	−62.7	−25.9	−18.9	4.4
Assets	−19.6	−24.2	−53.0	−80.3	−100.1	−160.6	−264.8	−74.0	−103.7	−108.1	−98.1
Liabilities	14.9	45.3	58.6	109.4	152.0	289.8	167.4	11.4	77.3	87.9	101.5
Developing Asia											
Private Financial Flows, Net	24.6	79.4	163.2	129.2	94.9	212.5	79.5	196.1	319.5	320.7	308.2
Assets	−34.8	−23.8	−53.3	−114.8	−227.0	−247.1	−169.0	−84.8	−233.9	−192.5	−255.4
Liabilities	58.6	102.8	216.2	243.8	321.7	459.1	247.7	280.9	553.6	513.2	563.8
Latin America and the Caribbean											
Private Financial Flows, Net	38.1	17.0	15.1	45.2	38.0	108.9	66.3	34.4	99.3	160.4	128.7
Assets	−30.8	−33.5	−45.4	−49.7	−90.5	−114.8	−75.6	−93.9	−161.5	−70.7	−87.6
Liabilities	68.5	49.2	60.2	94.3	128.1	223.4	140.5	129.0	260.9	231.2	215.8
Middle East and North Africa											
Private Financial Flows, Net	−7.9	9.8	−2.9	−3.2	−9.6	63.5	31.1	62.1	10.5	−20.0	17.1
Assets	−12.7	−22.5	−71.5	−93.6	−238.0	−355.8	−21.4	22.9	−22.5	−83.0	−60.3
Liabilities	4.8	32.3	68.7	90.4	228.3	419.3	52.5	39.2	33.1	63.0	77.4
Sub-Saharan Africa											
Private Financial Flows, Net	1.9	1.6	10.7	21.0	10.1	18.5	13.5	11.0	−0.7	32.9	43.0
Assets	−7.7	−11.1	−12.3	−12.8	−28.6	−29.3	−12.9	−12.4	−30.0	−19.0	−24.9
Liabilities	9.7	12.8	23.0	33.7	38.5	47.8	26.2	23.2	28.8	51.5	67.1

[1]Private financial flows comprise direct investment, portfolio investment, and other long- and short-term investment flows.
[2]Georgia and Mongolia, which are not members of the Commonwealth of Independent States, are included in this group for reasons of geography and similarities in economic structure.

Table A15. Emerging and Developing Economies: Reserves[1]

	2003	2004	2005	2006	2007	2008	2009	2010	Projections 2011	Projections 2012
					Billions of U.S. Dollars					
Emerging and Developing Economies	**1,341.4**	**1,792.0**	**2,304.4**	**3,073.6**	**4,368.4**	**4,950.0**	**5,596.1**	**6,486.8**	**7,616.9**	**8,678.2**
Regional Groups										
Central and Eastern Europe	114.5	134.0	164.3	208.9	264.8	261.5	300.4	337.5	360.0	375.5
Commonwealth of Independent States[2]	91.8	148.2	213.8	355.3	547.9	502.2	512.3	565.5	662.6	746.1
Russia	73.8	121.5	176.5	296.2	467.6	412.7	417.8	454.5	527.4	582.5
Excluding Russia	18.0	26.7	37.3	59.1	80.4	89.5	94.5	111.0	135.2	163.6
Developing Asia	670.3	934.6	1,156.1	1,489.6	2,128.9	2,534.1	3,077.9	3,669.1	4,380.5	5,125.9
China	409.2	615.5	822.5	1,069.5	1,531.3	1,950.3	2,417.9	2,889.6	3,479.5	4,112.7
India	99.5	127.2	132.5	171.3	267.6	248.0	266.2	291.5	319.7	354.9
Excluding China and India	161.6	191.8	201.1	248.7	330.0	335.8	393.9	488.0	581.3	658.2
Latin America and the Caribbean	195.4	220.6	255.3	310.3	445.1	497.3	547.8	651.3	771.5	834.1
Brazil	48.9	52.5	53.3	85.2	179.5	192.9	237.4	287.5	366.1	412.9
Mexico	59.0	64.1	74.1	76.3	87.1	95.1	99.6	120.3	140.3	150.3
Middle East and North Africa	230.3	293.8	434.1	595.5	836.9	999.5	1,001.2	1,104.0	1,249.0	1,371.1
Sub-Saharan Africa	39.1	60.7	80.9	114.0	144.8	155.4	156.4	159.4	193.2	225.6
Excluding Nigeria and South Africa	25.3	30.4	33.8	48.4	63.6	71.6	76.2	84.9	98.5	122.1
Analytical Groups										
By Source of Export Earnings										
Fuel	291.7	419.1	612.9	927.2	1,343.1	1,473.5	1,442.6	1,582.4	1,843.2	2,065.8
Nonfuel	1,049.6	1,372.9	1,691.5	2,146.4	3,025.3	3,476.5	4,153.5	4,904.4	5,773.7	6,612.4
Of Which, Primary Products	31.8	35.4	38.7	46.9	58.5	71.4	82.0	99.9	123.4	133.3
By External Financing Source										
Net Debtor Economies	564.5	664.8	773.6	971.7	1,350.4	1,398.5	1,584.6	1,825.0	2,061.0	2,240.1
Of Which, Official Financing	11.7	14.3	31.9	34.8	41.5	44.3	54.4	59.7	66.9	71.8
Net Debtor Economies by Debt-Servicing Experience										
Economies with Arrears and/or Rescheduling during 2005–09	35.9	46.4	60.1	73.2	101.5	105.2	119.2	130.4	140.6	153.6
Other Groups										
Heavily Indebted Poor Countries	18.6	23.3	24.3	31.4	41.5	45.1	54.1	61.7	71.2	80.9

Table A15. Emerging and Developing Economies: Reserves[1] *(concluded)*

	2003	2004	2005	2006	2007	2008	2009	2010	Projections 2011	Projections 2012
				Ratio of Reserves to Imports of Goods and Services[3]						
Emerging and Developing Economies	**59.6**	**62.6**	**67.2**	**75.5**	**86.9**	**80.0**	**109.1**	**102.4**	**100.1**	**103.9**
Regional Groups										
Central and Eastern Europe	38.4	34.3	36.1	37.8	37.5	30.5	49.6	48.0	41.6	41.2
Commonwealth of Independent States[2]	52.2	65.1	76.6	100.9	115.4	81.1	118.0	106.1	98.6	101.8
Russia	71.5	93.0	107.4	141.7	165.5	112.3	164.8	141.6	129.4	130.2
Excluding Russia	24.7	27.5	32.5	41.3	41.9	35.5	52.4	52.4	51.1	57.4
Developing Asia	74.4	79.4	81.7	89.5	107.1	106.3	145.0	131.2	130.3	135.6
China	91.1	101.5	115.5	125.4	148.0	158.2	217.2	190.0	188.4	195.4
India	107.1	97.0	72.8	75.5	95.1	71.3	73.8	66.4	62.1	60.3
Excluding China and India	44.9	43.6	38.6	42.6	49.1	41.7	60.6	58.3	58.2	60.6
Latin America and the Caribbean	47.1	44.3	43.4	44.8	53.9	49.8	70.4	65.2	63.4	64.9
Brazil	76.8	65.6	54.4	70.7	113.8	87.6	135.9	117.7	120.3	128.0
Mexico	31.3	29.7	30.5	27.4	28.5	28.5	38.7	36.8	35.9	37.1
Middle East and North Africa	72.9	74.7	90.0	104.3	113.6	104.5	115.8	118.9	117.6	116.5
Sub-Saharan Africa	27.4	34.7	38.3	47.9	49.1	41.8	48.7	42.8	44.9	48.5
Excluding Nigeria and South Africa	34.8	33.9	31.4	39.8	41.3	35.0	39.6	40.2	40.1	45.5
Analytical Groups										
By Source of Export Earnings										
Fuel	66.7	76.8	89.6	112.8	123.4	104.8	122.0	119.2	117.4	119.3
Nonfuel	57.9	59.3	61.6	66.1	76.8	72.7	105.3	98.0	95.6	99.9
Of Which, Primary Products	56.7	51.7	45.6	48.0	47.1	43.7	63.4	59.3	59.7	60.3
By External Financing Source										
Net Debtor Economies	45.8	42.9	41.7	44.0	50.1	42.3	60.0	56.7	53.4	53.9
Of Which, Official Financing	21.8	22.1	40.8	39.4	38.0	32.2	43.3	37.9	36.1	35.6
Net Debtor Economies by Debt-Servicing Experience										
Economies with Arrears and/or Rescheduling during 2005–09	31.1	31.3	33.4	34.4	38.5	31.6	43.7	39.3	34.6	35.4
Other Groups										
Heavily Indebted Poor Countries	32.0	32.1	27.4	30.1	32.6	28.1	38.1	37.7	37.8	40.4

[1]In this table, official holdings of gold are valued at SDR 35 an ounce. This convention results in a marked underestimation of reserves for countries that have substantial gold holdings.
[2]Georgia and Mongolia, which are not members of the Commonwealth of Independent States, are included in this group for reasons of geography and similarities in economic structure.
[3]Reserves at year-end in percent of imports of goods and services for the year indicated.

Table A16. Summary of Sources and Uses of World Savings
(Percent of GDP)

	Averages		2005	2006	2007	2008	2009	2010	Projections		
	1989–96	1997–2004							2011	2012	2013–16
World											
Savings	22.2	21.8	22.7	24.0	24.2	24.1	21.8	23.3	24.2	24.9	26.2
Investment	23.1	22.0	22.5	23.3	23.8	23.8	21.7	22.9	23.6	24.2	25.5
Advanced Economies											
Savings	21.9	20.8	20.1	20.9	20.7	19.8	17.2	18.2	18.6	19.4	20.4
Investment	22.5	21.2	21.2	21.7	21.7	21.0	17.8	18.6	19.1	19.6	20.6
Net Lending	−0.6	−0.4	−1.0	−0.7	−1.0	−1.2	−0.5	−0.4	−0.5	−0.1	−0.1
Current Transfers	−0.4	−0.6	−0.7	−0.7	−0.8	−0.8	−0.8	−0.9	−0.8	−0.8	−0.7
Factor Income	−0.5	0.3	0.7	1.1	0.5	0.5	0.3	0.7	0.5	0.5	0.6
Resource Balance	0.4	−0.1	−0.9	−1.0	−0.5	−0.7	0.1	0.0	0.0	0.3	0.1
United States											
Savings	15.8	16.7	15.2	16.4	14.6	13.4	11.5	12.5	12.8	14.1	15.9
Investment	18.3	19.7	20.3	20.6	19.6	18.1	14.7	15.8	15.8	16.2	18.0
Net Lending	−2.4	−3.1	−5.1	−4.2	−5.0	−4.7	−3.3	−3.3	−3.0	−2.1	−2.1
Current Transfers	−0.4	−0.6	−0.8	−0.7	−0.8	−0.9	−0.9	−0.9	−0.8	−0.8	−0.7
Factor Income	−0.8	0.9	1.3	2.2	0.8	1.0	0.4	1.1	1.3	1.4	1.6
Resource Balance	−1.2	−3.3	−5.6	−5.6	−5.0	−4.9	−2.7	−3.4	−3.6	−2.8	−3.0
Euro Area											
Savings	...	21.4	21.2	22.1	22.7	21.4	19.1	19.7	20.0	20.4	21.1
Investment	...	20.9	20.8	21.7	22.5	22.1	18.9	19.2	19.7	19.8	20.4
Net Lending	...	0.6	0.4	0.4	0.2	−0.7	0.1	0.5	0.3	0.7	0.7
Current Transfers[1]	−0.6	−0.7	−0.9	−1.0	−1.1	−1.1	−1.1	−1.2	−1.1	−1.1	−1.1
Factor Income[1]	−0.7	−0.5	−0.2	0.1	−0.4	−0.7	−0.3	0.1	−0.5	−0.5	−0.4
Resource Balance[1]	1.0	1.8	1.6	1.2	1.6	1.1	1.5	1.6	1.7	2.0	2.0
Germany											
Savings	22.6	20.7	22.3	24.4	26.7	25.6	22.2	23.0	24.1	24.4	24.5
Investment	23.3	20.1	17.3	18.1	19.3	19.4	16.5	17.3	19.1	19.4	20.1
Net Lending	−0.7	0.6	5.1	6.3	7.5	6.3	5.6	5.7	5.0	4.9	4.4
Current Transfers	−1.6	−1.3	−1.3	−1.2	−1.4	−1.3	−1.4	−1.5	−1.5	−1.5	−1.5
Factor Income	−0.3	−0.3	1.1	1.9	1.8	0.9	1.6	1.3	1.2	1.3	1.9
Resource Balance	1.1	2.2	5.3	5.6	7.0	6.7	5.4	5.9	5.4	5.1	4.1
France											
Savings	20.0	20.5	19.4	20.3	21.0	20.1	17.5	18.6	18.5	19.2	19.7
Investment	19.8	18.7	19.9	20.9	22.0	21.9	19.0	19.2	21.2	21.7	22.2
Net Lending	0.2	1.8	−0.5	−0.6	−1.0	−1.7	−1.5	−0.6	−2.7	−2.5	−2.5
Current Transfers	−0.6	−1.0	−1.3	−1.2	−1.2	−1.3	−1.4	−1.4	−1.3	−1.3	−1.3
Factor Income	−0.4	1.1	1.4	1.6	1.7	1.7	1.7	3.0	1.6	1.6	1.6
Resource Balance	1.2	1.7	−0.6	−1.0	−1.4	−2.2	−1.7	−2.3	−3.0	−2.8	−2.8
Italy											
Savings	20.5	20.6	19.0	19.0	19.4	18.3	16.8	16.9	16.5	16.9	18.4
Investment	20.6	20.4	20.7	21.6	21.9	21.2	18.9	20.2	19.9	19.9	20.5
Net Lending	−0.1	0.2	−1.7	−2.6	−2.4	−2.9	−2.1	−3.3	−3.5	−3.0	−2.1
Current Transfers	−0.5	−0.5	−0.7	−0.9	−0.9	−1.0	−0.8	−1.0	−0.8	−0.8	−0.8
Factor Income	−1.5	−1.1	−1.0	−0.9	−1.3	−1.2	−0.7	−0.5	−1.7	−1.6	−1.4
Resource Balance	1.9	1.7	0.0	−0.8	−0.3	−0.7	−0.6	−1.8	−1.0	−0.6	0.1
Japan											
Savings	32.5	27.6	27.2	27.7	28.5	26.7	22.9	23.8	23.9	25.0	25.1
Investment	30.4	24.8	23.6	23.8	23.7	23.6	20.2	20.2	21.4	22.2	22.6
Net Lending	2.2	2.8	3.6	3.9	4.8	3.2	2.7	3.6	2.5	2.9	2.5
Current Transfers	−0.2	−0.2	−0.2	−0.2	−0.3	−0.3	−0.2	−0.2	−0.2	−0.1	−0.1
Factor Income	0.8	1.5	2.3	2.7	3.1	3.1	2.5	2.4	2.7	2.5	2.8
Resource Balance	1.5	1.5	1.5	1.4	1.9	0.4	0.5	1.4	0.0	0.5	−0.2
United Kingdom											
Savings	15.6	15.8	14.5	14.1	15.6	15.0	11.8	11.8	11.3	12.0	14.9
Investment	17.8	17.4	17.1	17.5	18.2	16.6	13.5	15.0	14.1	14.3	16.0
Net Lending	−2.2	−1.6	−2.6	−3.4	−2.6	−1.6	−1.7	−3.2	−2.7	−2.3	−1.1
Current Transfers	−0.7	−0.8	−0.9	−0.9	−1.0	−1.0	−1.1	−1.4	−1.2	−1.1	−1.1
Factor Income	−0.4	0.9	1.7	0.6	1.4	1.9	1.5	1.6	0.6	0.4	0.4
Resource Balance	−1.1	−1.7	−3.4	−3.1	−3.1	−2.6	−2.1	−3.4	−2.1	−1.6	−0.4

Table A16. Summary of Sources and Uses of World Savings *(continued)*

	Averages		2005	2006	2007	2008	2009	2010	Projections		
	1989–96	1997–2004							2011	2012	2013–16
Canada											
Savings	16.5	21.3	24.0	24.4	24.1	23.6	17.9	19.1	19.9	20.2	21.3
Investment	19.3	20.1	22.1	23.0	23.2	23.2	20.9	22.2	23.2	24.0	24.2
Net Lending	–2.8	1.2	1.9	1.4	0.8	0.3	–3.0	–3.1	–3.3	–3.8	–2.8
Current Transfers	–0.1	0.1	–0.1	–0.1	–0.1	–0.1	–0.2	–0.2	–0.2	–0.2	–0.2
Factor Income	–3.6	–2.7	–1.7	–0.9	–0.9	–1.1	–1.0	–1.0	–1.1	–1.2	–1.1
Resource Balance	0.9	3.9	3.7	2.4	1.9	1.5	–1.8	–2.0	–2.1	–2.4	–1.6
Newly Industrialized Asian Economies											
Savings	35.0	32.3	31.8	32.5	33.4	32.8	31.6	33.4	32.4	32.3	31.4
Investment	32.5	27.3	26.1	26.4	26.1	27.7	23.6	26.4	26.1	26.2	26.0
Net Lending	2.5	5.1	5.7	6.1	7.3	5.0	8.0	7.0	6.4	6.1	5.4
Current Transfers	–0.1	–0.5	–0.7	–0.7	–0.7	–0.6	–0.6	–0.7	–0.7	–0.7	–0.6
Factor Income	0.9	0.4	0.1	0.6	0.7	0.9	1.0	0.6	0.6	0.6	0.6
Resource Balance	1.7	5.2	6.3	6.2	7.3	4.7	7.6	7.1	6.5	6.2	5.4
Emerging and Developing Economies											
Savings	23.5	25.5	30.7	32.8	33.0	33.6	31.9	33.0	34.0	34.2	34.9
Investment	26.0	25.0	26.9	27.9	29.1	30.1	30.4	31.1	31.7	32.3	33.2
Net Lending	–1.9	0.5	3.8	4.9	3.9	3.4	1.6	1.9	2.3	1.9	1.7
Current Transfers	0.6	1.2	1.7	1.7	1.6	1.5	1.4	1.2	1.2	1.1	1.1
Factor Income	–1.6	–1.9	–2.1	–1.8	–1.7	–1.7	–1.5	–1.6	–1.6	–1.6	–1.3
Resource Balance	–0.9	1.2	4.2	5.1	4.0	3.7	1.7	2.2	2.8	2.3	1.9
Memorandum											
Acquisition of Foreign Assets	1.5	4.1	9.2	11.5	13.5	6.8	4.5	6.6	6.2	5.8	5.1
Change in Reserves	1.0	1.9	5.4	5.8	7.7	3.8	2.8	4.1	4.5	4.0	3.7
Regional Groups											
Central and Eastern Europe											
Savings	20.7	17.7	16.2	16.6	16.3	16.7	16.1	16.5	16.6	17.4	17.6
Investment	22.4	21.3	21.4	23.4	24.8	25.0	19.1	21.0	22.8	22.6	23.0
Net Lending	–1.6	–3.6	–5.2	–6.8	–8.5	–8.3	–3.1	–4.6	–6.2	–5.3	–5.4
Current Transfers	1.7	2.0	1.7	1.8	1.6	1.5	1.7	1.5	1.4	1.4	1.3
Factor Income	–1.6	–1.4	–2.0	–2.4	–2.9	–2.4	–2.3	–2.3	–2.4	–2.5	–2.3
Resource Balance	–1.7	–4.3	–5.0	–6.3	–7.2	–7.5	–2.6	–3.9	–5.3	–4.3	–4.5
Memorandum											
Acquisition of Foreign Assets	0.7	2.4	5.0	6.1	4.7	1.6	1.8	2.6	0.5	1.3	1.4
Change in Reserves	0.2	1.1	3.7	2.5	2.3	0.2	1.8	2.1	1.2	0.8	1.0
Commonwealth of Independent States[2]											
Savings	. . .	25.9	30.0	30.2	30.7	30.1	21.7	26.0	28.7	28.0	26.8
Investment	. . .	20.3	21.2	23.0	26.7	25.2	19.0	22.1	24.0	25.1	26.1
Net Lending	. . .	5.6	8.8	7.3	4.0	4.8	2.7	4.0	4.7	2.9	0.7
Current Transfers	. . .	0.5	0.5	0.4	0.3	0.4	0.4	0.3	0.1	0.2	0.2
Factor Income	. . .	–2.9	–2.7	–3.3	–2.9	–3.4	–3.6	–3.6	–3.4	–3.1	–2.3
Resource Balance	. . .	7.8	11.0	10.3	6.8	8.0	5.8	7.2	7.9	5.8	3.0
Memorandum											
Acquisition of Foreign Assets	. . .	7.7	15.4	14.9	17.5	10.0	1.5	6.1	7.1	5.5	3.1
Change in Reserves	. . .	3.1	7.7	9.8	9.8	–1.2	0.5	2.7	3.9	3.0	0.8
Developing Asia											
Savings	31.3	33.7	39.7	42.5	43.5	43.9	45.1	44.9	45.6	45.7	46.6
Investment	33.6	31.7	36.3	36.9	36.9	38.4	41.4	41.6	42.3	42.3	42.5
Net Lending	–2.4	2.0	3.4	5.5	6.6	5.5	3.7	3.3	3.3	3.4	4.0
Current Transfers	1.0	1.6	2.2	2.2	2.2	2.0	1.9	1.7	1.7	1.7	1.6
Factor Income	–1.7	–1.4	–1.3	–0.8	–0.5	–0.3	–0.4	–0.3	–0.3	–0.3	–0.1
Resource Balance	–1.5	1.8	2.6	4.2	4.9	3.9	2.3	1.9	1.9	2.0	2.6
Memorandum											
Acquisition of Foreign Assets	2.5	4.9	9.0	11.2	13.4	7.6	6.6	8.4	7.2	7.2	7.0
Change in Reserves	1.7	3.1	6.8	7.4	10.3	6.8	5.7	6.2	6.4	6.1	6.1

Table A16. Summary of Sources and Uses of World Savings (continued)

	Averages 1989–96	Averages 1997–2004	2005	2006	2007	2008	2009	2010	Projections 2011	Projections 2012	Projections 2013–16
Latin America and the Caribbean											
Savings	18.7	18.7	21.9	23.2	22.7	22.7	19.4	20.4	20.7	20.9	21.2
Investment	20.1	20.6	20.4	21.6	22.5	23.8	20.0	21.7	22.3	22.9	23.5
Net Lending	−1.4	−1.9	1.5	1.6	0.2	−1.1	−0.6	−1.4	−1.6	−2.0	−2.3
Current Transfers	0.8	1.3	2.0	2.1	1.8	1.6	1.5	1.3	1.1	1.1	1.2
Factor Income	−2.2	−2.9	−2.9	−3.1	−2.8	−2.9	−2.6	−2.6	−2.7	−2.7	−2.7
Resource Balance	0.0	−0.4	2.4	2.6	1.3	0.3	0.5	0.0	0.0	−0.4	−0.8
Memorandum											
Acquisition of Foreign Assets	1.0	2.0	3.4	3.2	6.2	2.2	3.7	4.8	3.1	2.1	1.5
Change in Reserves	0.8	0.4	1.4	1.7	3.6	1.2	1.2	2.1	2.1	1.1	0.8
Middle East and North Africa											
Savings	21.6	27.9	39.7	41.3	40.6	42.5	31.5	34.8	37.1	36.1	35.1
Investment	24.5	23.4	23.5	23.3	26.6	27.4	29.1	27.1	25.7	26.8	23.0
Net Lending	−3.0	4.6	16.4	18.2	14.3	14.8	2.9	8.1	11.7	9.5	−5.4
Current Transfers	−2.2	−1.1	0.0	−0.4	−0.8	−0.8	−1.4	−1.3	−1.3	−1.4	1.3
Factor Income	1.1	0.6	−0.3	0.7	0.8	0.5	0.0	−0.5	−0.9	−0.7	−2.3
Resource Balance	−1.9	5.2	16.8	18.1	14.4	15.4	3.8	9.6	13.5	11.1	−4.5
Memorandum											
Acquisition of Foreign Assets	1.0	6.7	22.2	31.6	34.9	15.0	3.3	7.8	12.1	10.6	1.4
Change in Reserves	0.7	2.4	9.8	9.6	12.4	7.9	−1.0	4.3	5.5	5.2	1.0
Sub-Saharan Africa											
Savings	15.8	16.2	18.4	24.3	22.2	21.9	19.3	19.8	21.4	20.7	20.4
Investment	16.8	18.5	19.4	20.4	21.2	22.4	22.1	21.5	21.4	21.8	22.4
Net Lending	−1.0	−2.2	−1.0	3.9	1.0	−0.5	−2.8	−1.7	−0.1	−1.2	−2.0
Current Transfers	2.0	2.3	2.5	4.5	4.5	4.4	4.6	3.8	3.7	3.4	3.2
Factor Income	−3.1	−4.4	−6.2	−5.0	−6.2	−6.5	−4.6	−5.1	−5.9	−5.8	−5.6
Resource Balance	0.3	−0.1	2.6	4.3	2.7	1.5	−2.9	−0.6	2.0	1.1	0.3
Memorandum											
Acquisition of Foreign Assets	0.6	2.3	5.0	9.7	8.0	3.8	2.5	4.1	5.8	6.0	4.6
Change in Reserves	0.8	1.0	3.7	3.9	3.4	1.8	−1.0	0.3	2.8	2.5	1.6
Analytical Groups											
By Source of Export Earnings											
Fuel Exporters											
Savings	21.8	28.6	37.3	39.2	37.6	38.1	28.2	31.8	34.6	33.4	31.4
Investment	25.5	22.8	22.2	22.9	26.2	25.5	24.5	24.2	24.3	25.4	26.2
Net Lending	−1.8	5.9	15.1	16.3	11.5	12.3	4.0	7.7	10.4	8.0	5.1
Current Transfers	−3.3	−1.7	−0.6	−0.3	−0.7	−0.6	−1.0	−1.1	−1.0	−1.0	−1.1
Factor Income	0.2	−1.4	−2.6	−2.1	−2.2	−2.7	−2.4	−2.8	−3.0	−2.8	−1.9
Resource Balance	1.5	9.0	18.4	19.0	14.5	15.9	7.1	11.3	14.2	11.6	8.3
Memorandum											
Acquisition of Foreign Assets	1.1	7.6	20.6	25.1	27.0	13.7	3.0	7.5	11.1	9.3	6.2
Change in Reserves	0.2	2.6	9.1	10.1	10.8	3.6	−1.4	3.2	5.1	4.5	2.4
Nonfuel Exporters											
Savings	23.8	24.9	29.0	31.0	31.7	32.2	32.9	33.3	33.9	34.4	35.8
Investment	25.7	25.5	28.1	29.3	30.0	31.6	31.8	32.8	33.6	34.0	34.9
Net Lending	−1.9	−0.6	0.8	1.7	1.7	0.6	1.0	0.5	0.3	0.4	0.9
Current Transfers	1.4	1.8	2.3	2.3	2.2	2.1	2.0	1.8	1.7	1.7	1.6
Factor Income	−1.9	−2.0	−1.9	−1.8	−1.5	−1.4	−1.3	−1.3	−1.3	−1.3	−1.1
Resource Balance	−1.4	−0.5	0.4	1.1	1.0	−0.1	0.3	−0.1	−0.2	−0.1	0.3
Memorandum											
Acquisition of Foreign Assets	1.6	3.3	6.1	7.6	9.6	4.6	4.9	6.4	4.9	4.9	4.8
Change in Reserves	1.2	1.8	4.4	4.6	6.8	3.9	3.9	4.4	4.4	3.9	4.0

Table A16. Summary of Sources and Uses of World Savings *(concluded)*

	Averages 1989–96	Averages 1997–2004	2005	2006	2007	2008	2009	2010	Projections 2011	Projections 2012	Projections 2013–16
By External Financing Source											
Net Debtor Economies											
Savings	19.8	19.3	21.6	22.5	22.9	22.0	20.8	22.0	22.1	22.6	23.7
Investment	21.9	21.4	23.2	24.2	25.5	25.9	22.9	24.5	25.0	25.6	26.8
Net Lending	−2.1	−2.0	−1.6	−1.7	−2.6	−3.9	−2.1	−2.5	−2.9	−3.0	−3.1
Current Transfers	1.7	2.4	2.9	3.0	2.8	2.8	2.9	2.6	2.5	2.4	2.4
Factor Income	−1.9	−2.2	−2.5	−2.6	−2.6	−2.6	−2.4	−2.4	−2.6	−2.6	−2.5
Resource Balance	−1.9	−2.2	−2.1	−2.1	−2.9	−4.1	−2.7	−2.7	−2.8	−2.9	−3.0
Memorandum											
Acquisition of Foreign Assets	1.0	2.1	3.2	4.5	6.2	1.4	2.4	3.7	2.3	2.0	1.8
Change in Reserves	0.9	0.9	2.1	2.5	4.1	1.0	1.6	2.3	2.0	1.4	1.3
Official Financing											
Savings	16.6	18.9	21.6	23.6	23.6	22.6	22.5	23.4	22.9	22.6	23.6
Investment	19.3	20.9	23.2	23.5	23.4	24.5	24.1	25.2	25.8	26.2	26.1
Net Lending	−2.6	−2.0	−1.5	0.1	0.2	−1.9	−1.5	−1.7	−2.9	−3.7	−2.5
Current Transfers	4.6	6.8	10.2	10.3	10.8	10.5	10.6	10.6	9.7	9.3	8.8
Factor Income	−2.6	−2.8	−2.2	−2.2	−1.1	−1.5	−1.6	−1.4	−2.4	−2.7	−2.4
Resource Balance	−4.6	−6.0	−9.6	−8.1	−9.5	−11.1	−10.8	−11.2	−10.3	−10.4	−9.0
Memorandum											
Acquisition of Foreign Assets	1.5	1.9	0.3	1.9	2.7	0.5	1.4	1.8	1.0	0.7	0.7
Change in Reserves	1.5	1.2	0.6	1.2	2.4	1.2	1.9	1.6	1.7	1.0	1.2
Net Debtor Economies by Debt-Servicing Experience											
Economies with Arrears and/or Rescheduling during 2005–09											
Savings	14.6	15.8	20.9	22.7	21.9	20.7	19.1	19.9	20.3	20.7	21.6
Investment	18.2	19.0	22.2	23.3	24.4	25.0	22.4	24.4	24.9	25.1	25.1
Net Lending	−3.5	−3.1	−1.2	−0.6	−2.4	−4.2	−3.3	−4.5	−4.7	−4.5	−3.5
Current Transfers	1.9	3.5	5.5	5.5	5.0	4.5	4.6	4.3	3.7	3.5	3.4
Factor Income	−3.5	−4.5	−4.3	−3.9	−4.1	−4.6	−3.7	−4.5	−4.4	−3.9	−3.8
Resource Balance	−1.9	−2.1	−2.6	−2.3	−3.4	−4.3	−4.4	−4.4	−4.0	−4.1	−3.1
Memorandum											
Acquisition of Foreign Assets	2.3	2.6	2.5	3.8	5.7	1.0	1.1	2.1	2.0	1.5	1.6
Change in Reserves	0.4	0.4	3.2	2.2	3.7	0.6	1.4	1.3	1.0	1.1	1.2

Note: The estimates in this table are based on individual countries' national accounts and balance of payments statistics. Country group composites are calculated as the sum of the U.S. dollar values for the relevant individual countries. This differs from the calculations in the April 2005 and earlier issues of the *World Economic Outlook*, where the composites were weighted by GDP valued at purchasing power parities as a share of total world GDP. For many countries, the estimates of national savings are built up from national accounts data on gross domestic investment and from balance-of-payments-based data on net foreign investment. The latter, which is equivalent to the current account balance, comprises three components: current transfers, net factor income, and the resource balance. The mixing of data sources, which is dictated by availability, implies that the estimates for national savings that are derived incorporate the statistical discrepancies. Furthermore, errors, omissions, and asymmetries in balance of payments statistics affect the estimates for net lending; at the global level, net lending, which in theory would be zero, equals the world current account discrepancy. Despite these statistical shortcomings, flow of funds estimates, such as those presented in these tables, provide a useful framework for analyzing developments in savings and investment, both over time and across regions and countries.

[1]Calculated from the data of individual Euro Area countries.

[2]Georgia and Mongolia, which are not members of the Commonwealth of Independent States, are included in this group for reasons of geography and similarities in economic structure.

Table A17. Summary of World Medium-Term Baseline Scenario

	Averages				Projections			
	1993–2000	2001–08	2009	2010	2011	2012	2009–12	2013–16
	Annual Percent Change Unless Noted Otherwise							
World Real GDP	**3.4**	**4.0**	**−0.7**	**5.1**	**4.0**	**4.0**	**3.1**	**4.7**
Advanced Economies	3.1	2.1	−3.7	3.1	1.6	1.9	0.7	2.6
Emerging and Developing Economies	4.1	6.6	2.8	7.3	6.4	6.1	5.6	6.6
Memorandum								
Potential Output								
Major Advanced Economies	2.5	2.1	0.9	1.1	1.2	1.4	1.1	1.6
World Trade, Volume[1]	**7.7**	**6.1**	**−10.7**	**12.8**	**7.5**	**5.8**	**3.6**	**6.9**
Imports								
Advanced Economies	7.7	4.6	−12.4	11.7	5.9	4.0	1.9	5.4
Emerging and Developing Economies	7.7	10.1	−8.0	14.9	11.1	8.1	6.1	9.0
Exports								
Advanced Economies	7.4	4.9	−11.9	12.3	6.2	5.2	2.5	5.5
Emerging and Developing Economies	9.2	9.2	−7.7	13.6	9.4	7.8	5.4	9.1
Terms of Trade								
Advanced Economies	−0.1	−0.3	2.4	−1.1	−0.4	−0.1	0.2	−0.4
Emerging and Developing Economies	0.5	1.4	−4.7	3.0	2.9	−0.7	0.1	−0.8
World Prices in U.S. Dollars								
Manufactures	−1.1	3.9	−6.5	2.6	7.0	1.1	0.9	0.3
Oil	5.1	16.7	−36.3	27.9	30.6	−3.1	0.8	−1.1
Nonfuel Primary Commodities	−0.8	8.3	−15.7	26.3	21.2	−4.7	5.3	−3.6
Consumer Prices								
Advanced Economies	2.3	2.2	0.1	1.6	2.6	1.4	1.4	1.6
Emerging and Developing Economies	34.6	6.8	5.2	6.1	7.5	5.9	6.2	4.6
Interest Rates (in percent)								
Real Six-Month LIBOR[2]	3.6	0.7	0.1	−0.6	−1.7	−0.5	−0.7	0.5
World Real Long-Term Interest Rate[3]	3.6	1.8	3.2	1.6	0.4	1.9	1.8	3.1
	Percent of GDP							
Balances on Current Account								
Advanced Economies	−0.1	−0.9	−0.2	−0.2	−0.3	0.1	−0.2	0.0
Emerging and Developing Economies	−1.1	2.8	1.6	2.0	2.4	2.0	2.0	1.9
Total External Debt								
Emerging and Developing Economies	37.0	31.0	27.0	25.2	23.6	23.7	24.9	22.9
Debt Service								
Emerging and Developing Economies	8.2	10.0	9.6	8.1	8.0	8.3	8.5	8.7

[1]Data refer to trade in goods and services.
[2]London interbank offered rate on U.S. dollar deposits minus percent change in U.S. GDP deflator.
[3]GDP-weighted average of 10-year (or nearest maturity) government bond rates for Canada, France, Germany, Italy, Japan, United Kingdom, and United States.

WORLD ECONOMIC OUTLOOK
SELECTED TOPICS

World Economic Outlook Archives

I. Methodology—Aggregation, Modeling, and Forecasting

II. Historical Surveys

III. Economic Growth—Sources and Patterns

IV. Inflation and Deflation, and Commodity Markets

V. Fiscal Policy

VI. Monetary Policy, Financial Markets, and Flow of Funds

VII. Labor Markets, Poverty, and Inequality

VIII. Exchange Rate Issues

IX. External Payments, Trade, Capital Movements, and Foreign Debt

X. Regional Issues

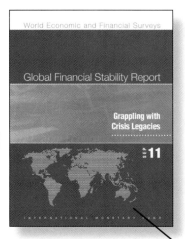
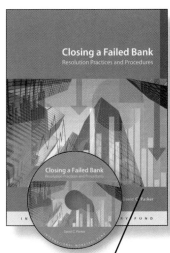
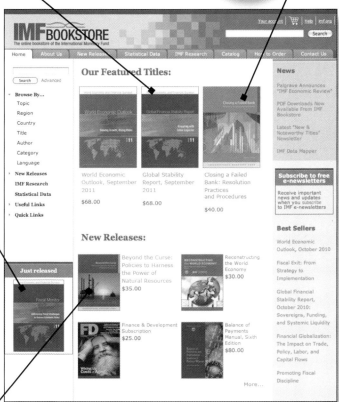
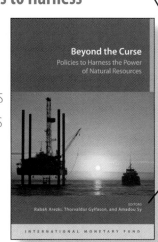